The AIDS Crisis

Other books in the Current Controversies series:

Drug Trafficking
Energy Alternatives
Iraq
Police Brutality
Women in the Military

The AIDS Crisis

David L. Bender, *Publisher*
Bruno Leone, *Executive Editor*
Bonnie Szumski, *Managing Editor*
Carol Wekesser, *Senior Editor*

Charles P. Cozic, *Book Editor*
Karin L. Swisher, *Assistant Editor*

Current Controversies

362
.19697
A2.8

Library of Congress Cataloging-in-Publication Data

The AIDS crisis / Charles P. Cozic, book editor : Karin L. Swisher,
    assistant editor
       p. cm. — (Current controversies)
    Includes bibliographical references and index.
    Summary: An anthology of articles debating AIDS-related issues,
including the prevention and treatment of AIDS, the necessity of
AIDS testing, funding for research, and the seriousness of the
epidemic.
    ISBN 0-89908-578-4 (lib.) — ISBN 0-89908-584-9 (pap.)
    1. AIDS (Disease) — United States.   [1. AIDS (Disease)]
    I. Cozic, Charles P., 1957-   . II. Swisher, Karin L., 1966-   .
III. Series.
RA644.A25A3552   1991
362.1'969792'00973—dc20   91-30034

Printed on
recycled paper

Contents

No: AIDS Testing Violates Civil Liberties

Chapter 4: How Can AIDS Be Treated?

Medical Methods Can Effectively Treat AIDS

Nonmedical Methods Can Effectively Treat AIDS

improved health and decreases in AIDS-related symptoms.

Chapter 5: How Can the Spread of AIDS Be Prevented?

Foreword

By definition, controversies are "discussions of questions in which opposing opinions clash" (*Webster's Twentieth Century Dictionary Unabridged*). Few would deny that controversies are a pervasive part of the human condition and exist on virtually every level of human enterprise. Controversies transpire between individuals and among groups, within nations and between nations. Controversies supply the grist necessary for progress by providing challenges and challengers to the status quo. They also create atmospheres where strife and warfare can flourish. A world without controversies would be a peaceful world; but it also would be, by and large, static and prosaic.

The Series' Purpose

The purpose of the Current Controversies series is to explore many of the social, political, and economic controversies dominating the national and international scenes today. Titles selected for inclusion in the series are highly focused and specific. For example, from the larger category of criminal justice, Current Controversies deals with specific topics such as police brutality, gun control, white collar crime, and others. The debates in Current Controversies also are presented in a useful, timeless fashion. Articles and book excerpts included in each title are selected if they contribute valuable, long-range ideas to the overall debate. And wherever possible, current information is enhanced with historical documents and other relevant materials.

Thus, while individual titles are current in focus, every effort is made to ensure that they will not become quickly outdated. Books in the Current Controversies series will remain important resources for librarians, teachers, and students for many years.

In addition to keeping the titles focused and specific, great care is taken in the editorial format of each book in the series. Book introductions and chapter prefaces are offered to provide background material for readers. Chapters are organized around several key questions that are answered with diverse opinions representing all points on the political spectrum. Materials in each chapter include opinions in which authors clearly disagree as well as alternative opinions in which authors may agree on a broader issue but disagree on the possible solutions. In this way, the content of each volume in Current Controversies mirrors the mosaic of opinions encountered in society. Readers will quickly realize that there are many viable answers to these complex issues. By questioning each author's conclusions, students and casual readers can begin to develop the critical thinking skills so important to evaluating opinionated material.

Current Controversies is also ideal for controlled research. Each anthology in the series is composed of primary sources taken from a wide gamut of informational categories including periodicals, newspapers, books, United States and foreign government documents, and the publications of private and public organizations.

Readers will find factual support for reports, debates, and research papers covering all areas of important issues. In addition, an annotated table of contents, an index, a book and periodical bibliography, and a list of organizations to contact are included in each book to expedite further research.

Perhaps more than ever before in history, people are confronted with diverse and contradictory information. During the Persian Gulf War, for example, the public was not only treated to minute-to-minute coverage of the war, it was also inundated with critiques of the coverage and countless analyses of the factors motivating U.S. involvement. Being able to sort through the plethora of opinions accompanying today's major issues, and to draw one's own conclusions, can be a complicated and frustrating struggle. It is the editors' hope that Current Controversies will help readers with this struggle.

Introduction

On June 25, 1981, the U.S. Centers for Disease Control (CDC) published the first reports of a mysterious disease that afflicted five men in Los Angeles. These men suffered from high fevers, weight loss, and unusual lung infections. By the end of 1981, nearly one hundred people in the U.S. had died of this disease, which came to be known as acquired immunodeficiency syndrome, or AIDS. By June 1991, approximately 116,000 of 182,834 people diagnosed with AIDS had died.

The CDC estimates that one million Americans are infected with human immunodeficiency virus, or HIV, which is believed to cause AIDS. The time it takes to develop the disease, the incubation period, has been known to last ten or more years. Researchers predict that a high percentage of those infected with HIV will develop AIDS and eventually die from the disease.

Because of the thousands of people who have already developed AIDS and the vast number of future cases predicted, many researchers and others dispute what effect AIDS will have on the nation's health-care system. While some researchers predict that AIDS will have a minor, manageable impact on health-care resources, others envision a more devastating effect.

These AIDS researchers and health officials are concerned with the potential of hundreds of thousands of future AIDS cases. They fear the economic toll the disease will take on hospitals, insurance companies, and the nation as a whole.

A study by the Society of Actuaries estimates that life-insurance policies already in force will generate AIDS-related claims totaling $50 billion by the end of the century. AIDS researchers William B. Johnston and Kevin R. Hopkins of the Hudson Institute state: "In scope and impact on the health-care system, the HIV epidemic will resemble the aftermath of a major, protracted war." According to Johnston's and Hopkins's worst-case scenario, the epidemic will cost the U.S. $79 billion per year in direct health-care costs by the year 2002.

Other analysts, however, are more optimistic about the crisis, claiming that AIDS will not cause a health-care catastrophe. They cite the fact that more medical care than ever is being provided at home or in outpatient clinics, where expenses for AIDS care are far less than in a traditional hospital setting. One such type of care is an AIDS hospice, a residential facility that cares for the long-term needs of AIDS patients. Many hospices have successfully provided AIDS care at a fraction of the cost incurred in hospitals. In San Francisco, the Coming Home Hospice spends $150 to $200 a day per patient—one-fourth the daily cost of hospital care. A similar type of care is known as case management, in which a case manager, who may be a nurse, a social worker, or a physician, carefully monitors AIDS treatment in a patient's home or in an outpatient clinic. The case manager sees that the patient's financial, social, and other needs are being met. In addition, he or she insures that the most cost-effective care possible is provided, in part by controlling the charges for drugs and medical supplies whenever possible.

Case management is an attractive concept to insurance companies because the benefits paid for an AIDS patient's care are much less than if such care had been provided in a hospital. According to Gordon Nary, executive director of the AIDS Medical Resource Center in Chicago, insurance companies can reduce future claims for AIDS care by 20 to 50 percent by implementing a case management program. Indeed, since 1987 the John Alden Life Insurance Co. has successfully used case management programs to trim the average AIDS patient's diagnosis-to-death medical expenses from $64,000 to $51,000.

While these treatment alternatives have reduced the cost of AIDS care in many instances, the specter of a growing number of future AIDS patients poses a threat to the health-care system in the U.S. Until a medical breakthrough against the disease is discovered, the issue of health care for present and future AIDS patients will remain a vital one.

In addition to the health-care system, AIDS impacts society in many other ways. For example, the AIDS crisis has raised controversial questions concerning sexual behavior and the spread of AIDS, civil liberties and AIDS testing, and governmental and medical strategies against AIDS. *The AIDS Crisis: Current Controversies* examines these and other issues surrounding this threatening and deadly disease.

Chapter 1:
How Serious Is the AIDS Epidemic?

Preface

Because an AIDS sufferer can have the disease for several years without experiencing any symptoms, the exact number of Americans who are infected with the AIDS virus is unknown. Estimates have ranged from approximately 500,000 to more than 3 million. The wide variation in these figures makes it difficult to determine how serious the current AIDS epidemic is and how serious it will be in the future.

Perhaps the most important source of information about the number of AIDS cases is the U.S. Centers for Disease Control (CDC). The CDC is the governmental body responsible for reporting such figures in the United States. In addition to tabulating the total number of AIDS cases and deaths reported to it, the CDC collects data from many sources, monthly and annually, on new cases of AIDS and on factors relating to the spread of the disease. Based on this data, the CDC makes estimates of the number of Americans currently infected and likely to be infected with the human immunodeficiency virus (HIV), the virus believed to cause AIDS. These estimates are a source of confusion about the prevalence of AIDS precisely because they *are* estimates.

The CDC's estimates are based on analyses of current cases of AIDS and an estimate of the disease's incubation time. While the CDC's studies are among the most complete available, the very uncertainty of the data upon which they are based makes the agency's estimates, and the estimates of others, subject to debate. As Michael Fumento, a former AIDS analyst with the U.S. Commission on Civil Rights, points out, "These models [are] no better than the numbers fed into them, many of which [are] shaky estimates. Economists call this 'black boxing': You put figures into a black box and pull out whatever ones you wish."

Another factor that makes the seriousness of AIDS difficult to estimate is that the groups most affected by the disease have continuously changed. For instance, in the early 1980s, homosexual males were most likely to contract AIDS. By the middle of 1987, AIDS had slowed among this group, and the disease came to be more prevalent among intravenous drug abusers (IVDAs). But by 1991, people who reported heterosexual contact with IVDAs and bisexuals became the fastest-growing groups with AIDS. This changing nature of the disease's victims magnifies the difficulty of estimating its extent. For example, the CDC reported in 1986 that as many as 1.5 million people in the U.S. were infected with HIV. However, it was not until 1988 that the CDC conducted an expansive survey of the general population for HIV infection. Due to more precise data, the CDC reduced its estimate to 1 million as of July 1991.

The Future of AIDS

Other researchers and organizations have also formed theories concerning the future of the AIDS epidemic. In 1987, Theresa Crenshaw, a member of Ronald Reagan's AIDS commission, announced perhaps the most ominous prediction. Crenshaw told Congress that if the spread of AIDS continued at the present rate, 1 billion people worldwide could be infected by 1996. In 1988, noted sex researchers William H. Masters and Virginia E. Johnson also maintained that CDC researchers were seriously underestimating the seriousness of the AIDS epidemic in order to avoid public panic. Based on other studies and their own research of sexual behavior among high-risk AIDS groups, Masters and Johnson said, "It is quite likely that there are now three million or more 'carriers' of the AIDS virus in the United States."

In 1988, the Hudson Institute, a public policy research center, conducted a study using data on actual AIDS cases, AIDS transmission rates, and the progression rate from HIV infection to full-blown AIDS. The study concluded that "between 1.9 million and 3 million Americans probably were infected with HIV." The study also found that 850,000 to 1.4 million heterosexuals were likely to be infected, one of the highest estimates of heterosexual AIDS at the time. To calculate different scenarios of the future of AIDS, Hudson researchers William B. Johnston and Kevin R. Hopkins considered variables such as future sexual behavior, future intravenous drug use, and future medical advances in treatment. In the worst-case scenario, they projected that nearly 11 million people would be living with HIV by the year 2002. Their best-case scenario, however, placed the figure at slightly more than 500,000.

CDC researchers, however, continue to stand by their estimates. James W. Curran, director of the AIDS program at the CDC, believes the CDC estimate of people with HIV is a reasonable one: "The 1 million estimate seems to be neither too low nor too high. If there were 2 million to 2.5 million [HIV] positive [cases] out there, then we would be seeing more AIDS cases reported."

Although researchers are striving to understand the progression of AIDS and predict its future course, there is still no consensus concerning how many Americans the disease will affect. The authors in this chapter debate the severity of the AIDS epidemic.

How Serious Is the AIDS Epidemic?

The AIDS Epidemic Is Worsening

The AIDS Crisis Will Worsen

AIDS Is Spreading Rapidly Among Heterosexuals

AIDS Is a Health Risk for Women

AIDS Poses a Threat to Teenagers

The AIDS Crisis Will Worsen

Nancy F. McKenzie

About the Author: *Nancy F. McKenzie is executive director of the Health Policy Advisory Center, a New York City health care organization. McKenzie is editor of* The AIDS Reader: Social, Political, Ethical Issues, *from which this viewpoint is excerpted.*

What is unique, terrifying, and challenging about the HIV epidemic is its position within the current institutional and economic crisis of non-prosperous America. With respect to the populations affected, we are in an economic situation unparalleled in this century of American history, with the exception of the 1930s. The disarray is primarily seen in our unfulfilled housing, education, and medical and mental health needs. Of course, all directly affect any national health crisis, for sick people need a stable environment, relevant information, and ultimately, a permanent continuum of health care resources. Sick people who are also *poor* people spend most of their waking, energy-expending hours trying to procure one or all three.

The people affected by the HIV virus are now largely poor. When they manage to secure their institutionally unmet housing, education, and medical needs they do so through a network of resources which is now acknowledged to be an alternative health care system—a community born equally of care and necessity. This network—led by the Gay Men's Health Crisis in New York City, the Shanti Project at San Francisco General Hospital and the City of San Francisco itself, as well as a host of community-based care groups in other major cities—exemplifies a decentralized way of organizing health care and,

like the community health clinics of the 1960s, carries with its existence an indictment of the current organization of health care in the United States. . . .

Scientific and medical initiatives in the first ten years of the epidemic have been largely organized around the morphology of the virus and the possibility of interventions—either through vaccine, through the direct cellular interdiction of the virus as it assaults its hosts, or through ways of shoring up the host to meet the assault. The other place energies have been almost single-mindedly directed has been in the area of transmission—the public health need for containment.

Perhaps because no one could predict the course of the HIV disease; or perhaps because the reality of suffering and death is eclipsed by our emphasis on bureaucracy and technology; or because the American media has conditioned us to expect medical bad news to have a rapid solution; or because the HIV-affected themselves have become the scapegoats of a public reluctant to take responsible action, very little attention has been paid to the fact that *the meaning of the HIV epidemic is the suffering it causes the individual.* The current medical crisis is singular in its wholesale lack of compassion for its casualties.

> **"The HIV-affected themselves have become the scapegoats of a public reluctant to take responsible action."**

Understanding the HIV epidemic means understanding the significance of HIV infection in someone's life. It cannot be viewed as though its significance lay in the numbers of people affected. (Although the numbers are daunting—1.5 to 2 million Americans known to be HIV-antibody-positive; 135,000 AIDS cases; 83,000 dead. AIDS has already become the leading cause of death among people under forty in some large cities.) Its significance may be how close it lies to you, or how far away from me, or from "us," but that is only a way of putting off the question of its actual significance in our lives.

"AIDS has already become the leading cause of death among people under forty in some large cities."

The significance of the HIV epidemic is not that it now affects blacks and Hispanics at higher rates than whites but that it is unnecessary that anyone get it at all. And if they do, eight years after we have figured out how AIDS is transmitted and eliminated the infection from our blood supply, what does that say about "a country within a country"—about who counts in this country and who does not?

The significance of the HIV epidemic is not its existence in someone as the result of "high-risk behavior" but what it means for people to *blame* the affected—people they may already hate or fear—for being gravely ill.

The significance of the HIV epidemic is not how it is transmitted, as if the process were mysterious and the intentional result of cunning and deceit. (HIV is transmitted through blood injection and the sexual exchange of semen and vaginal fluid.) The significance is that the almost single-minded focus on transmission allows us to continue to internalize medical technology as The Answer and to continue to deny that our institutions are largely unable to offer comfort or care to the HIV-affected, and most other individuals suffering a debilitating chronic disease. It allows us to continue the illusion that we as a society are all educated individuals living, working, and playing within functioning institutions. It allows us to disregard the fact that our health care facilities are, for fully one third of the population, impoverished and worn out. It allows us to ignore our predominantly two-class system of medical care; to ignore the medical triage that substitutes for sustained medical care in most urban hospitals. Wholesale, it allows us to fail to focus on the criminal inadequacies of our health, education, employment, and justice systems. Finally, more than anything else, it allows us to deny what we intuitively know is true: As people lose their communities, their social and interpersonal networks, because of sickness or through employment and housing displacement, they lose a major basis for good health. By focusing only on issues of transmission, we give ourselves license to ignore the relation between homelessness, drug abuse/mental illness, and HIV infection and to fail to understand how the three relate to the worsening economic condition of our cities.

HIV and AIDS

The HIV virus may or, as it turns out, may *not* be the cause of the myriad catastrophic conditions we call AIDS. Only time will tell whether the single invasive agent theory will prevail historically. The alternative—that the HIV virus is one factor among many undermining already immunosuppressed human organisms—has many implications, not the least of which involve the *general* state of Americans' health. The medical exigencies of HIV infection nonetheless require that we "medicalize" the condition of those who are infected. This simply means that it is imperative that health professionals speak out about the epidemic and give those infected a hand with their uphill battle to be respected as sick people, not shunned as moral deviants. An indication that this imperative has not been met, ten years into the epidemic, is the data on physician willingness to treat the HIV-infected. Another important indication that the HIV-infected are not considered first and foremost sick people, and thus deserving of the same rights as others, is the New York State decision to *waive* the ethical and legal requirements for providing contraception and abortion services, safer sex and drug education in skilled nursing facilities that predominantly house people with AIDS. At this late juncture in the epidemic, it remains urgent to remind ourselves to focus on the over

1.5 million HIV-positive people, as well as the over 135,000 people with AIDS as individual people in great physical and mental need.

While it is important to focus on the spread of the disease, the fear of spread is, in fact, only a direct result of the dire consequences of being infected. We must begin to affect the medical urgency of HIV infection, to redirect its focus from those who aren't infected to those who are.

Medical Needs

The needs of the HIV-infected highlight inequities in our economic and health care systems. They are needs left unmet that, when we focus upon them, appall us in their magnitude. Only the judgment that the afflicted somehow *deserve* what they get can insulate us from the person with AIDS—the PWA. Data from New York City and San Francisco provide two major profiles. The profiles are not meant to depersonalize but to draw into the medical outline features that point to structural resources not ordinarily focused upon.

Fifty to 60 percent of the over 200,000 intravenous drug users in New York City are HIV-antibody-positive. Of these, approximately 25 percent are women and 75 percent are men. Most of the women have at least one child, and that child or those children on average are under ten years old. Of the men, two-thirds have children with average ages between eleven and sixteen.

Consider the fate of the HIV-affected drug user. Naturally, intravenous drug use introduces a complex picture, one that includes unnecessary deprivation. While intravenous drug use designates a troubled individual, it also often indicates one who cannot find a treatment program and one who is primarily unemployed, and often because of addiction, unemployable. The economic outlook for this individual is now predictable. Unemployment means public assistance and drug use without treatment. No job and public assistance means housing instability —transient residences in hotels or shelters or with intolerant family members. Add children; add a public entitlement bureaucracy designed

to thin out assistance rolls; add stigma; and, most important, subtract medical, emotional, or social support except through entirely overcrowded public hospitals. The total picture is beyond tragedy.

Treatment of people with AIDS is largely treatment of people bereft of family, community, or medical support. It is treatment that requires long-term care in a context that is totally devoid of *locations* for it. It is treatment that places a heavy burden on families and communities when they do exist and a crushingly impossible burden on social workers and advocates when they don't. PWAs stay in the hospital for months longer than they have to for lack of a place to live. Their attempts at parenting, at partnership, at life continuity are thwarted not only by their illness but, given a brief respite from the latest medical crisis, by their addiction. Transportation to and from public assistance agencies may, in fact, be an impossible $1.15 away. Inadequate shelter may kill a body already weakened. Looking at urban centers, we see, clearly and startlingly, how vital the physical resources of housing and home care are to wellness and, shamefully, how inaccessible these two have become, to the point that they are practically nonexistent for people who are slowly dying.

"The needs of the HIV-infected highlight inequities in our economic and health care systems."

The elderly, the disabled, and the terminally ill have long tried to express the real impossibility of obtaining care for chronic conditions as middle- or low-income Americans. They have continually pleaded that we recognize the lack of home care structures; child care resources; humane policies for the difficulties of procurement in general (entitlement applications, transportation, groceries, etc.) for those who are "differently abled" but become "handicapped" by structures; for those who have the will, if not the complete stamina, to lead a meaningful life; and for those who hope and plan for a meaningful death. Continuity of medical care, hospice care, group residences, support groups, meal groups, recreational outlets, and child care are all necessities for those who have a catastrophic illness. They are crucial elements of health care for those who lack meaningful social networks. If the intravenous drug user who has AIDS cannot find a program in which he/she can be helped to get off drugs, is it likely that this individual could find these other ancillary but necessary medical services? The situation is impossible. It leads those medical professionals who work with people who have AIDS to reflect upon this system as one they no longer understand, one that frightens them and makes them regard it as a political more than a medical reality. One social worker concerned about the PWAs he works with revealed the potential seriousness of this problem when he said, "I'm hopeful that quarantine or encampment never becomes a reality in this country like it was during the Second World War for Japanese citizens." Ernest Drucker's investigation of intravenous drug users with AIDS in New York City makes it clear that the picture of the person with AIDS in New York City is a picture of a person who is twice ill, a person whose children will probably grow up in foster care or be raised by a grandmother. The picture is contrasted by the picture of the white gay male who first made the American epidemic visible. That picture, in turn, is different from the picture of the intravenous drug user, although the gay PWA meets the same debilitated medical/social system as the nonwealthy. In the gay-identified male population, drug addiction is less frequent than in other population groups intimately tied to the epidemic. But the lack of social support because of the stigma of sexual preference is still operative. To understand the situation of gay men in the epidemic, one must recognize the violence directed against gay males and the complexities of internalized oppression. Almost invariably the PWA is

at the mercy of public programs inadequately funded and stressed beyond responsiveness because the insurance industry refuses to underwrite them. A focus on the person with AIDS forces a confrontation with the unfulfilled promises of the American way of life that most Americans so studiously avoid until they are seriously ill and find (as many Americans are only now finding) that they cannot afford help. It is a focus, when trained on medical and social services, that darkens rather than illuminates. It demoralizes quicker than it informs. But this will change. As we truly confront the medical requirements of the HIV-affected, we will come to terms with the need for medical insurance for everyone and for a health care system that is truly responsive to medical needs rather than to esoteric research agenda.

No Emotional Help

Judging by the extent to which the HIV-infected are *not* being studied or treated, psychological and psychiatric help for those with HIV disease has yet to be invented. And yet, what could be more stressful, more catastrophic, more debilitating than finding out that one is HIV-antibody-positive; that one has an almost always fatal disease; or that this almost always fatal disease causes severe neurological disorders in one-third of the afflicted? Again, most of the professional energy with respect to the psychological and neurological dysfunction that is associated with the virus has been focused upon detection—finding out who is likely to suffer the impairment so that they can be screened out of employment and insurance rolls.

"Treatment of people with AIDS is largely treatment of people bereft of family, community, or medical support."

There has been no national call from the American Psychological Association or from the

American Medical Association's psychiatric division for stepped-up efforts to treat the various emotional and neurological disturbances related to HIV infection. Few programs have been designed to deal with the problems of addiction that are so much a part of the American way of life and of poverty. What little help there is comes from "support groups" provided by communities meeting the needs of addiction, bereavement, depression, suicide prevention, and stress-related illnesses. Mental health experts have largely ignored the HIV-affected.

Of the 1.5 to 2 million Americans who are HIV-antibody-positive, perhaps half have knowledge either that they are at risk or that they are infected. This translates into the fact that over 1 million Americans are trying to negotiate their lives with the knowledge that they possibly have only a few years, even a few months, to live. They are facing these prospects with the social encouragement that they internalize a shame and an exaggerated notion of personal choice that makes them responsible for their own addiction, their own destitution, and ultimately, their own death. The HIV-affected carry not only a view of their own imminent dysfunction, deterioration, and demise but also a social guilt *undeserved and intractable*—the burden of culpability for their own illness.

"Psychological and psychiatric help for those with HIV disease has yet to be invented."

What has not been sufficiently investigated and documented and, more important, for which few interventions have been devised, is the sheer physical and mental discomfort and dis-ease of the HIV-affected. This medical and human concern requires that we begin to set up a broad range of medical responses to HIV infection that emphasizes *caretaking:* drug/alcohol rehabilitation; stress management; residential treatment centers; support networks; pain man-

agement; grief counseling; family therapy; child care and child therapy; rehabilitation therapy; suicide prevention; life-continuity counseling; recreational therapy; and psychotherapy. If HIV infection is, in the final analysis, an epidemic, it is in the *first* analysis an individual medical and psychological catastrophe. It makes little sense to be urgent about its spread, if we cannot muster urgency about its victims. . . .

Success and Failure

There have been criticisms by public health officials that different groups have refused to cooperate in the standard public health efforts necessitated by the epidemic. And it is true that public health measures in response to this epidemic *have* been influenced by political decisions. Groups have resisted standard public health measures, wishing to find measures with some promise of efficacy. It is undeniable that the homosexual community has interrupted the transmission of HIV. The rate of new infection among homosexual men is much lower than anyone thought it could be. And it is undeniable that the gay community has accomplished this without the traditional strategies of mass testing, isolation, and contact tracing. By not opting for mass testing, the communities of New York City and San Francisco took a microscopic approach to HIV. They had to define individual and collective practices that were dangerous and go about convincing each other how to avoid those dangers. The homosexual community has indeed made a difference in this epidemic. They have highlighted the extent to which only communities themselves and individuals within communities can deal with the transmission of disease. Any larger or more depersonalized measures like mass screening or contact tracing do little to stop the spread of disease and much to further demoralize and depress individuals who need every optimistic hope and incentive to believe that their behavior will make a difference to their health and the health of their partners. What is different about the HIV epidemic is that a group of people took into their own hands the job of educating themselves to the dangers of the virus. They did yell a collective "foul" when it seemed that they could be scapegoated for the epidemic.

Homosexuals not only have been effective in the area of transmission, where no one else has, they have been imaginative and resourceful in responding to the illnesses that accompany HIV infection—something that has not happened at any governmental level. Gay Men's Health Crisis in New York City, the Shanti Project in San Francisco, the Community Research Initiative, and Project Inform are at the forefront of knowledge about the epidemic and about the medical and psychological needs of the HIV-affected. As the epidemic progresses, the federal government increasingly adopts medical measures that were originated by these communities.

"It is undeniable that the homosexual community has interrupted the transmission of HIV."

Epidemics are highly complex phenomena. They involve not only a "germ," they involve practices that transmit it, and probably what will prove ultimately to be the most important factor, "hosts" that are vulnerable to the "germ." The host factor, besides the myriad practices that are involved in epidemics, is the individuating factor of epidemics. Populations, according to their lifestyles, nutrition, and relative ease or difficulty in maintaining continuity of health care, differ in their susceptibility to disease. But these factors are rarely emphasized by the epidemiologist. Only communities themselves have access to this information and the will to address the issues in the way that they have to be addressed if epidemics are to be halted. To say that epidemics largely affect the ignorant or the disenfranchised is to say little; it is to view the epidemic from the height of the unaffected. To say that they affect communities of differing vulner-

abilities and resources is to say quite a lot and to commit oneself to allowing the differences to emerge and play their part in resolving the epidemic. It is to view the epidemic from the base of community.

Transmission of the virus has not been halted. This is not because the virus takes advantage of every opportunity to infect the unwary but because the populations that are currently being affected are ones that have no institutional affiliation. The high school dropout is also the unemployed, the medically invisible, the person confronting psychological problems alone. For instance, there is no realistic appraisal of the extent of illness among intravenous drug users, their partners, and their children, as well as the growing numbers of women and adolescents at high risk for their addictions to alcohol and cocaine, heroin and crack. Nor have there been attempts to understand the intertwining epidemics of drug use, homelessness, and HIV infection or the extent of their reflection upon poverty and its ranks. No plans for drug treatment—none at all. And short-term preventive interventions like the education about cleaning needles or exchanging old ones for clean ones meets the same resistance that condoms do with the Catholic Church, despite very effective containment programs around the globe through state-sponsored needle-exchange schemes or programs.

Health Information

People with no formal affiliation with health professionals or educators will not be reached by public health information packets or posters. Certainly not when they distrust health systems that might report their immigration status; or require cash; or find out about a stigmatizing condition such as drug use, unemployment, or homosexuality. It is far too easy to avoid a health care system altogether—one that has been wholesale in its callousness. It is not easy to bring a person who may be at risk for HIV into a health care system that is largely nonexistent or whose experience with that system has involved enduring long, numbing waits for less-than-compassionate caregivers. Transmission of the virus continues because the people most at risk are unreachable through "normal" institutional channels and no one has been imaginative enough or courageous enough to fund the use of the "media" that serve as a network within *communities*—radio, TV, churches, bars, and community organizations.

"It is not easy to bring a person who may be at risk for HIV into a health care system that is largely nonexistent."

The transmission issue as it is defined by the American media is a red herring. The true issues of transmission relate more to *disconnectedness and concealment* than they do [to] morality and responsibility. The greatest tool for halting transmission is the assurance of a lack of reprisals for those who are infected.

If one begins to imagine the concrete measures needed to create a climate in which people will come forward to health centers for treatment and testing, one sees first a health care system that does not rely primarily on the emergency room and that has physicians willing to treat the HIV-affected. In addition, one envisions an effective application of law and effective leadership. Amnesty proved more effective in documenting immigrants than punishment and reprisals for illegal status. HIV-affected people, or those who suspect that they may be affected, are not "illegal." They don't require amnesty. They require help against threats and abandonment. They require protection. A national effort to enforce federal antidiscrimination laws would do more to bring people forward than all the public health or police restrictions one could invent. It is that simple. Strict enforcement of antidiscrimination law at the federal level with highly visible encouragement of state enforcement would bring people closer to those centers

that can help them and interrupt the spread of the HIV virus.

But this is not enough. Like the issues of the medical and psychological needs of the HIV-affected, effective transmission policy cannot be formulated within structures that are moribund and cynical. Effective public health policy, like effective medical policy, cannot be developed within the usual institutional settings, settings that have been more gatekeeping and warehouses for the poor than places of responsiveness. The epidemic requires wholly new structures, not new policies installed within old structures. The issues of transmission require that people police themselves and that they do so with respect and dignity. This requirement is hard met by public health officials within medical and social service institutions designed more for efficiency and compliance than responsiveness and compassion. . . .

Evaluating AIDS Treatment

One further set of issues concerns testing for the HIV virus in order for people to get treated by drugs that might stave off those symptoms of HIV infection that result in the disease of AIDS. There are many drugs now available that offer some hope of longevity with an HIV diagnosis. Given that these drugs currently make up the American arsenal of "treatments," many are calling for larger numbers of people to be tested for the virus. Sometimes these calls are directed at certain groups that are at risk, such as those most vulnerable to infection—the newborn of HIV-affected mothers. The basic assumption here is that because there are "treatments," it is irresponsible not to somehow force people to know their serostatus or the status of their child. A word of caution should be expressed. Relative to the first five years of the epidemic, the current pharmaceutical methods of staving off infection do constitute "treatments" for, or interventions into, the progress of the HIV virus. But only *relatively* speaking. The current drugs are highly toxic, largely untested, and, equally important, available only to the affluent. They are effective only in conjunction with very close monitoring by a physician—who for a large percentage of the infected is not available. As more drugs come on the market, it is necessary to re-evaluate the national consensus against involuntary testing. But this re-evaluation should always be done with a realistic appraisal of what medical (and not just pharmaceutical) interventions are available to patients with HIV and their children. The ethical issue here is whether the knowledge of one's HIV status can bring about any change in one's condition. The issue is one of knowledge and its efficacy. If we have no treatment of newborn infants who are HIV-antibody-positive (but who have only a 30 percent chance of developing AIDS), is it necessary that they be tested, since what this may tell us is that their mothers were or are HIV-antibody-positive—jeopardizing not only her fundamental right to refuse consent to the HIV antibody test herself but also jeopardizing her standing with respect to private insurance, job security, and housing? The debate will continue as drugs and other treatments develop. We should be armed with the proper kinds of questions not merely with respect to the progress of medical technology but equally with respect to access to health care and the importance of official respect for the rights of the affected.

"The epidemic requires wholly new structures, not new policies installed within old structures."

What the last ten years has taught us is that very little of traditional public health thinking "works" with this epidemic. The epidemic requires us to think anew—both about transmission and response. It requires that we address as indicated above what we have singularly refused to acknowledge about current inadequacies in our national systems. In an attempt to give an overview of the epidemic so far, I've offered the above points as ways to *reorient* our thinking to more adequately respond to the epidemic as it really is.

AIDS Is Spreading Rapidly Among Heterosexuals

Kevin R. Hopkins

About the Author: *Kevin R. Hopkins is an AIDS research director for the Hudson Institute, a public-policy research center in Indianapolis, Indiana.*

From a public-policy perspective, AIDS is a major health problem that will not go away any time soon. And conservatives can no longer follow the perilous course of ignoring the problem, as suggested by people like Michael Fumento, the leading apostle of the "closed eyes" school.

As Fumento explained it to a Heritage Foundation audience in July 1988, the "correct" theory of AIDS is that "it will continue to plague those who exchange bodily fluids . . . but will pose far less of a threat to the general heterosexual population." According to Fumento, conservatives should "let the disease run its course," and sit back and wait "until all the evidence is in" before attempting to put together any kind of program to control the spread of the virus. In that way, he argues, conservatives will save themselves from buying into a liberal agenda that they will regret "come the morning after."

But there are several problems with Fumento's theory of AIDS, not the least being that it is wrong—perhaps dangerously so. Infection with the AIDS virus is not a small and isolated affliction, but a large and growing one. It is not a blight just on those who transgress on conventional morality, but is a threat as well to people firmly in the mainstream of society.

The epidemic and its long-term implications are not things that conservatives can ignore.

Kevin R. Hopkins, "Heterosexuals and AIDS," *Conservative Digest,* October 1988. Reprinted with the author's permission.

Over the next decade, the disease will pose many serious challenges to public compassion, public institutions, and the public purse. To be able to contribute intelligently to what may become the most contentious domestic political struggle of the 1990s, conservatives need to replace the seven deadly misperceptions with a greater understanding of the disease and the extent to which it has already spread through the population.

The most critical facts about our knowledge of AIDS and the human immunodeficiency virus (HIV) that causes it can be summarized in seven points that directly counter these common misimpressions:

1. *The disease of most concern is infection with HIV, not AIDS.* Many commentators on AIDS gauge the size of the epidemic by the number of reported AIDS cases—about 70,000, by mid-August 1988—but this is not a useful indicator. While undercounts and delays in reporting cause this figure to be about a third below its actual value, the more important problem is that the collection of symptoms known as AIDS is only the end-stage of the disease, the most obvious sign that a person is infected with HIV. For every identified AIDS case, there are probably dozens of persons carrying the virus, who themselves will eventually come down with end-stage AIDS, and who in the interim may pass the virus on to others.

"[AIDS] is a threat . . . to people firmly in the mainstream of society."

This seems such an obvious aspect of the disease that no one could seriously take AIDS case data to be a true picture of the epidemic, and yet many people do. A typical mistake is relying on AIDS case trends as an indicator of the speed with which new infections are taking place, especially among heterosexuals. But observations of new AIDS cases tell us nothing about current trends in new *infections*. Like the rays from a star several light-years distant, AIDS cases reflect events—infections—that took place a number of years in the past. They give no indication of infection trends *today*. As MIT's [Massachusetts Institute of Technology] Jeffrey Harris has remarked, there could be one million or 100 million people now infected, and there would be no way to tell just by looking at the current AIDS case levels.

"We simply do not know whether there are '400,000 or 4 million people' infected with the virus."

Indeed, it has become clear in the past few months that the incubation period of AIDS infection may be much longer than originally thought. Early reports indicated that most of those infected with the virus who were going to contract AIDS would do so within four or five years, with the remainder escaping the debilitating end-stage of the disease. But more recent studies now place the average incubation period at eight years or more, with some eventual AIDS patients expected to remain free of symptoms for as long as 15 years. Hence, persons infected today might not show up on the CDC [Centers for Disease Control] AIDS register until the turn of the century, and could continue to transmit the virus in the interim.

In this sense, AIDS infection is fundamentally different from the diseases that ravaged earlier societies, from the Black Death of the Middle Ages to the U.S. influenza epidemic of 1918. In each of these instances, it was readily apparent within days or, at most, weeks who the victims and hence carriers of disease were. That is clearly not the case with AIDS. Asymptomatic carriers are no different in appearance than those who are completely free of the infection. No one can tell by merely looking who is and who is not harboring the disease. Most infected

people do not even know they are carrying the virus. AIDS is thus a silent stalker of the population—a quiet plague—thankfully much smaller in number yet far more insidious in its stealth than its historical precedents. That alone will make the public and private response to AIDS an extremely sensitive and complicated undertaking.

Even so, there should be no mistake about the condition that defines the beginning of the disease process and hence the true scope of the epidemic: *infection with HIV*. For in the absence of dramatic medical progress, there appears to be little hope that persons infected with the virus will be able to escape AIDS's ultimate sanction: According to current estimates, fully 99 percent of those infected can be expected to die from the disease.

2. No one knows how many people are infected with HIV. If AIDS cases do not accurately measure the extent of the epidemic, why don't federal officials rely more heavily on the reported number of HIV infections? The reason is that HIV infections are not reportable to health authorities, like syphilis and other venereal diseases are. No one in the United States keeps track of the number of people carrying the virus—in large part because the great majority of infected people have never even been tested for the presence of HIV. As [former] Surgeon General C. Everett Koop has warned, we simply do not know whether there are "400,000 or 4 million people" infected with the virus.

Random AIDS Testing

Yet even without testing the entire population—an enormously expensive and intrusive operation that would be impractical at this time even if it were desirable—there are other ways for officials to approximate how many people are carrying the AIDS virus. The most promising is to conduct a limited number of tests on a nationally representative random sample of people, a method similar to that used by the U.S. Census Bureau in measuring overall population levels in the country. With such information in hand, officials could determine with a high degree of accuracy not only how many people were infected, but how the disease was distributed among different demographic groups.

Unfortunately, the United States still has not undertaken this kind of survey. As Dr. William Haseltine of Boston's Dana-Farber Cancer Institute and one of the nation's leading AIDS researchers explains, the "tools for the determination of the infection of the population have been available for three years. It is a major failure of government's response to the epidemic that a cross-sectional survey of the population for HIV-I infection is not completed." As a result, he points out, "we are 'flying blind' with respect to this fundamental aspect of the epidemic."

"The study concluded that between 1.9 million and 3.0 million Americans probably were infected with HIV."

To its credit, the Atlanta-based CDC, the nation's top AIDS watchdogs, has at last recognized this problem and has planned such a survey.... The first CDC testing effort, in Washington, D.C., was indefinitely delayed after resistance from the black community forced a restructuring of the testing process. Until such problems are resolved and a national survey is actually completed, no one will know how many Americans are infected with HIV.

3. Conventional estimates of HIV infection levels may severely understate the spread of the disease. In the absence of data from a national sample, the CDC has used test results from small population subgroups—such as IV [intravenous] drug users visiting treatment centers, gay men visiting sexually transmitted disease (STD) clinics, blood donors, and military recruits—as one means of gauging the extent of infection in the country. The process works like this: The average infection rate for each subgroup (for example, gay men) is calculated and multiplied by the total

number of people in that group to give the number in the subgroup who are infected. These subtotals are then added up to yield an overall total of infection in the United States. Using this method, the CDC estimated in 1987 that between 945,000 and 1.4 million people were HIV carriers.

Infection Rates

There are two serious problems with this estimate, however. One concerns the infection rates derived from tests in drug treatment and test clinics. Most of these surveys involve only people who voluntarily agreed to have their blood tested for HIV. But a study in New Mexico found that those people who refused to be tested had infection levels *five times higher* than those who volunteered. Thus, the reported infection rates may be significantly below the actual percentages for the subgroups.

More important is the rate applied to the 142 million non-drug-using heterosexuals. The CDC uses the figure of 2/100s of one percent—two out of every 10,000 people—derived from blood donor and military recruit samples as the average for the whole population. But officials of both the American Red Cross and the U.S. military admit that there is no way to tell whether blood donors or recruits are representative of the rest of the population. Indeed, because these institutions actively discourage people from giving blood or applying for military service if they believe they may be infected, the samples are likely to be highly *un*representative of the general populace.

Other studies suggest this may be so. Blood tests on mostly poor heterosexual women in New York and Baltimore revealed infection rates as much as *100 times as high* as in the blood donor and recruit samples. Fewer than one-third of the women in the Baltimore study were members of clearly identified risk groups, and therefore did not contract the disease through needle-sharing or sex with drug users. Thus, the infection rates used to produce the national estimate of HIV levels among heterosexuals may be greatly understated, meaning that the overall totals of infection may be as well. Again, without a nationally representative survey, there is no way to tell for sure.

Given these deficiencies in the small-sample infection rates, the only reasonably accurate method for estimating infection levels in the country is to "work backward" from AIDS case data to derive the time-path of HIV infections that would have generated the observed AIDS cases. The Hudson Institute, a public-policy research group noted for its futures studies, completed such an analysis that carefully adjusted the AIDS data for underreporting and delays in reporting, used medical evidence on the progression from infection to AIDS, and incorporated the best available information on people's actual sexual and drug-using practices. The study concluded that between 1.9 million and 3.0 million Americans probably were infected with HIV—*more than twice the conventional estimates*—and that those numbers were continuing to grow.

Infected Heterosexuals

4. AIDS is not just a gay disease. It remains a common perception that AIDS is a "gay disease." One frequently hears, for instance, that only two percent of all AIDS cases are the result of transmission of the virus between American-born heterosexuals. Of course, because these are AIDS cases, they represent infections that took place many years in the past, and so, as before, they say nothing about current HIV infections resulting from heterosexual intercourse. The category of "heterosexual transmission" is probably understated anyway, since the CDC includes in that category only people who meet a very restrictive standard for how they might have contracted the disease.

But there is a larger issue here. The number of heterosexual *transmission* cases of AIDS (that is, people who contracted the disease through heterosexual contact) is not the same thing as the number of heterosexuals who *have* AIDS. Excluding gay men, who constitute some 70 per-

cent of AIDS cases reported as of mid-1988, the vast majority of the remaining AIDS patients (IV drug abusers, hemophiliacs, and transfusion recipients as well as heterosexual contact cases) are heterosexuals. And at least some of the men classified as having received the disease homosexually may be mainly heterosexual. Taking these factors into account, and adjusting the data for reporting delays, shows that nearly *one-third* of all AIDS cases have occurred among heterosexuals—as have more than half of all AIDS cases among minority members. The point is, these people, no matter how they contracted the disease, can pass it on to other heterosexuals. . . .

> ## "Most of these heterosexuals are drug users . . . [but] they can still spread the disease heterosexually."

---

5. The number of HIV-infected heterosexuals may be greatly underestimated. The most frequently cited estimate of infected heterosexuals is the 30,000 figure derived by CDC. Not only is this number understated because it relies on nonrepresentative infection surveys, but it applies only to heterosexuals "without other identified risks." The total number of heterosexuals carrying the virus, including drug users, is more than 10 times as high, even according to official calculations. But the Hudson study, using the adjusted data and more sophisticated estimation techniques, found that from 850,000 to 1.4 million heterosexuals probably were infected, some *300 to 450* times the most commonly cited figure.

To be sure, most of these heterosexuals are drug users—which takes nothing away from the fact that they can still spread the disease heterosexually—but as many as a third or more are not. The Hudson study estimated that the number of infections among non-drug-using heterosexuals was far from minor—from a minimum of some 200,000 to as many as 500,000, with the most likely number around 330,000. Together, heterosexuals appear to account for more than 45 percent of all HIV infections, and non-drug-using heterosexuals for about 14 percent of infections. If it ever was, AIDS is certainly no longer just a "gay disease."

Middle-class Problem

6. *HIV infection is making its way into the middle-class.* Even if one concedes that HIV infection has become a problem of heterosexuals as well as of gay men, the point is often made that only the poor or the partners of IV drug abusers are at risk. Presumably, middle-class conservatives do not need to be concerned in that case, since AIDS is yet another problem the poor, supposedly bent on short-term gratification, are "bringing on themselves."

This is not warranted by the evidence. The Hudson study found that as many as 120,000 middle-class non-drug-using heterosexuals, including 85,000 whites, were already infected with the virus. This may be a small number when compared to a million or more gay men, but it still represents as many as a third of all infected non-drug-using heterosexuals, and a significant outlet for the further spread of HIV among the middle-class.

At least two carefully conducted surveys document that this spread is already occurring. One, carried out by researchers William Masters and Virginia Johnson, looked at 400 mostly young, mostly white, mostly middle-class heterosexuals who led active sex lives—an average of six partners per year for each of the past five years. The investigators found that between five and seven percent of these sexually active men and women were already infected, as were 12 to 14 percent of the most sexually active persons. Another survey in New York, reported at the Fourth International AIDS Conference, evaluated 39 heterosexual contacts of HIV-infected persons in a largely white, middle-class borough of the city, and found that 30 percent were already infected. The researchers concluded: "Heterosexual HIV spread is occurring in the middle-class. The predominant sources are IV [drug users] who do

not fit the stereotype of being minorities and lower class.". . .

7. *HIV can be transmitted in the course of conventional heterosexual sex.* In light of everything that has been said above, perhaps it is unnecessary to state the obvious: HIV infection can be passed from one person to another through "normal" intercourse. Although it is much more difficult to catch HIV than, say, syphilis, there are recorded cases of HIV being transmitted in a single sexual act. Among the steady sexual partners of HIV-infected persons, anywhere from 20 percent to 70 percent contract the disease within one to three years.

"HIV infection can be passed from one person to another through 'normal' intercourse."

In sum, conservatives may be inviting a serious medical and moral crisis, in both their political and public lives, if they ignore the evidence and import of the mounting AIDS catastrophe. As former Presidential Science Advisor Dr. George A. Keyworth has cautioned, recent findings are a "sober warning" that "we may be gravely underestimating the extent of the epidemic. The disease may be spreading much faster than has been generally believed." Not only do such results argue for more thoughtful consideration of how to handle the future strains on our national health and economic systems, he contends, but they also pose "important implications for individual behavior in the face of this increased hazard."

To fail to face up to this challenge, with the dispassion and common sense that has typified conservative public policymaking in the past, would be to do more than miss a major opportunity to help protect the American people from the tragedy of a terrible disease. It would be to forfeit the decency, humanity, and compassion that must lie at the heart of good conservative leadership.

AIDS Is a Health Risk for Women

Sue Halpern

About the Author: *Sue Halpern is a frequent contributor to* Ms., *a monthly feminist magazine. Halpern, who lives in the Adirondack Mountains of New York, has written magazine articles on the topics of abortion and the homeless.*

"This is ridiculous," I tell the nurse as she primes my arm for the "AIDS test"—the test that determines the presence of antibodies to the human immunodeficiency virus (HIV) known to cause AIDS—required by the company to which I am applying for health insurance. "What chance do I have of testing positive? I'm a woman. I'm married. I've never had a transfusion, never injected drugs."

"It's a lot cheaper for them to do this now," she says, sticking me with a needle, "than to pay for it later."

I don't argue. What she says makes good sense, but it's beside the point, the real point of my objection: people like me—white, middle class, female—don't get AIDS.

I am right, in a way, and I am wrong. There is a lawyer my age in New York City who has no idea how she contracted the disease. There is a 16-year-old high school student at the other end of the country who has no doubt where she got it since she's only had sex with one boy. There is the daughter of doctors in Westchester whose parents thought she had lupus. And then there is Anita Wexler, who used to be the director of finance for ABC-TV. "I bet Metropolitan Life wants to kill me," she says of the company that is paying for her thousands of dollars of medical expenses each year. When she was younger,

Sue Halpern, "AIDS: Rethinking the Risk," *Ms.*, May 1989. Reprinted with permission of *Ms.* magazine, © 1989.

Anita Wexler had an IV [intravenous] drug habit. She knew it could kill her, but not in this way, with fungus under her nails and a tuberculosis-like infection and hallucinations induced by a toxic liver.

"There are documented cases of transmission of HIV on one sexual contact, male to female," says Dr. Tedd Ellerbrock, a medical epidemiologist at the Centers for Disease Control [CDC]. "Yet, on the other side, which women are really at risk? Those who are doing IV drugs and those who are sexually involved with high-risk partners."

This is the conventional wisdom, the one borne out by the statistics, the demographics, the impressionistic data. "We are seeing many more women than ever before," says Ronald Johnson, executive director of the Minority Task Force on AIDS in New York City. "Our population is shifting away from gay and bisexual men as the AIDS population shifts to substance abusers. The women we see are mostly substance abusers or women who are the sexual partners of substance abusers. In New York City, AIDS is becoming a poor person's disease."

> **"There are documented cases of transmission of HIV on one sexual contact, male to female."**

The problem with the conventional wisdom is that some women may take it too seriously—that women who are not IV drug users, say, or have no reason to suspect that their male lover has had a male lover—will cease to be concerned with the disease or those it affects, that they will feel exempt. It wasn't long ago that all women felt this way.

There are, at this writing in May 1989, in this country, 7,220 diagnosed cases of AIDS in women—9 percent of the total number of diagnosed cases. By 1992, women are expected to account for 10 percent or more of 365,000 cases of AIDS in the United States. But this projection fails to illustrate with sufficient detail the extent of the epidemic. AIDS is the end stage of a much more widespread condition, the very tip of an iceberg that will not remain submerged much longer—HIV disease. There are an estimated 1.5 to 3 million Americans currently infected with the human immunodeficiency virus, the agent that causes AIDS. At the moment, most are asymptomatic, unaware that they are infected. Nonetheless, they are capable of transmitting the virus. No one knows how many will get sick, develop AIDS, die. Dr. Mathilde Krim, founding cochair of the American Foundation for AIDS Research, estimates that "75 percent of them will become very ill within seven years of acquiring their infection." The Public Health Service suggests that 30 percent will become ill within five years of infection. The fact is, it is still too early to tell.

HIV and AIDS are not the same thing. This is a critical distinction, one that is often lost in the confusion of learning that someone, possibly yourself, tests positive for HIV. There is no test for AIDS itself; that determination is made by a physician after a patient has had one or more of the various opportunistic infections or malignancies included in the CDC's definition of the disease, such as *Pneumocystis carinii* pneumonia (PCP), Kaposi's sarcoma, dementia, wasting syndrome. The infections that overwhelm AIDS patients are unusual or nonthreatening in people who do not have the virus. In people with AIDS, the virus has attacked and killed certain white blood cells called T-helper cells that are essential to the body's immune system. As these cells are destroyed, the body becomes more vulnerable to illnesses that otherwise it would be able to resist. The illnesses are considered "opportunistic" because they move in on and take advantage of the damaged immune system.

Gender-neutral Disease

The CDC, which has been tracking AIDS since 1981, does not include people infected with HIV in its weekly morbidity and mortality reports. Nor does it include people with AIDS-related complex (ARC). People with ARC suffer many of the same illnesses as do people with AIDS; they have night sweats, persistent diarrhea, fungus infections, chronic fatigue. Because they have not been stricken with one of the "major" infections within the CDC's definition of AIDS, though, they are not diagnosed as having the disease. ARC is thought to be the prelude to AIDS. It does not always segue into AIDS, however; sometimes it leads directly to death. In certain cases it may be more benign than AIDS, but that may not be saying a lot. Women seem especially prone to ARC.

"Women seem especially prone to [AIDS-related complex]."

"Everyone I know who is serving women has said they are seeing a lot more ARC cases than AIDS cases," says Maria Maggenti, a member of the AIDS Coalition To Unleash Power, ACT UP, a New York City activist organization. For Catherine Maier, coordinator of the Women's Services Program of the San Francisco AIDS Foundation, this has certainly been the case. Of 102 clients, 30 have AIDS, while 72 have ARC.

When the history of the AIDS epidemic is finally written, the absence of ARC from the public record may prove to have been the page that would have made women understand that this disease is gender neutral. It's possible to be complacent about an epidemic that has affected *only* 7,220 women. But what if the number were actually higher, the disease more widespread? What if, as researchers are now beginning to think, the virus may follow a different course in women than in men? Women, for instance, appear to be more susceptible to some illnesses, like respiratory infections, and less susceptible to others, like Kaposi's sarcoma. What if the CDC definition of AIDS does not accurately identify the disease as it is manifest in women because the definition was derived from a caseload that is overwhelmingly male? It's conceivable. Since 1981 the CDC has changed the definition of AIDS three times, as researchers have learned more about the disease. In 1988, the Presidential Commission on the Human Immunodeficiency Virus Epidemic stated in its report: "With little exception, HIV research and programs have focused exclusively on homosexual men and intravenous drug users. As a result, there is limited information about the course of HIV infection in women."

Just a few months before the report was issued, Dr. Iris Davis, who runs an AIDS clinic in Brooklyn, told Congress: "The statistics presently available to public health officials often do not describe the extent of spread of HIV disease or may be understated. For women alone, attempting to determine the true extent of HIV-related disease, we have to look at overall death statistics and I looked at those in New York City. In 1986, there was a 5 percent increase in deaths in women from 14 to 44 years of age, in addition to the recorded cases of AIDS. Numbers of deaths due to illnesses such as pneumonia/influenza have risen by approximately 150 percent."

Although Anita Wexler had been sick for two years with AIDS-related complex, she wasn't officially counted in the AIDS statistics until 1988, after a long bout with PCP. She had left her job before that, when she no longer had the strength to get out of bed. These days she feels well enough to go to the movies now and then, to work as a volunteer with hospitalized AIDS patients, and to serve on the board of New York's People with AIDS Coalition. Still, her life—especially her social life—is circumscribed. "It's hard not being in a relationship going through this," says Wexler. "Ninety percent of the people I hang out with are gay men. I'd like to meet a straight man with the disease but they are all drug addicts."

Chances of Infection

So what is the chance that you, personally, are infected? Statistically, not very great. In 1988, for example, the state of Illinois instituted mandatory testing of couples applying for marriage li-

censes and found 28 positives in 155,000 people. Of the 12 women who were infected almost all had used drugs intravenously or had been sexually involved with someone who used drugs intravenously. It's the same across the country. According to the CDC, of the 7,220 women with AIDS, 52 percent are current or former IV drug users, 29 percent were the sexual partners of infected men, 11 percent received infected blood products (before 1985, when the antibody test was developed). The cause of the disease in the remaining cases is undetermined.

"Women can contract the virus from . . . vaginal and anal intercourse and oral sex with someone who is carrying the virus."

And what are the chances that you, personally, *risk* infection? It depends on how you live, where you live, where you've been, who you've been with, what you have done. Like men, women can contract the virus from a dirty syringe, and from vaginal and anal intercourse and oral sex with someone who is carrying the virus. Researchers at the University of California determined that the likelihood of infection from having vaginal intercourse once with an infected partner without a condom is one in 500. The odds change dramatically with the number of sexual encounters. Having sex 500 times with an infected partner without using a condom raises the probability of infection to two in three. But for a disease with a 100 percent mortality rate, betting on these odds is not like stacking your chips on the red or the black—it's like playing Russian roulette. "If there is a one percent or two percent risk of getting infected, that, to me, is a risk," says Solveig Hover, a counselor at one of New York City's AIDS test sites. "As long as there is one person whose history you don't know, it's a risk."

According to the University of California researchers: "Choosing a partner who is not in any high-risk group provides almost four orders of magnitude (5,000 fold) of protection compared with choosing a partner in the highest risk category. . . . Condoms, in contrast, are estimated to provide only one order of magnitude." But who can be certain that their partner isn't infected, especially when so many people are unaware of their HIV status? Even the antibody test is not a guarantee, since the window between the time of infection and the development of antibodies may be open for as long as six months. These days, people who are not in long-term, monogamous relationships are told to be cautious when considering a new sexual relationship. They are told that they'd better find out that person's sexual history, drug history, and medical history before learning if he or she prefers the eggs scrambled or over easy.

"How do you know where your partner has been?" Hover says. "Most people should be practicing safe sex."

"[AIDS] travels as easily between men and women as it does men and men."

Safe sex, in a heterosexual relationship, means that a condom is used. It seems quite simple, but isn't. Unless a woman knows how to "negotiate" safe sex, condoms may make her more vulnerable to harm, not less. According to Maria Maggenti of ACT UP, battered women's shelters and rape crisis centers lately have been receiving calls from women who have been attacked for asking husbands and boyfriends to use a condom. According to Karen Solomon, the HIV test site coordinator for the New York City Department of Health: "When a woman asks her lover to use a condom, he may accuse her of cheating on him or not trusting him. If they are in a battering relationship her life could be at risk." Asking a man to wear a condom, a report issued by the Women and AIDS Resource Network (WARN) states, "only serves to magnify the larger societal problem—females who are powerless in a male-dominated society are just as powerless in a male-dominated bedroom. If a man does not want to wear a condom, he won't. With the coming of AIDS, the age-old battle of the sexes is literally becoming a life-and-death struggle for women."

Public Nightmare

When Faye Grant (not her real name), a 33-year-old New Yorker, married her husband in 1983, it didn't even occur to her to ask him to use a condom. She was aware that he had had homosexual relationships in the past, but they were in love and AIDS wasn't something that concerned them—it wasn't their disease. Not long after they were married and working together as interior designers, her husband began to come down with a series of inexplicable illnesses. At the time, the HIV antibody test had not been developed. In two years, when it was, it confirmed what they had already figured out. Her husband was seropositive. So was she. Her husband died a year later.

From the beginning, heterosexual transmission has been the nightmare of the public at large. As long as AIDS was the "gay plague," people who were not gay could rest assured at night, often next to a lover they barely knew. But then it turned out that the disease does not have sexual preferences, that it travels as easily between men and women as it does men and men (and now, in two reported cases, women and women). According to an article in the *Journal of the American Medical Association*: "Although AIDS is not 'exploding' into the heterosexual population relative to other risk groups, the increase in the number of heterosexual cases is proportional to increases in other risk groups. These increases are resulting in a doubling of heterosexual cases every 14 to 16 months."

As it became clear that heterosexual transmission was occurring, female prostitutes were typically considered to be the source, the operators in a big game of Telephone: a man would have sex with an infected prostitute, then have sex with another woman—his wife, a girlfriend—and infect her, maybe she'd get pregnant and infect the baby, and so on. But according to researchers at the CDC, the game doesn't quite work that way. As with anyone else, infection is dependent upon risky behavior like sharing unsterilized needles and having unprotected intercourse with an infected partner. In Las Vegas, for example, where prostitution is legal and IV drug use among prostitutes is nil, the seroprevalence rate is zero. In Newark, where drug use is rampant, it is estimated that more than 60 percent of prostitutes who work the streets are infected. Many prostitutes make it a practice to slip condoms on johns, but now some report offers of $50 and $100 more if they don't. "Do you know what an extra $50 means to someone whose nose is running and bones ache?" says Gina (not her real name), a 30-year-old Boston woman who has ARC and a drug habit she supports by prostitution. "These men don't live in caves. They know AIDS exists, but they pay extra for sex without a rubber and then go home and have sex with their wives. A lot of men think they'll take their chances because they say it's harder for a woman to pass the virus than a man."

> ## "Public recognition that women are susceptible to HIV disease . . . has come almost by accident."

This assumption—that female to male transmission is less likely than male to female transmission—although widely believed, is unfounded, according to Dr. Ellerbrock and his colleagues at the CDC; no evidence yet has been produced to substantiate it. They suggest that AIDS in America could someday parallel the course of AIDS in Africa where the rate of infection is equal between the sexes. On the other hand, genital ulcers, which provide openings for the virus, are more common in both men and women in Africa than they are here. Because of such factors the comparison may turn out to be inapt. In either case, it is important to recognize that when the CDC states that no evidence has been found, it is not reporting that no evidence will ever be found. It is saying that it does not yet know what it will find.

AIDS Effect on Women

As the President's Commission noted, not much research has been done on women and HIV disease. This wasn't malice aforethought, just oversight—the kind that hindsight usually reveals. Not much is known about drug therapies for infected women, either, but this, it turns out, is the result of something far more pernicious, the systematic exclusion of women from experimental drug tests. According to Nan Hunter of the American Civil Liberties Union [ACLU], in 1988 only 142 women—4 percent—were enrolled in the National Institute of Allergy and Infectious Diseases' trials of new drugs, because the government, like private drug companies, made it a practice to exclude women of childbearing age, the age of most women infected with HIV, from experimental drug protocols. This practice is not exclusive to HIV drug testing; researchers typically consider women improper experimental subjects if there is a chance that their reproductive systems or fetuses could be harmed.

As a consequence of pressure brought to bear on the National Institutes of Health, the Food and Drug Administration, and private drug companies by the ACLU, ACT UP, and others, the "overt exclusion of women has stopped," says Deborah Ellis, Hunter's colleague at the ACLU. More entrenched problems persist, however, that keep women out of clinical trials, like having no child care, no help at home. "If you have HIV disease and you are a 35-year-old woman with four kids and you still have to get dinner made for your husband, you are not going to travel all the way into midtown Manhattan in the middle of the day for treatment," Dr. Davis says.

And then there is the problem of information, of knowing where and when new protocols are being held. How can poor women (or any poor person, for that matter) find out about medical research when they don't have primary care physicians, when the emergency room and public clinics serve as their doctor's office, and when the doctors they see there are not aware of new drugs and new drug protocols themselves? Women who are HIV infected tend to be isolated, atomized, observes Catherine Maier. They do not have a natural community, as gay men have had, from which to draw support and from which can emerge a network of self-taught experts that stays on top of the latest medical information and disseminates it to their peers. The most resourceful women have been able to tap into this network, but even for them it's a party line, not a direct connection. They may not be hearing what they need to hear if the drugs and dosages are different for men and women. They may not be talking to each other. There are a few groups devoted to the special needs of seropositive women—from health care to child care—but they are far between. "I get calls from women in Pittsburgh and Ohio and Canada," says Marie St. Cyr-Delpe, director of WARN. "They have nothing where they are. It's only been in the last year that the issue of women with AIDS has scratched the surface."

Public recognition that women are susceptible to HIV disease—that women die from AIDS—has come almost by accident, second-hand to the rising number of babies with AIDS. "When people talk about women and AIDS, they talk about women who give AIDS to children," says Lynne McArthur, cochair of New York State's Women and AIDS Project. In some urban hospitals, one in 22 women delivered HIV positive infants. Anywhere from 30 to 60 percent of these babies will actually develop the virus. If they do, routine childhood illnesses like chicken pox and measles can kill them. By 1991, according to the President's Commission, as many as 20,000 children may be infected with the virus, and their mothers may not have known they

were themselves HIV positive until after their babies were tested at birth and found to be carrying their antibodies. In one study, at New York City's Bellevue Hospital, 24 out of 28 new mothers were unaware they were seropositive. Even if they had known, though, it would not have necessarily led to the termination of the pregnancy.

"Statistically, women die much more quickly than men from AIDS."

"Some of my clients have gotten pregnant," Catherine Maier says. "We talk about it, but it's up to them. They have to make up their own mind. It takes away their dignity to tell them what to do. I tell them that there is a fifty percent chance that their baby will be infected. Fifty percent to you and me may sound like pretty bad odds, but a fifty percent chance to them may sound pretty good. The chance of dying of a heroin overdose is much greater than that. But I always ask them, 'Have you ever heard a baby with AIDS cry?'"

Empowering Women

Infected women who do have children—HIV positive or negative—often as not find the combination of child-rearing and sickness debilitating. They tend to neglect their own health to care for their family, which often includes an infected spouse or lover, and seek treatment for their own illness only when they are too sick to take care of anybody else. Statistically, women die much more quickly than men from AIDS once they are diagnosed, which may be because they enter treatment at a much later stage when the illness is acute. Describing her own case, Faye Grant says: "When I found out I was infected I didn't really get full of tears. At the time I really wasn't concerned for myself. I was taking care of my husband, who was dying. I wasn't the issue."

Talk to anyone counseling women about the

human immunodeficiency virus, and before long they will all mention the same word, the same goal for their clients—empowerment—empowering women to control their own lives. At first it sounds out of place, especially in the context of a fatal disease like AIDS. And it sounds out of date, a rhetorical riff left over from the sixties. But for many women with AIDS and ARC and other manifestations of HIV disease—women whom the Women's Movement largely left behind—learning to assert themselves, learning to get what they need, learning to like themselves, may be the best treatment there is. To Karen Solomon, empowerment means that women will begin to demand the medical care they need. To Catherine Maier, it means that women who early in their lives turned to drugs or men will get the chance to do the things they have always wanted to do and be the people they have always wanted to be—finish high school, be good mothers.

"Every day I look in the mirror and tell myself that I love myself, that I'm doing the best I can," Anita Wexler says. She also says that now that she spends so much time in her apartment she's getting it redecorated, in lavender and pink. "I should be dead, according to the statistics," she says. "I refuse to be a victim."

AIDS Poses a Threat to Teenagers

Jean Fain

About the Author: *Jean Fain is a free-lance writer in Cambridge, Massachusetts. She has written articles for the* Wall Street Journal *and the* Los Angeles Times *newspaper syndicate.*

One recent hot afternoon at Revere Beach [near Boston], just before fall, teen-age beachgoers were doing what they do every sunny summer day: strutting, posing, and preening along the beach strip. Lithe bodies clad in unofficial uniforms — French-cut bikinis, gold chains, and moussed hairdos for girls; shorts, white leather hightops, and gelled, spiked hair for boys—hang out here to catch some rays, some fun, and, who knows, maybe some action.

Stretched out on colorful towels along the beach wall and on adjacent car hoods, teen-agers talk over blaring radios about pressing issues like who's that hunk and what's happening this weekend. Subjects of delayed consequences, such as the ozone layer, cholesterol, or AIDS, don't naturally come up. On this sunny day, AIDS is the last thing on their minds. But with some prompting from a visitor, several of the beachgoers are willing to discuss the deadly virus.

"I usually don't talk about AIDS with the girls I go out with," one 19-year-old from Everett authoritatively tells his younger cousin from Ohio. "I instinctively know they don't carry a sexual disease because of their age, their family background—white, middle or upper class—and because of where they hang out."

Down the wall, only one of a group of five girls glistening with tanning oil says she would discuss AIDS with a new date. But all five are concerned, to varying degrees, about catching the virus.

"I worry about it," says an 18-year-old blond in a faux reptile-skin suit. "But not a lot." The girl who said she would talk with a new date about AIDS reprimands her friend. "Even if you've been going with a guy for two years," she says, "you don't know how many people he's been with."

"I do worry about it," the blond girl insists, "but it's not always on my mind." Her friend is quick to respond. "I worry about it as much as I worry about nuclear war. All the time."

Not far away, four Medford guys relaxing in lounge chairs in the parking lot talk about protection methods in good-buddy banter.

"Get a good girl," suggests one 17-year-old, from behind purple shades. "A nice, respectable girl."

"Don't go with pigs," translates his buddy.

Abstinence, they all agree, is a fine concept, but condoms are essential. Unless, of course, it's 3 a.m. and Store 24 is closed. "What are you going to do, ring the doorbell the next day and say, 'Hey, I got one?'" asks an 18-year-old with John Travolta looks and a deep tan.

"I usually don't talk about AIDS with the girls I go out with."

At this point, his idea of feminine perfection walks by in a hot-pink halter and black shorts. "I'd give my left arm for that," he says.

"Would you do 'that' without a condom?" a friend asks.

"If I didn't have one," the 18-year-old says with a grin, "I think I'd have to say I would."

What would he do if he then contracted AIDS, the visitor wants to know.

The teen-ager's smile vanishes. "I'd buy a bike and drive off the nearest cliff."

Like those on Revere Beach that summer day, more and more adolescents can accurately recite AIDS-prevention methods, but some still have life-threatening misconceptions, and many acknowledge that in the heat of the moment they probably wouldn't practice what they preach.

Until recently, it's been all too easy to dismiss the threat of AIDS to adolescents. Teen-agers account for fewer than 1 percent of all AIDS case, 568 of the 146,746 cases diagnosed, according to the Centers for Disease Control in Atlanta. But given what we know now about the long latency of the virus (approximately eight to 10 years) and the number of young adults in their 20s who have contracted AIDS (one-fifth of all reported cases), it seems likely that some, if not many, young adults contracted the virus in their teens.

"That sense of invulnerability keeps kids from perceiving the threat of AIDS."

Unless drastic measures are taken quickly, the teen-age population is likely to become, as the American Pediatric Association fears, the epidemic's "next hot spot." Calling it the next death march may be more apt, especially when you consider teen-agers' interest in sex, drug use, and other risky behaviors. More teen-agers are "doing it," and doing it younger, than they were a generation ago. According to the US Sex Information and Education Council, a New York-based nonprofit organization concerned with sex education, more than half of all American teen-agers aged 15 to 19 are already sexually active—primarily, but not exclusively, in heterosexual activity.

But most kids aren't really worried, says Mary Jane Rotheram-Borus, an associate professor of clinical psychology at Columbia University who runs an AIDS-prevention program for runaway and gay youths. "Adolescence is characterized developmentally by a sense of invulnerability," Rotheram-Borus says. "And that sense of invulnerability keeps kids from perceiving the threat of AIDS."

More teen-agers are using condoms but, in light of the rising rates of sexually transmitted disease, still too few, too infrequently. Twenty-five percent of Massachusetts teen-agers contract such a disease every year. According to researchers Ralph Hingson and Lee Strunin at Boston University's [BU] School of Medicine, 69 percent of adolescents in the commonwealth have reported that they've never used condoms or that they use them inconsistently.

Teenage Experimentation

All this unprotected sex affords America the unfavorable distinction of having the highest teen-age birthrate in the industrialized world—1 million teen-age girls, nearly 1 in 10, get pregnant every year. More teen-agers are saying no to drugs, but the teen-age years remain a time to experiment, Hingson and Strunin reported. The two conducted statewide telephone surveys of teen-agers in 1986 and in 1988. The proportion of Massachusetts teen-agers (in homes with telephones) using drugs other than alcohol and marijuana declined by 4 percent, from 13 percent to 9 percent, and intravenous drug use declined from 1 percent to 0.1 percent. The danger for teen-agers experimenting with drugs is not only in sharing dirty needles but in having sexual contact with older, IV [intravenous]-drug-using individuals. What is particularly disturbing, the BU researchers concluded after their 1988 survey, is the fact that although most adolescents have been informed of the dangers of high-risk activities through school- and community-based programs, many maintain perilous attitudes and behaviors. Random telephone calls to 800 teen-agers, aged 16 to 19, revealed that the proportion of teen-agers who had discussed AIDS in the classroom increased from 52 percent to 82 percent in two years. Yet 37 percent reported having never used condoms, and 33 percent reported using them only some of the time. Eighteen percent of the respondents reported having had unprotected sex with more than one partner in the previous year, and 3 percent had had unprotected sex with IV-drug users.

And misconceptions persist. In the 1988 survey, some teen-agers still believed that AIDS can be acquired from toilet seats (5 percent), eating and drinking utensils (11 percent), airborne germs (6 percent), or by giving blood (51 percent). Five percent believed that men can't catch the virus sexually from women. Single adults score similarly to teen-agers in surveys about HIV [human immunodeficiency virus] transmission and condom use; teen-agers and adults from low-income, minority, and inner-city households generally score lower than average on such surveys and account for a higher percentage of the nation's AIDS cases.

Preventing the disease among teen-agers is going to take more than feeding adolescents the right answers, experts agree, especially when so much in our culture keeps encouraging youths to have sex. "I was on the stump all the time, exhorting young people to listen to what I was saying about AIDS and its sexual transmission," C. Everett Koop, former US surgeon general, has said. "And yet young people who watch soap operas got the impression the only reason you got out of bed in the morning was to jump into somebody else's."

> **"It seems clear that teen-agers . . . are transmitting the virus through heterosexual intercourse."**

Pop-music influences such as Madonna's sexual gesturing and 2 Live Crew's moan-filled lyrics glamorize wantonness. The hip teen-agers in such movies as *Heathers* and *About Last Night* jump into bed within a few hours of meeting one another. Teen-age film characters rarely discuss prevention methods, even in *Casual Sex?*, a movie about safe sex in the age of AIDS. The covers and advertisements of teen magazines continue to feature models with bedroom eyes and sexy outfits.

"People need to recognize that this is a critical situation," says Devon Davidson, a national AIDS curriculum consultant and the director of the trilingual Viviremos AIDS Education Project in Boston. "Kids' lives are at stake, a lot more than most people realize. What's really scary is, adolescents exhibit many of the same risk behaviors and attitudes that caused the virus to spread in other populations." Like many in the gay population, teen-agers generally have a higher number of sexual partners than do older heterosexuals. And much like addicts, Davidson notes, adolescents lack the ability to anticipate consequences, their own reactions, and their own feelings.

Teens at Risk

For many teen-agers, it's hard to believe that everyone, not just gays and junkies, is at risk of contracting AIDS. Comparing the male-female ratio of AIDS cases among New York City teen-agers (2.9 males for every 1 female) with that among New York City adults (7 to 1), it seems clear that teen-agers, more than any other age group, are transmitting the virus through heterosexual intercourse. A study of HIV infection among college students shows that of 16,861 students who sought blood tests in 1989 at 19 college health centers nationwide, an average of 2 per 1,000 tested positive. These figures indicate that even one promiscuous student infected with HIV on a college campus could make for a bleak scenario.

Twenty-four-year-old Alison Gertz has gone public with her story, as did Ryan White, the Indiana teen-ager who died of AIDS in 1990, to help teen-agers realize that clean-cut heterosexuals can indeed get AIDS. At age 16, this popular, pretty, straight-A student caught the virus, probably from a 25-year-old she met at a New York nightclub.

"I had suspicions that he was bisexual," Gertz

says. "I even asked him if he were bisexual, but he said he wasn't," she recalls tiredly, exhausted from having told her story so many times. Since developing full-blown AIDS in 1987, Gertz has given interviews to publications (including the *New York Times, People,* and *Mademoiselle*), ABC's *20/20,* and college audiences.

"It wouldn't have mattered, anyway," Gertz continues. "When I was with this man, it wasn't even called AIDS yet."

Bradford, who asked that his last name not be used, is a 20-year-old office worker in Boston. He's at far greater risk for contracting AIDS than most teen-agers, because he's gay and he has tested HIV-positive.

Bradford, like Gertz, was completely surprised by his diagnosis. "Clearly, we had unsafe sex," Bradford says, referring to the man who infected him at age 17. "I had heard about AIDS, but I didn't realize I had anything to be concerned about." Not until months later, when he came down with a severe case of strep throat, a 104-degree fever, and mononucleosis—symptoms of a failing immune system—did Bradford become concerned. Yet he put off having "safer" sex for a year and getting tested for another six months. Two weeks before he got his braces off, he tested positive for HIV.

Bradford, like Alison Gertz, now talks to teen-agers at schools and community centers in an attempt to help others understand. His prognosis is uncertain, but doctors generally agree that virtually everyone infected with the HIV virus will eventually develop AIDS and, most likely, die.

"I want to know why . . . we're held back from talking about necessities to save teens' lives?"

If they had protected themselves then, Bradford and Gertz know, they'd likely be healthy now. The gay community has shown that education can prevent the spread of this virus that devastates the immune system. Years after the dis-

ease was named, there's been a significant decline in the number of new AIDS cases among homosexuals. The number of teen-age AIDS cases increased by 40 percent from 1988 to 1990.

Fingers have been pointed at government, communities, schools, religious organizations, parents, and teen-agers. AIDS activists and educators see the root of the problem as a general discomfort and unwillingness to talk about subjects that have never been easy to discuss.

Saving Lives

"We're living in a society closed to issues of sex, drug use, death, and dying," says Maurice Melchiono, the program coordinator for adolescent AIDS education and outreach activities at Children's Hospital. "We can't say the word 'condom,'" Melchiono continues. His eyes linger on a photo above his desk of a handsome teen-ager, the first client he lost to AIDS. "I want to know why . . ." he says, "we're held back from talking about necessities to save teens' lives?"

Many leaders and institutions that could facilitate life-saving talk and action have become expert at avoiding questions like that one, says Melchiono. Not a word has been heard from President Bush on the subject of teen-agers and AIDS, although Bush did plant a tree in memory of Ryan White in 1990. The last loud, official words from Washington specifically about teen-agers and AIDS came from former Surgeon General Koop in his landmark 1986 "Report on AIDS," which bemoaned the public's reticence in dealing with the subject of sexual practices.

The federal government hasn't been inattentive to the teen-age problem. The federal Centers for Disease Control in Atlanta funds AIDS educational programs and research. The CDC has also developed general guidelines, but no specific mandate, for AIDS education. [Massachusetts'] response echoes Washington's: Fund, educate, but mandate nothing. Cutting through political red tape, state employees like Shoshana Rosenfeld, adolescent HIV prevention coordinator for the Department of Public Health, and Kevin Cranston, AIDS health-education consultant to the Department of Education, have launched innovative educational programs, organized opportunities for educators to share ideas, and drafted policies that affect teen-agers in and out of school.

AIDS activists lambast the state for not doing more. The complaints boil down to two: that Massachusetts does not put enough money into education and that it doesn't allow enough leeway in terms of what can be said—like the word "condom." When Linette Liebling, president of the board of directors for the AIDS Action Committee, was editing the state-sanctioned AIDS curriculum back in 1986, she was instructed, after much debate, to delete that six-letter word. "It took the guts out of the program," Liebling says, the outrage still evident in her voice.

The Department of Public Health released its 19-page report *Adolescents at Risk: Sexually Transmitted Diseases*. The report clearly documents that 15- to 19-year-olds have the highest rates of gonorrhea, syphilis, chlamydia, and other STDs [sexually transmitted diseases]—and that those rates are going up. In 1990, despite a new advertising campaign launched by the state promoting condom use, then-Gov. Michael S. Dukakis showed no sign of taking a stand on condoms and teen-agers.

A historical survey shows that mass condom distribution has been the only sure-fire weapon for combating STDs among teen-agers. In his book, *No Magic Bullet: A Social History of Venereal Disease in the United States*, Harvard University professor Allan M. Brandt explains that lectures on the dangers of unprotected sex did little to dissuade young World War I recruits from having unprotected sex and thus bringing home STDs. Providing condoms to World War II recruits did, however, markedly reduce infection rates. "The long-standing debate about teenagers has been, do you try to discourage them from engaging in sexual activity as a means of prevention, or do you recognize that teen-agers are sexually active and try to develop means to protect them?" Brandt asks.

Both, progressive educators believe. "It's

pretty tough, in the back seat of a car, to decide what to do about AIDS," says Bill Timmins, an AIDS educator at Cambridge Rindge and Latin School. "It has to be done ahead of time."

Educators may argue fiercely about school curriculum, but all agree that AIDS/HIV education should be tailored to the needs of each culture, community, and age group. Ideally, AIDS education should be offered as part of an ongoing, multilingual, comprehensive health program, beginning in kindergarten. But few existing programs live up to these standards. In 1989, 434 of the commonwealth's 526 high schools reported offering HIV/AIDS education. Only 58 percent of the schools said they presented those lessons in the context of comprehensive health education.

"It's pretty tough, in the back seat of a car, to decide what to do about AIDS."

Peer-leadership programs offer the most hope and promise in AIDS education today. The hope is that young people can talk to each other about subjects that can be difficult to discuss with adults. Teen-agers would lead teen-agers in lively discussions about risk reduction and role-playing that help clarify values.

"But no one knows what's going to work," says Amy Jacobson, a physician's assistant at Holyoke High School's teen-age clinic who also serves as an AIDS educator. "There's no data to show that kids' understanding intellectually is changing behavior. I have a feeling that we're going to have to see a lot of kids dying before teens really get it."

AIDS Awareness

"Tell us what you guys know about AIDS," Lea Gillis, a sophomore, asks four rows of slouching students, as a lawn mower whines outside the open windows.

Gloria Wong, a senior and the other AIDS

peer leader invited to teach Judy Hibert's freshman math class, eagerly scans the room for raised hands. Many students cradle their faces, blank as the blackboard, in their palms. Up front, a boy wearing a Simpsons sweat shirt drops his head to his desk.

"Of the 55 US states and territories, 29 mandate AIDS education."

"Does anyone know one way of getting AIDS?" Wong's enthusiasm meets glazed stares.

Welcome to Brookline High School, one of the most culturally diverse, academically advanced, all-around-privileged public schools in the area.

"Drug use, sexual intercourse, blood," the class finally drones, as if reciting multiplication tables.

Of the 55 US states and territories, 29 mandate AIDS education. Massachusetts is not one of them. The Department of Education offers training, technical assistance, and funding ($1.35 million to 35 of 286 Massachusetts school districts). Each school system independently makes its own decisions about offering an AIDS curriculum—some tailor existing curricula to fit their needs, others create their own, and others do nothing.

"Funding is our biggest problem in this state," laments Kevin Cranston, the AIDS health-education consultant to the Department of Education. "At the same time that schools are being decimated by Proposition 2 ½ cuts we're facing the onset of the most significant epidemic our society has ever faced."

Schools also face community resistance, as Cambridge Rindge and Latin did before winning the right to distribute condoms in the school clinic, and resistance from the church. In 1988, when the Boston public school system introduced its AIDS-prevention program, which included specific instructions on condom use,

Cardinal Bernard F. Law urged parents to keep children home. That year, 278 parents kept their kids out of the two-session program.

"What brand of condoms do you suggest?" a muscular Brookline freshman asks with an embarrassed grin.

Gillis prints "Nonoxynol-9" on the blackboard, as Wong discusses the difference between latex and sheepskin.

"Ask more questions," Wong urges, as she roams the room.

A girl with cornrow braids raises her hairbrush: "If you get AIDS, how long do you have to live?"

"Can you catch AIDS in a pool? Can you get AIDS from shooting steroids? What about tattoos?" While the same three students fire questions, another rummages through her purse.

The kid in the Simpsons sweat shirt closes his eyes.

Health centers and community agencies offering AIDS education to school dropouts confront the same roadblocks as schools, plus one: elusive clients. Even given the enormity of the population—the high school dropout rate is approximately 25 percent statewide and about 40 percent in Boston—these young people are hard to find.

"Many of these kids—runaways, addicts, prostitutes—don't think they're going to be alive at 25," says Dr. Cathryn Samples, director of the adolescent program at the Martha M. Eliot Health Center in Jamaica Plain. "So they're not worried about having a fatal disease at 25."

Peer Education

Peer educators at Dimock Community Health Center in Roxbury present teen-agers seeking medical treatment with videotapes and discussions about HIV and sexuality. Children's Hospital offers AIDS education over free pizza in its basement drop-in center at Arlington Street Church.

The staff at Bridge Over Troubled Waters, the Boston-based multiservice agency for runaways and homeless youth, urges high-risk clients to get tested. They were finally able to convince one young woman to take the test after she lost 40 pounds and fistfuls of hair. In a Bridge counseling room, the woman, now 21 and robust, admits she doesn't know who gave her the virus, but she thinks she caught it before she swore off alcohol and marijuana at 18.

"I left home when I was 12 and lived on the streets on and off for six years," she says, dragging on a cigarette. "To survive, there are things you have to do." She has a veteran smoker's cough. "Like prostitution. I could have gotten HIV anywhere."

The woman's doctor has told her to give up smoking, take care of herself, and get a physical every six months. "But I don't have any symptoms," she says exhaling.

Getting teen-agers who lack strong social supports to comply with medical treatment is a big problem, but not the only one doctors face in treating teen-agers. According to a Columbia University study, young people may view a negative test result as a green light for engaging in high-risk behaviors. And 21 percent of high school students surveyed individually, when asked what they would do if they tested HIV-positive, answered "commit suicide."

Teens' Hopes

Extensive and uniform counseling for teenagers who seek testing is one item that tops AIDS activists' long wish list. The Department of Public Health hopes soon to release guidelines for teen-age testing and counseling. Also on the list: stronger government leadership, better communication between parents and kids, more comprehensive health education. And, of course, more money.

"Young people may view a negative [HIV] test result as a green light for engaging in high-risk behaviors."

Alison Gertz steadfastly maintains her lifelong hopes: marriage, children, career success, and health. Bradford, on the other hand, used to think about going to college, buying a condo by the age of 25, a house by 35. Now he asks himself if he's got four years to spend in college. [His] doctor tells him that he does, tries to convince him that a cure will be found long before he gets sick, but [Bradford] is not so sure.

Back at the beach, a 19-year-old Revere native ponders the future. "I worry about AIDS because of him," this young man says, pointing to a stroller, where an infant snoozes among quilted clouds.

"I worry about when he grows up," the young man says to his 16-year-old girlfriend, the mother of his child.

"I think, in 10 years," he begins, and she finishes, "Everyone will probably be dead." She adds, "I hope they find a cure."

How Serious Is the
AIDS Epidemic?

The AIDS Epidemic Is Exaggerated

The AIDS Epidemic Is Waning
The Rate of Heterosexual AIDS Is Exaggerated
Women Are Not a High-Risk AIDS Group

The AIDS Epidemic Is Waning

Dennis J. Bregman and Alexander D. Langmuir

About the Authors: *Dennis J. Bregman is an assistant professor of preventive medicine at the University of Southern California in Los Angeles. Alexander D. Langmuir is a former chief of epidemiology for the U.S. Centers for Disease Control in Atlanta.*

The current acquired immunodeficiency syndrome (AIDS) epidemic presents a major challenge to epidemic theorists to find a rational basis for projecting future incidence of the disease. Purely empirical approaches cannot be expected to provide as relevant projections as one based on epidemiologic inference. The theory of AIDS projections should have a biologic foundation supported by epidemiologic precedent. With this proposition in mind, we proposed in 1985 that Farr's Law of Epidemics be invoked. Two years later, we extended our views in more detail.

We have analyzed 2 more years of experience and are able to reaffirm our previous conclusions. Our findings indicate that the AIDS epidemic in the United States crested in 1988. The incidence of new cases has started to decline and will continue downward to a still to be determined but probably low endemic level before the year 2000. The total accumulated incidence of cases of AIDS in the United States by that time will be in the range of 200 000.

In 1840, William Farr included a section enti-

Dennis J. Bregman and Alexander D. Langmuir, "Farr's Law Applied to AIDS Projections," *Journal of the American Medical Association,* March 16, 1990, vol. 263, no. 11, pp. 1522-1525, © 1990, American Medical Association. Reprinted with permission.

tled "The Laws of Epidemics" in his second annual report to the Registrar General of England and Wales. He begins by stating the following:

> Epidemics appear to be generated at intervals in unhealthy places, spread, and go through a regular course, and decline; but of the cause of their evolutions no more is known than of the periodical paroxysms of ague. . . . If the latent cause of epidemics cannot be discovered, the mode by which it operates may be investigated. The laws of its action may be determined by observation.

He then proceeded to analyze mortality from smallpox in England and Wales for 1838 and 1839, when a severe epidemic was on the wane. He showed that "the fall in the mortality took place at a uniformly accelerated rate."

In that earliest era of modern epidemiology and before Robert Koch and Louis Pasteur kindled the bacteriologic revolution, Farr described the first measure of epidemic theory. He expressed his abiding faith that epidemics were natural phenomena controlled by forces that could be divined by scientific inquiry and expressed in mathematical terms. Surely, he was one of the earliest modern epidemic theorists—if not the first.

"Our findings indicate that the AIDS epidemic in the United States crested in 1988."

At the beginning of the 20th century, during the years in which Sir Ronald Ross (1908 and 1915) and William Hamer (1906) developed the basis of today's classic epidemic theories, John Brownlee, an inveterate Scottish public health physician and statistician, resurrected and embellished the mathematics of Farr's ideas. Brownlee showed how a normal bell-shaped curve is produced by following the same arithmetic calculations used by Farr to measure a constant deceleration in the mortality rates of smallpox. He studied the records of large epidemics from various parts of the world over several centuries and was impressed by how many tended to be symmetrical in shape. He struggled rather unsuccessfully to derive a rational biologic process that explained either the prominence of the bell-shaped curve or the pattern of epidemic transmission it may represent. Others have since confirmed Brownlee's mathematical derivation of the normal curve. We simply reiterate the relationship between Farr's Law of Epidemics and the normal curve in contemporary epidemiologic terms: in large epidemics, the incidence of new cases tends to rise to a crest and then fall in a manner so that the entire curve forms the shape approximately described by a normal curve.

"In large epidemics, the incidence of new cases tends to rise to a crest and then fall."

Farr did not publish further on his epidemic theories until 1866, when a severe epizootic of cattle plague (rinderpest) struck in England. Beginning in the fall of 1865, incidence grew steadily, reaching a cumulative total of 73 549 attacks by the end of December. To most observers, it was rising on an unrestrained upward course. Although it was beyond his official responsibilities, Farr studied the reports of the royal commission that published cumulated figures by 4-week periods. On February 16, Farr wrote to the *Daily News of London* a letter in which he challenged the prevailing view of an impending disaster. . . .

> It will be observed that, although the attacks in the second period of four weeks were nearly double those in the first period, that rate of increase did not continue; otherwise on the principle of doubling, the numbers should have run up from 9,597 to 19,194 to 38,388 to 76,776. But the attacks in the last four weeks were only 47,191; and the real law implies that the ratio of increase goes on rapidly decreasing until the ratio itself is decreasing.
>
> Thus the increase in the first interval was at

the rate of 96.07 percent [18,817/9,597]—in the second interval it was 79.81 percent [33,835/18,817]—and in the third or last interval under observation it was only 39.47 percent [47,191/33,835].

Farr then went on to predict that the epizootic was about to crest and then decline rapidly. He was a little overenthusiastic. It crested 2 weeks later than he predicted, but then did decline rapidly.

The analogy between Farr's cattle plague epizootic and the present AIDS epidemic in the United States is sufficiently close to warrant careful study. The annual incidence of cases of AIDS in the United States by year of diagnosis is [applied to] three major transmission categories: (1) homosexual or bisexual male, (2) heterosexual intravenous drug abuser, and (3) homosexual or bisexual male intravenous drug abuser. The data have been drawn directly from the July 1989 AIDS Public Information Data set provided by the Statistics and Data Management Branch in the Division of HIV/AIDS of the Centers for Disease Control in Atlanta, Ga. The cases are presented separately for the pre-September 1987 and post-September 1987 diagnostic criteria.

The data are graphed in Figure 1 using a logarithmic scale to compare trends. The three curves rise steeply from 1982 to 1983, but already by 1984 the tendency for them to veer off to the right is evident. This trend continues progressively through 1987. The data for 1988 and the first 6 months of 1989 are not charted because the shape would be misleading. The lag in reporting would cause a greater flattening of the curves than warranted.

Diagnostic Criteria

The effect of the change in the Centers for Disease Control diagnostic criteria introduced in September 1987 is apparent. Additional cases have been reported with dates of diagnosis going back to the beginning of the epidemic in 1981. The increase in case counts became appreciable in 1984, when 1% of the total cases for that year were based on the new criteria. This percent increased steadily to approximately 30% by 1988. The increase affected the homosexual or bisexual male group the least, 22% in 1988 and 23% in the first 6 months of 1989, whereas the comparable increases for the heterosexual intravenous drug abuser group were 45% and 50%, respectively. The increases for the homosexual or bisexual male intravenous drug abuser group fall between the homosexual or bisexual male and heterosexual intravenous drug abuser groups.

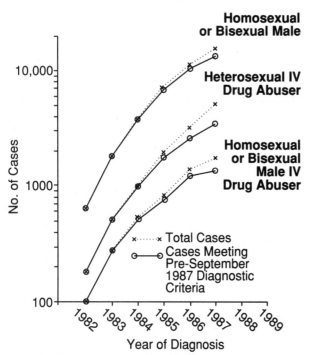

Figure 1: The rate of the spread of AIDS for three major transmission groups has decreased after each year of diagnosis.

Despite the substantial and disproportionate impact of the revision of diagnostic criteria, the effect has not changed the underlying configuration of the curves. All give the impression of moving in a parallel fashion. They look a lot like parabolas—the shape of a normal curve plotted on a logarithmic scale.

In attempting to invoke Farr's law with these data, we have chosen, as our first approxima-

tion, to limit our calculations to cases in which the diagnosis was made prior to 1988 and classified by the Centers for Disease Control with the pre-September 1987 diagnostic criteria. This provides a certain degree of consistency in diagnostic standards in the cases being analyzed and eliminates most of the knotty problems created by lags in reporting cases to the health department. Based on inspection of the intervals between diagnosis and report, we found that approximately 90% of cases are reported within 18 months of diagnosis. By using cases diagnosed before 1988, the need for extensive and somewhat uncertain adjustments is minimized. The counts for 1985, 1986, and 1987 are adjusted upward by 0.5%, 4.0%, and 8.0%, respectively, to account for cases diagnosed in those years that may still be reported to the health department. Furthermore, if there is any validity to Farr's law, it should become apparent with 6 years of consecutive data.

We have combined the data for the three major transmission categories. During these 6 years, 1982 through 1987, these three groups have consistently made up from 89% to 91% of the total adult cases. Combining the groups provides the stablest numbers and eliminates the difficult problem of how to subdivide the homosexual or bisexual male intravenous drug abuser group between the two possible transmission categories.

Slowing Epidemic

We have applied Farr's simple, but elegant, arithmetic method of fitting a normal curve to the combined data. The first ratio is calculated by dividing 1 year of data by that of the immediately preceding year. For example, the 2573 cases in 1983 divided by the 920 cases in 1982 give a first ratio of 2.7967. By subtracting 1.0 from this ratio, one obtains the percent increase, or 179.67%. The first ratios progressively decline with time, so that the ratio of 1.3148 in 1987 signifies that the increase over 1986 was only 31.48%. When the ratio reaches 1.0 the epidemic crests, and thereafter it declines as the ratio becomes lower.

The second ratios are calculated by dividing the first ratio for 1 year by that of the preceding year. The second ratio measures the rate of change of the first ratio, or in mathematical terms the acceleration. For a normal curve the second ratio is constant, having a value between

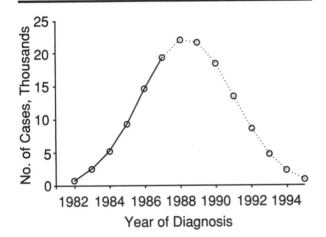

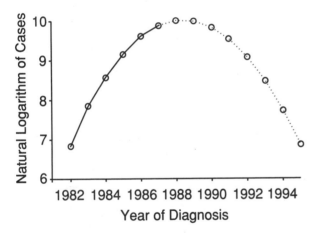

Figure 2: Annual AIDS cases in the U.S. from 1982-1987 (solid line) for combined study groups. Using future projections (dashed line), the authors report a decrease in annual AIDS cases after 1988. The upper panel is charted on an arithmetic scale and the lower panel on a logarithmic scale.

0.0 and 1.0, which signifies a constant deceleration in the rate of change. For 1984 the second ratio is 0.7278, and for the ensuing years it varies from 0.8850 to 0.8341. To fit a normal curve to

these data, we have chosen the mean of the second ratios for 1985, 1986, and 1987, which is 0.8647. By back calculation the first ratios after 1987 can be estimated and from them the projected incidence for each succeeding year.

The epidemic can be seen to crest at the end of 1988 and begin its decline in 1989 to a yet to be determined endemic rate, which we believe will be low. The incidence falls symmetrically to an annual incidence of fewer than 1000 cases in 1995.

The data are graphed in Figure 2 on an arithmetic scale in the upper panel and on a logarithmic scale in the lower panel. The classic bell-shaped appearance of the arithmetic chart and the parabolic shape on the logarithmic chart are evident. The total number of cases observed from 1981 through 1987 plus those projected to the end of 1995 is 144 339, or in round figures 150 000.

We wish to reemphasize that this projection is a crude first approximation. Many factors must be incorporated into its evaluation. Some might lead to a reduction in the total, most will increase it. For example, the choice of 0.8647 as the constant for fitting the approximate normal curve may be a bit high. If the second ratio for 1984 of 0.7278 had been included in the estimate, or if a normal curve had been fitted to the full 7 years of data, the resulting projection would have crested somewhat earlier and the total projection would have been a little smaller.

More significantly, the projection was based only on adult cases—among homosexual or bisexual males, heterosexual intravenous drug abusers, and homosexual or bisexual male intravenous drug abusers. These make up about 90% of the total cases, which implies the projection must be increased by at least 10%. Likewise, to correct for the omission of the pediatric cases, an additional increase of about 2% is indicated.

A more imponderable problem was created in September 1987 when the Centers for Disease Control broadened the case definition, encouraging a greater variety of manifestations of AIDS to be reported. Experience during the ensuing 21-month period shows that "new criteria" cases make up about 30% of the total cases. The homosexual or bisexual male group contributes about the same numbers of new criteria cases as both the heterosexual intravenous drug abuser and the homosexual or bisexual male intravenous drug abuser groups. The impact of the new criteria still has to be evaluated. It depends on what proportion of patients who meet the new criteria go on to develop the signs and symptoms compatible with the old criteria. Two extreme contingencies can be considered. First, suppose all the patients who meet the new criteria proceed to develop old criteria manifestations. Then the effect will be to put a somewhat asymmetrical cap on the top of the curve, with a compensatory decrease on the down curve. The total projection based on the old diagnostic criteria would stand unchanged, since the effect would be to accelerate the rate of reporting, but not to affect the total recorded cases in the long run. Second, if none of the patients who meet the new criteria develop old criteria manifestations, the estimated curve should be evenly increased by about 30%. For these reasons, we state that the projected total would be in the range of 200 000.

Reasonable Estimate

We have made no effort to calculate confidence limits for these projections. We humbly submit that we do not know how to account for the error due to biases in the reporting system. Furthermore, we believe it would be futile and meaningless to place a 95% confidence interval based on random error about the projections that extend out for a decade. To do so would suggest a greater confidence in both the method used and the data available than is justified.

By invoking Farr's law with Brownlee's expanded interpretation that many large epidemics tend to be symmetrical, we introduce a new and epidemiologically reasonable estimate into the debate over AIDS projections. The use of the normal curve was chosen partly in respect to the Farr-Brownlee tradition but more practically because of the stark simplicity of the method. Others have also discussed the complexity of modeling the infinite number of events, circumstances, and relationships that have conspired to create the epidemic of AIDS. There is reluctance to accept simple explanations of complex phenomenon.

In spite of problems with the lag in reporting of cases and the change in diagnostic criteria in September 1987, we believe the AIDS epidemic has crested and will steadily decline. However, while the number of new cases starts to decline, those who chart prevalence statistics will find the number of living cases will continue to increase as medical treatment prolongs the duration of disease.

We note with interest the 1989 official report of the US General Accounting Office on AIDS forecasting. In it, 13 national forecasts of the cumulated total of cases through 1991 are identified. None of these considered the concept that the epidemic might crest and then decline. We believe the evidence presented is sufficient to indicate that the Farr-Brownlee ideas are worthy of consideration. The passage of time, perhaps only 1 more year, will serve to confirm or refute their validity.

The Rate of Heterosexual AIDS Is Exaggerated

Michael Fumento

About the Author: *Michael Fumento is the author of* The Myth of Heterosexual AIDS, *from which this viewpoint is excerpted. Fumento is a former AIDS analyst for the U.S. Commission on Civil Rights.*

Nineteen eighty-seven was to have been the year of the heterosexual AIDS epidemic. Not heterosexuals infected through needle sharing, or blood transfusions, or clotting factor for hemophiliacs, or even through sex partners of any of the above. No, this was to have been a bona-fide epidemic, going from heterosexual to heterosexual, finding "fertile growth"—as *U.S. News* put it—without need of the original connections to the risk groups. The debate on *whether* having ended, it was now all a matter of reaction, with *Time, The Atlantic,* and other magazines, newspapers, and television networks commissioning reports to write profound essays on how heterosexuals were coping with what they called "the new realities."

But a funny thing happened on the way to the apocalypse. By the end of the year, heterosexuals still were not dropping like flies, and it was looking more and more as if they were not about to start. Much of the media and the Public Health Service began to switch sides and state—cautiously, to be sure—that not only had there been no heterosexual explosion, but one was not imminent or even probable. In the course of that one short year, those who had created the fear—

and to a great extent profited by it—were left standing on the dock, binoculars in hand, waiting for a ship that would not come in. Many of them would persist in their vigil, of course, screaming "It's here!" at the sight of any sail, or semblance of one, on the horizon. Yet time and again, they would be disappointed.

> ## "Not only had there been no heterosexual [AIDS] explosion, but one was not imminent or even probable."

The "myth" of heterosexual AIDS consists of a series of myths, one of which *is not* that heterosexuals get AIDS. They certainly do get it, from shared needles, from transfusions, from clotting factor, which hemophiliacs use to control internal bleeding, from their mothers at or before birth, and sometimes through sexual intercourse with persons in these categories and with bisexuals. The primary myth, however, was that the disease was no longer anchored to these risk groups but was, in fact, going from heterosexual to heterosexual to heterosexual through intercourse, that it was epidemic among non-drug-abusing heterosexuals. As Dr. Robert Redfield, an infectious disease specialist at Walter Reed Army Hospital in Washington, D.C., articulated the myth (in which he believed) in 1985, "This is a general disease now. Get rid of the high-risk groups, anyone can get it."

Through August 1989, there were 106,000 AIDS cases reported to the federal Centers for Disease Control (CDC). Of these, 61 percent were homosexual or bisexual males presumed to be infected through sexual intercourse, 21 percent were intravenous drug abusers (IVDAs) presumed to have gotten infected through sharing needles with infected persons, 7 percent were both homosexual males and IVDAs, 1 percent were hemophiliacs, 2 percent had received blood transfusions infected with HIV [human immunodeficiency virus], the cause of infection in 3 percent had yet to be determined, and 4.5 percent were listed as having probably been infected through heterosexual intercourse. Of this 4.5 percent, however, more than one third were "born in countries in which heterosexual transmission is believed to play a major role although precise means of transmission have not yet been fully identified"—a longhand way of saying "natives of Haiti and central and East Africa.". . . Of native-born Americans, about 3,300 of the 106,000 AIDS victims, about 3 percent, were listed as victims of heterosexual transmission. The proportion had been just about 2.5 percent eighteen months earlier, but the new case definition of AIDS, which added such symptoms as wasting syndrome and dementia, caused a sudden jump in both heterosexually transmitted and IVDA cases. About three fourths of these were men. Despite the media's and the various federal, state, and local public health services special targeting of the white middle class for "education," only 960 of those 3,300 were white. In fact, only about nine tenths of 1 percent of all AIDS victims are whites who are thought to have become infected through heterosexual intercourse, of which assuredly a much smaller percentage yet are members of the middle class. (Heterosexual transmission usually means the partner of an IVDA, and most infected IVDAs are lower class.) Thus, it is probably fair to say that this, the most heavily targeted of all groups, accounts for less than one half of 1 percent of all AIDS cases diagnosed in this country.

"It is difficult to name any broad category of death that will take fewer lives than heterosexually transmitted AIDS."

Further, there is evidence that even the 700 and 2,500 figures may include many persons who did not, in fact, become infected through heterosexual intercourse. In New York City, the heterosexual AIDS capital of the United States,

out of 18,000 cases diagnosed by early 1989, only 7 males have been identified as having gotten AIDS from heterosexual intercourse. Consider, on the other hand, that New York has slightly over one third of all female IVDA cases, and that male infections come almost exclusively from IVDAs. (After all, female bisexuals pose men no threat and female hemophiliacs are extremely rare.) The explanation, it would seem, is that while some cities and states simply take a man at his word when he says he was infected by a woman, New York City thoroughly investigates each such claim, rejecting the vast majority as other risk factors come to light. Considering that New York City has about one third of all female IVDA AIDS cases, if other health departments interviewed patients as carefully as New York does, efficiently screening out those who don't admit to homosexual intercourse or shared needles but who have in fact done so, we would expect to find only about a score of such men in the entire country. As it was, in early 1989, 600 men were listed as infected through heterosexual intercourse throughout the nation.

AIDS Alarmists

The alarmists were highly distressed by the low number of men classified in New York as victims of heterosexual transmission. One of them, the author Chris Norwood, wrote that the figure

was so incredible that the Commissioner of Health finally had to say he would appoint a special panel to review the city's casecounting methods. One reason the city "found" so few heterosexual men was, almost certainly, a refusal to look for them. When a man who said he was heterosexual didn't know for sure whether any woman he had slept with was at risk for AIDS, the Health Department made no attempt to test his present or past girlfriends for HIV infection. Instead, his case was simply assigned to the "no known risk" caseload.

Au contraire, according to Rand Stoneburner, director of AIDS research for the city, who told me the panel "found no bias involved that would undercount significantly male heterosexual cases any more than any other city in the country has. Ours was found as good or better than any in the country." In fact, speaking at a time when 8 men were in the heterosexually transmitted category, according to the city's then-chief interrogator, Anna Lekatsas, "I have doubts about seven of them, but we couldn't prove anything." Since she said that, one of the men was found to have other risks and was dropped from the category.

Heterosexual Infections

Considering that the great majority of female heterosexual infections come from IVDAs as well, and that New York City has about half of the male IVDA cases in the nation (about 5,000 out of 12,000 at the end of January 1989), yet less than one third of the female heterosexual transmission cases (about 500 out of 1,800 nationally), this also indicates that female infections outside of New York City are being misclassified as heterosexually transmitted. Thus, it is possible that even among that 3 percent, nearly one half of the cases had other risk factors they would not admit to.

Nevertheless, let us assume for the sake of argument that all 3,300 of those native-born cases were indeed heterosexually transmitted, as were the 960 cases among whites. During the eight years those cases were being racked up, about 380,000 Americans, the vast majority of whom were white heterosexuals, were killed in automobile accidents. About 10,000,000 more suffered disabling injuries. Almost half those deaths and more than half of deaths and injuries combined could, according to the National Highway and Transit Authority, have been prevented by the simple buckling of a safety belt, an act the victim neglected because he or she did not think the risk was great enough. Indeed, a majority of Americans do not wear safety belts. If we look at AIDS in the short-term future, at the present rate of case reporting, there will be somewhere in the range of 1,000 new native-born heterosexual cases reported to the Centers for Disease Control during 1989, of which about 300 will be white and a significantly smaller portion of these

middle class. During the same period, 475,000 Americans will die of cancer and over 750,000 of heart disease.

In fact, other than fairly spectacular rare occurrences, such as shark attacks and maulings by wild animals, it is difficult to name any broad category of death that will take fewer lives than heterosexually transmitted AIDS. In 1985, there were 19,628 murders, 12,001 fatal falls, 5,316 drownings, 4,938 deaths related to fire, 4,091 accidental fatal poisonings by solids or liquids, 3,551 deaths by suffocation or ingested objects, and 1,649 fatal firearms accidents. Murder will claim perhaps twenty times as many heterosexual lives in 1990 as AIDS; falls, eleven times; and so on. A middle-class non-IVDA heterosexual in the Chicago suburbs or Orange County, California—or, indeed, in almost any area of the country—has less of a chance of getting AIDS than of being struck by lightning or drowning in a bathtub (about 360 direct lightning strikes are recorded in the United States each year, and about 350 Americans drown in a bathtub a year). Most of us, while acknowledging the existence of these threats, be they murder or drowning, do not live in terror of them.

"The level of infections in the general population is declining as persons with AIDS die off."

Indeed, if heterosexuals treated other risks as they have been told to treat the threat of AIDS, life as we know it would cease to exist. Heterosexuals have simply too many activities far riskier than sex that are nevertheless essential to conducting life or at least very important to a useful and enjoyable existence. Not so for homosexuals and IVDA. While I will discuss their individual risk factors later, suffice it for now to say that a homosexual having unprotected (without a condom) intercourse in most areas of the United States, or an IVDA sharing needles in an area where needle sharing is common, runs a risk of infection far, far greater than of dying in an automobile accident, much less of drowning or dying in a fire.

One common objection to this line of reasoning is that one cannot look at present AIDS caseloads. After all, it often takes years before an infected person develops the full-blown disease. Thus, the sex therapists William Masters, Virginia Johnson, and Robert Kolodny declared in their controversial *Crisis: Heterosexual Behavior in the Age of AIDS* that there were probably 200,000 or more infected non-IVDA heterosexuals in the United States, and that the virus was therefore "running rampant in the heterosexual community." The Hudson Institute fellows Kevin Hopkins and William Johnston, in their "preliminary report" *The Incidence of HIV Infection in the United States,* said there were anywhere from 200,000 to 500,000 such infections. Unfortunately, none of these people bothered to show how they arrived at their figures.

The best answer to such fictitious estimates is to look at blood-testing figures, most of which to date are from military applicants and active-duty personnel and from blood donors.

Military Testing

In October 1985, the Department of Defense began testing all applicants to the armed forces as well as active-duty servicemen. The first test results from the military were immediately interpreted as bad news, in great part because of the role of Redfield, the military's most outspoken AIDS doctor. The CDC announced in July 1986 that 15 out of every 10,000 applicants to the armed forces tested positive for HIV. Much of the attention focused on New York City applicants, where the rate was 6 per 1,000. In Manhattan, it was 17 per 1,000, almost 1 in 50. It might have occurred to some reporters and doctors who were sounding the Klaxons that the fact that New York City has the largest number of IV drug users and homosexuals, and the highest level of HIV-positivity in drug users, in the country was simply being reflected in the statistics. But no, declared the NBC [National Broadcast-

ing Company] science writer Robert Bazell in the *New Republic,* probably relying on Redfield (whom he quoted later in the article), "It appears that most of [the seropositive military applicants] are neither intravenous drug users nor homosexuals. They are just ghetto kids."

"Hopkins and Johnston . . . claimed that heterosexual infections were increasing dramatically."

Redfield's chief ally in the media, Ann Guidici Fettner, remarked, "Think about it: Six of every 1,000 young women from New York trying to enlist in military are carrying HIV," having just stated that "given the highly publicized policy of testing recruits for the HIV virus, it seems unlikely that swarms of 'at-risks' would be signing up."

Some people were just a little less trusting of the Redfield interpretation than were Bazell and Fettner. In defense of a major article refuting the practicality of premarital testing (which Redfield continues to advocate), a group of Harvard Medical School researchers headed by Paul Cleary stated, "Army recruits are demographically different from the premarital population, and more likely to be sexually active homosexual men and drug abusers."

But Redfield told his critics, "The Army population is the same as the population of the country." In fact, he later told me that the army is almost certainly less likely to have members of risk groups than is the general population. As an army veteran who left the service just three years before Redfield made that statement, I found it difficult to believe an army officer could suffer such delusions. The two most obvious differences between the military and the civilian population are that applicants to the military are of the age category most at risk for AIDS and are several times more likely to be of races and ethnic groups (black and Hispanic) much more at risk for AIDS than are whites. Indeed, the rate among white applicants was only 1.0 per 1,000; while blacks were over four times more likely to be infected, at 3.9 infections per 1,000.

In fact, it appeared that military applicants testing positive had the same old risk factors AIDS victims had. Writing in the *New England Journal of Medicine*, Stoneburner and others reported that 23, or about one fourth of the first set of rejected applicants to the military from New York City, had been located and interviewed. Of these, 10 turned out to be intravenous drug abusers, 7 were bisexuals, 1 was homosexual, and 1 woman knew that she had had contact with an infected man. Three of the infected men claimed no risk other than prostitute contact, a claim the report viewed with skepticism, especially because the only chance for interview was over the phone. The final infected person claimed no risk factors. Upon retest he was negative, which doesn't say much for military testing procedures.

"It can be said of the heterosexual AIDS alarmists that they have . . . little idea of how epidemics work."

A presentation at the Fourth International AIDS Conference in Stockholm in June 1988 stated that while approximately 20 percent of active-duty male soldiers testing positive for HIV originally deny identifiable risk factors (intravenous drug use, homosexuality, and so on), an additional 60 percent of these are, upon further investigation, reclassified into traditional risk groups.

Thus, researchers have estimated that the prevalence of HIV infection in military recruits not belonging to such high-risk groups is about 0.02 percent, or 2 in 10,000, or less. Since then, the testing of recruits has not revealed increasing levels of infection, as Redfield and other alarmists declared they would; by the middle of

1988, infections were down significantly to 12 per 10,000. The greatest percentage drop was among white males, who fell from 10 per 10,000 to only 5 per 10,000. This overall reduction in infections may simply represent a greater awareness on the part of applicants that they will be tested; hence, they are self-selecting out more efficiently than they formerly did. It may also mean that the level of infections in the general population is declining as persons with AIDS die off and are replaced by fewer newly infected people. Either way, it's certainly not bad news.

Blood Donations

Blood donations constitute the single largest blood-testing program in the nation. By the end of 1988, over 17,000,000 tests had been performed. In the first two years of such testing, 43 per 100,000 first-time donors proved to be infected. In more recent testing, that figure has fallen to 40 per 100,000—though, again, whether that represents better screening or a declining level of infection in the population is difficult to determine. Even though persons at high risk for HIV are meticulously screened through questionnaires, 80 percent to 90 percent of infected donors interviewed nonetheless turn out to be from high-risk groups. When members of high-risk groups are excluded, therefore, the level of infection falls to only 6 per 100,000.

Thus, both the military and blood donor figures sound like wonderful news for sexually active heterosexuals. But not so said Hopkins and Johnston, whose report claimed that heterosexual infections were increasing dramatically. Responding to an article critical of that report (my own), which invoked the military recruit and blood donor figures, they stated, "The Red Cross actively discourages donors with risk factors, and systematically excludes donors who have previously tested positive [and the] military does not test recruits until after they have already passed through a recruiting screen, including checks of school and police records.". . . Likewise, Chris Norwood told her readers that, while "among more than 300,000 donors tested from late 1985 to late 1986, the Red Cross of Minnesota did not uncover one infected woman," this "encouraging fact loses significance when we remember that women who even suspect they may be at risk are no longer supposed to donate blood." The point all three missed was that, while certainly IVDA women or men, and homosexual or bisexual men, might know to avoid blood testing, their unwitting heterosexual sex partners, whom Norwood and Hopkins wanted us to believe were being infected in massive numbers, would not. And they simply aren't showing up. If there were 200,000 to 500,000 non-IVDA-infected heterosexuals out there, as the Hudson Institute report claims, or 200,000-plus as Masters, Johnson and Kolodny claim, the majority of whom would be of eligible age to join the military, they would not know to self-select out and would undoubtedly start showing up in blood testing of either the military or the blood banks. They aren't showing up for the simple reason they don't exist.

"The great majority of AIDS carriers are unable to infect their steady partners heterosexually."

A team of CDC scientists, writing in *Science* about these donor and military figures, has concluded, "These preliminary data suggest that the proportion of 'unexplained' heterosexual HIV transmission is not much higher than predicted from analysis of reported cases of AIDS." In an editorial in the 7 October 1988 *Journal of the American Medical Association*, Dr. H. Hunter Handsfield, director of the Seattle-King County Department of Health, stated even more forcefully that "even when the prolonged interval from HIV infection to overt AIDS is taken into account, it is likely that the classification of reported cases accurately reflects the actual patterns of transmission."

More recently, CDC has begun numerous other testing programs, some of which are partially blind (no names are taken), fully blind (no names or even demographic information taken), and some of which allow identification of the individual. Where demographic information is kept, the results always reveal the same basic pattern: infection rates are much higher in inner cities and much higher among blacks and Hispanics than among whites.

The largest of these studies (in terms of geographic area and size of potential pool) was a statewide survey in late 1988 in which for three whole months the blood was tested from all women giving birth in California. Of 135,762 tests, only 101 proved positive, for a rate of 7.4 per 10,000. This is the land of east Los Angeles, Watts and Oakland—all high drug abuse areas—and these women are by definition heterosexual, sexually active, and of the ages during which IV drug use is most common. Yet purely random sampling found far fewer infections in heterosexual women than in the population of military recruits that many were saying was *underrepresentative* of the general population. Released in September 1989, it was wonderful news. Or should have been. The media greeted the release of the study with complete silence. More good news had come in May of 1989. A massive sampling of students on American college campuses revealed an infection rate in women of only 2 per 10,000. The media did make reference to this study, but failed to specify that even this low figure included needlesharers and transfusion recipients as well as victims of heterosexual transmission.

Future Infections

As the heterosexual epidemic continued to fail to show up, either in actual cases or in infections, the alarmists took a series of fall-back positions. By early 1988, the alarmists had fallen back to Masters, Johnson, and Kolodny's, "The AIDS *virus* is now running rampant in the heterosexual community" (emphasis added). By late 1988, the alarmists were couching their threats in the future, as with the Hudson Institute's concession that many middle-class heterosexuals were "at little immediate risk of catching HIV." Thus, long after non-IVDA heterosexuals were supposed to be dying in droves, the warnings had gone from "they've got AIDS," to "they've got the virus," to "they're going to get the virus."

"Heterosexual partners of IVDAs are, in fact, also shooting drugs themselves and using their partners' needles."

Somehow the alarmists failed to see (or at least claimed to fail to see) how the current low level of AIDS cases and infections in the heterosexual population was tied to a *continuing* low level. It was as if being spared the epidemic early on was simply a matter of luck, luck that could not hold out forever. No doubt this is how many people felt 150 years ago when they saw some cities devastated by the "Red Death" (cholera) while others were spared completely. Blind luck or the wrath of God or "miasma" (evil vapors) was blamed for epidemics back then, although we now know that the selectivity of cholera depended on the efficacy of a city's sewage system. Similarly, blind luck plays no part in accounting for the low levels of AIDS and AIDS virus infections in heterosexuals, especially white middle-class heterosexuals.

It can be said of the heterosexual AIDS alarmists that they have, with few if any exceptions, little idea of how epidemics work. This is no less true of the average person, the difference being that the average person does not broadcast his or her ignorance. The first point to recognize, in comprehending the heterosexual non-epidemic, is that *disease* and *epidemic* are not synonymous. In 1987, 14 cases of bubonic plague were reported in the United States, yet no plague flags were flown, no red crosses painted upon the doors of quarantined households. For reasons that are unclear, there have been no plague epidemics since just after the turn of the century (the vaccine now used in some countries is a recent development); yet every year a few people will get plague, and a small percentage of those will die. Likewise, there is no reason simply to assume that because some heterosexuals are getting AIDS, there will be an epidemic of AIDS among heterosexuals.

In the hysteria surrounding the AIDS crisis, one of the tenets of epidemiology (the study of epidemics) which has been virtually ignored is that for an epidemic to spread, each case has to give rise to, on average, slightly more than 1 additional case. If, say, 100 cases give rise to 500 cases, the epidemic will spread quickly; if they give rise to 101, it will spread slowly, though inexorably. But if, say, 100 cases lead only to 100 more, the numbers will never increase; and if they lead to only 99, the incidence of disease will fall back upon itself or "implode" as some have put it. Of the aforementioned 14 plague cases, none spread to other human beings (they all originated with animals); hence, the disease quickly imploded. Nobody knows exactly how many cases 100 heterosexual AIDS cases will lead to; but for our purposes, all that must be figured is whether it is over 100 or under.

While extremely elaborate formulae can be concocted to try to give an exact answer to the $100 \gtreqless X$ problem, the basic formula depends on three factors: how long infected people remain infectious; how efficient is HIV transmission from men to women and women to men; and how often these men and women switch partners. There are no exact answers to these, but continuing research gives us figures that should suffice for our basic purpose. . . .

Length of Infectiousness

Into the first part of the formula, length of infectiousness, one might plug a number of about nine years *except* that the development of symptoms indicating HIV infection tends to show up much sooner—in fact, on average about four and one half years. Thus, this will be a tipoff both to the HIV carrier and a potential sex partner that something is wrong. The question, then, is how likely is one heterosexual to infect another before developing symptoms that will tend to negate the possibility of that transmission?

Measuring Infection Rate

One way of measuring is to look at the possibility of infection on a per-contact basis, multiplying this by average number of sexual acts of a heterosexual couple in one year, about 100. The only such study to provide an accurate quantification of the per-contact risk was conducted by Dr. Nancy Padian, then at the Berkeley School of Public Health in California. She found that women in the study averaged about 1,000 sexual contacts with infected men before becoming infected. Thus, according to this formula, a man would only have about a 50 percent chance of infecting a woman before becoming symptomatic.

"If there were heterosexual spread, after twelve years it would be showing up."

But one problem with the Padian study, which she readily acknowledges, is that the risk may not be evenly distributed. It may be that some women will become infected easily, while others will become infected only after a period of many years or not at all. This, indeed, was the probable conclusion of a study by Dr. Thomas Peterman of CDC and Rand Stoneburner. In their study of transfusion victims and their female sexual partners, these researchers found a couple of women who became infected after only a few contacts each, and many women and men who remained uninfected after hundreds or even more than a thousand contacts. This finding indicates that while as a crude measuring stick of a woman's risks it may be useful to use the 1-in-a-1,000 figure, to measure the spread of the epidemic it may be better to look at the overall chance an infected individual has of infecting a partner.

In the Peterman-Stoneburner study, about 20 percent of the men ended up infecting their partners, while 10 percent of the women did. These numbers seem to be about par for the course. Contrary to the assertion of *USA Today* in 1987 that "dozens of studies indicate that spouses spread the virus to each other more than half of the time by vaginal intercourse alone," a compilation of such studies from around the world in the 18 December 1987 CDC *Weekly Mortality and Morbidity Report* noted a total of only 22, of which only three showed partners seroconverting over half the time. Another compilation of such studies—this one by the director of the CDC AIDS program, James Curran; the CDC chief AIDS epidemiologist, Dr. Harold Jaffe; and other doctors at CDC—in *Science* found that the great majority of AIDS carriers are unable to infect their steady partners heterosexually even over a period of years. Among female partners of bisexuals, about 25 percent become infected. Female partners of men who received HIV from transfusion have only about a 20 percent seroconversion rate. Among partners of hemophiliacs, this rate falls to less than 9 percent. Only two categories show much higher seroconversion rates. One of these consists of both female and male partners of patients born in Haiti or Zaire. The number of couples here, however, was so small (35, as opposed to 288 partners of hemophiliacs) as to make the results questionable. The other category comprised female partners of IV-drug abusers, of whom just fewer than 50 percent seroconvert; and male partners of female IV-drug abusers, among whom a full 50 percent seroconvert. Fewer than 15 percent of male partners of female transfusion recipients seroconvert by contrast (although both cohorts were small).

This difference in transmission rates has puzzled some alarmists. Chris Norwood offers her bizarre explanation that "some unknown aspect of hemophilia may inhibit or retard replication of the virus, making sexual transmission less likely." In fact, the hemophiliac-transmission figure is probably not so different from the blood-transfusion and bisexual categories as to require any explanation other than that they are all within the range of statistical error. It's the extraordinarily *high* rate of IVDA transmission that needs explanation.

Higher rates of sexually transmitted diseases (STDs) among IVDAs and their partners may help account for this. But perhaps the best explanation is that it probably is not more efficient: that heterosexual partners of IVDAs are, in fact, also shooting drugs themselves and using their partners' needles. There is anecdotal evidence to this effect. In one reported case in New York, an AIDS victim kept denying risk factors other than heterosexual intercourse. But a wily investigator, excusing himself to go to the bathroom at the victim's house, found there syringes and needles. This clearly has ramifications beyond establishing that partner studies overstate the risk of heterosexual transmission. Over three fourths of all heterosexually transmitted AIDS cases of native-born Americans occur in women, of whom over 80 percent are partners of IV-drug users. If, as the partner studies would seem to indicate, a significant proportion of the women who claim to have gotten HIV sexually from their IV-drug-abusing male partners were, in fact, infected through needles, then that portion of AIDS cases attributed to heterosexual transmission among native-born Americans would be cut dramatically. This could well account for the disparity with New York City where, with over a third of the nation's IVDA AIDS cases, the city has less than one fourth of the national total of cases listed as being heterosexually transmitted—because of its excellent re-interviewing techniques.

Partner Switching

At a glance, then, from studies that show only 10 percent to 20 percent of heterosexuals infecting their steady partners over a period of years, one might assume that the "more than 100 cases

for each original 100 cases" threshold could not be reached. Unfortunately, it's not quite that simple. Another factor that has to be figured in is nonsexual transmission: that is, to what extent is HIV entering relationships due to reasons other than sex? For middle-class heterosexuals, this is not a significant factor. As noted, intravenous drug abuse, especially with needle sharing, is largely confined to the lower economic class. Indeed, the needle-sharing aspect of it (and of course it's the sharing of needles, not the actual drug use itself, that spreads disease) tends to be much more of a black and Hispanic problem than a white one. The only other ways the virus is going to enter nonsexually into a relationship is through infection with hemophilia-clotting factor or blood transfusions. Yet only a small portion of the population has been infected this way (about 22,000, according to CDC estimates); in addition, many, if not most, have been identified through testing and counseled to avoid infecting others. Finally, since testing of blood and heat treating of clotting factor were introduced in 1985, very few new infections have come about in these manners. Through attrition by death, the number of people infected through these methods continues to dwindle.

"It should be clear by now that there is no single 'AIDS epidemic.'"

But this lack of outside infusion for white middle-class heterosexuals doesn't hold true for lower-class black and Hispanic ones living in America's inner cities. They have a constant infusion of new virus into their relationships because of the drug problem. This has also proved problematic in Africa, where tainted blood transfusions were and continue to be a much greater problem than in the United States and Europe, and where reuse of needles in hospitals has also contributed to, again, a constant infusion of virus into relationships. Even American homosexuals, at least those in the big cities, seem to have a much closer connection to the intravenous drug abuse culture than does the heterosexual middle class. . . .

At this point, I have discussed the factors that go into determining whether 100 cases will equal more or less than 100, but have come to no solid conclusion other than of the absurdity of comparing the spread of the disease in the middle-class heterosexual population of the United States and Europe with the spread among homosexuals and Africans. In every way, the homosexuals and Africans had the odds stacked against them. If, for example, homosexuals had engaged in lots of partner switching but anal sex were a poor way of transmitting the virus, they would not have nearly the problem they do today. Likewise, even if anal sex were comparatively dangerous but homosexuals were essentially monogamous, they would not have had the same problem. But both of these factors were multiplied to create the homosexual epidemic. Similarly, in every way middle-class heterosexuals have the odds on their side.

Less than an Epidemic

While we just do not have enough data to make an exact statement of exactly what 100 cases do equal, as Dr. Alexander Langmuir, the founder of the modern epidemiology branch at CDC, has stated with all these facts in mind, "Everything I have seen says that outside of the high-risk groups, the spread is less than epidemic survival." Indeed, the evidence for this goes right back to the case figures and blood-test figures given earlier. If there were heterosexual spread, after twelve years it would be showing

up. It is not. As the New York City Department of Health paper presented at the Fourth International Conference in Stockholm stated in 1988, "In the city with the world's highest reported incidence of AIDS, these results suggest that HIV infection was primarily limited to known AIDS risk group members and their sexual partners.". . .

It should be clear by now that there is no single "AIDS epidemic." There is an epidemic among homosexuals and bisexuals and their sex partners. There is an epidemic among intravenous drug abusers and their sex partners, which may widen slightly in some areas to include the partners of those partners. But among the great wide percentage of the nation the media calls "the general population," that section the media and the public health authorities has tried desperately to terrify, there is no epidemic. AIDS will pick off a person here and there in this group, but the original infected partner will be in one of the two groups in which the disease is epidemic. Most heterosexuals will continue to have more to fear from bathtub drowning than from AIDS.

Thus, the folly of slogans like "Everyone is at risk," or "AIDS doesn't discriminate," and of such broad-based educational approaches as sending a version of the Surgeon General's Report on AIDS to every household in the country. Such a mailing makes every bit as much sense as sending a booklet warning against the dangers of frostbite to every home in the nation, from Key West, Florida, to San Diego, California. But the slogans and the mailings did make sense in one very important way. They were essential to spreading the myth of heterosexual AIDS.

Women Are Not a High-Risk AIDS Group

Robert E. Gould

About the Author: *Robert E. Gould is a professor of obstetrics and gynecology with Cornell University Medical College in New York City. Gould is also a member of the AIDS committee for the New York City branch of the American Psychiatric Association.*

You are a healthy, vital American woman, and just when you've decided to have an active love life, everyone tells you that sex kills. You're cautioned to hold onto chastity for dear life or face the deadly risk of contracting AIDS, the fatal disease. Meanwhile, all about you, policemen, firemen, law-court personnel, health-care workers are donning gloves, masks, outer-space wear—and even with the protective gear, they are afraid of being within spitting distance of a person with AIDS or suspected of carrying the virus.

Where does all this panic leave you? Is the hysteria justified? In my opinion and from objective evidence, the answer is *no:* In all probability, you won't catch the virus by inhaling it, ingesting it, or, more to the point, by having vaginal or oral sex. Even the experts who have come to specialize in the disease admit that the fear of AIDS transmission through vaginal intercourse has been greatly exaggerated, that the epidemic is not spreading through the population in this way, though many authorities had predicted it could. In the words of Dr. B. Frank Polk, an AIDS epidemiologist at the Johns Hopkins School of Hygiene and Public Health in Baltimore, "A number of scientific leaders in AIDS have overstated the risk in the absence of data."

Robert E. Gould, "Reassuring News About AIDS," *Cosmopolitan,* January 1988. Reprinted with the author's permission.

And according to Dr. Harold Jaffe, chief AIDS epidemiologist at the Centers for Disease Control in Atlanta, "Those who are suggesting that we are going to see an explosive spread of the virus into the heterosexual population have to explain why this is not happening."

"There is almost no danger of contracting AIDS through *ordinary sexual intercourse.*"

Why it isn't happening, I believe, is that there is almost no danger of contracting AIDS through *ordinary sexual intercourse,* a conclusion I have reached from my own studies and after having gone over most of the published reports on AIDS, visited hospital wards, and talked with leading researchers in virology. Let me be very specific about what I mean by ordinary sexual intercourse. As I define it, it is penile penetration of a well-lubricated vagina—penetration that is not rough and does not cause lacerations (as it might in rape or violently macho thrusting or in the presence of severe vaginismus). Assuming that the genitals of both partners are healthy and intact—that there are no lesions or other openings due to infections—the virus, I contend, will not be transmitted during vaginal sex from an infected person to his or her partner. (Anyone not sure whether she has any open vaginal lesions or infections would, of course, be safer and feel more comfortable with her partner if he were to use a condom.) Nor do I believe there is a danger of AIDS transmission by oral sex or deep kissing or the exchange of body fluids. Although not all experts agree with my conclusions, there is no denying that the only undisputed route of transmission is through direct introduction of the virus into the bloodstream. And I maintain it is the *only* route. Which is why I believe that if the conditions of heterosexual intercourse as I have outlined them are met, a woman is quite safe from contracting AIDS.

To begin with, the secretions of a healthy vagina are very inhospitable to the AIDS virus, so that normal lubrication from one's own secretions not only serves as a preventive measure against lacerations but would also tend to neutralize the virus if present. In other words, if you are aroused, your own body is the best protection against injury. Nature has arranged this so that sex will feel good and be good *for* you.

Then, too, in order to become infected with AIDS, you need a really large dose of the virus, because it is so low-grade. As Dr. Howard Bierman, director of the Institute for Cancer and Blood Research in Beverly Hills, told me, "The AIDS virus should not be likened to hepatitis B [which it often is], because it takes several thousand times the AIDS virus to equal the infective strength of the hepatitis virus."

Last, you should know that the AIDS virus is very fragile, a medical finding frequently downplayed because of the disease's inevitable fatality. But the severity of the disease should not be confused with its degree of contagion, and the fact remains that it is hard, if not impossible, to contract the virus outside of direct entry into the bloodstream.

"No researcher . . . could state with certainty that *any* cases of AIDS have occurred through conventional intercourse."

Let's look at the figures. The latest survey available at press time having to do with heterosexual AIDS victims in the United States puts the number of such cases since June 1981, when the disease was first diagnosed, at 1,375 out of a total of 35,477, or roughly 3 percent. That percentage includes 661 victims with no known cause of the disease but who contracted AIDS in another country (mostly in Africa, where heterosexual transmission of AIDS, according to the survey, "is believed to play a role"). This puts the number of American heterosexual cases at 714 and

reduces the 3 percent to some 2 percent. So imprecise are the data that no breakdown as to gender has been published, but even assuming that fully one-half of the 714 are women, the number is further reduced to 357 and the percentage to just 1. Not only is the 1 percent estimate a very small fraction of the whole of AIDS victims but for various reasons people afflicted with AIDS may not give a true history of the source of their infection, so it is not really known how many women even in that tiny percentile fit the category of engaging in ordinary heterosexual intercourse as I have just defined it. To be sure, no researcher with whom I talked could state with certainty that *any* cases of AIDS have occurred through conventional intercourse. That it may occur in this way is a theory yet to be proved.

High and Low Risks

Anal intercourse is another matter. Because hemorrhoidal vessels are very near the surface of the anus, because the mucosa is delicate, and because the insertion of the penis in an orifice so small and tight is often traumatic, bleeding and/or lacerations may occur. And this is what makes anal intercourse a high-risk activity, regardless of whether the recipient of the penis is a man or a woman, heterosexual or gay.

The other main high-risk activity is intravenous drug use, which may entail injection with a contaminated needle, thereby introducing the virus directly into the bloodstream. (Blood transfusions, previously a source of transmission, are generally thought not to be a risk factor for new cases, since all donated blood is now tested for the AIDS virus. It should be noted, however, that there can be a time lag—sometimes longer than a year—during which the virus, though present in the blood, may not be detected by the test.)

As for another reported method of acquiring the virus, the exchange of body fluids—tears, saliva, semen, secretions from the vagina—there is no documented evidence that anyone has ever become infected in this way. True, the virus has been isolated in these substances, but all the evidence indicates that contact will not result in transmission unless there is ready access to the bloodstream.

Soul, tongue, or deep kissing has also been reported as risky, yet *not one case* of transmission in this way has ever been discovered during the recorded history of AIDS. Furthermore, the clinical observation that the mouth often has open lesions (think of bleeding gums), certainly more than the vagina, only supports the view that the AIDS virus is not very contagious.

What about oral sex? A number of authorities are still calling it risky behavior, yet, again, there are *no* reported cases of AIDS having been transmitted through cunnilingus or fellatio (mouth-vagina or mouth-penis sex). Now suppose your partner did have the virus and you swallowed his semen. What would happen? The virus would be diluted and neutralized by the secretions of your gastrointestinal tract. Of course, one can speculate on the unlikely situation that a person ingesting semen might have an acutely bleeding ulcer through which the virus could gain entry into the bloodstream. A highly improbable situation, to be sure, but it and other equally improbable situations keep me from saying with 100 percent certainty that AIDS could *never* be transmitted by oral sex—or, indeed, that anything is *ever* 100 percent certain.

"It is probably through the needle, not routine intercourse, that the virus is transmitted."

It has been said that in Africa heterosexual intercourse is a documented mode of transmission of the AIDS virus, the implication being that it is just a matter of time before the disease will spread throughout the world in this manner. As with so many other medical reports, I would recommend this one be viewed with strong skepticism. Cultural differences must be taken into account—which I can attest to from firsthand experience. For six years, the Family Life Division

of Manhattan's Metropolitan Hospital offered a three-month course in family planning to nurses from various countries in Africa; I taught the section on sex education. Year after year, the African nurses would confirm that homosexuality, although commonplace among their people, was not talked about or even acknowledged. And not until the very end of the course did the nurses themselves begin to speak openly on the subject. So considering just how reluctant Africans are to talk about their homosexual practices even among themselves, I would question the information reported by African researchers and collected by western researchers regarding AIDS in the African heterosexual community. Given my own experience, it is not farfetched to assume that the data may well reflect infection by homosexual activity (i.e., anal sex).

AIDS in Africa

In addition, the data I gathered concerning heterosexual intercourse in Africa show marked differences from the way it is usually practiced in the United States. Example: Anal intercourse is often used as a means of preventing pregnancy (and the more anal intercourse, the more risk of AIDS). Then, too, many men in Africa take their women in a brutal way, so that some heterosexual activity regarded as normal by them would be closer to rape by our standards and therefore be likely to cause vaginal lacerations through which the AIDS virus could gain entry into the bloodstream. Furthermore, in many areas, clitoridectomy (surgical excision of the clitoris) is still practiced as a tribal custom and the vagina sewn up to insure chastity, so that sex, when it occurs for the first time, often involves serious tearing and lacerations in an organ that has already been scarred and weakened (thus creating access to the bloodstream). Still another factor pertinent to Africa is that family members may all receive injections from a clinic routinely using nonsterile needles and syringes. Infected couples, not knowing this, may therefore mistakenly report contracting the AIDS virus from heterosexual intercourse.

Misreporting in the U.S. is also not uncommon. Not long ago, a published report described men who claimed to have caught AIDS from infected female prostitutes, a group known to have a high incidence of the disease. Yet closer investigation revealed these men had, in fact, contracted the virus through homosexual anal intercourse but found it more palatable to report otherwise.

Promiscuity and AIDS

Promiscuity, incidentally, has been identified as a risk factor among prostitutes, but it would seem to be a risk factor only in the narrowest sense—i.e., the more partners you have, the more likely it is for one of them to engage in anal intercourse or in sexual behavior that will lacerate the vaginal walls, thereby making the woman vulnerable to an AIDS infection (this would be true, too, of women in general, not merely of prostitutes). Since prostitutes comprise a high proportion of IV drug users, it is very likely that drug abuse (i.e., using needles that may carry the AIDS virus) is the source of infection rather than number of partners.

"Prospective victims inhabit the known high-risk groups."

Along with prostitutes, another high-risk group has been identified as "IV drug users and their sexual partners," a phrase that conveys the false impression that an IV drug user passes the AIDS virus on to his or her partner through vaginal intercourse. In truth, the sexual partner of a drug user is often a drug user as well, and it is probably through the needle, not routine intercourse, that the virus is transmitted.

Finally, we are told that there will be many more AIDS sufferers over the next few years. True, but considering the gestation period—typically from one to five years—the increase will reflect mostly the people who *already* carry the

virus. Their number is estimated at 1.5 million, with perhaps 25 percent of them eventually developing the disease—although some medical opinion holds that every last carrier will eventually come down with AIDS. In any event, these prospective victims inhabit the known high-risk groups: those who had blood transfusions before there was a screening test for the AIDS virus, gay men who have engaged in anal sex (a practice now becoming relatively rare even among homosexuals), and IV drug users, who will undoubtedly account for the vast majority of new cases.

Can recurrent sexual activity with a person who does carry the AIDS virus cause *you* to develop AIDS? Not if you subscribe to the theory, supported by considerable fact, which I have just put forward: that you don't get AIDS from sexual activity with a man who has the disease or carries the virus unless you engage in anal sex or there is an open lesion in the vagina when you are having vaginal intercourse. Otherwise, you will not be vulnerable to the disease.

If, then, there is so little likelihood and no solid proof of AIDS spreading to women practicing healthy heterosexual intercourse, you have to ask why so few experts are saying so. And I think it is possibly because certain organizations and groups have specific agendas for not acknowledging just how risk-free conventional heterosexual intercourse actually is. Researchers, for one, will receive larger grants and be funded more readily if AIDS is thought not to be largely restricted to the out-groups of IV drug users (encompassing mostly minorities) and homosexual men but rather is believed to include the heterosexual white middle-class population. Many gay organizations, too, are not unhappy with the warnings that the virus is spreading into the larger community—and understandably so, since the warnings not only spur greater efforts to find a cure but also dilute the burden these organizations would otherwise have to bear of AIDS being labeled a gay disease (which it is not; it is only that anal intercourse is such an efficient conduit for the virus). And the media, of course, thrive on disaster reports and so are quick to take up the cry that all of us are in peril.

Caution and Fear

As for government and public-health officials, they feel they must err on the side of extreme caution and thus cover themselves if there is *any possibility* that the virus might be spread through heterosexual intercourse or the exchange of body fluids. As [former] Surgeon General C. Everett Koop said, "As a health officer . . . if I were to spread the word that you don't have to worry about AIDS, I could really besmirch the office of the Surgeon General." And so we are told that chastity is the only sure way of avoiding the disease. You cannot argue with that. Next best is monogamy, after knowing the other person well and taking screening tests for the presence of the virus. Finally, if you are going to be sexually active, the advice is to use condoms at all times.

"Despite the hysteria, sex itself is not and never has been a killer."

Some health officials have told me that although they cannot prove transmission of the virus does occur in heterosexual intercourse, they cannot rule out the possibility "and so let's be overly cautious—it can't hurt." But it can. The hurt exists in the continually mounting fear and false alarm that may make it difficult for any of us to enjoy sex.

Irrational fear that AIDS is spreading or soon will spread rampantly through heterosexual intercourse is having enormous repercussions in our society. The most serious: that guilt and fear are again taking hold of people who have learned to be comfortable with their sexuality. Many of us have invested a great deal of time in learning to accept our sexual feelings, to understand that behaving sexually is both natural and healthy. Now, that painfully slow process of education is being rapidly undermined. The door to old feelings of fear, guilt, sinfulness, and immorality is being reopened. We are once again being persuaded that sex is wrong, dirty, bad for us, even deadly.

I don't mean to underestimate or downplay the horror of AIDS, the pain and torment it causes not only the people afflicted with the disease but their family and friends as well. Still, this killing of our sexual selves, I feel, may prove more destructive in the long run than the AIDS virus itself. We need to remember that sex, which can be used in a multitude of ways, some of them destructive, under the right circumstances expresses love, warmth, togetherness, as well as just plain fun.

Through the tumultuous 1960s and the sexual revolution of the '70s, sex emerged as a natural part of our being alive. We need to hold onto that enlightenment. We need to believe we can enjoy sex without fearing that our life is in danger with every sexual encounter. We need to know that despite the scary condom ads on TV, despite the panic, despite the hysteria, sex itself is not and never has been a killer. And this knowledge should give us all the right to continue to behave as fully sexual beings. God and nature made us that way.

Chapter 2

Has America Adequately Funded AIDS Research and Treatment?

AIDS Funding: An Overview

Marlene Cimons

About the Author: *Marlene Cimons is a staff writer for the* Los Angeles Times, *a daily newspaper.*

Editor's note: *When AIDS was first reported in the early 1980s, response to the disease from the government, the medical community, and society in general was indifference. Many people believed AIDS was a disease solely affecting homosexual men and therefore not a matter for general concern. In response to this indifference, some gay Americans formed lobbying groups to pressure the nation to recognize what they believed was a growing crisis. Today, the AIDS lobby has grown to encompass a diverse collection of people. Primarily through this group's work, more people became aware of the disease and of ways to prevent it.*

The AIDS lobby, consisting of such diverse groups as ACT UP (AIDS Coalition to Unleash Power) and the National Institutes of Health (NIH), worked vigorously and successfully to prod Congress to allocate $1.7 billion toward AIDS research, testing, and education programs in 1991. The lobby based its urgency on two facts: The first was that AIDS is always fatal, and the second was that many people who had the disease remained unaware of it and continued to spread it.

Congress' favorable response to the AIDS crisis has provoked a backlash from the medical community. Lobbying groups for other diseases such as cancer and Alzheimer's disease have begun to question the fairness of AIDS receiving high levels of limited government funding. These lobbyists argue that cancer and Alzheimer's affect many more people than does AIDS, and funding levels should be allocated in proportion to these statistics. In the following overview, Marlene Cimons, a Los Angeles Times *staff writer, discusses the impact the AIDS lobby has had on Congress and*

whether this lobby's actions are fair to the rest of the medical community.

Jean McGuire, an accomplished AIDS policy lobbyist, is accustomed to a Congress that has been extraordinarily willing in recent years to approve dramatic increases in AIDS spending.

So she was more than a little startled during a recent Capitol Hill visit to hear the following comment from a key Senate appropriations official:

"You know," said the aide, who works for the labor-health and human services subcommittee, chaired by Sen. Tom Harkin (D-Iowa), "there are many times more people in Iowa who are living with Alzheimer's than are living with AIDS."

To McGuire, who had gone to plead the case for funding the "disaster relief" bill, a measure that would provide money to the hardest-hit cities to help care for AIDS patients, the message was shockingly clear:

When critical money decisions are made—in an era of no-growth federal spending—members of the panel may be reluctant for the first time in recent history to afford special treatment to AIDS over other diseases.

There appears to be a growing resentment over the status given AIDS over numerous other diseases which, the advocates for those illnesses argue, strike and kill many more people every year than AIDS.

"There appears to be a growing resentment over the status given AIDS."

"We're starting to hear that now wherever we go: 'OK, you guys have got your growth—now it's somebody else's turn,'" says Jeff Levi, a Washington-based consultant on AIDS issues. "There is the misconception that the acceleration in AIDS funding has occurred at the expense of other diseases."

To be sure, a range of groups from the radical ACT UP (AIDS Coalition to Unleash Power) to the prestigious Institute of Medicine believes that AIDS funding has been inadequate to meet the needs of the burgeoning epidemic. Thousands of activists recently demonstrated outside the sprawling National Institutes of Health (NIH) in Bethesda, Md., demanding more money for AIDS research, and numerous reports by respected think tanks have urged that AIDS funding be increased far above the current levels.

"AIDS patients have accomplished so much through civil disobedience."

Nevertheless, recognizing the special urgency of the AIDS epidemic, Congress specifically earmarked research dollars for AIDS through much of the decade until 1989—which it did not do for any other disease—and awarded much more AIDS money in every budget than was requested by either the Ronald Reagan or George Bush Administrations. But starting with fiscal year 1990, research monies have no longer been directed specifically at AIDS, but have been included in the overall budget of each federal research institute to parcel out as it wishes.

"AIDS patients have accomplished so much through civil disobedience, and we know of many organizations that work for diseases that are just as deadly and just as horrible," said Abbey Meyers, executive director of the National Organization for Rare Disorders. "They are saying: 'Maybe we should go down to Washington and block traffic.'"

Stephen McConnell, vice president for public policy for the Alzheimer's Disease Assn., agrees.

"When they were out there demonstrating, I thought: 'What can we learn from that?'" he said. "I have read up on the AIDS lobby to see what we can do."

Non-AIDS lobbyists are not the only ones who are disgruntled. There is also a considerable degree of unhappiness from laboratory researchers in other fields who are frustrated because it has become more difficult to get funding grants. One major reason is that there is less money available overall for new grants. But there is no question that there has been an emphasis on grant money for AIDS research.

"There is the idea that if you do AIDS research, it's easy to get funded," said one specialist in infectious diseases who often reviews grant proposals for the National Institutes of Health and who requested anonymity.

"In general, it's very tough to get funded," he continued. "So now I'm seeing researchers who are trying to make their work AIDS-related. I read many grant proposals in which the principle investigator—who has never done any AIDS work—is trying to slant what he has been doing for 10 or 20 years to make it sound like it has something to do with AIDS. But when you read the grant, it's clear that the relationship is a funding ploy."

Lobbying for Funds

Dr. Anthony Fauci, director of AIDS activities for the NIH and director of the National Institute of Allergy and Infectious Diseases, acknowledges that "there are people who feel that the amount of support AIDS is getting is taking away the support they could be getting—but it's not as bad as they think. Non-AIDS is not suffering."

Others would not necessarily agree with that assessment. McConnell of the Alzheimer's Disease Assn., for example, says that when he lobbies, he never suggests that AIDS spending be reduced. But he does make a point of asking lawmakers to compare AIDS funding levels to those for other diseases that are more widespread than AIDS—such as cancer, heart disease and Alzheimer's.

"There are now 4 million people affected by Alzheimer's in this country at a cost of caring for them estimated at $80 billion to $90 billion a year," he said. "We've never said bring theirs down—we've only said bring ours up to a comparable level."

The total fiscal 1991 budget for Alzheimer's is $153 million, according to McConnell. The

Bush Administration's budget for AIDS for fiscal 1991 is $1.7 billion.

Health and Human Services Secretary Louis W. Sullivan acknowledges that he has experienced pressure over AIDS funding from other groups, most often those lobbying for cancer research. He says he tells them that "we have an opportunity now . . . if we can find better ways to treat the [AIDS] virus or to prevent its spread."

AIDS, as compared to cancer, for example, "represents a spreading infection . . . a disease that is going to continue to escalate significantly in our society," he says. "And we're making progress. We're not simply throwing money blindly at the AIDS problem, we really do have a number of promising leads for better therapies or better ways in preventing it. Therefore, that kind of investment is worth it."

Further, those who support increased AIDS funding insist that AIDS research has contributed to all fields of biomedicine. They point to a recent survey conducted among scientists by the Congressional Office of Technology Assessment that concluded that numerous areas of medicine—including infectious diseases, cancer, neurology, hematology, pulmonary medicine and immunology—have all benefited from AIDS research.

"Research monies have no longer been directed specifically at AIDS, but have been included in the overall budgets."

Moreover, the report said, AIDS research has also contributed to advances in drug and vaccine development, epidemic modeling techniques, and health care delivery systems.

"There are many positive spinoffs from AIDS work," Fauci said.

Lobbyist McGuire, who is known in Washington as a skillful coalition builder, understands that AIDS organizations need the support of other health groups to use their combined clout to achieve legislation and other priorities. She and others organized such a union to achieve passage of several measures, including the disaster relief bill passed by the House, which would provide money for AIDS counseling and treatments, and the Americans With Disabilities Act, which would forbid discrimination in the private sector against those with disabilities, including AIDS and AIDS infection. With the latter bill, for example, AIDS groups joined forces with disability rights groups and made a powerful impact.

AIDS Funding

During the budget process, McGuire said, a coalition of health groups lobbied for an overall health dollar figure. But, she said, when it came to money for their own special interests, "We knew we would have to carry our own line."

There are some signs on Capitol Hill that the growing tension is beginning to have some effect.

"There just aren't as many AIDS cases as there are cancer cases—that's just simple fact," said a Senate appropriations committee official, who requested anonymity. "The scientific evidence is that everyone who gets AIDS will die—that's scary. But there still aren't as many AIDS victims as there are cancer victims—and now we're spending as much on AIDS as cancer.

"It's talked about all the time—how AIDS [funding] has grown very rapidly," he continued. "Everyone feels they would have had a higher funding level but for AIDS. But there's no way to know if that's true."

During the appropriations process, each institute of the National Institutes of Health receives a lump sum, which the appropriations committees do not break down by specific diseases. In recent years, AIDS has been the only disease so designated.

But in 1989, the House Appropriations Committee decided to stop earmarking AIDS money after fiscal 1989. The committee said that the "rapid expansion" of AIDS research between 1982 and 1989 "required this unusual treatment," but that AIDS research should now "be managed by the NIH using the same system as it uses for other critical illnesses, such as diabetes and Alzheimer's."

Appropriations sources also note that, in the early 1970s, with former President Richard M. Nixon's "war on cancer," cancer received similar singular treatment, including "radically increased funding, much as we have with AIDS." Further, they say, this approach "cooled in the '80s as well."

"There just aren't as many AIDS cases as there are cancer cases."

One congressional source involved with the appropriations process during early years of the AIDS epidemic says that the specially earmarked AIDS spending "was supposed to be new money—we didn't take it from one institute and give it to another. Every institute got an increase. But AIDS got a big increase."

The source added: "The real problem is that there just isn't enough money in the overall pot to do everything. Is that the fault of AIDS? I don't know. I don't know that the non-AIDS NIH appropriations would have been different if AIDS hadn't been in the picture. We were in the middle of a public health crisis. Based on what we were hearing from the scientists, it looked to us that this was where the additional dollars needed to go."

The real problem, Fauci and others say, is that "there are more research opportunities than there are resources.

"What has to happen is that the American public and the nation have to relook at how much we're willing to spend on biomedical research as an entity," Fauci said. "Perhaps the American public is not as well-informed as to its importance and what dividends it holds for their lives and health."

Meyers and others agree that ultimately there must be a fundamental change in priorities.

"Congress has to make up its mind that certain things matter," she said. "If health is a top priority, it can't be a top priority for just one disease. It has to be health for everybody."

Has America Adequately Funded AIDS Research and Treatment?

Yes: America Has Adequately Funded AIDS

The Government's Funding for AIDS Is Adequate
America's Response to AIDS Is Adequate
AIDS Funding Should Be Reduced

The Government's Funding for AIDS Is Adequate

Elizabeth M. Whelan

About the Author: *Elizabeth M. Whelan is the president of the American Council on Science and Health in New York. The council monitors and publishes reports on health and science issues.*

If your only sources of information about our nation's AIDS crisis were AIDS activists—as represented at the Sixth International Conference on AIDS in San Francisco in June 1990, in associated newspaper editorials, op-eds and other public statements by leaders of the homosexual community—you would conclude that the United States government and its political leaders were blind, deaf, uncaring, passive and uninvolved in the struggle against the health devastation of HIV [human immunodeficiency virus], the AIDS virus.

This view is best summarized in a recent *New York Times* opinion article by Larry Kramer, a founder of the Gay Men's Health Crisis and ACTUP (AIDS Coalition to Unleash Power), "It is beyond comprehension why, in a presumably civilized country, in the modern era, such a continuing, extraordinary destruction of life is being attended to so tentatively, so meekly in such a cowardly fashion."

In a similar vein, activists are charging that there has been insufficient presidential-level involvement in AIDS; not enough money dedicated to AIDS research or patient care; a cruel, bureaucratic holdup in life-saving drugs for persons suffering with AIDS; and that AIDS is ultimately the government's fault. Each of these

Elizabeth M. Whelan, "Rhetoric, Finger Pointing: Obstacles to Progress Against AIDS," *Priorities,* Fall 1990. Reprinted by permission of the author and the American Council on Science and Health.

premises needs a closer, more critical look.

"There's no presidential leadership. . . ." During the AIDS convention, the Gay Men's Health Crisis took out advertisements in national newspapers claiming, "throughout the AIDS crisis, our nation's efforts have been sorely lacking in leadership from the highest level of federal government."

The *San Francisco Examiner* editorialized, "Neither (Presidents Reagan or Bush) has treated AIDS as the disaster it is . . . we are living in a time of plague and two Presidents in a row have refused to stem it."

President Bush evoked scorn from participants at this year's AIDS Conference ("Where's George? Where's George?" the crowd chanted) when he declined to address the convention, sending Secretary Louis Sullivan in his stead. Writing of President Bush, the *San Francisco Examiner* noted, "by refusing to come to the meeting himself, President Bush missed a chance to show that 'kinder, gentler' is more than words. He missed a chance to use the bully pulpit of the presidency in a life-and-death cause. He missed a chance to be compassionate to reach out to people who have suffered greatly. . . ."

> ## "Activists are charging that there has been insufficient presidential-level involvement in AIDS."

In reality, of course, President Bush had every legitimate reason *not* to attend. When in 1987, as Vice President, he attempted to address the Third Annual International AIDS convention in Washington, DC, he was hissed and booed. And in June 1990 when Dr. Sullivan attempted to deliver a message from the Bush Administration—his speech was completely drowned out—"Shame, Shame," the crowd intoned. No one heard a word he was saying as a result of an AIDS activists' demonstration. Why would any President wish that upon himself? And what would it accomplish?

If President Bush did attend the conference—as a show of "leadership" on the AIDS front—what could he possibly say that would be acceptable to that audience? Should he have dared mention the options of abstinence, monogamy, and a "just say no" message to drugs as a primary means of preventing AIDS transmission, he would have been jeered off the stage. Unless he were to come dressed as RubberMan (a caricature of the gay community in San Francisco), lecture on the Joy of Condoms and endorse the role of BleachMan to clean dirty needles, which he clearly would not have done, he would have been viewed as Public Enemy #1. Better for him to stay at home.

Government Response to AIDS

"*There's not enough federal dollars going into AIDS research.*" "Only the Federal Government can manage the project to find, as quickly as possible, the cure that top scientists believe there is. . ." wrote Larry Kramer, lamenting that the "government" was not investing enough in AIDS research.

The reality is, of course, that, after an arguably slow start in the early 1980s, the U.S. government's (read that: taxpayers') investment in AIDS has been *unprecedented*. Since early in this decade, we have spent at the federal level almost 5 billion dollars in research, and AIDS now receives more government research money than any other individual illness, and more than heart, cancer, and stroke combined, despite the fact that the numbers of diagnosed cases in the whole decade is but a minute fraction of cases of cancer, heart disease and other chronic illnesses which occur each year in the U.S.

Of course AIDS *is* different. It is a new, infectious disease and it demands our research attention. But to conclude that we have been negligent in pursuing AIDS research is nothing short of absurd. Indeed, there are those who are increasingly arguing that our spending on AIDS is seriously and negatively affecting our research on other more extensive medical problems, such as heart disease, cancer and Alzheimer's disease.

In their claim that we are "not doing enough," AIDS activists overlook some bleak realities about HIV. They demand a cure, yet cures for viral diseases are rare. Viruses make bacteria look like laboratory child's play: bacteria are independent life forms—they exist by themselves, separate from the organs which they infect. They are thus relatively easy to target and kill. But with a virus, we are dealing with a phenomenon which only takes on life once it has entered another cell—and becomes part of the host cell. To thus go after the virus, you must invade the very cell itself. In the case of herpetic kerato-conjunctivitis, a "cure" is attained only by killing the infected cell. There is no immediate "magic bullet" for the AIDS virus. Indeed, if every U.S. scientist with any understanding of virology and immunology were subject to mandatory conscription to work seven days a week to seek a "cure" for AIDS, the "cure" might still be decades away. Simply throwing more money at AIDS does *not* mean that we will conquer HIV any sooner.

"*There is insufficient money dedicated to take care of AIDS patients.*" The U.S. Congress recently took an unprecedented move: it approved a bill designating 4 billion dollars over 5 years to assist in the care of AIDS patients in areas of the country hardest hit by the disease. This decision caused much concern for, among others, the White House Office of Management and Budget which noted that "the bill's narrow, disease-specific approach sets a dangerous precedent, inviting treatment of other diseases through similar ad hoc arrangements."

"The U.S. government's investment in AIDS has been *unprecedented*."

Indeed, it raises some very disturbing questions, namely, how much is *too much* to spend on

AIDS care? From where will this money come, that is, what cure for what disease will be delayed because of greater spending on AIDS? Questions of this type will become even more intense as efforts for "early intervention" are launched: it is estimated now that 600,000 to 1 million Americans infected with the AIDS virus, but not yet manifesting AIDS disease, might benefit from treatment with AZT and aerosol pentamadine before serious AIDS symptoms occur.

For the cost of the drug AZT alone (not counting medical care costs), it is estimated that if all potential candidates seek treatment, the bill could reach $1.62 billion annually. How much is too much to keep mortally ill persons alive for an additional 6 months?

"AIDS more than any other disease has successfully confronted the problem of 'drug lag' head on."

"Life-saving AIDS drugs are not being made available in a timely manner." ACTUP writes that "effective AIDS treatments . . . are now being denied millions of people by government red tape," noting that what they are really attacking is the slow pace of development and approval of new drugs, a system that relies on contributions from academic institutions, government agencies and pharmaceutical companies.

Actually, AIDS more than any other disease has successfully confronted the problem of "drug lag" head on. AZT was approved for use in AIDS in record time—and any promising new drug is being given top priority treatment. But given that the ultimate goal here is extension of life of AIDS patients, it helps no one to abandon efficacy tests and practice (in the words of Dr. Arnold Relman, editor of the *New England Journal of Medicine*) "black magic." Responding specifically to claims being made by Martin Delaney, head of Project Inform, an AIDS activists' group concerned with approval of new AIDS

drugs, that "Compound Q" was safe and effective, Relman noted "if (inaccurate information) gets out without being reviewed by unbiased experts and gets acted upon, it leads to a lot of bad possibilities . . . money is wasted, time is wasted . . . there is great initial enthusiasm and then despondency, pessimism and despair."

Drug Trials

Understandably patient advocates seek faster introductions of new, effective therapies and are impatient with the slow and deliberate scientific methodologies which have served well in the past. But in demanding approval of various antiviral drugs and immune-system enhancers, patient advocates come with a paucity of data on both safety and efficacy. How will we *ever* identify an effective agent against AIDS unless scientific protocol is maintained?

"AIDS is ultimately the government's fault and thus the solution is in the hands of the government." "Only an all out effort by the Federal Government can defeat AIDS. . . . History will record (that the war on AIDS) was lost because two U.S. Presidents and the entire Federal Government surrendered," wrote Larry Kramer, and in vintage-Kramer style he adds, "we are being exterminated just like the Jews were in the Holocaust."

Given what we know about the epidemiology of AIDS, these statements are clearly ridiculous. With rare exceptions, AIDS doesn't come out and get you—you have to go out and seek it. Over 90% of AIDS transmissions are related to specific consensual activities, those relating to sexual activity and IV [intravenous] drug use. As Charles Krauthammer correctly pointed out in his recent *Time* essay, "AIDS is far less an act of God than, say, cancer or diabetes."

What we need as we enter the second decade of AIDS is less emphasis on "government" and more on personal introspection about self-selected lifestyle factors. Government can educate, but it can't in itself change personal behavior. Only individuals can do that. Ronald Reagan and George Bush did not cause the 140,000 AIDS cases we have seen to date. Nor are they responsible for the frightening new trend among homosexual men who after a few years of "safer sex" are reverting to anal intercourse which carries the highest of risk of AIDS transmission.

Promiscuous sexual patterns, particularly those involving the practice of anal sex, and sharing of contaminated needles caused and still cause AIDS. Is, then, AIDS a self-inflicted disease? While it is not popular to so state in this age of "blamelessness," AIDS was and is largely self-inflicted. Even before the acronym "AIDS" came into our vocabulary, prior to 1980 when we had not yet officially diagnosed even one case, the health risks of sexual promiscuity, anal sex and sharing needles were well known.

AIDS did not strike like lightning on a clear day. AIDS occurred in the context of an epidemic of other sexually transmitted diseases (hepatitis B, rectal gonorrhea, genital herpes, and other bowel infections) among homosexual men.

Risk-Taking Behavior

Risk taking, in terms of engaging in health-threatening behavior, was part of the homosexual scene of the 1970s—with the risk taker's complacency based on the premise that antibiotics could cure almost everything. AIDS, a deadly viral disease that scoffs at antibiotics, was the unknown risk assumed at the same time. This is not a point to be belabored—nor is it grounds for withholding our compassion for AIDS victims who now suffer from the relentless horrors of a devastated immune system, but it is a significant factor to weigh in against the strident chants of AIDS activists that they were to-

tally helpless victims and that "government" is the real villain. This absurdity of "the government did it to me" came into focus in New York City during a Gay Rights parade where one sign read, "Reagan and Bush have blood on their hands" and another adjacent one said, "Legalize Sodomy—For the Fun of it."

"AIDS doesn't come out and get you—you have to go out and seek it."

AIDS will remain a heavy tax burden for every taxpaying American citizen well into the 21st century. Progress will be impeded with further finger pointing and name calling. There is no room in our struggle against the AIDS virus for unjustified discrimination against those infected or for indifference to the suffering caused by this disease. But activists and spokesmen for AIDS patients and those at high risk for the disease should recognize that it is time to turn down the volume on the rhetoric and work within the system to focus rage not on the very establishment which is struggling to cope with this national disaster, but on the common enemy, HIV. Compassion can quickly be in short supply when there are no acknowledgments of the enormous investment already made in AIDS research and when epithets of blame are randomly assigned without even a pause for some serious personal introspection about the role one's own personal behavior played in the evolution of a tragedy.

America's Response to AIDS Is Adequate

Charles Krauthammer

About the Author: *Charles Krauthammer, a well-known writer whose works have appeared in such publications as* The New Republic, *is an essayist for* Time, *a weekly newsmagazine.*

In May 1990, a thousand demonstrators camped outside the National Institutes of Health [NIH] near Washington, and with a talented display of street theater protested governmental and scientific neglect of AIDS. If not the angriest demonstration Washington has seen in a long time, it was certainly the most misdirected. The idea that American government or American society has been inattentive or unresponsive to AIDS is quite simply absurd. Consider:

Treatment. Congress is about to do something extremely rare: allocate money specifically for the treatment of one disease. The Senate voted $2.9 billion, the House $4 billion over five years for treating AIDS. And only AIDS. When Senator Malcolm Wallop introduced an amendment allowing rural districts with few AIDS patients to spend the money on other diseases, the amendment was voted down, 2 to 1.

Research. Except for cancer, AIDS now receives more Government research money than any other illness in America. AIDS gets $1.2 billion to $1.3 billion. Heart disease, for example, receives about half as much, $700 billion. The AIDS research allocation is not just huge, it is hugely disproportionate. AIDS has killed 83,000 Americans in nine years. Heart disease kills that

many every six weeks.

Testing. Under pressure from AIDS activists, the FDA [Food and Drug Administration] has radically changed its regulations for testing new drugs. The Administration has proposed "parallel track" legislation that would make drugs available to certain patients before the usual testing process is complete. Nothing wrong with this. But this exception is for AIDS patients only—a fact that hardly supports the thesis that government is holding back an AIDS cure or discriminating against AIDS patients.

> **"The idea that American government or American society has been inattentive or unresponsive to AIDS is quite simply absurd."**

The suffering caused by AIDS is enormous. Sufferers deserve compassion, and their disease deserves scientific inquiry. But AIDS has got far more. AIDS has become the most privileged disease in America. Why? Mainly because its victims are young, in many cases creative and famous. Their deaths are therefore particularly poignant and public. And because one of the two groups that AIDS disproportionately affects (gay men) is highly organized. This combination of conspicuousness and constituency has allowed AIDS activists to get more research funding, more treatment money and looser drug testing restrictions than any comparable disease.

Nothing wrong with that. The system for allocating research and treatment money in American medicine is archaic, chaotic and almost random anyway. Under the "Disease of the Month Club" syndrome, any disease that has in some way affected a Congressman or some relation gets special treatment. There is rough justice in this method of allocation because after a while Congressmen and their kin get to experience most of the medical tragedies that life has to offer. At the end of the day, therefore, funds tend to get allocated in a fairly proportionate way.

AIDS is now riding a crest of public support, won in the rough and tumble of politics. All perfectly legitimate, and a tribute to the passion and commitment of AIDS activists. But that passion turns to mere stridency when they take to the streets to protest that a homophobic society has been ungenerous and stinting in its response to the tragedy of AIDS. In fact, American society is giving overwhelming and indeed disproportionate attention and resources to the fight.

At first the homosexual community was disoriented and defensive in reaction to AIDS. In the quite understandable attempt to get public support, it fixed on a strategy of claiming that AIDS was everyone's problem. Since we were all potential sufferers—anyone can get AIDS, went the slogan—society as an act of self-protection should go all out for cure and care.

This campaign was initially successful. But then it ran into an obstacle. It wasn't true. AIDS is not everyone's problem. It is extremely difficult to get AIDS. It requires the carrying out of specific and quite intentional acts. Nine out of ten people with AIDS have got it through homosexual sex and/or intravenous drug use. The NIH demonstrators, therefore, now appeal less to solidarity than to guilt: every person who dies is more blood on the hands of a society unwilling to give every dollar demanded for a cure.

Contracting AIDS

But society has blood on its hands every time it refuses to give every dollar demanded by the cancer lobby, the heart disease lobby, the diabetes lobby. So now a different tack: the claim that the AIDS epidemic is, of course, not an act of government but an act of God—and government has not done enough to help its helpless victims.

In fact, AIDS is far less an act of God than is, say, cancer or diabetes. Apart from a small number of relentlessly exploited Ryan White-like exceptions, the overwhelming majority of sufferers get AIDS through some voluntary action: sex or drug abuse. You don't get AIDS the way you used to get TB [tuberculosis], by having someone on the trolley cough in your face. You don't get it the way you get, say, brain cancer, which is through some act of God that we don't understand at all.

"AIDS is in the class of diseases whose origins we understand quite well."

AIDS is in the class of diseases whose origins we understand quite well. It is behaviorally induced and behaviorally preventable. In that sense it is in the same moral class as lung cancer, the majority of whose victims get it through voluntary behavior well known to be highly dangerous. For lung cancer the behavior is smoking; for AIDS, unsafe sex (not, it might be noted, homosexuality) and IV [intravenous] drug use.

As a society we do not refuse either to treat or research lung cancer simply because its sufferers brought it on themselves. But we would find it somewhat perverse and distasteful if lung cancer sufferers began demonstrating wildly, blaming society and government for their problems, and demanding that they be first in line for a cure.

Many people contracted AIDS before its causes became known, about six years ago. For them it is truly an act of God. For the rest (as the word has gone out, an ever increasing percentage), it is an act of man. They, of course, deserve our care and treatment. But it is hard to see from where they derive the claim to be first in line—ahead of those dying of leukemia and breast cancer and stroke—for the resources and compassion of a nation.

AIDS Funding Should Be Reduced

Michael Fumento

About the Author: *Michael Fumento is the author of* The Myth of Heterosexual AIDS. *He also contributes to* The New Republic, *a weekly journal of opinion.*

If there is one thing Americans seem to agree upon about AIDS, it is that we are not spending enough on the disease. "The government has blood on its hands," reads a bumper sticker that is ubiquitous in major cities, "one AIDS death every half hour." AIDS activists, who are fond of asserting that AIDS is "not a homosexual disease," tell us in the same breath that the failure to spend more on it constitutes genocide against homosexuals. A recent public-opinion poll shows, indeed, that most Americans favor increasing spending on AIDS.

But consider. In 1989, reported cases of AIDS in the U.S. increased only 9 percent over the previous year's tally. The federal Centers for Disease Control (CDC) of the Public Health Service (PHS) has been forced to lower greatly both its estimate of current infections and its projections of future cases. The World Health Organization, similarly, has lowered its original estimate of as many as 100 million infections by 1990 to a current eight to ten million. New York City, AIDS capital of the nation, has lowered its estimate of current infections from 500,000 to about 150,000.

Nor has the long-expected "breakout" of AIDS into the heterosexual middle class shown any sign of occurring. Former Surgeon General

C. Everett Koop, who probably coined the expression "heterosexual AIDS explosion," now claims he knew "from the very beginning" that such a thing would never happen; Gene Antonio, author of *The AIDS Cover-Up?* (300,000 copies in print), which predicted as many as 64 million infections by 1990, now denies having made such a prediction. At the 1990 AIDS conference in San Francisco, Dr. Nancy Padian put another nail in the coffin of the "breakout" theory when she reported the results of her study of 41 couples among whom the woman was originally infected and the man was not: over a period of years, only one man became infected, and that only after both he and his partner had experienced penile and vaginal bleeding on over 100 occasions.

In 1990, AIDS dropped from being the 14th biggest killer of Americans to number 15. Heart disease this year will kill about 775,000 Americans, a figure perhaps 20 times as high as the number of Americans who will die of AIDS in the next twelve months. In the next two months cancer will kill almost as many people as have died of AIDS in the course of the entire epidemic.

> ## "AIDS dropped from being the 14th biggest killer of Americans to number 15."

Nevertheless, the *current* PHS allocation of about $1.6 billion for AIDS research and education is higher than that allocated for any other cause of death. In 1990, the CDC will spend $10,000 on prevention and education for each AIDS sufferer as opposed to $185 for each victim of cancer and a mere $3.50 for each cardiac patient. Total federal research expenditures on AIDS this year will be more than 100 percent of nationwide patient costs; in the case of cancer, the corresponding ratio of research-and-development spending to patient costs is about 4.5 percent, in the case of heart disease about 2.9

percent, and in the case of Alzheimer's disease, less than 1 percent.

AIDS Activism

AIDS activists have answers to these statistics. Since AIDS strikes most often in the prime of life, they urge us to consider the years of lost productivity as a cost that could be avoided by more spending now on AIDS research. Yet every year cancer and heart disease *each* kills more than 150,000 Americans below the age of sixty, while this year AIDS will kill around 30,000 persons of all ages. Nor do the calculations of years lost take account of the fact that intravenous drug abusers, who make up a growing portion of those affected by the disease, have a very low life expectancy and an even lower expectancy of productivity.

But, say AIDS activists, the disease is overwhelming the nation's health-care system, and this alone justifies increased spending on research. A figure repeated often in the media has been the Rand Corporation's estimate that by 1991, direct medical costs for AIDS (that is, medical expenses only, with lost wages not included) could be as high as $133 billion, with up to $38 billion in 1991 alone. *U.S. News & World Report* flatly declared, "What is now becoming clear to an array of leaders—in medicine, business, government, and academia—is that AIDS not only threatens untold death and suffering but could bankrupt America's health system as well." In fact, however, a typical AIDS case costs approximately the same as a terminal cancer case, about $40,000 to $50,000, which means that the 35,000 reported AIDS cases in 1989 will end up costing the nation something less than $2 billion, or considerably less than 1 percent of this year's total U.S. medical costs of approximately $650 billion.

Of course, localized emergencies can exist. New York City's hospital system, running poorly even before AIDS, is clearly in a state of crisis even though cases in that city have peaked. The reason New York, San Francisco, Los Angeles, and other such cities have been hit so hard by AIDS is that they are refuges for homosexuals and drug abusers. With that in mind, the House and Senate are seeking to authorize $2.9 billion and $4 billion, respectively, over the next six years, mostly for these hard-hit cities and states. (Ironically, the bill has been cast as emergency relief for *rural* areas, apparently in the belief that voters have more sympathy for the problems of Peoria than for those of San Francisco or New York.) This special allocation for AIDS, which comes on top of an earlier special allocation to subsidize the drug AZT, is almost without precedent. There is nothing similar for people with heart disease or cancer or diabetes or lupus or any number of other potentially fatal diseases (with the exception of end-stage renal disease).

What about the assertion that AIDS deserves more funding because it is contagious, while heart disease and cancer are not? In fact, AIDS is contagious almost exclusively through behavior, and modification of that behavior could in theory reduce future AIDS cases virtually to zero without another penny spent on research and without a single medical breakthrough. An as-yet-uninfected homosexual who avoids high-risk behavior will almost certainly never contract AIDS; but his chance of dying of cancer remains one in five. Indeed, male homosexuals outside of such high-incidence areas as San Francisco, Los Angeles, and New York, and whose HIV status is unknown, currently have less chance of getting AIDS than of dying of either heart disease or cancer.

"A typical AIDS case costs approximately the same as a terminal cancer case, about $40,000 to $50,000."

It is said that even if research on AIDS does not yield a cure, spin-offs from that research could lead to cures and treatments for other diseases. In line with this idea, Congressman Ted Weiss (D.-NY) requested the Office of Technology Assessment (OTA) to prepare a report titled, "How Has Federal Research on AIDS/HIV Contributed to Other Fields?" The reviewer in the British medical journal *Lancet*, struck by the contrast between this tiny report and OTA's customary "behemoth, exhaustive" efforts, noted that it was comprised of nothing more than opinions from an "unspecified organization of 'distinguished biomedical and social scientists,'" and that "For policy or polemics, this OTA production is a bust."

"An as-yet uninfected homosexual who avoids high-risk behavior will almost certainly never contract AIDS."

Nevertheless, Dr. Anthony Fauci, the director of the National Institutes of Allergies and Infectious Diseases (NIAID), a branch of the National Institutes of Health (NIH), and long an advocate of increased spending on AIDS, declared that "There's positive spin-offs already and certainly in the next decade or two you'll see more," adding that these included cancer. In fact, no life has ever been saved, no disease ever ameliorated, by AIDS spin-offs. As former NIH director Donald Fredrickson has pointed out, most AIDS research is far too narrowly targeted to lead to significant spin-offs. Indeed, most of the money spent by the PHS on AIDS (including for advertisements on late-night television like the one featuring a man who resolves not to go out on the town and "bring back AIDS to my family") does not involve clinical research at all.

This is not to say that no spin-offs are ever possible. After all, no one knew that the space program would end up introducing the world to velcro. But we did not embark on the space program because we wanted a new kind of fastener. If it is a cure for cancer we seek, we should spend money on cancer research, not on another disease entirely. As it happens, increasing spending on cancer at the expense of spending

on AIDS might do more for both diseases: of the first three drugs approved for treatment of AIDS or its conditions, two—AZT and alpha interferon—were spin-offs of cancer research.

Disproportionate Spending

Among the deleterious effects of disproportionate spending on AIDS have been inevitable boondoggles, as great a problem in medicine as in national defense. In December 1988, NIAID announced two grants totaling $22.8 million to study non-drug-using heterosexuals in order, as the Associated Press put it, to "prevent a huge new epidemic." Speaking on condition of anonymity, one prominent federal epidemiologist said of the study, "I think it's complete bullshit." He added, "My sense was that a huge amount of money got dumped on NIAID and that by the time they got around to awarding the money a lot of good institutions had already been funded and all that was left was schlock."

Concentration on AIDS has in general prompted a de-emphasis of other medical diseases like Alzheimer's, a cruel, debilitating malady that will continue to exact an ever-higher yearly toll unless medical intervention becomes possible. Nobody is more conscious of this than researchers themselves. It takes up to a decade to put a high-school graduate through medical school; thus, for now and for the immediate future, AIDS researchers are being drawn from other research areas, primarily cancer, and the rumblings from traditionally nonpolitical laboratories are growing louder and louder. Some are calling it "AIDS Resentment Complex," a play on "AIDS Related Complex." Dr. Vincent T. DeVita, Jr., just before stepping down from his position as director of the National Cancer Institute (NCI), said that AIDS "has been an extraordinary drain on the energy of the scientific establishment." In fact, AIDS research has now weakened cancer research to the point where NCI's ability to fund promising new proposals is lower than at any time in the past two decades.

Two top doctors left NCI in late 1988, partly out of frustration over this state of affairs. According to one of them, Dr. Robert Young, now president of the American Society of Clinical Oncology, "the superstructure of cancer research is being dismantled." Indeed, for non-AIDS work, NIH lost almost 1,100 employees between 1984 and 1989. At the same time, according to *Science* magazine, the number of NIH employees engaged in AIDS work increased by more than 400 to 580 workers or their full-time equivalents.

"Among the deleterious effects of disproportionate spending on AIDS have been inevitable boondoggles."

The most vocal opposition to spiraling federal AIDS expenditures has probably come from women concerned about breast cancer, which kills about 44,000 a year; every two years as many women die of breast cancer alone as the number of men and women who have died of AIDS over the course of the entire epidemic. True, Congress is now considering bills that would appropriate funds for cancer screening in women, but the total to be allocated for both breast cancer and cervical cancer—the latter kills 6,000 women a year and is virtually always preventable if caught early enough—is only $50 million, as contrasted with the $3 to $4 billion which Congress wants to spend for AIDS treatment programs over the next six years and which will probably not save a single life, from AIDS or anything else.

The blunt fact is, then, that a great many people will die of other diseases because of the overemphasis on AIDS. We will never know their names and those names will never be sewn into a giant quilt. We will never know their exact numbers. But they will die nonetheless.

Is this right? Should a compassionate society allocate funds and research on the basis of media attention, on the basis of whoever makes the loudest noise? Or should it, rather, put its appropriations where they can do the most good for the greatest number of people?

Has America Adequately Funded AIDS Research and Treatment?

No: America Has Not Adequately Funded AIDS

America's Response to AIDS Is Inadequate
The U.S. Government Needs a National AIDS Policy
Women with AIDS Need More Government Help

America's Response to AIDS Is Inadequate

Jessica Portner

About the Author: *Jessica Portner is a free-lance writer in Washington, D.C.*

A student at Howard University in Washington, D.C., was admitted to the university hospital for psychiatric care after attempting suicide. When the doctors discovered from her medical charts that she had tested positive for the HIV [human immunodeficiency virus] virus, which causes AIDS, they refused to admit her to the psychiatric ward.

According to the Whitman Walker Clinic, which represented the student in a suit against Howard, "Hospital staff had strapped the woman to a bed for five days, [and] left her wallowing in her own feces," in an out-of-the-way facility. Howard University was found guilty of discrimination and now allows any person with HIV infection equal treatment in any unit of the hospital.

Two lesbians working in a manufacturing plant for Johns Hopkins University in Baltimore were almost fired recently because co-workers suspected them of "spreading AIDS." The National Organization Responding to AIDS (NORA) stepped in with an impromptu educational seminar about transmission and risk factors on the job, preempting any lawsuit.

A young black man in Detroit recently entered the U.S. Department of Labor's Job Corps, which provides residential training for disadvantaged youth. Six weeks after testing him without his knowledge, the administrators told him,

Jessica Portner, "Fighting Back," *The Progressive,* August 1990. Reprinted by permission from *The Progressive,* 409 E. Main St., Madison, WI 53703.

"You have AIDS and you can't stay here any more," according to attorney David Barr, who filed suit on the youth's behalf.

AIDS is becoming as much a legal as a medical battle. And 1990 may be remembered as the year the balance for people with AIDS was tipped. Congress recently passed the Americans with Disabilities Act (ADA), which extends civil-rights protection to people with AIDS under a definition of "contagious diseases." The law wasn't advanced in Congress or elsewhere as an "AIDS bill." If it had been, proponents argue, the bill never would have passed. So AIDS activists joined forces with the disability community, tacking it onto a disability-rights law.

"People don't want to be seen as enemies of the disabled," says Kurt Decker of NORA. "There is safety in numbers."

Federal law previously protected only those people employed in and served by institutions that receive Federal funds (excluding military personnel and Federal prisoners). The ADA now extends this ban on discrimination against sufferers of contagious diseases to the private sector as well. It also protects people *perceived* as HIV-positive. Barr, who is on the staff of the New York-based Lambda Legal Defense Fund, the country's oldest and largest gay legal-defense organization, explains, "It's one thing to say, 'You have AIDS and you're fired,' and another thing to say, 'I think you have AIDS and you're fired.'"

> ## "AIDS is becoming as much a legal as a medical battle."

Businesses may no longer legally refuse service to patrons they "perceive" to have AIDS. For example, hotels may now be fined for refusing rooms to guests who fall into high-risk categories.

The inclusion of AIDS in the ADA's definition of "contagious disease" is a victory not only for AIDS patients, but for the AIDS activists who made it happen. With the paltry $1.1 billion allocated to AIDS education and prevention by the Reagan and Bush Administrations from 1982 to 1988, AIDS activists have become political organizers, lobbyists, and on-the-spot virologists to deal with the epidemic effectively. Pooling resources from such groups as the American Foundation for AIDS Research (AMFAR), local governments, and concerned citizens, community-based organizations have grown larger and gradually stronger.

In major cities from Los Angeles to New York, activists are plastering kiosks with posters announcing AIDS education meetings, rallies, and fundraisers. Privately funded AIDS hotlines are operating in dozens of metropolitan areas, providing referrals to hospitals, clinics, law offices, and crisis centers.

"It's clear that if AIDS were primarily affecting middle-class straight white America, it would be more thoroughly reported."

Twenty-five-year-old Scott Sanders, the public-relations director of the Whitman Walker Clinic in Washington, D.C., sits in his white-walled office, which is decorated with photos of fundraisers and a fluorescent poster of a red-eyed Reagan with the word AIDSGATE in black letters underneath. Sanders calmly discusses the clinic's innovative AIDS prevention program, which provides free testing, counseling, and health care to Washington residents. But when he talks about the mainstream press's response to the epidemic, he becomes visibly angry.

"If you look at Legionnaires' disease [a virus which mysteriously killed about twenty middle-aged white men in the early 1980s], and you compare how the press responded to that to how they're dealing with AIDS, the difference is overwhelming," says Sanders. "It's clear that if AIDS were primarily affecting middle-class straight white America, it would be more thoroughly reported."

ACT UP (AIDS Coalition to Unleash Power)

of New York, the country's largest and arguably most militant gay-rights group, lashes out at judges, pharmaceutical companies, or the Bush Administration, depending on the crisis of the week. The group has a highly focused mantra that kicks off every Monday-night meeting: UNITED IN ANGER AND COMMITTED IN ACTION AGAINST AIDS.

At its now-infamous demonstration at St. Patrick's Cathedral in December 1989, a group of ACT UP protesters stormed into the church with banners and placards denouncing John Cardinal O'Connor as a "devil" while the cardinal delivered his Sunday-morning sermon. Evening television reports showed young men in black T-shirts feigning death in the aisles and chomping on communion wafers.

But ACT UP's goal is not just to advance the struggle on the evening news. The group often and effectively uses civil disobedience to challenge what it sees as a prejudicial legal system. Currently, ACT UP is on an "illicit campaign" to distribute clean needles to drug users around the city. Possession of any drug-related paraphernalia is illegal in New York State.

In March 1990, ACT UP deliberately announced the time and place of the needle distribution, sparking a counterdemonstration at which ten ACT UP members were arrested. "The purpose was to get them arrested," Barr explains, "so we could challenge the law."

Media Messages

Though ACT UP/New York may be the national model, each AIDS group has to adapt its style to its constituency. "We're all media queens out here," says Jesse Dobson, an organizer for ACT UP/San Francisco who discovered that he is HIV-positive. "In our sound-bite society," he says, "we have to have a concise *Entertainment Tonight* message to get people's attention."

His chief focus now is drug testing. Dobson and others are putting pressure on the Food and Drug Administration to adopt "parallel track" guidelines for releasing AIDS drugs immediately after safety testing, without waiting for clinical trials to assess possible health complications. "Let the patient take the risk," Dobson says, "because the downside is pretty bad."

And in May 1989, the Hoffmann-LaRoche pharmaceutical company, which manufactures the newest antiviral drug DDC, filed an early-release application with the FDA. "It's one of the things we're most jazzed about these days because it's been a successful effort," Dobson says.

Political and Economic Pressure

While some concentrate on this kind of political pressure, other AIDS activists muster entrepreneurial energy to get results. William Waybourn, president of the Dallas Gay Alliance and a consummate businessman, boasts a $1.2 million budget for 1991, 70 per cent of which comes from individual contributions of $20 or less. "We have taken modern marketing techniques and applied them to gay rights," he says. "People say gays have been devastated by AIDS, but my budget proves them wrong. AIDS has dramatically galvanized our society."

The Alliance provides a myriad of AIDS-related services from testing to counseling to inventive educational outreach. "We have an antiviolence project where volunteers patrol certain neighborhoods," Waybourn notes. The Alliance runs a resident facility, a food pantry, a family registry, and a weekly radio show. There is even a program called "Pet Pals" where volunteers help people with AIDS care for their pets by soliciting donations or taking animals to veterinarians.

Julian Rush, executive director of the six-year-old Colorado AIDS Project, is a veteran activist. He runs a controversial outreach program that is being duplicated in urban areas across the country. Volunteers go into local bars and "do one-to-one contacts about safe sex." Rush points out that safe-sex dialogue has to be direct because of the rate of relapse behavior. "Safe sex isn't second nature to them; they need to be reminded," he says. A poll the project conducted showed a 20 per cent increase in AIDS awareness among contacts, beating the state's education track record by a large margin.

With the success of these gay-based AIDS coalitions as models, many new groups have organized around the concerns of women, blacks, and Hispanics. "HIV infection among women, especially women of color, is increasing rapidly," explains Jacquelyn Wilkerson of the Women's Council on AIDS in Washington, D.C. "And because most organizations are targeted at men, women are falling through the cracks." Wilkerson advocates a positive approach to education, pointing to her group's Valentine's Day drive. "We said the ideal gift would be a dozen roses and a dozen condoms," she says.

The Council passes out its leaflets in "nontraditional settings," such as laundromats, churches, and town meetings. One innovative program is the Beauty Shop Project, where volunteers go into salons and distribute safe-sex manuals and condoms to the customers. "It's a good way to reach women in a nondiscriminatory way. And it's also convenient because they're not going anywhere," Wilkerson says.

"Because most organizations are targeted at men, women are falling through the cracks."

Robert Garcia heads ACT UP/New York's Latino Caucus, formed recently to address the growing AIDS crisis in the Hispanic community. He charges Latino leaders are "in a deep state of denial" about the impact of AIDS. "They think junkies are the only members of their communities dying of AIDS," he says. "And these people have no political clout, so the leadership can't afford to care about them." In poor Hispanic neighborhoods, says Garcia, AIDS is one epidemic of many and can only be seen "within the context of malnutrition, lack of education, crime, and drug use."

"AIDS is just one of many oppressions," he says.

It is clearly less popular these days to publicly argue that "deviant" behavior warrants violent punishment. Many AIDS activists say the pace of change in the public's attitude quickened in 1987, when Rock Hudson died of AIDS. Americans suddenly wanted to know more about the disease. Such celebrities as Elizabeth Taylor started holding galas and chic fundraisers that made the pages of *People* magazine. And when actor Paul Michael Glazer's daughter died of AIDS—a contaminated blood transfusion her mother received shortly after giving birth was transmitted through breast feeding to the child—Ted Koppel devoted a *Nightline* show to the growing number of pediatric AIDS cases in the United States.

Unfortunately, the media attention does not ensure quick release of affordable drugs, nor does it alter national policy. And, for many Americans, AIDS still generates a fear that they feel justifies differential treatment of those suspected of having contracted the disease.

Michael Perelman, a twenty-six-year-old visual artist in New York City, took a job at Clyde's restaurant in the West Village in 1986 and paid $59 a month for a group health plan. When he sent in his first doctor's bill, the insurance company canceled his policy. The company, Perelman says, claimed he had lied about a preexisting condition. "The company threatened to revoke the policies of two other waiters and a bartender, all of whom just happened to be gay," he says, noting the company offered to reinstate the policies if they agreed to take an HIV test. All refused. The bartender died last year of AIDS.

"AIDS is a disaster that demands a response by the American people."

Insurance companies are, according to many AIDS activists, the greatest villains in America's AIDS saga. Many companies require new enrollees to take HIV tests, even if they do not fall into high-risk categories.

That means the estimated one to two million Americans with HIV infection who may be asymptomatic may have no medical option if they become ill. "You'd have to quit your job, become disabled, and spend all your money so you'd be eligible for Medicaid," says Barr.

And the new disability act doesn't remedy that. "The insurance companies have a very powerful lobby," says NORA's Decker, who notes that the chances of passing a law requiring companies to end their biased practices were so remote that a bill was never even introduced in Congress.

Empolyers will, however, be required by the act to find an insurance company to sign people with HIV infection, and cannot refuse to hire anyone because of the increased cost of a health policy—a measure that affects insurance companies indirectly.

The ADA won't transform society's fear into compassion or create an accessible health-care system. Attorney Catherine O'Neill of the Legal Action Center in New York, who has been representing disadvantaged clients for more than a decade, sees the ADA as a Bandaid measure which will have little effect for her clients unless it is coupled with outreach and education.

But the ADA is a crucial first step toward giving AIDS sufferers—increasingly the poor, minorities, women, and children—the tools to fight back. . . .

Senator Edward Kennedy, Democrat of Massachusetts, wants to move beyond the ADA. His AIDS funding bill, which would provide $600 million in "emergency funds" for "hard-hit" cities and states to develop HIV care programs, recently passed both houses of Congress but has not yet been signed into law. . . .

"AIDS is a disaster that demands a response by the American people," he said recently. "It is not a question of resources—because we can find the resources. What we need is the political will."

The U.S. Government Needs a National AIDS Policy

Robin Weiss

About the Author: *Robin Weiss is the director of the AIDS program at the Institute of Medicine in Washington, D.C. The institute studies and reports on the nation's major health problems.*

In four years in this nation, the epidemic of human immunodeficiency virus (HIV) infection and its most severe manifestation, acquired immune deficiency syndrome (AIDS), will claim over 200,000 lives. The U.S. Public Health Service estimates that 1 million to 1.5 million people are currently infected with the virus. In the absence of effective therapy, the vast majority of those infected will develop AIDS and die. Although AIDS now kills fewer people than heart disease or cancer, its rank as a cause of mortality is quickly rising, and the primary sufferers of AIDS come from what is ordinarily a healthy and productive population group: young adults.

Stemming this agonizing epidemic requires presidential leadership. The epidemic poses dilemmas both for the public and the private sectors which will best be solved by forceful, coherent national policy. The obligation to formulate AIDS policy spans a variety of federal government departments and reaches beyond the Department of Health and Human Services (HHS) to the departments of Justice, Education, State, Defense, Energy, the Veterans Administration, and other components of the Executive Branch. In addition, private organizations, foun-

dations, volunteer groups, professional organizations, and state and local governments already have taken the initiative to create educational programs, formulate laws and regulations, and address other aspects of the epidemic. These efforts are an enormous contribution to the progress that has been made thus far against HIV infection and AIDS. Nevertheless, the absence of coherent national direction condemns many localities to begin anew when it comes to setting local policy and increases the likelihood that failed experiments will be repeated from place to place. The Bush administration can furnish overarching direction for all segments of the government and the private sector. Equally important, the president can set a tone that encourages aggressive action yet resists hysteria and insensitivity to the civil rights of infected persons.

Furthermore, foreign leaders will turn to the president of the United States for assistance and wisdom in addressing their own countries' HIV problems. The World Health Organization estimates that between 5 million and 10 million persons are infected with HIV worldwide. AIDS may double the mortality rate for young and middle-age adults in some developing countries, and perinatal transmission in those countries may reverse hard-won advances in child and infant survival.

"The primary sufferers of AIDS come from what is ordinarily a healthy and productive population group: young adults."

This paper proposes that the Bush administration take several actions, which we believe will help slow the spread of HIV and limit its damaging effects on this nation and on other countries: (1) Use the National Commission on AIDS effectively; (2) protect HIV-infected persons from discrimination; (3) develop a comprehensive plan for financing the care of those with

HIV infection and AIDS; (4) initiate a forceful program for the treatment of substance abuse and the prevention of the associated spread of HIV; (5) institute aggressive and unambiguous educational programs and evaluate their effects; (6) ensure that HIV testing and other public health measures are used only when their purposes are clear and their results productive; (7) bolster efforts in surveillance, case reporting, and the gathering of information about risk behavior; (8) ensure that biomedical research (including drug and vaccine development and regulation) continues to follow fruitful paths; and (9) recognize our special responsibility in international health efforts to control AIDS.

"There are no grounds for discriminating against persons with HIV infection or AIDS."

Use the National Commission on AIDS effectively. President Ronald Reagan signed into law the AIDS Amendments of 1988, which establish a National Commission on Acquired Immune Deficiency Syndrome. Although the creation of a national commission is an important step, the commission's existence alone does not guarantee its effectiveness. The Bush administration can maximize the commission's impact in the following ways:

• The president will appoint five members of the 15-member body, two of whom will be selected from the general public (the other three are the Secretary of Health and Human Services, the Administrator of Veterans' Affairs, and the Secretary of Defense). The two other appointees should be senior experts of national stature in areas of particular relevance to AIDS. They should not be chosen because they hold any particular political ideology.

• The commission will submit its reports to the president and to the appropriate committees of Congress. In addition, however, the chairman should have direct access to the Oval Of-

fice. The work of the commission will have the greatest possible effect on policy if it is widely perceived that its chairman has the ear of the president. The president can endow the commission with sufficient national stature and credibility for its advice to influence all participants in the struggle against AIDS.

• The commission is required to report its recommendations one and two years after its constitution. Although the reports will identify needed action, the commission will be most valuable if it is also consulted on a continuing basis as policy questions arise within the executive branch.

Protect HIV-infected persons from discrimination. HIV transmission occurs through sexual contact, the use of contaminated needles or syringes, exposure to infected blood or blood products, transplantation of infected tissue or organs, and from mother to child either across the placenta or during delivery (and probably during breast-feeding). There is no evidence that HIV is transmitted by casual contact or by insects. Therefore, there are no grounds for discriminating against persons with HIV infection or AIDS because of fears that they pose a health risk through casual contact in schools, in the workplace, in housing, or in customary social interchanges.

Discrimination Exists

However, such discrimination does exist, and fear of discrimination discourages some individuals at risk for infection from participating in testing programs, contact notification, and other potentially effective public health measures. Public health measures crucial in controlling the HIV epidemic depend on voluntary cooperation; for that cooperation to occur, people must believe that they will be protected from discrimination.

• The president should ask Congress to enact legislation designed to prevent discrimination on the basis of HIV infection or AIDS in both the public and the private sectors.

Develop a comprehensive plan for financing the care of those with HIV infection and AIDS. The average lifetime medical expenses per AIDS patient in the United States, from diagnosis to death, are from $65,000 to $80,000. In 1986, estimated total direct costs for AIDS were approximately $1.64 billion—.$1.1 billion for personal medical care and $542 million for nonpersonal expenses—representing 0.4 percent of total U.S. health expenditures. By 1991, direct costs associated with AIDS are projected to be $10.8 billion and to account for approximately 1.5 percent of national health care expenditures. Although the proportion of total health care expenditures devoted to AIDS will continue to be small through 1991, in certain metropolitan areas the economic burden to the health care sector will be great. For instance, in San Francisco, AIDS patients are expected to occupy 12.4 percent of all medical/surgical hospital beds.

"Information about the modes of HIV transmission must be conveyed in an understandable, yet scientifically accurate form."

According to the Health Care Financing Administration, Medicaid provides health care coverage for approximately 40 percent of all patients with AIDS. Public hospitals in states with stringent Medicaid eligibility requirements are faced with growing numbers of uninsured AIDS patients; the result is that many public hospitals are incompletely reimbursed for the care they provide. Medicare currently covers only 1 percent of AIDS patients, in part because they often do not survive the required 24-month waiting period to qualify for benefits. Private health insurance may pay for a dwindling share of AIDS patients as more poor and nonworking persons become sick and because insurers are making plans to limit their exposure to financial risk.

Solutions to financing AIDS health care can reflect the pluralism of the current health care financing system. Elements of a comprehensive financing strategy could include: enabling HIV-infected persons to secure or maintain private insurance through insurer tax incentives and government subsidy of premiums; modifying existing state Medicaid programs to make them more uniform and more efficient; shortening or eliminating the 24-month waiting period for Medicare benefits; establishing state risk pools; and establishing an AIDS federal grant program to direct funds to the states on the basis of a formula that reflects individual states' AIDS caseloads and resources.

• The Secretary of HHS should develop an AIDS federal grant program to the states to ensure that AIDS patients and those with HIV-related conditions have access to appropriate and cost-effective care. This approach would offer some immediate financial relief to those hard-hit states and medical institutions that currently bear a disproportionate burden of AIDS care.

• Another immediate need is to remove financial barriers to drug therapies. The Secretary of HHS should require all state Medicaid programs to reimburse for costly AIDS drugs that have been approved for marketing or that are under the Food and Drug Administration's (FDA) new mechanism allowing certain drugs still under investigation to be distributed.

• Piecemeal solutions to the problems of health care financing must not sidetrack the need for a more comprehensive scheme. The Secretary of HHS should take the lead in developing a comprehensive national plan for delivering and financing care for needy HIV-infected and AIDS patients. The following principles should guide the development of such a financing strategy: (1) coverage from the time HIV infection is discovered, (2) consideration of relief for hard-hit communities, (3) shared responsibility between public and private sectors, and (4) payment mechanisms that encourage the most cost-effective types of care.

AIDS and Addiction

Initiate a forceful program for the treatment of substance abuse and the prevention of the associated spread of HIV. The gross inadequacy of efforts to reduce HIV transmission among intravenous (IV) drug abusers, when considered in relation to the scope and implications of such transmission, is the most serious deficiency in current programs to control HIV infection in the United States. IV drug abusers are the second largest group of AIDS sufferers, and the most likely to transmit HIV beyond the current high-risk groups. Several actions are necessary:

"The president can encourage a level-headed approach to testing strategies."

• First, the Secretary of HHS should order a rapid, large-scale expansion of residential drug-free treatment, outpatient treatment, and methadone maintenance in order to provide immediate access for all addicts who request treatment. Methadone maintenance, an effective therapy for some heroin addicts, does not treat cocaine addiction. Yet IV cocaine abuse is increasingly related to transmission of HIV infection. Research to find effective treatment for cocaine addiction is urgently needed.

• Second, innovative intervention programs must be begun to reach those IV drug abusers who are not in treatment. Former IV drug abusers, functioning as community health workers, can provide individual risk-reduction counseling; in addition, trials of sterile needle exchange programs, in which sterile needles and syringes are provided to drug abusers, should be implemented and evaluated.

• Finally, long-term drug abuse prevention strategies are needed that begin with teens and preteens. Research and evaluation are necessary to determine which prevention methods work best.

Institute aggressive and unambiguous educational programs and evaluate their effects. Educational efforts to foster and sustain behavioral change are the only practical means now available to stem the spread of HIV infection. Information about the modes of HIV transmission must be conveyed in an understandable, yet scientifically accurate form. The message of AIDS education programs must also address sexual behavior and drug abuse, matters that are regarded by some as morally unsuitable for description in public health campaigns. Unsubstantiated concern that frank, straightforward educational programs can encourage IV drug abuse or sexual relations has stymied educational efforts. Explicit information on the risks associated with unsafe sex and drug abuse, and the way those risks can be minimized, does not promote or encourage such activities. Its sole function is to help people avoid an illness that endangers their lives and those of their sexual partners and children, and costs the nation billions of dollars.

• Government at all levels should continue to fund factual educational programs designed to foster behavioral change. This may mean supporting AIDS education efforts that contain explicit, practical, and perhaps graphic advice, targeted at specific audiences, about safer sexual practices and how to avoid the dangers of shared needles and syringes. This is the approach followed in the United Kingdom and in other western European countries.

• In addition, the Secretary of HHS should see that more studies are conducted to determine the effects of various types of educational campaigns on specific populations. For example, there have been few systematic assessments of the effect of AIDS education programs or media presentations on the behavior of heterosexuals (as opposed to the impact on their beliefs or understanding about the disease). It is also essential to develop effective methods for reaching school-age children, youth who are just becoming sexually active, and persons at risk for HIV infection within minority communities.

Education Needed

The urgency of the HIV epidemic warrants a multiplicity of educational efforts, including the use of paid advertising to convey all types of AIDS-prevention messages on television and in other media. Although a number of federal government entities, including the military, the postal service, Amtrak, and the U.S. Mint, currently spend more than $300 million yearly for advertising, administrative restrictions from HHS have precluded the Centers for Disease Control (CDC) from paying for advertising in the past. But the recently enacted AIDS Amendments of 1988 now allow the CDC to purchase advertising time.

• The Secretary of HHS should direct the CDC to purchase advertising for educational messages and should make certain that funds are supplied to do so.

Ensure that HIV testing and other public health measures are employed only when their purposes are clear and their results productive. The ability to detect antibodies to HIV has prompted various proposals for testing individuals and screening populations for evidence of HIV infection. However, these proposals must be assessed carefully to evaluate what they might add to interventions that are possible in the absence of testing. The president can encourage a level-headed approach to testing strategies by conveying the belief that HIV testing alone is not a panacea. Several considerations follow.

AIDS Testing

First, it is essential that the purpose of any proposed testing plan be clearly spelled out; test results should be linked to actions that achieve individual or public health objectives. For example, donated blood, tissue, organs, and semen can be tested, and infected material discarded, thereby preventing transmission. This purpose is sound and has been achieved: The screening of blood for antibodies to HIV, combined with self-disqualification by potential donors at high risk for infection, has almost eliminated the transmission of HIV through blood and blood products. A common rationale for medical testing—to identify infected, asymptomatic persons so that they can be treated early—cannot be applied to HIV infection, since no therapy yet exists that prevents the progression of HIV infec-

tion to overt illness.

Another frequently cited purpose of testing, that knowledge of one's antibody status may encourage behavioral change, is a hoped-for but still unproven effect. In addition, it has been argued that uninfected persons can use the knowledge of others' test results to protect themselves from infection; or, in some situations (e.g., the military, jails, and other closed populations), authorities can intervene to protect uninfected persons by testing and then segregating infected persons. Extension of these strategies to the general population, however, is inappropriate and infeasible because 1 million or more people may be infected, the mean incubation period is eight to nine years, and the virus is not transmitted by casual contact. The testing of applicants for marriage licenses has also been tried, but such testing is costly, identifies very few infected individuals, and is not clear in its intent (if one of the applicants were infected, would marriage or pregnancy be prohibited?).

• At this time, the only mandatory screening appropriate for public health purposes is that of donated blood, tissue, and organs. Voluntary testing, however, will play an increasingly useful role against the spread of HIV infection. The Secretary of HHS should ensure that voluntary testing, combined with pretest and posttest counseling, is available to all those who may be at risk for exposure to HIV. For example, serologic testing and counseling should be extended immediately to all settings in which IV drug abusers are seen or treated.

> **"It is essential to maintain reliable data on current AIDS cases, to refine estimates of the extent of current HIV infection."**

The technical aspects of HIV testing must also be considered. Although the current tests for HIV antibody are highly accurate, there will inevitably be false-positive and false-negative results (and the proportion of positive test results that are false is largest when the test is applied to populations with a low prevalence of infection).

• The federal government should give more attention to establishing standards for laboratory proficiency in HIV antibody testing, setting criteria for interpreting assays, and instituting quality assurance procedures.

Other public health measures should also be carefully considered for their potential effectiveness in controlling the spread of HIV and for their conformity with social values.

Voluntary contact notification, for instance, may be useful in preventing the spread of HIV infection.

Contact notification programs allow local public health officials or physicians to inform the sexual or needle-sharing partners of HIV-infected individuals who are afraid, embarrassed, or unwilling to notify partners themselves. These programs are of greatest value when directed at those who otherwise could be unaware that they had risked infection.

"The National Institutes of Health should provide wider access to clinical trials."

Mandatory reporting of persons who test positive for HIV antibodies, on the other hand, should not be required at this time. In fact, the effect of mandatory reporting may be to discourage individuals from seeking voluntary testing, a cost that does not justify its potential benefit. For determining how many people in a population are infected, well-designed studies are more useful than random reporting of cases.

Bolster efforts at surveillance, case reporting, and the gathering of information about risk behavior. By November 1988, over 76,000 AIDS cases had been reported to the CDC. Of these, over 40,000 have died. An additional 10 to 20 percent of cases are believed to have been missed by the case surveillance system. The Public Health Service predicts that by the end of 1992, 365,000 cases of AIDS will have been diagnosed.

Estimating Infection

Estimates of the total number of persons infected with HIV are less certain. Methods used to estimate the number of currently infected persons rely on information that is itself uncertain—for example, the prevalence of infection in certain subgroups (such as homosexual men and IV drug abusers), the sizes of these subgroups, and the latency period between infection and the onset of AIDS.

It is essential to maintain reliable data on current AIDS cases, to refine estimates of the extent of current HIV infection, and to predict accurately future trends in the epidemic. Several actions will serve these ends:

• The Secretary of HHS should ensure that the CDC's personnel, space, and technical resources are adequate to the task of continuing epidemiological research and surveillance, including the development of mathematical models of the HIV epidemic.

• The Secretary should also see that adequate research support is provided to the social and behavioral sciences so that more can be learned about sexual behavior, IV drug abuse patterns, and how to influence behavioral change.

Ensure that biomedical research continues to follow fruitful paths. Substantial progress has been made in defining the genetic structure of HIV and understanding how the virus replicates; less well understood, however, is how HIV compromises the human immune system and causes disease. Understanding the processes and consequences of HIV infection is crucial to the development of therapies and vaccines against HIV and AIDS. This understanding, in turn, is rooted in all basic research in the areas of cellular biology, virology, immunology, and genetics. For this reason, increasing the amount of funds devoted to AIDS at the expense of all other basic biomedical research is shortsighted.

• Funding for basic research in all areas of biology should remain strong rather than be reduced in favor of AIDS-targeted research.

Current knowledge of the HIV proteins and their functions offers several potential targets for rational drug design. The search for therapeutic agents must also encompass the screening of existing compounds for potential antiviral activity. Both of these approaches to drug development require organizational cooperation among the government, the pharmaceutical industry, and academic health centers.

AIDS Drugs

Once a drug appears to be a candidate substance for the treatment of HIV infection or AIDS, it begins the long journey toward licensure. The U.S. drug approval process, which is regulated by the FDA, is the most rigorous in the world; it generally involves tests in animals and then a three- or sometimes four-phase series of clinical (human) trials for safety and efficacy. Although the process has been criticized as slow and cumbersome, it has also been credited with protecting the American public from the harmful effects of inadequately tested drugs. In response to the AIDS crisis, the FDA has moved to speed up some portions of its review and has established a category of investigational new drugs (IND) called the "treatment IND," which allows manufacturers to distribute a drug for use (if the drug meets certain criteria) while it is still under investigation. Zidovudine (AZT), which was approved in September 1986 under a prototype treatment IND mechanism, received the fastest evaluation that has ever occurred within the FDA. In addition, new FDA regulations will allow the approval and marketing of certain drugs after Phase II testing.

However, the diversion of FDA personnel necessary to approve zidovudine resulted in a backlog of applications in the FDA's Division of Anti-Infective Drug Products. As the number of applications for treatment IND status grows, these personnel problems may become more severe. At present, the FDA is not a bottleneck in the availability of new drugs to treat HIV infection and AIDS. The paucity of new drugs is related more to shortcomings in the science of antiviral agents than to the drug approval process. However, as more promising new drugs are discovered or designed, the FDA, without additional resources, could become an impediment to speedy availability.

• FDA's resources for new drug approval should be commensurate with the task. The need to borrow personnel from other parts of the agency should be relieved; the need for work space, which appears to be particularly acute, should also be addressed.

Although the FDA has responded with ingenuity to hasten the availability of new drugs against HIV, a note of caution is warranted. The treatment INDs (and certainly the widespread use of unapproved drugs obtained here or abroad) could interfere with the ability to execute conclusive clinical trials because new experimental drugs will be available to patients earlier than in the past.

"The FDA is not a bottleneck in the availability of new drugs to treat HIV infection and AIDS."

• In light of these concerns, the Secretary of HHS should direct the FDA to seek an outside evaluation of the treatment IND process and other new regulations designed to hasten drug approval or availability. This evaluation should take place after enough time has elapsed to determine whether new regulations have unanticipated consequences for any new drugs.

Criticizing Drug Trials

The urgency of the AIDS situation has brought the traditional scientific method for evaluating the effectiveness of treatment—randomized controlled clinical trials—under scrutiny. Criticism of this method grows in part from the frustration, fear, and anger of people with HIV infection, who may feel a lack of urgency in the drug development process. Yet, carefully controlled trials remain the fastest, most efficient way to determine what treatments work. Conducting well-designed trials from the beginning will benefit more patients, sooner, than any other approach. Poorly designed trials, or administering drugs without controls and "observing" the course of disease, can be inconclusive or lead to incorrect conclusions. The widespread distribution of untested drugs makes it difficult to determine whether they are effective, especially if the benefits are real but small. The result of these approaches could include the continued prescribing of useless or harmful therapies.

"A further resource in the nation's efforts against AIDS is solely the provenance of the president."

Although the best-designed clinical trial would enroll the fewest people needed to demonstrate drug effectiveness, many persons with HIV infection want to participate in clinical trials.

• The National Institutes of Health (NIH) should provide wider access to clinical trials by broadening their geographic base; by extending trials to previously untapped populations including women, IV drug abusers, and pediatric patients; and by testing all compounds that appear to have a possibility of effectiveness.

The prevention of HIV infection by vaccination continues to pose fundamental difficulties. Experiments with candidate vaccines in animals induce antibodies that fail to block subsequent HIV infection. These experimental results tend to mirror clinical observations of natural infection in patients, in which disease progresses despite the presence of antibodies and other immune responses. The advent of a licensed vaccine against HIV remains a distant prospect. Nonetheless, innovative research continues and

may produce more promising results in the future.

Human Vaccine Trials

In the meantime, the FDA has approved human trials for two vaccine candidates. These tests, designed to assess the safety and immunogenicity of the vaccine candidates, were approved in the absence of proof of protective efficacy in animals, a generally accepted prerequisite to human vaccine trials.

• In the future, the FDA should approve human trials for HIV vaccine candidates only when protection against infection has been demonstrated in a suitable animal model or when the candidate rests on new knowledge of the relevant human response that cannot be adequately modeled in animals.

• In addition, NIH, CDC, and other relevant government agencies should begin now to plan for large-scale human efficacy trials of as yet undeveloped vaccines. Such trials are complex to design, and their results will be difficult to evaluate. Because the trials must enroll sufficiently large numbers of subjects at sufficiently high risk of infection, the sites for vaccine efficacy tests will most likely include African and other developing countries. A process should be agreed on for joint decisionmaking among the countries involved; the World Health Organization is currently developing guidelines for the conduct of these trials.

The development of model systems, in which an animal infected with HIV or a similar animal virus shows the same symptoms and exhibits the same course of disease progression found in human AIDS patients, is essential to the campaign against the disease. Yet there is currently no such model. Chimpanzees and other primates are imperfect but nevertheless useful animal models, but they are in short supply for research purposes.

• Plans for breeding, conserving, and otherwise expanding the present stock of chimpanzees should be examined. This expansion may require increased funding. In addition, the development of a mouse (or other small animal) model for AIDS is of utmost importance. A promising development in this area is the transplantation of human fetal immune system elements into immunodeficient mice. As long as efforts to develop small animal models are carried out under safe laboratory conditions, further work in this area should be strongly supported.

Existing facilities are inadequate for further advances in research against HIV: Very few laboratories are equipped to handle the virus safely.

• The director of NIH, in consultation with research scientists from within and without the institutes, should assess the need for and costs of new intramural and extramural facilities for AIDS research. This information should be forwarded to the Secretary of HHS and to Congress for evaluation and subsequent action.

Federal Appropriations

Federal appropriations for AIDS research have been growing steadily. At the present rate of increase, funding will reach the goal (previously recommended by the Institute of Medicine and the National Academy of Sciences) of $1 billion annually by 1990.

• When federal research expenditures for AIDS reach this figure, an assessment of the need for further increases should be made. It is important to ensure that other research programs are not penalized by a long-term disproportionate growth of the AIDS budget.

Recognize our special responsibility in international health efforts to control AIDS. The rationale for U.S. involvement in international AIDS activities is more broadly based that the protection of American troops and tourists. AIDS can destabilize the work forces and the economies of developing countries whose advancement has been aided by U.S. dollars. AIDS can also reverse the child survival figures in countries where our help only recently has improved infant and child survival. Finally, some countries of the world offer important opportunities for collaborative AIDS research because they present varieties and prevalences of disease that do not exist in the United States.

The United States has an additional responsibility to international health efforts to control AIDS because of our exceptional resources in public health specialists and biomedical scientists, the large number of infected persons in the United States, and our relative affluence. American activities in international work against AIDS are conducted by many federal agencies. In addition, U.S. contributions to the World Health Organization Global Programme on AIDS (which provides support to national AIDS control and prevention programs and conducts global AIDS surveillance and research) were $1 million in 1986, $5 million in 1987, and about $15 million in 1988.

The Bush administration should plan now to provide a substantial increase in resources over the next few decades to be devoted to international AIDS prevention and control, reaching $50 million annually. Funds will also be needed to ensure that today's predominantly educational methods for preventing HIV transmission can be supplemented with appropriate vaccines and drugs if and when they become available.

Important as the above responses are, a further resource in the nation's efforts against AIDS is solely the provenance of the president— a resolve that the devastation caused by HIV infection will be prevented and its sufferers provided compassionate care, and an attitude that bespeaks the resolve.

Women with AIDS Need More Government Help

Peg Byron

About the Author: *Peg Byron is a New York-based reporter for United Press International, an international wire news service. Byron, who completed a Knight Journalism Fellowship in medicine, writes on health and public policy issues. She is also a contributor to* Ms., *a bimonthly feminist magazine.*

Harlem Hospital's HIV outpatient clinic was emptying into the gray afternoon and Wilda Correa was still waiting to see the doctor. Nervous, but trying to be cooperative, she had already waited three months for the appointment since taking the blood test for HIV, the human immunodeficiency virus responsible for AIDS. Inside the crowded clinic, Correa, a 43-year-old mother of three, knew it would take a lot to keep the once-silent virus from totally destroying her immune system.

In many ways, Correa epitomizes the people who are at great risk yet are most ignored in the U.S. AIDS epidemic: poor women of color and IV [intravenous] drug users, who, because of sex, race, and class, are viewed as the "throwaways" of society. But Harlem is not the only place in the U.S. where women must wait too long to get HIV care. And delays mean deterioration as the infection destroys the immune system and spirals into devastating diseases and, often, death.

AIDS might be described most accurately as a late stage of HIV disease. There are some long-term AIDS survivors, but the outlook for most women is bleak. One small New Jersey survey found that women diagnosed with AIDS live an average of barely four *months*, while white gay men with AIDS live 1.3 to 1.7 *years*; studies conducted in New York and San Francisco corroborate the differential. African American women in 1988 died at nine times the rate of European American women. Does this reflect the difference in the quality of health care available to these groups? Is HIV affecting women in different ways? Are different epidemics striking different communities? Experts say they don't know.

They don't know because these questions remain unexplored. But the lack of interest and the high death rate for women are two sides of the same crime: women are being ignored in the AIDS epidemic.

Women continue to get the attention of most AIDS researchers only as possible infectors of children and men. It is as if HIV-infected women are viewed solely as carriers of disease. Seen as pregnancy risks and troublesome with their child care and transportation problems, women also are widely excluded from experimental drug trials—making up only 7 percent of the enrollment in AIDS treatment research. Yet such drug trials are usually the only sources of potentially crucial medicine for this as yet incurable condition.

"Women with HIV/AIDS suffer from lack of money or insurance for basic care."

More often than men, women with HIV/AIDS suffer from lack of money or insurance for basic care. Yet without the data to define how they get sick with HIV differently from men, many women are denied desperately needed disability benefits.

Still, no major research has addressed the question of whether women may experience any symptoms different from men's. Dr. Daniel

Peg Byron, "HIV: The National Scandal," *Ms.*, January/February 1991. Reprinted with permission of *Ms.* magazine © 1991.

Hoth, AIDS division director for the National Institute of Allergy and Infectious Diseases (NIAID), a man who controls millions of research dollars, reluctantly concedes he has sponsored no studies about women's health. And the situation is the same at the National Cancer Institute; together, the two institutes get the bulk of U.S. AIDS research dollars, but neither has gotten around to asking what AIDS looks like in women.

According to Dr. Kathryn Anastos, director of HIV primary care services at Bronx-Lebanon Hospital Center in New York, one third to one half of all HIV-infected women have gynecological complications before the appearance of any other symptoms, except possibly fatigue; 32 percent to 86 percent of HIV-infected women have abnormal Pap smears and are at risk for cervical cancer; there is some evidence that pelvic inflammatory disease (PID) is more aggressive and caused by a wider array of organisms; irregular periods and infertility have been reported, suggesting unknown hormonal effects.

Women's Health

For at least three years, reports in medical journals have warned about severe, hard-to-treat gynecological infections linked to HIV. But not a single female genital complication is included in the federal guidelines set by the Centers for Disease Control (CDC) for AIDS diagnoses or even as signs of HIV infection.

"It's a major problem," said Dr. Mardge Cohen, who is the director of the Women and Children with AIDS Project at Cook County Hospital in Chicago. "It would make more sense to consider gynecological manifestations as representative of the clinical spectrum of AIDS. If it's not AIDS by the official definition, we see women who are desperate for those benefits."

The very definition of AIDS, as set forth by the federal government, excludes women. The CDC has characterized AIDS based on what government scientists knew when clusters of gay men were stricken in the early 1980s. Originally called GRID, for Gay-Related Immune Deficiency, AIDS was gradually defined. If many women or intravenous drug users were dying in similar ways then, they were not noticed and their particular symptoms were not included in the AIDS definition. The human cost of that exclusion continues today each time a woman confronts her HIV problems.

"Women throughout the country are the fastest growing part of the AIDS epidemic."

"Look at my hands," Correa says, still waiting for her clinic appointment. They are covered with strange, reddish-brown spots, a few of which faintly scatter her cheek. "It feels like something crawling up my face. They itch." The spots appeared during the summer when Correa first got sick and lost 30 pounds with a severe bout of diarrhea.

She saw a doctor about fatigue and shortness of breath just two years earlier. He did not suggest an HIV test, though intravenous drug use accounts for over 50 percent of all U.S. women who have been diagnosed with AIDS and he knew she had a ten-year-long heroin habit. He diagnosed an enlarged heart and warned her to clean up her lifestyle. Since then, she's been off both heroin and methadone.

Dr. Wafaa El-Sadr calls Correa into one of the clinic's examining rooms and decides to hospitalize her to get her heart and blood pressure under control before starting HIV treatment. Chief of the hospital's infectious disease department, El-Sadr says Correa does not have what is officially AIDS. She will try an antibacterial ointment on Correa's rash, which she says is not Kaposi's sarcoma lesions (common among gay men with AIDS but almost never seen on others diagnosed with AIDS).

Did Correa have any unusual gynecological symptoms? The doctor says she doesn't know. While the city-run clinic supplies at no cost an expensive regimen of drugs, it does not have the equipment to do pelvic exams. The examining tables don't even have stirrups.

The doctor describes the clinic's almost 600 patients as "desperately poor," many of them homeless. Women make up 30 percent of her AIDS caseload—triple the national AIDS rate for women. The Egyptian-born El-Sadr says the high percentage of women she treats are the leading edge of the epidemic. "We're seeing the evolution of the epidemic."

Women throughout the country are the fastest growing part of the AIDS epidemic. Several years ago, they made up 7 percent of all those who were diagnosed. Now, women with AIDS number about 15,000; of these, 72 percent are African American or Latina. "If AIDS has done anything for us, it has magnified the other social and health problems that exist for women of color," said Dàzon Dixon, executive director of SISTERLOVE, an affiliate of the National Black Women's Health Project.

By 1993, women will make up 15 percent of the people with AIDS in the U.S., according to the CDC; several AIDS researchers argue that the CDC's figures on women are at least 40 percent too low, in part because of its failure to count many of women's HIV-induced illnesses as AIDS.

AIDS and Pregnancy

Even when examining tables have stirrups, most researchers aren't interested in the woman, but in the fetus she is bearing.

For a new national AZT study called protocol 076, 700 pregnant women are being sought to determine if the drug reduces the chance of an infected woman transmitting the virus to the baby. The protocol, still under review, as recently as March 1990, included no evaluation of the women's health or the drug's impact on the mothers. A letter from NIAID's Hoth explained that protocol 076 "was not designed to be a study of pregnant women, although this topic is most important.". . . NIAID has since revised the study to include a maternal health component, but it is not for purposes of the woman's health. Hoth said in an interview, "As we move on in our thinking, we realize we have two patients to

account for in pregnancy studies." This startling revelation is a chilling reminder of the history of interference with women's reproductive choices, from forced sterilizations and denial of abortions to the current concern for fetal rights.

For a woman with HIV, pregnancy poses a dilemma: if she wants to deliver (the odds of having a healthy baby are estimated to be 70 percent), she may be pressured to end the pregnancy. But if she chooses to abort, many clinics refuse to assist anyone who has HIV, and 37 states do not allow Medicaid or other public funds to be used for abortion.

In the limited studies that do involve pelvic exams, abnormal cervical Pap smears have been detected at rates five to eight times greater than in non-HIV women in the same communities. Other studies suggest a dangerous synergy between HIV and a common virus that causes genital warts, called the human papillomavirus, or HPV. Women with both HIV and HPV infections are 29 times more likely than non-HIV women to have cervical cancer, one study found.

"HPV is a ubiquitous virus. It is found in the inner cities, the upper classes. Some studies suggest that it is found in a third of all adolescents in the inner cities and a quarter of all women," said Dr. Sten Vermund, chief of epidemiology for NIAID. He warns that once HIV-infected women start reaching the same life expectancy as HIV-infected men, an epidemic in cervical cancer may emerge due to the HIV-HPV combination.

***

"The battles pit the sick against the dying in a fight over money."

***

Doctors who treat many women with HIV infections (in clinics with properly equipped examining tables) say they already see higher rates of abnormal cervical conditions rapidly progressing to invasive cancers.

Advanced HPV with HIV, argues Vermund, should be considered one of the opportunistic infections that define AIDS—making many more women count in both the AIDS toll and benefit programs. "I'm having trouble getting people's attention on this matter. I have had a paper about it in review at the *American Journal of Obstetrics and Gynecology* for a god-awful long time," said Vermund. Dr. Mathilde Krim of the American Foundation for AIDS Research (AmFAR) says how women are counted "matters a lot when it comes to entitlement to disability payments or Medicare. The rest of the government relies on this definition. And where women are left out of the system, the lack of treatment can shorten their lives."

There are conflicts over the hierarchy of AIDS illnesses, which not only affects who qualifies for limited disability benefits but how the shape and scope of the epidemic is defined. And that affects how both public and private agencies must respond.

Fighting for Limited Resources

The battles pit the sick against the dying in a fight over money. Scientists and doctors, for example, are in a fierce competition for limited research funding: the scientists are focused on long-range goals to stop HIV with the development of antiviral drugs and a vaccine, while doctors are desperate for ways to treat people already infected. But President Bush and the Congress—which will spend a projected $800 billion on the S&L [savings and loan] crisis and $2.2 billion a month in the Persian Gulf—have capped NIAID's AIDS research funding at $432.6 million and NCI's at $161 million for fiscal year 1991.

AIDS activist Maxine Wolfe, who demonstrated and sat in at CDC and NIAID offices as part of the Women's Caucus of AIDS Coalition to Unleash Power (ACT UP), says: "The whole size of the epidemic is being squashed. Can you imagine if they added TB [tuberculosis] with HIV, or vaginal thrush with HIV, or PID [pelvic inflammatory disease] or syphilis with HIV? The number of cases out there would be enormous. By not having that number, they [the feds] justify so little government money for research and treatment."

"Given the barriers women face getting diagnosed correctly, . . . women are falling through the cracks."

Following pressure from activists as well as the Congressional Caucus for Women's Issues, NIAID sponsored a special conference on women and HIV in December 1990 to help prioritize women's needs. At another meeting at NIAID in 1990, Wolfe, a professor at the City University of New York Graduate Center, and other ACT UP activists confronted NIAID chief Dr. Anthony Fauci, Hoth, and other officials to demand that "women be treated as women and not as fetus-bearers." Even Fauci had to concede that there had been few women included in AIDS drug trials.

Not surprisingly, the blind sexism of the NIH establishment is also reflected in the institute's attitudes toward women researchers. According to Dr. Deborah Cotton, an assistant professor of medicine at Harvard Medical School who chaired the session on women in clinical trials at NIAID's December conference, condescension was the typical response to criticisms from her and other women of the Food and Drug Administration committee reviewing protocol 076.

"As a woman, part of the problem in talking about clinical trials in women is that people don't listen," said Cotton. "They consider it a political statement . . . as if we are overstating what the scientific issues are." Pressure from women's advocates has helped, she said. "I think it did take that kind of advocacy to put women at the top of the agenda."

Legal pressure may also help. A class-action lawsuit has been filed against Health and Human Services Secretary Louis Sullivan, who oversees the Social Security Administration as well as CDC, NIH, and NCI. The suit seeks to grant disability benefits for a broader range of HIV diseases, including HIV-induced gynecological diseases. Legal services attorney Theresa McGovern filed the case from her cramped New York City office after hearing from dozens of people like S.P., a 23-year-old with two children in foster care.

S.P. said she can't have her name published because she must keep her HIV condition a secret from her father, with whom she shares a tiny, dilapidated apartment. She can't afford her own apartment unless she receives Social Security Disability insurance and Supplemental Security Income benefits. Without adequate housing, she has been unable to convince the family court to return her children.

"I get headaches, throw up a lot. I've got a lot of pain in my side," S.P. said. She has outbreaks of painful pelvic inflammatory disease for which she has been hospitalized. Her immune system is nearly depleted.

The benefits would mean a monthly grant of $472 instead of the $113 she gets from local assistance programs. Despite her own doctor's testimony at a hearing that she is unable to work, an administrative law judge deemed the rail-thin woman's testimony "not credible" and denied her claim. The class-action suit, in U.S. District Court in Manhattan, could affect thousands of women as well as male IV drug users.

> **"Viewing women as hysterics . . . is a common reason given to deny better research and medical care to women."**

"This should have been a national class action but we just didn't have the money to do it," McGovern says. Other nonprofit legal service groups joined in the suit, including the gay-rights oriented Lambda Legal Defense and Education Fund. But McGovern said that support from major AIDS groups has been slower in coming.

McGovern's lawsuit—like the Women's AIDS Network in San Francisco and the handful of other such efforts for women—has been run on a shoestring. These groups get little of the money that flows, for example, to New York's Gay Men's Health Crisis (GMHC), the country's biggest AIDS service group. GMHC, for its part, did not join the lawsuit, though it made a small donation.

Programs for Women

Even when better funded AIDS groups sponsor programs needed by women with HIV, they may set entrance criteria women can't meet. Even large groups like GMHC have restricted their client services to serve only those diagnosed with AIDS or AIDS-related conditions, as set by the male-oriented CDC definition; GMHC has long refused services to anyone still using drugs. Given the barriers women face getting diagnosed correctly, plus the high percentage who get AIDS from IV drug use, women are falling through the cracks even in community HIV service groups.

Some doctors are uneasy about women bringing new demands to the fray. They are critical of demands to include women's genital tract infections among AIDS-defining illnesses. "Some of these infections are very common," said Dr. Paula Shuman, infectious disease specialist at Wayne State University School of Medicine in Detroit. "It would terrify a lot of women into thinking it means they have HIV." No one wants to promote unnecessary anxiety, but viewing women as hysterics who would place extra demands on doctors is a common reason given to deny better research and medical care to women.

Women's organizations themselves are also guilty of ignoring the threat of HIV to women. Center for Women Policy Studies executive Director Leslie Wolfe says her group will be pushing women's organizations to start giving AIDS priority, after years of groups insisting HIV is not a women's issue.

If women don't fit some stereotype, HIV

won't be considered," said Cohen of Chicago's Cook County Hospital. For women of color, the poor, and IV drug users who are the majority of women with AIDS, HIV adds a grim dimension to the neglect they always have experienced; for middle-class European American women, HIV is often missed because AIDS is what happens to other people.

Older women also suffer from doctor biases. According to Dr. Mary A. Young, who sees scores of infected women at her office in the Georgetown University Medical Center in Washington, D.C., one 62-year-old was given cancer tests for a year before anyone thought to take her sexual history and recommend an HIV test. It was positive. "No one had considered this widow might be sexually active," Young said.

But women with HIV have been organizing among themselves to try to answer the questions that the AIDS establishment has ignored. Michelle Wilson, 39, a legal services aide from Washington, D.C., started a newsletter and an organization called "The Positive Woman" for women like herself who live with the virus. Sex is one of the toughest topics.

"The answer to uncertain risk— 'just wear a condom'—ignores the fact that women don't wear condoms."

"Initially, it made me feel unclean," she said about trying to have sex after learning of her infection. "I felt like my husband couldn't touch me without infecting himself." For a while, he didn't wear a condom because he thought it would make her feel bad. "It was hard to relax and feel good. I couldn't keep feeling sexually aroused because I knew what that condom meant. But at some point, a coping mechanism kicks in and you feel, 'Now what a guy—our lovemaking remains unchanged because he really loves me.' And that keeps us a loving and sexual couple."

Wilson gets calls from around the country about the newsletter. Many women describe frustrations when they look for support from male-oriented service groups. "You're reluctant if you're in a room filled with men to raise your hand and say, 'I have lesions on my vagina,'" Wilson said.

Women with AIDS

Lesbians with HIV find their existence even more widely denied. Drug use, alternative methods of fertilization, blood transfusions, and sex with infected men are known routes of HIV into the lesbian population. As for lesbian sexual HIV transmission, several possible cases have been reported in letters to medical journals, but the risk remains unclear. CDC epidemiologist Susan Chu, the lead author of a report that looked for AIDS in lesbians, said she found no cases of female-to-female transmission.

But Chu states flatly her study did not rule out HIV risks in lesbian sex. Notably, the study used the CDC's narrow definition of AIDS, not a cross section of HIV-infected women. And the authors defined "lesbian" more strictly than would many lesbian women: they omitted any women mentioned in CDC AIDS reports through 1989 who had had sex with men since 1977, leaving 79 lesbians, or 0.8 percent of all reported adult women with AIDS in the country. Almost all were intravenous drug users and 5 percent were described as infected through transfusions. This gives no help for lesbians who, for whatever reason, are infected. The CDC has not found the question of lesbian risk significant enough to warrant safer sex guidelines.

As far as menstrual blood is concerned, Chu said she doesn't know if it is as HIV-laden as circulating blood in infected women. She could not say if sex during menses was riskier for one's sex partner, although the menstruating woman might be at more risk of infection herself, because her cervix is more open.

In trying to assess their own risk, women probably should consider the geographic prevalence of the virus where they or their sexual partners have had sex, shared hypodermic needles, had blood transfusions, maybe even had tattoos and electrolysis performed since the late 1970s. Perhaps most tangled is the daisy chain of sex tied to everyone's history that is both invisible and sometimes distorted by guilt.

The answer to uncertain risk—"just wear a condom"—ignores the fact that women don't wear condoms. Men do and most don't like it; some admit it gives them performance anxiety and others say it is "unnatural." For some, says Dooley Worth, Ph.D., an anthropologist and adviser to New York's Health and Hospitals Corporation, condoms are unwelcome symbols of extra-relationship activity. Worth also warns that no relationship is static and commitment to condom use can diminish over time. And condom campaigns ignore the real pressures in women's relationships that sometimes make unsafe sex seem the less risky alternative.

"Women may be getting battered, or fear the possibility of battery or of losing the relationship," said Sally Jue, the mental health program manager for AIDS Project Los Angeles. "For many Asian and Hispanic women, being assertive and getting their men to wear condoms is a ludicrous idea."

In one study of women in prostitution, only 4 percent of nearly 600 women reported they regularly had customers use condoms. In a more encouraging study, the Alan Guttmacher Institute recently reported that levels of condom use among Latino teenagers had tripled during the 1980s.

But if condoms are not known as perfect birth control, why are they so great when it comes to a question of life and death? After all, condom failure in pregnancy prevention ranges between 3 percent for older, white married women and 36 percent for younger, nonmarried women of color. With HIV protection, less is known. One study concluded that condom use reduces HIV infection risk for women by a factor of 10.

There are mixed recommendations about antiviral spermicides, containing nonoxynol 9, sodium oxychlorosene, or benzalkonium chloride. Although these are in the woman's control, they are less effective than condoms. . . .

As a long-term public health strategy, condoms are not the answer for women wanting control over their health. But federal officials were dumbfounded when Representative Constance Morella (R.-Md.) and other congresswomen asked what was being done to give women control of HIV protection. "They have not been doing anything," said Morella, whose district includes the NIH's sprawling research campus.

"Condoms are not the answer for women wanting control over their health."

The concept that women's health counts as much as men's is long overdue. In the summer of 1990, the Congressional Caucus for Women's Issues forced the formation of an Office of Research on Women's Health at NIH. The caucus also introduced the Women's Health Equity Act, which includes AIDS initiatives written by the Center for Women Policy Studies in Washington.

"The activists are right," said AmFAR's Krim. "But unless politicians also feel pressure from the mainstream, from groups like NOW [National Organization for Women] and the League of Women Voters, they won't do it for women." Certainly, scientists and doctors, when asked to spend time and money on women's health, must stop reacting like men who have been asked to wear condoms.

Women cannot afford to let the Health Equity Act follow the path of the ERA [Equal Rights Amendment]. Unless true health equity is addressed, thousands and thousands of women, especially in the inner cities and gradually across the country, are sentenced to death as HIV in the U.S. begins to take on the global pattern of AIDS.

Chapter 3

Is AIDS Testing Necessary?

AIDS Testing: An Overview

Ronald Bayer

About the Author: *Ronald Bayer is an associate professor at the Columbia University School of Public Health in New York City. He was co-chairman of the first national project to study the ethical and social challenges posed by AIDS.*

Editor's note: In July 1990, the U.S. Centers for Disease Control reported the first case of a doctor infecting a patient with AIDS. Prior to this, many doctors and others considered such a possibility highly unlikely. But the doctor, a dentist who later died from the disease, was also discovered to have infected four other patients. Kimberly Bergalis, the first patient to publicly disclose her infection, subsequently became the focus of controversy over the issue of whether doctors and patients should be tested for AIDS. The 23-year-old Bergalis, who was near death as of August 1991 from an AIDS-related tuberculosis, devoted much of her time after her diagnosis to campaigning for health-safety regulations regarding HIV [human immunodeficiency virus]-positive physicians and dentists.

Because of the Bergalis case, many people have advocated that doctors and patients be tested for AIDS. One of these advocates is Representative William Dannemeyer, a California Republican. In June 1991, Dannemeyer proposed the Kimberly Bergalis Patient and Health Providers' Protection Act. The act calls for doctors, dentists, and other health-care providers who perform invasive procedures to undergo testing for diseases such as AIDS that pose a risk to public health. The bill also grants doctors the right to test their patients for these diseases.

Many people consider such mandatory testing an infringement on the civil right to privacy. They believe that doctors who test positive for AIDS may face job dis-

crimination from hospitals and that patients with AIDS may be denied access to necessary health care. In the following overview, excerpted from the book Private Acts, Social Consequences: AIDS and the Politics of Public Health, *Ronald Bayer explores the AIDS-testing controversy by analyzing the purpose of such testing and the public's reaction to it. Bayer explains the goals of those who advocate testing and perceive it as an opportunity to control the spread of the disease. He also discusses the apprehensions of those who fear that mandatory testing will lead to discrimination against AIDS patients.*

From the outset the test developed to detect antibody to the AIDS virus—and first used on a broad scale in blood banking—was mired in controversy. Uncertainty about the significance of the test's findings and about its quality and accuracy provided the technical substrate of disputes that inevitably took on a political character, since issues of privacy, communal health, social and economic discrimination, coercion, and liberty were always involved. For those who feared that public anxiety about AIDS would turn individuals identified as infected with the AIDS virus into targets of irrational social policy and practice, the antibody test became emblematic of the most threatening prospect in the community's response to AIDS. They believed that the ELISA [enzyme-linked immunosorbent assay] test would inevitably be extended beyond blood banking. Vigorous encouragement of testing would ineluctably lead to mandatory approaches as the impatient appealed to the authoritarian history of public health. Since confidentiality would not be preserved, the consequences would be stigmatization and deprivation of the right to work, go to school, and obtain insurance. Most ominously, the identification of the infected could threaten freedom itself. No marginal advance of the public health, those who argued against wide-scale testing asserted, could warrant such a catastrophic array of personal burdens.

Those who believed that the identification of the infected or potentially infected—through testing or other public health efforts—provided an opportunity for strategically targeted measures viewed the availability of the antibody tests as a great opportunity. Some advocates of testing, opposed to the use of coercion and attentive to matters of privacy so forcefully articulated by gay groups, would stress the importance of preserving the right of each individual to determine whether to be tested, protecting the confidentiality of test results, and guaranteeing the social and economic rights of those whose test results revealed infection with HIV. Theirs was a posture that sought to demonstrate the compatibility of an aggressive defense of the public health with a commitment to the privacy and social interests of the infected and those at risk of infection.

Others asserted that the defense of the public health required coercion and limitations on the liberty of the infected. For them screening on a compulsory basis was both necessary and inevitable. Assertions that the public health would not require such efforts merely masked, they argued, the willingness to sacrifice the communal welfare to private interests. The specter of such coercion haunted the discussion of all public health efforts, even the apparently voluntary attempts to facilitate identification of the infected.

"The defense of the public health required coercion and limitations on the liberty of the [HIV] infected."

Ultimately, the debate over testing and other public health measures designed to identify the infected would force a confrontation over which proposed interventions could most effectively contribute to the transformation of the private behaviors linked to the spread of HIV infection and the development of a public culture that would encourage and reinforce such changes. Bold moves might advance the cause of public health in the face of the AIDS epidemic, or they might subvert that very cause. Caution might

represent wisdom or a failure to grasp the opportunity to affect the pattern of HIV transmission. Appeals to the history of public health would inform the perspectives of those who encountered each other as antagonists; so too would profound differences over the weight to be given to communal well-being and personal liberty. Empirical considerations, historical perspectives, and philosophical commitments each thus helped to shape the fractious struggles that characterized the politics of identification.

AIDS Testing

Months before the AIDS virus antibody test was licensed by the Food and Drug Administration [FDA] for use in blood banks, anxiety had already surfaced in the discussions of gay leaders. "Don't take the test" became the rallying cry. In an editorial, the *New York Native* wrote, "No gay or bisexual man should allow his blood to be tested. . . . The meaning of the test remains completely unknown, beyond indicating exposure to the virus. The meaning of exposure to the virus is completely unknown. Scientists and physicians agree that a positive test result cannot be used to diagnose anything." What was far from uncertain, however, was the "personal anxiety and socioeconomic oppression that [would] result from the existence of a record of a blood test result. . . . Will test results be used to identify the sexual orientation of millions of Americans? Will a list of names be made? How can such information be kept confidential? Who will be able to keep this list out of the hands of insurance companies, employers, landlords, and the government itself?" What was critical was for gay and bisexual men to modify their behaviors in order to protect their own health and that of their sexual partners. For those purposes, what role could such an ambiguous and potentially dangerous test play? "If you test positive, will you act with any more wisdom or concern than if you test negative? Will you be less or more conscious of following safe and healthy sexual guidelines?"

In the same issue of the *Native* Stephen Caiazza, president of the New York Physicians for Human Rights, warned his readers that the test was "pernicious" and would cause great harm. "We have reached the point in medical technology where we can accumulate data upon data without knowing what they mean. Unfortunately, there are times when the information collected can hurt the individual. This is at present the case with AIDS." Here then, before the test was available, were the elements of what would harden into an orthodoxy among gay leaders: the test was technically limited; the findings it produced would be of no benefit to the individuals tested or to their sexual partners; those who were antagonistic to gay interests would seize upon the test to foster irrational discrimination wrapped in the mantle of public health.

But despite such opposition, gay leaders were driven by the imminence of blood bank screening in early 1985 and the FDA requirement that individuals whose blood was found to contain antibody to the AIDS virus be so notified to support, along with some public health officials, the creation of alternative test sites. Only such testing centers could protect the blood supply from the hazard that those at increased risk for AIDS might turn to blood banks for testing. Thus the American Association of Physicians for Human Rights [AAPHR] declared that while "current uncertainties about the accuracy or prognostic significance of the available antibody test mitigate against [its] widespread use . . . in screening individuals . . . some individuals will ultimately fail to be dissuaded from seeking testing." Confronted by the realization that an undetermined number of gay men would seek testing, AAPHR was compelled to advance protective guidelines for the governance of alternative test sites while opposing the use of tests for such extra-blood-banking purposes.

Opposition to AIDS Tests

Opposition to the use of the antibody test outside the context of blood banking and research protocols was not, however, restricted to gay groups. A number of health departments, some-times strongly influenced by concerns of gay medical and political leaders, also expressed alarm. The Philadelphia Health Department petitioned Secretary of Health and Human Services Margaret Heckler to revise her decision to provide federal funds for the creation of alternative test sites. "We believe that the Public Health Service loses credibility when it tells Americans that they should not have the test, but then makes it generally available anyway. . . . If we expect the public to believe us on complicated and sensitive issues, we should be consistent and credible in our scientific and public position." The insistence of the Public Health Service on the notification of blood donors about their test findings had *created* the need for the new sites. Eliminating that requirement would also eliminate the need for special settings where testing could be done. Chicago joined Philadelphia in challenging the public health grounds for creating the alternative sites. And in New York City the health commissioner not only refused to establish alternative sites but sought by every means at his disposal to create impediments to the use of the test outside of blood banking. New York, the epicenter of the American AIDS epidemic, thus became the only major American city where testing would not be readily available.

"Gay groups intensified their efforts to discourage use of the test."

Perhaps most striking, the Association of State and Territorial Health Officials [ASTHO], which ultimately was to become a strong proponent of broad-scale voluntary testing, expressed doubts about the use of the test. In early February 1985 ASTHO noted that the ELISA test would simply generate too many false positive results, and the association, like others, stressed the unknown prognostic significance of the results that were truly positive. In all, the test was not appropriate for public health screening purposes. One month later, on the eve of the licensing of the antibody test, ASTHO convened a national consensus conference designed to provide guidance to public health officials. The final report of the meeting asserted that beyond the screening of blood and in research protocols the test was of "extremely limited utility."

"The presence of the antibody was indicative of current infection with the AIDS virus."

Despite the award of $9.7 million by the Centers for Disease Control [CDC] to more than fifty localities to facilitate the establishment of alternative test sites, it took many months for such centers to become operational. Even in California, where the legislature moved aggressively to provide funding for such sites, where testing could be conducted under conditions of anonymity, and where the nation's most stringent confidentiality legislation was enacted to protect those who took the test, it was not until July 1985 that testing was begun. During this period, gay groups intensified their efforts to discourage use of the test. In New York City, the Gay Men's Health Crisis—the city's largest AIDS service organization—warned in a paid advertisement, "The test can be almost as devastating as the disease." In Washington the AIDS Action Council, speaking for a coalition of gay political and health organizations, urged, "If you are a member of a group at risk for AIDS, you have it within your power to short circuit the dangers that this test poses for you and millions of others. How? By refusing to be tested yourself and by refusing to let any of your friends be tested. Don't donate blood and don't ask your physician, clinician, or public health service to give you the test. It's that simple." This perspective was extended to those responsible for the treatment of drug users, as typically more sophisticated gay leaders counseled them about how testing could have only deleterious effects upon those who were in their care. And so such treatment personnel began to articulate positions indistinguishable from their gay tutors, despite the grave implications for the heterosexual transmission of the AIDS virus and the transmission of HIV to fetuses as a result of maternal infection.

The Antibody Test

At the same time that gay leaders were denouncing the antibody test, a countercurrent began to emerge that perceived in the test, especially when the ELISA was done in conjunction with the technically more difficult and more expensive Western Blot confirmatory test, a potentially invaluable adjunct in the struggle against AIDS. The proponents of testing did not deny that there were lingering technical problems with the test and especially with the standardization of the Western Blot procedure, but they asserted that similar problems were associated with virtually every test done in medicine. They did not view the test as a substitute for individual counseling and mass education but as a potent tool for fostering the behavioral modifications that everyone understood to be essential to any AIDS control program. They did not discount the risks posed by threats to confidentiality but sought to protect the privacy of those who needed testing, frequently by arguing that the option of anonymity be available. Finally, and most critically, those who supported the use of the test believed that the emerging understanding of the significance of confirmed positive findings was of great personal and public health relevance. Unlike those who persisted in asserting that the test demonstrated little about current infectivity, the test's proponents relied on studies revealing that the presence of the antibody was indicative of current infection with the AIDS virus and of a presumed capacity to transmit infection to others. In sum, at each juncture where uncertainty and ambiguity led opponents of the test to stress the threats to privacy and civil liberties and the absence of compensating public health benefits, proponents of testing underscored the potential for a contribution to the struggle against AIDS.

Thus in March 1985, when many public health officials were still counseling caution and when the precise significance of antibody test results remained very uncertain, Franklin Judson, an aggressive Colorado public health official and president of the American Venereal Disease Association, wrote to the association's membership, "I am concerned about the lack of movement towards an organized HTLV-III [human T-cell lymphotropic virus] control program." AIDS, Judson asserted, was "the most deadly" sexually transmitted disease in recent history, and yet the antibody test was being conceived of only as a way of preventing transfusion-associated cases—less than 1 percent of all cases. Neither technical limitations of the test nor fears about how results could be abused provided a warrant for inaction. "The realities of imperfect diagnostic tests and fear about confidentiality should not drive us to the sidelines to observe the natural history of this epidemic. In my mind the consequences to gay men and other high risk groups of doing nothing are far worse than the consequences of an active program that at least considers the use of traditional public health disease control measures." Among such measures would be the screening of high-risk group members, the reporting of the names of those found positive to well-guarded public health registries, contact tracing—a method commonly used in venereal disease control programs—and "legal restrictions on the sexual activities of seropositive individuals."

It was precisely the threat of such a broad-gauged public health program and the ominous implications of establishing registries as well as legal restrictions on sexual activities that provoked the reaction of gay leaders as they heard Donald Francis, a virologist on the staff of the Centers for Disease Control, address a meeting in the spring of 1985, just before the commencement of the First International AIDS Conference in Atlanta. Francis called upon gay men to seek out testing voluntarily in order to limit the transmission of AIDS. There was no question

but that those who were positive for the antibody to the AIDS virus were infected. There was no question but that they could transmit the virus to others. They had to know those facts. Though Francis stressed that he was speaking in an unofficial capacity, to those who heard him the imprint of the government marked his words. Some in his fearful and outraged audience termed his proposal "unworkable," others "diabolical."

"For the CDC such identified [AIDS] reports were essential if an accurate . . . record of cases was to be developed."

But it was not simply those officially involved with public health who had begun to argue that testing for the antibody to the AIDS virus was important. A few gay leaders, most often physicians or scientists, began to break ranks on the issue. In April 1985 Bruce Voeller, former executive director of the National Gay Task Force, a member of a number of federal scientific advisory panels and an active participant in the early controversy over blood safety, published bold appeals for testing in the Los Angeles-based *Advocate* and in the *New York Native*. "Gay leaders have warned that lists of test-takers could fall into the wrong hands. Maybe so, but I'd rather be alive and on a list than dead because I'd been misled into believing I could get no value from knowing my test results. Lives are more important than lists." Unlike those who argued that the test produced no clinically or socially relevant information, Voeller argued that knowledge of one's own antibody status was necessary, not only to protect oneself, but to protect one's lovers. . . .

Public Health Reporting

As the dimensions of the threat posed by AIDS became increasingly apparent . . . state and local health departments moved to require that physicians and hospitals report by name those diagnosed with the new syndrome. Only such reporting would permit health officials to have an accurate epidemiological picture of the disease with which they were confronted. Only such reporting would permit the application of other appropriate public health measures to the sick. The public health required this abrogation of the principle of confidentiality, as had always been the case when epidemic threats were involved.

"Contact tracing is a euphemism. What they want to do is to keep a list of sexually active people."

The history of public health regulations requiring such reporting, with their obvious intrusions into the privacy of the physician-patient relationship, has been fraught with conflict. Disagreements over what the public interest required, over professional prerogatives, and over the rights of privacy have been as critical in these controversies as matters of science and therapeutics. However such conflicts were formally resolved, private physicians, in fact, dictated the ultimate pattern of reporting. Sheer resistance, especially when sexually transmitted diseases were involved, often limited dramatically the extent to which public health officials had before them a true picture of the pattern of disease in their communities. Promises, enshrined in legislation and regulation, that the identity of those reported would be shielded from the scrutiny of those with no public health interest, often did little to affect the willingness to report, especially when private patients were involved. It was in recognition of the capacity of private physicians to exercise a de facto nullification of public health regulations that in 1937 the Conference of State and Territorial Health Officials declared that "qualified physicians—with the approval of local health authorities—should be given the option of reporting their coopera-

tive patients by initials, date of birth, and community of residence, rather than by name."

It is thus remarkable, given the salience of concerns about the privacy of individuals with AIDS, that there was little resistance to efforts to mandate case reporting by name. Indeed, an appreciation that only accurate epidemiological information could unlock the mysteries associated with the transmission of the new disease led the Board of the American Association of Physicians for Human Rights in 1983 to call upon local health authorities to make the names of AIDS cases reportable. Controversy did emerge, however, when the CDC called upon local health departments to forward to Atlanta full case reports, including the names of those about whom they had been informed. For the CDC such identified reports were essential if an accurate unduplicated record of cases was to be developed for the nation as a whole. Distrust of the intentions of the federal authorities and anxieties about how such a national list might be abused led gay leaders to oppose such efforts. As a result, some treating physicians and local health departments began to resist the requests by federal health officials for case reports. Ultimately the CDC was compelled to agree, albeit reluctantly, to reporting by a unique coding mechanism—called Soundex—that would preclude duplicate reporting without the use of names or other personal identifiers such as social security numbers. James Allen—then chief of the Surveillance Section of the CDC AIDS Activities Branch—acknowledged that the compromise would complicate his efforts, but noted, "It's better than the alternative: persons refusing to cooperate by giving inaccurate information. That would make the situation worse. By agreeing to this compromise we can reassure them that we are acting in good faith and won't jeopardize their privacy." Others within the CDC expressed exasperation. "They say the government isn't doing anything, then they accuse us of breaching confidentiality when we try to carry out responsible studies."

The relative ease with which AIDS was incorporated under state and local health require-ments governing the reporting of communica-ble diseases did not extend to efforts to make re-sults of the antibody tests reportable. The first encounter over a proposal for such reporting oc-curred in New Jersey just a month after the test-ing of blood donations began in April 1985. Drawing a sharp distinction between reporting cases of AIDS and the results of the new anti-body test with its ambiguous clinical implica-tions, the local gay community denounced the proposal. Opposition came also from the na-tional Federation of AIDS-Related Organizations and the United States Conference of Local Health Officers. Confronted with so determined an opposition, the New Jersey Public Health Council decided to defer to the legislature rather than act through administrative determi-nation.

For those who had viewed New Jersey's effort as medically unwarranted and as a potential threat to the privacy of those whose names would be reported, the decision was an "impor-tant victory." But there was also some trepida-tion about whether other states would succeed where New Jersey had failed. "We are in the first skirmish," said Timothy Sweeney of the Lambda Legal Defense and Education Fund, a national gay civil rights organization. "This does not mean they will not come back and try again or [that] other states will not try this." Such fears were confirmed just days after New Jersey had held its hearings on reporting, when [former] CDC director James Mason declared in a May 1985 radio interview that public health depart-ments might seek to keep records of those who were antibody positive. Linking the reporting of such test results to standard public health prac-tice in venereal disease control, he asserted, "The same sensitive confidential system that has served this nation so well in the past for a series of other sexually transmitted diseases . . . doesn't have to be rearranged or reworked to serve equally well in the control of AIDS.". . .

In mid-1985, as part of an effort to limit the spread of AIDS among heterosexuals, San Fran-cisco launched a pilot program in which bisex-ual males reported to the health department as having AIDS were asked to provide the names of their female sexual partners so that these women might be notified about the possibility of exposure to the AIDS virus. In an editorial in the *Journal of the American Medical Association*, Dean Echenberg, the city's chief communicable disease officer, asserted that such a program was of critical importance since the mass educa-tional campaign designed to warn about the risks of HIV infection and transmission would inevitably have less impact among heterosexuals than among gay males. Furthermore, the female partners of bisexual men would have no reason to believe that they had been exposed to AIDS and would have little reason to modify their sex-ual and procreative behaviors. Only by warning them directly and by urging them to be tested would it be possible to avoid the unwitting trans-mission of the AIDS virus to others. "The foun-dation of this approach," wrote Echenberg, "rests on the assumption that no individual would want to unknowingly infect others."

"C. Everett Koop rejected proposals for mass mandatory screening."

Though limited in its scope—the program would not reach the female partners of asymp-tomatic but infected bisexual males—and com-mitted to the preservation of the confidentiality of the named partner as well as the anonymity of the "index case" (the patient with AIDS who had provided the contact's name), San Francisco's effort was denounced by representatives of gay and civil liberties groups as an "Orwellian night-mare." Thomas Stoddard of the New York Civil Liberties Union declared, "Contact tracing is a euphemism. What they want to do is to keep a list of sexually active people." Though acknowl-edging that contact notification had been used historically to interdict the spread of other sexually transmitted diseases, he argued that to become part of a list of those exposed to AIDS would have social consequences "far graver than with any other disease."

That so vigorous a response could be provoked by San Francisco's modest and circumscribed program of sexual partner notification was evidence of how intense anxiety about privacy and the power of the state had affected the milieu within which public health policy was being made. . . .

"The history of compulsory health measures revealed . . . that they had often been ineffective."

In New York City, where officials had in 1985 and 1986 adamantly resisted suggestions that contact notification had any role to play in the response to AIDS and where the provision of testing in alternative test sites came so late, the first moves were made in 1987 toward making third-party notification available to those who tested positive and requested assistance in alerting their sexual partners.

The gradual recognition that voluntary contact notification did in fact have a role—albeit limited—to play in the response to AIDS, especially where epidemiological circumstances made such labor intensive measures feasible, was a victory for those who believed that the history of public health interventions provided important lessons that should not be put aside. Contact notification did not represent a deviation from the broad consensus forged by public health officials, in large measure out of intense and often acrimonious confrontations with gay leaders and advocates of civil liberties. Voluntarist at its core, it was a consensus marked by an appreciation of the gravity of the AIDS epidemic and a recognition of the very limited role that coercive public health measures could play in the years ahead. Perhaps most critically, it was a

consensus which recognized that some coercive measures could harm the public health by driving those most at risk of infection into defensive postures by subverting the prospects for the broad-scale modification of private behavior so central to any effective campaign against AIDS.

Voluntary Testing Programs

Both the surgeon general of the United States and a special committee established by the Institute of Medicine of the National Academy of Sciences underscored these themes in reports issued in the fall of 1986. Coming just months after the Public Health Service had announced its grim forecast for the next five years—270,000 cases of AIDS by 1991, 179,000 AIDS-related deaths by that year—these recommendations were all the more striking. In his *Report on AIDS*—a pamphlet designed for broad-scale distribution—[former] Surgeon General C. Everett Koop rejected proposals for mass mandatory screening as "unnecessary, unmanageable, and cost prohibitive." Instead, voluntary testing conducted under conditions of confidentiality was recommended for those whose behaviors placed them at risk. Indeed, to foster a social climate of trust between those at risk and the nation's health institutions, Koop—going beyond the CDC's positions—rejected both the reporting of positive antibody test results to public health departments and sexual contact tracing. To mandate such procedures would, he asserted, drive the potentially infected "underground, out of the mainstream of health care and education."

The Committee on a National Strategy for AIDS, created by the Institute of Medicine and the National Academy of Sciences, similarly rejected compulsory testing as a method of identifying the infected. Its report, *Confronting AIDS,* argued forcefully that the history of compulsory health measures revealed not only that they had commonly been applied in an invidious and discriminatory manner but that they had often been ineffective. Its perspective on intervention was thus dictated by philosophical commitments as well as a concern for the efficient use of public health resources. In the case of AIDS, where so much irrational fear had already surfaced and where those at increased risk were socially vulnerable because of their sexual orientation or illicit behavior, the necessity of fashioning policies that would strike an appropriate balance was especially critical. It was thus that the committee sought to put forth proposals that would protect individuals from HIV infection "in a society that values privacy and civil liberties."

It followed that mass mandatory HIV antibody screening of the American people was "impossible to justify on either ethical or practical grounds." Furthermore, proposals for more targeted mandatory screening of at-risk individuals were rejected as impractical and infeasible in an "open society." Instead of such compulsory measures, the committee, albeit with less enthusiasm than the Public Health Service, endorsed the availability of wide-scale "voluntary, confidential testing (but with provision for anonymous testing if desired)." Both a commitment to privacy and concern about creating conditions conducive to voluntary testing led the committee, like the surgeon general, to oppose the reporting of antibody test results to local and state health departments.

Timid Response

But to those who viewed the future with a sense of not only gravity but alarm, the voluntarist consensus as expressed by the surgeon general, the Institute of Medicine, and the National Academy of Sciences represented too timid a response, too much of an accommodation with those who sought to restrain the effective use of the government's authority to intervene forcefully to protect the public's health. It was not the limits imposed by AIDS, its modes of transmission, and the absence of effective medi-cal prophylaxis, but rather the triumph of interests committed to the protection of privacy that accounted for the peculiar disjunction between the gravity of the situation confronting America and the prescriptions that had been put forth. At first this challenge was given articulate expression by those of the sectarian right wing of American politics. Eventually it would find a sympathetic hearing among America's politicians and by the White House itself.

"Mass mandatory HIV antibody screening of the American people was 'impossible to justify on either ethical or practical grounds.'"

If the fear of how public health authority could be abused had often compelled gay leaders passionately to oppose measures, like voluntary testing and sexual contact notification, that could have contributed to the overall strategy of limiting HIV transmission, those who were frustrated by the complex tasks imposed by the AIDS epidemic turned in a reflexive way to the authoritarian traditions of public health. Fear and frustration thus colluded ironically and inadvertently to weaken the goal of effecting long-term behavioral change: fear by seeking to thwart the implementation of public health policies designed to identify and counsel voluntarily those who could transmit HIV infection, frustration by threatening the infected in ways that would render collaboration with public health officials difficult to attain. Both subverted the prospects for the emergence of a public culture of restraint and responsibility that could affect the course of the epidemic.

Is AIDS Testing Necessary?

Yes: AIDS Testing Is a Public Health Necessity

AIDS Testing Can Control the Spread of AIDS
Health Care Workers and Patients Should Be Tested for AIDS
High-Risk Groups Should Be Tested for AIDS

AIDS Testing Can Control the Spread of AIDS

Frank S. Rhame and Dennis G. Maki

About the Authors: *Frank S. Rhame is an assistant professor of medicine at the University of Minnesota School of Medicine in Minneapolis. Dennis G. Maki is head of the Infectious Disease Section at the University of Wisconsin Medical School in Madison.*

A decade into the most serious pandemic of infectious disease in modern history, we possess the technology and resources to test for evidence of human immunodeficiency virus (HIV) infection accurately and economically. Yet there has been great reluctance on the part of the federal government and medical leaders to advocate extensive use of HIV testing as a public health measure. We believe that a very strong case can be made for wider HIV testing.

Most discussions of HIV testing reach a conclusion on whether testing should be encouraged, at least in populations in which the prevalence of infection with the virus is high. Although R.A. Weiss and Samuel O. Thier in their *New England Journal of Medicine* editorial found no basis for testing beyond screening before blood and tissue donation, most national bodies have favored the broader use of HIV testing. The Committee for the Oversight of AIDS Activities of the Institute of Medicine favored "expanded voluntary testing combined with counseling of all those whose behavior may have put

Frank S. Rhame and Dennis G. Maki, "The Case for Wider Use of Testing for HIV Infection," *The New England Journal of Medicine*, vol. 320, no. 19 (May 11, 1989), pp. 1248-1254. Reprinted with permission.

them at risk for exposure to HIV." Likewise, the Presidential Commission on the Human Immunodeficiency Virus Epidemic recommended that "people who fall into any of the [high-risk] categories should seek testing and counseling services from their physician or public health agency, regardless of the presence or absence of symptoms." Even more strongly, the Centers for Disease Control (CDC) has endorsed routine testing of persons who may have a sexually transmitted disease, intravenous drug abusers, and others who consider themselves at risk of HIV infection. The Canadian National Advisory Committee on AIDS has also recommended voluntary HIV testing in persons whose histories put them at risk. In endorsing HIV testing, none of these groups has presented a rationale beyond the reduction of transmission of HIV. We offer here additional public health reasons for much wider use of HIV testing, and we argue further that persons infected with HIV can gain important, direct health benefits from learning of their infection as early as possible.

> **"The Centers for Disease Control (CDC) has endorsed routine testing of persons . . . who consider themselves at risk of HIV infection."**

We advocate only voluntary testing, by which we mean that the test must be discussed with the person before testing, and that testing may be refused. Moreover, all HIV testing must be accompanied by stringent institutional and societal safeguards of confidentiality and privacy.

In November 1987, the Public Health Service estimated that there were between 945,000 and 1,400,000 persons infected with HIV in this country. Most of them do not know that they are infected, although HIV testing has been available since 1985. Since September 1985, it has been necessary to report all cases of HIV infection in Minnesota. (This has brought, incidentally, no known harm to those whose infection has been reported.) As of April 1, 1989, there have been 1100 reported cases of HIV infection in addition to 504 reported cases of acquired immunodeficiency syndrome (AIDS). The Minnesota Department of Health estimates that there are between 10,000 and 30,000 Minnesotans infected with HIV. If one uses the low end of this range and allows for substantial underreporting of diagnosed HIV infections, less than 20 percent of Minnesotans infected with HIV know of their infection. The situation in Wisconsin is quite similar: 318 cases of residents with AIDS and an additional 1065 cases of HIV infection have been reported; and an estimated 7000 to 11,000 residents of Wisconsin are thought to have HIV infection. Nationally, the percentage of persons infected with HIV who know of their infection is probably smaller, because the level of acceptance of HIV testing in the upper Midwest is thought to be relatively high and the prevalence of HIV infection is relatively low. The continuing detection of HIV infection among blood donors (0.043 percent of first-time donors through 1987), applicants for military service (0.15 percent), and Job Corps applicants (0.33 percent) is strong evidence that many—and probably most—Americans infected with HIV are not aware of it, although nearly all infected persons will ultimately report histories that put them at risk of HIV infection. Thus, current efforts to make persons infected with HIV aware of their infection are failing. We argue here that widespread voluntary HIV testing based within the health care system must be promoted nationally to bring us nearer the goal of informing all persons infected with HIV about their condition.

Testing the Healthy

Before focusing on the testing of apparently healthy, asymptomatic persons, we should address two related issues. First, our views on the testing of asymptomatic persons do not apply to the testing of those with symptoms compatible with illness caused by HIV, for whom few would

argue with the clinical value of an HIV test. Second, there are several specific clinical situations in which persons without HIV-related symptoms should be tested routinely. The CDC has explicitly recommended that an HIV test be performed in all persons with syphilis or active tuberculosis, because the presence of HIV infection alters the suggested therapy and follow-up. It is, we believe, a logical extension of the CDC recommendation to advocate testing for HIV infection in all tuberculin-positive persons. Although the current policy of smallpox vaccination in U.S. military forces can be questioned, it seems wise to recommend an HIV test before vaccination. Finally, the CDC has also implicitly recommended testing before vaccination in persons in whom bacille Calmette-Guérin vaccine is indicated and—when health care personnel have been exposed to a patient's blood through injury such as a needle stick—explicitly recommended testing the patient for HIV infection. . . .

"HIV testing appears to have reduced unsafe sexual behavior in those infected with HIV."

We believe that a recommendation to undergo HIV testing as part of routine health care would also have important benefits to society. General acceptance of HIV testing would reduce the reluctance to be tested of persons who know they are at increased risk. Taking the test would heighten the sense of vulnerability that is a necessary part of decisions to adopt more healthful behavior. Although there are many sexually transmitted disorders that should convince all persons to avoid unprotected coitus, the fear of HIV infection may foster most powerfully the changes in sexual behavior our society must make. Taking the test would enhance appreciation of the fact that AIDS is a problem that society at large must face. It would help undercut the pernicious we-they mentality that feeds the social stigmatization associated with AIDS and HIV infection.

HIV Testing

There has been widespread discussion of the public health benefit of HIV testing—primarily as an adjunct to counseling—as part of the efforts to reduce the transmission of HIV. In their editorial, Weiss and Thier describe this rationale, without detailed analysis, as "unproved." We agree that the available studies are not conclusive, but in the populations studied, HIV testing appears to have reduced unsafe sexual behavior in those infected with HIV. The effect of testing on those who are found not to be infected with HIV is admittedly less clear, but it too appears favorable. If one presumes that most people do not want to hurt others and that the gravity of HIV infection is becoming more widely recognized, the beneficial effects of testing should grow with time. In any case, these studies are only indirectly relevant to the context we discuss, because they were limited to homosexual men who volunteered for HIV-related studies, attended counseling and testing centers, or otherwise came forward voluntarily. Such persons had already broken through some of the denial that acts as a barrier to changing their behavior. Our greatest concern is to reach the great number of persons infected with HIV who are not availing themselves of any current options in testing and who are not confronting their risk of HIV infection.

As evidence that identifying persons infected with HIV through more widespread testing would reduce risk through more intensive counseling, we offer the findings of a study in blood donors and our experience with patients with hemophilia. A.E. Williams et al. found substantial reductions in unsafe activities—reductions considerably greater than those likely in society as a whole—during the year after blood donors were notified of their infection. Patients with hemophilia are even more relevant to the context we discuss—the widespread testing of persons in the general population receiving health care. Most patients with hemophilia are already under close medical supervision, and because their physicians recognize that their patients are at increased risk of infection with HIV, most patients have been encouraged to undergo testing. There is ample evidence that in spite of general educational messages about their very substantial risk of HIV, many patients with hemophilia engage in unprotected sex. Although we know of no systematically collected data on the point, we are convinced that many patients with hemophilia do not begin to pay attention to the risk of sexual transmission of HIV until they are tested. Furthermore, we have found that intensive, repeated counseling, ideally involving the patients' regular sexual partners, is often required to reduce unsafe sexual practices among those whose tests are positive to their current levels, which are still unsatisfactory. Finally, we believe that persons infected with HIV who are tested through the health care system serve as the best starting points for programs to notify sexual partners. . . .

"Physicians and other health care providers should assume a much more active role in promoting HIV testing."

Another current issue bears on the testing of hospitalized patients for HIV. The CDC and the Department of Labor have recommended the adoption of "universal precautions"—precautions in the care of all patients, not just those known to be infected with hepatitis B or HIV. Efforts to encourage the careful handling of specimens from untested patients are certainly laudable, because some infectious materials will inevitably be unrecognized as such. But the adoption of universal precautions is sometimes used as an argument against HIV testing, and some hospitals have removed warning designations for patients known to be infectious and their specimens. This approach has been advocated without careful study of whether health care workers are in practice as vigorous in exercising precautions when the patient has no known infection as they are when the patient is known to be infectious. The concept of universal precautions clearly deviates from that of targeted precautions concerning patients with known infection, which has been the approach for the past 20 years to preventing cross-infection and transmission with virtually all other contagious diseases. Universal precautions might provide less protection than routine HIV screening and targeted precautions in hospitals with a low prevalence of HIV and hepatitis B among their patients or in situations—such as certain types of surgery—in which very heavy exposure to blood and a high incidence of percutaneous injury occur. We believe that the effectiveness of universal precautions should be evaluated scientifically. The outcome of such studies may provide a basis for the institution of routine screening of hospitalized patients in at least some contexts.

Having established that there are personal as well as public health benefits in increasing the percentage of persons infected with HIV who know of their infection, we are still left with difficult issues. Would an extensive HIV testing program based within the health care system have paradoxical effects on public health? Does the diagnosis of an asymptomatic HIV infection constitute a *net* benefit to the infected person?

Adverse Effects

HIV testing based within the health care system could paradoxically have adverse effects on public health in two ways. It is often asserted that aggressive testing programs could drive underground, or away from the health care system, those who fear or know that they are infected with HIV. We believe those likely to respond in this way are already underground, and every person retains the right to refuse testing. Aggressive testing programs could also lead to the rejection of all efforts at testing, even at centers for counseling and testing. We believe, however, that raising the issue with all patients increases the probability that those who refuse the test in a hospital or office will use such centers.

"The benefits to those infected with HIV are outweighed by the potential for discrimination."

The disruption caused by a false positive test is uniformly advanced as an argument against the wider use of testing. However, screening with sequential enzyme immunoassays followed by confirmation with Western blot testing according to current, more stringent criteria should produce a false positive test only rarely.

It must be acknowledged that the studies cited were done in high-quality laboratories and may suffer from spectrum bias. . . .

How then can persons infected with HIV be harmed by learning of their infection? Most go through a period of intense emotional distress after diagnosis. This period, however, seldom lasts more than several weeks. Since the reality of HIV infection will ultimately make itself known to most or all persons infected with HIV, to put off learning of an HIV infection postpones but does not eliminate the period of anguish. And in any case, the potential anguish should be weighed against the aggregate anxiety of those who know they are at risk yet remain untested. It is tempting to try to shield anyone from harsh and unfair realities, but this somewhat paternalistic temptation runs counter to the prevailing trend toward a patient's right to know, a trend that has arisen in this generation. Part of the physician's responsibility is to be the bearer of bad news.

It could be argued that counseling and testing centers are better able to mitigate the initial distress associated with the diagnosis of an HIV infection. A substantial fraction of HIV testing, however, already occurs in physicians' offices and hospitals, and counseling by a physician with whom one already has an established relationship should be advantageous. Moreover, an extensive program of HIV testing based within the health care system would stimulate physicians to acquire the requisite skills. It has been argued that HIV testing serves the tested best when it is performed in settings that offer anonymity. Although many who would be tested prefer anonymity, it is nonetheless an elusive goal for most persons who find themselves infected with HIV, even while they remain asymptomatic. It is psychologically burdensome to withhold the information from all friends and loved ones. In addition, virtually all counseling and testing centers advise persons infected with HIV to obtain a physician. We believe that persons who do not contact a physician immediately are more apt to delay seeking medical care if HIV-related symptoms occur. Recommendations to inform dentists and other health care workers about one's HIV infection are uniform.

"HIV testing provides a net benefit both to the public health and to persons infected with HIV."

Finally, it can be argued that the benefits to those infected with HIV are outweighed by the potential for discrimination. Most discrimination related to HIV—in the workplace, in housing, in schools, and in society—is irrational, notwithstanding substantial public sentiment to the contrary. Some types of discrimination, although unfair, are understandable in economic terms. An employer motivated by economic considerations will tend not to hire, promote, or specially train infected persons because they are more likely to use sick-leave and health-insurance benefits. Similarly, an insurer will prefer not to offer health insurance to persons with HIV. Because discrimination will subvert the good that wider HIV testing can produce, we must vigorously fight it. Physicians should also fight for society's acceptance of homosexuality

and for improved funding for drug abuse treatment and related research. We have a special responsibility to advance these positions because of their importance in the fight against AIDS. In essence, we are arguing that HIV infection should be treated as much as possible like any other infectious disease. We should fight the unfair consequences that interfere with this goal.

Broader HIV Testing

We have concluded that HIV testing provides a net benefit both to the public health and to persons infected with HIV. We now turn to the issue of implementing broader testing. We believe that the nation's physicians and other health care providers should assume a much more active role in promoting HIV testing. Before presenting our argument we digress to assert two important underlying premises. We believe that a thorough sexual and drug-use history must be part of any routine health assessment. Patients should find physicians they trust, and they should be candid about these aspects of their history. These premises should be supported by advocates for gay and bisexual persons and substance abusers.

How could routine recommendation of HIV testing affect interaction between patient and physician? We believe it would provide a focus for and enhance efficiency of taking a history of risk for HIV. It would act as a probe to make the history more accurate—a good outcome if our earlier premises are correct. The interaction would begin with the physician saying in effect, "I recommend an HIV test to all my patients because some people who have risked exposure to HIV don't realize it, and many persons whose activities put them at risk find it difficult to disclose them." A brief risk history would follow.

The patients' responses would fall into three groups. The largest group would deny any risk history and would not object to being tested. Brief counseling would be given before the test. Those with absolutely no risk history would make a small financial sacrifice on behalf of those who are infected with HIV. Among those who have a risk history but deny it would be most of the people infected with HIV who would benefit from expanded testing.

A second group of patients would acknowledge risk histories. Of these, some would have done so whether a test had been recommended or not. In others, the reluctance to be tested can be used to elicit a more accurate history. All these patients should receive lengthy counseling. Some will and some will not permit testing. For those tested and found to be seronegative, counseling after the test must include information about the possibility of false negative tests.

The smallest group of patients would decline an HIV test without acknowledging activities putting them at risk. The physician's judgment would dictate the appropriate level of counseling. If broader HIV testing becomes the norm, the presence of a negative test in a patient's medical record will no longer be suggestive of a risk history for HIV. Those who refuse testing are more likely to be infected with HIV. Whether they acknowledge a risk history or not, they should be encouraged strongly to seek public health facilities that offer anonymous testing.

"We are recommending HIV testing vigorously to all U.S. adults under the age of 60 regardless of . . . risk history."

We believe it no longer tenable to do less than strongly recommend an HIV test to all patients who acknowledge any sexual contact with homosexual men, any needle sharing, or multiple unsafe heterosexual contacts. Physicians should vigorously elicit such histories. Testing should also be recommended to those who received unscreened blood transfusions after 1977 (many of whom are unaware that they received them), those with a history of any sexually transmitted disease (including acute hepatitis B), and those with lymphopenia, unexplained elevation of hepatic enzymes, or positive status for hepatitis

B markers. Testing should also be encouraged for those who have been exposed sexually to any person who has tested positive for HIV or any untested person in the above categories.

HIV Testing for Most Adults

We also strongly favor universal prenatal testing for HIV. The American Academy of Pediatrics and the American College of Obstetricians and Gynecologists currently recommend counseling and HIV testing of pregnant women who are "at increased risk of HIV infection." This selectivity is inconsistent with the U.S. and Canadian decision to extend hepatitis B testing to all pregnant women because risk histories are often inaccurate. Comparison with universal prenatal screening for rubella, which has been advocated since 1984, is instructive. From 1985 to 1989, there have been 21 cases of congenital rubella in the nation. Since thousands of babies infected with HIV are born annually, universal prenatal screening will prevent many more than five cases of neonatal HIV infection a year through decisions to have abortions or to limit the number of future pregnancies. If routine screening of pregnant women is accepted nationwide, its extension to the general population is logically only a small step.

Is it economical to recommend HIV testing to all adults who enter the health care system? Elderly women with negative risk histories are extremely unlikely to be infected with HIV. Perhaps our recommendation should be abridged to include only adults under 60 or in some parts of the country only men under 60. The problem of course is that if testing is justifiable in any segment of an apparently uninvolved population, the boundary between that segment and the rest of the population will inevitably be arbitrary. We urge serious consideration of recommending the test to populations with no apparent risk histories for HIV, especially if the prevalence of infection exceeds some very low threshold. We are recommending HIV testing vigorously to all U.S. adults under the age of 60 regardless of their reported risk history.

Health Care Workers and Patients Should Be Tested for AIDS

Marcia Angell

About the Author: *Marcia Angell is the executive editor of* The New England Journal of Medicine, *a weekly medical publication. Angell is also a lecturer on social medicine at Harvard Medical School in Cambridge, Massachusetts.*

Ten years ago five homosexual men in Los Angeles were reported to have acquired a mysterious and profound immune deficiency associated with pneumocystis pneumonia and other opportunistic infections. The report on these men, published in the *Morbidity and Mortality Weekly Report* on June 5, 1981, marked the beginning of the AIDS epidemic. Within weeks, similar cases were being described elsewhere. Even before the isolation of the causative virus in 1983 and the introduction of serologic testing in 1985, it was clear that a major epidemic had begun.

Now, a decade later, well over 100,000 Americans have died of AIDS and an estimated 1 million are currently infected with the virus, of whom more than 125,000 are thought to have clinical AIDS. Women and children are affected, as well as both heterosexual and homosexual men. Although the rate of spread in the homosexual community has slowed, the reservoir is now huge, and we can therefore expect to see the number of cases continue to grow. Thus, AIDS is no longer an obscure disease known only to the medical and homosexual communi-

Marcia Angell, "A Dual Approach to the AIDS Epidemic," *The New England Journal of Medicine,* vol. 324, no. 21 (May 23, 1991), pp. 1498-1500. Reprinted with permission.

ties; it is now a household word, of concern to most Americans and frightening to many. Not since the polio outbreaks of the early 1950s have we been faced with so threatening an epidemic. Furthermore, with the advent of expensive treatments that extend the lives of persons infected with the human immunodeficiency virus (HIV) for many years, the cost of this epidemic has become a troubling issue in a time of shrinking resources.

> **"AIDS . . . is now a household word, of concern to most Americans and frightening to many."**

In addition to the medical and economic issues surrounding AIDS, there are social issues unique to this epidemic that have greatly complicated our response to it. Unlike the polio epidemic of the 1950s or the influenza pandemic of 1918, AIDS tends to afflict people who are for one reason or another the objects of discrimination. Although increasingly a disease of inner-city black and Hispanic intravenous drug abusers of both sexes and their sexual partners, AIDS was at first almost exclusively a disease of homosexual men. It therefore carried the stigma of any sexually transmitted disease, but unlike syphilis or gonorrhea, it also carried the stigma of homosexuality—a double burden. Members of the homosexual community, articulate and well educated and accustomed to injustice, mobilized to protect themselves from a discriminatory backlash more effectively than the politically powerless drug abusers could possibly have done. Concerned that identification of those with AIDS would lead to loss of employment, housing, and medical insurance, as well as to social ostracism, they and others sensitive to civil rights issues argued successfully for confidentiality and against screening and efforts to trace sexual partners. Thus, although AIDS is reportable in all states, HIV infection is not, nor are contacts systematically traced. Instead, testing for infection is by and large voluntary, as is the notification of sexual partners.

We are now seeing growing opposition to this policy of strict confidentiality. With reports of the transmission of AIDS from patients to health care providers and, more recently, from a provider to patients, we hear calls for the routine screening of both groups—all patients admitted to hospitals and all doctors and nurses. There are also calls for the routine screening of pregnant women and newborns in response to the growing number of infants who contract AIDS from their mothers perinatally. Requiring the notification of sexual partners is less emphasized, perhaps because it is so difficult, but it, too, is receiving renewed attention.

Debates about these issues, it seems to me, too often confuse the social with the epidemiologic problems. To be sure, both sets of issues are closely enmeshed, but there seems to have been little effort to sort them out. Many of those who believe that controlling the epidemic should be our most important priority recommend draconian methods for doing so, including not only widespread screening, but also the removal of infected children from their schools, infected adults from their jobs, and both from the neighborhood. On the other hand, those moved primarily by compassion for AIDS sufferers and concern for civil rights are likely to resist the usual methods for monitoring and containing an epidemic—methods that might spare more people suffering.

"We hear calls for the routine screening of . . . all patients admitted to hospitals and all doctors and nurses."

I believe we need a dual approach that attempts to distinguish social from epidemiologic problems and that deals with both, simultaneously but separately. Clearly, HIV-infected persons need to be protected against discrimination and hysteria, but doing so requires social and political measures, not epidemiologic ones. Jobs, housing, and insurance benefits, for example, should be protected by statute. The economic consequences of HIV infection require additional attention, since they go far beyond the possible loss of employment and ordinary insurance benefits. Treating AIDS is expensive, and the disease lasts for the rest of a patient's life, during much of which he or she may be unable to work. Even the most generous medical insurance is unlikely to cover all the health care needs of a patient with AIDS; thus, as patients grow sicker they also stand to become destitute.

Devastating Consequences

We as a society should deal more systematically with the devastating economic consequences of HIV infection. I suggest we establish a nationally funded program, analogous to the end-stage renal disease program, for the medical care of HIV-infected persons. The end-stage renal disease program, established by Congress in 1972, extends Medicare coverage to all patients with kidney failure. This was a response to the development of effective but extremely expensive treatments for end-stage renal disease — namely, long-term dialysis and renal transplantation. Handling the AIDS epidemic in the same way would probably cost society no more than it spends on HIV infection now. Increases in costs due to expanded access would probably be offset by the elimination of the expensive practice of attempting to shift costs. Under the present patchwork system, each potential payer (employers as well as federal, state, municipal, and private insurers) naturally wishes to pass the costs to another. Thus, for example, a health care institution that finds itself possibly liable for the care of an employee who becomes infected with HIV takes an adversarial stance, asserting that there is no proof the infection was work-related. Whatever the outcome of any such dispute, some element in the system, often Medicaid, eventually must assume the costs. A nationally funded program would have the advantage of uniformity, simplicity, and efficiency. It would also give those at risk an incentive to be tested, thus allowing for earlier treatment and the protection of sexual partners. The present system, in contrast, is filled with disincentives for being tested.

"The present system . . . is filled with disincentives for being tested."

If by such measures we can soften the social and economic burdens on people with HIV infection, perhaps we will be freer to address the epidemiologic problems more rigorously. Concern about social issues now creates a reluctance to deal effectively with the epidemiologic problems. For example, systematic tracing of the sexual partners of HIV-infected persons is generally resisted because of the threat to confidentiality, although contact tracing makes sense from an epidemiologic standpoint and is officially required for other sexually transmitted diseases. Similarly, there is resistance to a screening program for all pregnant women and newborns, although such a program would be reasonable, given the accuracy of new confirmatory tests and the fact that perinatally acquired HIV infection is now more common than congenital syphilis or phenylketonuria, both of which are tested for routinely. Infected women could make more-informed choices about family planning, and infected newborns could be treated earlier.

Testing health care providers and hospitalized patients is also controversial, although it makes sense from several standpoints. Screening pa-

tients on admission would identify those with whom health care providers must be most alert; it is unrealistic to expect them to maintain the highest level of vigilance continuously. Similarly, because it is remotely possible that there could be an exchange of blood during a medical procedure, patients have a right to know whether a doctor or nurse who performs invasive procedures is infected with HIV. If necessary, retraining in noninvasive areas or early retirement could be provided for by special insurance programs for health care professionals. Screening both patients and health care providers would also, of course, identify those for whom treatment could be begun early and whose sexual partners could be protected.

I believe that, on balance, systematic tracing and notification of the sexual partners of HIV-infected persons and screening of pregnant women, newborns, hospitalized patients, and health care professionals are warranted. These populations are, after all, relatively accessible to the health care system and at some special risk. Attempting to screen the entire population would simply be impractical; on the other hand, targeting only high-risk groups would be unworkable, in part because it would entail making distinctions that are often impossible as well as invidious. With any increase in screening, however, the specter of discrimination arises once a person is known to be infected. Only if such discrimination, at least in its more tangible expressions, is countered by statute and if those with HIV infection are assured of receiving all the medical care they need, can we pursue the basic elements of infection control more resolutely and so spare others the tragedy of this disease.

High-Risk Groups Should Be Tested for AIDS

Brenda Almond

About the Author: *Brenda Almond is the director of the Social Values Research Center at the University of Hull in Hull, England. She is coeditor of the* Journal of Applied Philosophy.

Twice this century the world has been swept by global war, taking its massive toll of young lives. In recent years, the slogan "make love, not war" has understandably found favor with many young people as a personal reaction to the politics of destruction and aggression that have made these events possible. This is particularly so in countries where personal freedom is extended to matters of lifestyle and sexual behavior.

It is an irony—comparable to the twists of a Greek tragedy—that, without the firing of a shot, the world should now be on the brink of a third catastrophe of at least equivalent proportions. Responsible authorities speak of millions of anticipated deaths from AIDS, and figures bear comparison with estimates of the likely casualties of nuclear war. The *proportionate* figures are, however, possibly of more significance in relation to this disease, and there are towns in some countries of central Africa where local medicine and health workers estimate that a quarter of the population may be affected by the virus that causes AIDS, while authorities in the U.S. have put figures for men in the relevant age groups in the cities of New York and Philadelphia at one in 15. It is not difficult to forecast that once the virus that causes AIDS is as extensively distributed in a human population as

Brenda Almond, "AIDS and International Ethics," *Ethics and International Affairs,* volume 2, 1988. Reprinted with permission.

these figures suggest, control of further spread poses a problem of enormous dimensions.

It is not surprising, then, that AIDS should have become, as it has, a major political issue on both a national and an international scale—not only a concern of international agencies such as the World Health Organization, but also an addition to the agenda of world leaders at their economic summit in Venice in June 1987. The negative aspect of this otherwise welcome development lies in the fact that politics tends to divide when it is necessary to be united, to produce an adversarial response when what is needed is fellow-feeling and a common sense of human vulnerability. In the case of AIDS, there is an incipient tendency for nations to confront each other in a spirit of mutual recrimination and to deny unpalatable facts. There is also a tendency *within* countries toward polarization of the issue on a left-right axis, with the protection of civil rights being set against the taking of strong measures to control the spread of the virus. It would be absurd, however, and even potentially disastrous, if the public mind were to associate attempts to prevent or control the spread of the virus with the political right, and indifference to this issue with the political left. For the right is also concerned with civil liberties; the left is also concerned with survival.

> ## "AIDS is hardly a limited or modest problem on a world scale."

AIDS is hardly a limited or modest problem on a world scale. . . . The World Health Organization estimates that the number of people who are already carrying the virus (are seropositive) lies somewhere between five and ten million. . . . The proportion of those infected by the virus who it is expected will go on to develop AIDS and AIDS-related complaints (ARC) has risen from early lower estimates of perhaps 17 percent to 35 percent, 50 percent, and beyond. Finally, it is assumed, most chillingly, that all those who become ill will indeed die, not of AIDS itself, but of one of the many illnesses to which they fall victim as their immune system is destroyed.

Despite the limited and highly specific ways in which the virus is known to be communicated from person to person, sexual transmission alone is sufficient to provide for an exponential spread. Some figures from Belgium illustrate this in relation to the case of a single male engineer who died of AIDS. In the previous seven years, before he had had any reason to believe he was ill—and indeed before anyone could have been conscious of the deadly threat so recently arrived on the scene, he had had sexual relationships with 17 women—as well as two others who could not be traced—of whom no less than ten have now been found to be seropositive. Clusters of this nature illustrate the potential danger for metropolitan populations in countries, such as those of Western Europe, where health standards are high.

Globally, however, there are two main sites of the disease: sub-Saharan Africa, where it is believed that the disease may have originated, and the United States. . . .The U.S. Centers for Disease Control (CDC) in Atlanta estimates that one and a half million American men have the virus. This amounts to one in 30 American men aged between 20 and 50, so that already the chances of an American woman being at risk through a sexual relationship are not inconsiderable.

One other salient characteristic of the disease must be mentioned: this is that, unlike many other diseases, such as cancer, with which mankind has reluctantly learned to live, AIDS involves unacceptably *early* death, so that again, the CDC estimates that it will become the second largest cause of lost years of expected life in America. It may have already reached or exceeded this in some parts of Africa.

Global Outlook of AIDS

In considering the global situation, it is illuminating, and may be useful in responding to the threat, to see the world as divided into three areas: developed Western liberal nations, the countries of Eastern Europe, and Third World nations. The liberal democracies have taken individual freedom in the sexual sphere as part of their ethos and way of life; they have also embraced the principle of freedom of travel for their citizens. In their case, sexual liberation together with geographical mobility have provided the conditions for the rapid spread of the virus.

"In June 1987 President Ronald Reagan announced an intention to screen immigrants."

The countries of Eastern Europe have on the whole endorsed a sterner personal morality—they have tended to reject what they see as the permissiveness of Western society and have not attached value to individual freedom in the sexual sphere, other than in state-approved and regulated ways. Neither have their citizens been free to travel between countries with ease and frequency. These countries, it appears, are at the present time relatively free of the disease.

Certain Third World countries have borne the brunt of the disease, where problems caused by lack of resources for medical care, for education, and for the spread of information about the mode of transmission of the virus have added to the difficulties. These are the very countries in which the potential effects of AIDS on trade, tourism, and skilled labor could be the most dramatic. . . .

In the Western Hemisphere, where the United States, Brazil, Canada, and Haiti together account for 96 percent of reported cases, only three countries have not reported any cases at all. While the majority of cases are in the U.S., Brazil is very badly affected, particularly in the city of São Paulo.

Parts of Africa, however, are recognized as having the most serious AIDS problem in the world. Particularly affected are the regions around the great lakes Uganda, Burundi, Zaire, and Tanzania. In Africa, it is generally agreed that the spread of the disease is through heterosexual activity rather than homosexual, and through contaminated blood supplies and medical equipment. Frequently, the disease there is encountered as a concurrent infection with other diseases. The problem in Africa is compounded by the inadequacy of the resources available to cope with the scale of current AIDS cases; health expenditure may amount to no more than $4-$5 per person, while the cost of screening a single donation of blood would be $4. Syringes *have* to be used more than once and cannot be properly sterilized.

In the light of these economic and practical limitations, statistics from parts of the African continent are daunting. A quarter of the women tested at a leading anti-natal center in Kampala were found to be affected by the virus, and AIDS now accounts for a quarter of the deaths in one leading Kinshasa hospital. At the same time, ten percent of all blood stored for donation is believed to be infected.

Government Action

Action taken by governments, given their problems, or their perception of their problems, varies. In a growing number of countries, including France, Sweden, and the United States, the reporting of AIDS, and sometimes of positive test results, is mandatory. Places where this is not so include the United Kingdom, Belgium, and the Netherlands, all of which have decided to opt for voluntary systems. In contrast, the policy adopted by the state government of Bavaria has received considerable publicity, some of it hostile. This involves the screening of all legally registered prostitutes at least every three months, as well as the testing of prisoners, drug addicts, applicants for jobs in the public sector, and people applying for residence from outside the European area.

The United States was early in adopting screening for the military and for members of the Foreign Service and their families and in

June 1987 President Ronald Reagan announced an intention to screen immigrants, prisoners, and applicants for marriage licenses. Two days after his announcement a bill requiring mandatory screening of immigrants was passed by the Senate of the United States. A number of American states, however, have either taken or are considering further measures, some seeking the quarantining of infected persons who do not take steps to avoid spreading the disease, the so-called recalcitrant cases. Minnesota, Texas, Colorado, and Illinois are in the forefront of this move. The legislation places the burden of proof on the state to show that the individual is endangering other human beings, and it also contains strict confidentiality provisions, with fines or imprisonment as penalties for public disclosure of the results of an AIDS test.

A number of countries have limited policies of screening foreign students, workers, and business visitors. India, China, and Russia have been reported as adopting this stance. Russia has deported 221 people with positive test results, and India has ordered its five thousand or more African students to be tested or to leave the country. Belgium, too, has decided to insist on tests for students from the Third World who receive grants for their education. Eligibility will depend on a negative test result.

> *"Everyone* is at risk, and every sexually active person is a potential source of infection."

Other areas in which relevant legislation change has been initiated include access to and advertising of condoms—previously described as contraceptives, but now increasingly viewed in their prophylactic capacity—a change of emphasis that provides a sufficient reason for this change of terminology. France and Belgium have both passed legislation to liberalize access to condoms, while a number of countries which had legislated against the advertising of condoms on grounds of taste, or because of some people's religious objections, have reconsidered this policy. This includes the United Kingdom, which now permits condom advertisements on television.

Testing and Discrimination

Whatever the results of such enquiries, it is clear that governments are likely to be under increasing pressure to act against the threat of the disease. It is important, then, to consider, not only what laws might be effective but also what are the ethical constraints within which such legislation must operate. The debate on this issue, as was stated earlier, is frequently presented in terms of a conflict between public health and civil liberties—classic instance of utility (for many) versus liberty (for the few).

"Testing can tell the person tested whether or not he or she is carrying the virus."

In discussing the discrimination issue, it should first of all be said that there is more than one such issue. There is the issue of discrimination against high-risk groups, the issue of discrimination against people diagnosed as seropositive and the issue of discrimination against people with AIDS. The first of these should be, both rationally and ethically, a non-issue. *Everyone* is at risk, and every sexually active person is a potential source of infection. (This is because history and literature establish only one thing with certainty in the area of personal relationships, and this is that no one can be certain about someone else's fidelity.) So discrimination against particular groups, such as homosexuals, is a response to a phase of the virus that has already passed. In the San Francisco area, new cases amongst homosexuals have dropped dramatically; gay men have responded to the threat by taking precautions, something they are well able—practically and emotionally—to do (het-

erosexuals, as will be argued later, have a more difficult problem).

The term "discrimination" has also been applied to laws and policies relating to persons diagnosed as carrying the AIDS virus. It is also much bandied about in relation to the contentious question of establishing whether or not someone is in this category—the issue of testing. It must be said that these are very different issues from the first. The ethical basis for non-discrimination is the ancient principle that equals should be treated equally—that distinctions should be made between people only on grounds that are morally relevant. The significant thing about someone who is HIV positive is that, in specific situations, that person may be instrumental in bringing about the illness and death of another person. So if, for instance, within the closed and compulsory context of a prison, people are located in different places solely on the grounds that they are HIV positive or negative, then this is not a morally irrelevant ground for differentiation. Nevertheless, it has to be said that it is not a relevant ground for offering less exercise, worse facilities, or harsher treatment.

Within society at large, however, where people may choose their associates, such separation is both impractical and in most cases unnecessary. This means that discrimination against them in housing or employment is unjustifiable. However, if a duty to warn sexual partners is imposed on individuals who know themselves to be seropositive, this does not constitute discrimination or unfair treatment.

Finally, there is the question of discrimination against people suffering from AIDS. As in the case of the previous group, the protection of this group from arbitrary shunning in place of work or housing is a legitimate cause for campaigning by organizations interested in the preservation of civil liberties, for it is a consequence of the ethical principle that rules out discrimination on nonarbitrary grounds. The limited modes of transmission of the virus make attempts to curtail social contact in these ways an irrelevant and unjustifiable basis for discrimination.

The issue of testing is fraught with contention. The arguments, however, often fail to take account of the type and purpose of testing in question. Some of the objections offered to testing are practical rather than moral. There are three major practical objections. First, tests need to be offered repeatedly if they are to be effective, since a person may be found negative but shortly afterwards become infected. Second, tests themselves involve a built-in time lag. However, relevant to both these objections is the development of new forms of testing which may make it possible to establish within days, or at least weeks, whether a person has been infected. The possibility of a five-minute "frontier" test could also dramatically alter the possibilities of geographical control between countries. Third, it is pointed out that testing involves the misleading discovery of false positives and false negatives. As tests improve, however, the incidence of false test results is diminishing. Repeat testing will in general rule out the possibility that false positive test results will be left to stand, so that this particular problem may be confined to that of a small number of false negative results—to set against the vast body of accurate information that testing can generate.

Effects of Testing

Once these practical objections are dismissed, it is possible to turn to the moral reasons for dissent. In order to do this it will be useful to set out the various functions that testing may be expected to fulfill.

Testing can tell the person tested whether he or she is carrying the virus or not. This may be useful to the individual in two ways: first, it informs the individual of whether or not to expect the onset of a serious illness; and second, it tells the person whether or not he or she is likely to transmit a lethal virus to another person by intimate contact. Those who oppose testing tend to ignore the second extremely important function. As regards the first, they speak of a "right to ignorance." It is true that the news that one is suffering from something that may lead to fatal illness is unwelcome. Nevertheless, the second function of this knowledge should override the right a person might otherwise be considered to have to maintain peace of mind through ignorance.

"Common sense suggests some liberalization of controls in relation to testing."

Alongside the right to ignorance a "right to know" is sometimes mentioned. The right becomes relevant in relation to proposals for testing the blood supply, or for conducting anonymous surveys designed simply to establish the extent of the spread of the virus in the population. These further functions of testing merit separate discussion.

Also, testing can enable a medical professional to treat a person whose condition might otherwise be misunderstood; it can enable that medical professional to take appropriated measures to guard against infection in operating on or otherwise treating the person; and it can enable the medical professional to discover whether others are involved who might be at risk, in particular the spouse of a patient, and to consider whether they are adequately protected.

Finally, testing is an instrument for guarding the public health. Only if it is known that a person *is* a carrier of the virus can it be known also whether that person's sexual contacts are at risk, and are themselves liable to put others at risk. This is not a negligible function, and contact-tracing has long been accepted as a right and responsible strategy in relation to other less serious sexually-transmitted diseases. In addition, testing facilitates public health objectives in a more general way than this, by providing information not otherwise obtainable of the spread of the virus in the population, and of the groups amongst which it is most prevalent.

The strategies suggested by these various

functions of testing are sometimes discounted on the grounds that no cure can be offered to a person found carrying the virus. However, this is to overlook the message of the campaign of prevention currently being adopted by many governments. An individual can take self-responsibility for ensuring the safety of third parties, in some cases by avoiding the risk altogether, or by having sexual contact with people of the same HIV status, or at least by taking special precautions (the use of condoms). Where a person is prepared to take such a responsible attitude, the intervention of the state would be redundant.

Here the legislation enacted by Sweden on November 1, 1985 as an amendment to its Infectious Diseases Act may provide a model for other countries. This legislation classifies HIV infection as a venereal disease. Anyone who has reason to believe that he or she has been infected with the virus is *obliged* to contact a doctor, who *must* provide an examination and inform the authorities if the result is positive. An infected person is obliged to take measures to prevent the risk of spreading the disease, and to inform health and hospital personnel of the risk. In a recent incident, Swedes were scandalized to discover that someone had knowingly entered a hospital for major surgery without informing the medical staff of her positive HIV status. In Sweden, these measures are seen as consistent with maintaining the confidentiality of the patient, and a coded system for laboratory tests and special registration forms for AIDS patients have been introduced.

"The overwhelming moral priority . . . must be the protection of those who may receive donated blood."

There can, then, be no right to remain ignorant, unless indeed the desire to remain ignorant is combined with a willingness to behave as if one had been tested and the result was positive. (It is not inconceivable that some people might prefer this knowledge.) However, one should beware of using this as an argument for inaction, or as a facile solution to the problem. In a recent contribution to the discussion, Mark A. Rothstein echoes many others when he writes: "The same medical advice—in particular, avoidance of high risk activities—should be given to both seropositive and seronegative individuals."

Safe Sex

This sort of statement must be challenged on two counts. First to be considered are the psychological and practical assumptions involved. Anthony Coxon, a sociologist and gay rights advocate who has made a special study of these aspects in relation to homosexual and bisexual men, writes:

> A prevalent ideology among gays is that there is no need to take the HIV test: since the wise man will adopt safer sex practices anyway, taking the test will not affect his behaviour.

Coxon comments that this is "more a pious hope than a reality" and says that many take the test precisely to find out if they *need* to adopt safer sex measures. His own conclusions from his research are that the only event likely to precipitate a major change of lifestyle is the death from AIDS of a lover or close friend.

Second, the advice is advice *only* for homosexuals. To desist from "high-risk" sexual activities is a program of action that can only be recommended to heterosexual people if the necessity to propagate the species is ignored. Of course, not all heterosexual sex is engaged in for this end, but even here there are problems for securing adherence to "safe sex" guidelines. They stem from a double inequality in the male-female sexual situation: 1) an inequality of power in decision-making as to whether to take protective measures or not, and 2) inequality of risk; the receptive partner is at greater risk of infection, and females are always receptive partners in the biological sense.

So much then, for the right to remain ignorant, based on the assumption that "safe sex" will now become the norm for both homosexuals and heterosexuals. But what of the right to *know*, which appears to be violated in *anonymous* screening programs? Here it is important to keep the separate functions of testing clearly in mind, and it would be absurd if public health authorities in various countries were unable to obtain epidemiological information without at the same time pursuing the personal and pastoral aims that are alternative objectives of testing. If the doctrine of informed consent means that people's blood cannot be investigated for disease without their specific consent, to every contingency and illness for which it might be tested being given, then, to modify another saying, the doctrine's an ass. Few people know of all the complaints that laboratory examination of their blood might reveal, and the doctrine of informed consent has not normally been extended to such matters. Indeed, it could be argued that informed consent is essentially only necessary for *treatment*, and that a sample of blood that has been donated, for whatever purpose, is not a person being treated, but an object being scrutinized.

Routine Testing

Voluntary testing allied with counseling, while this should certainly be offered, may not provide a complete answer to the problem. For those who will not volunteer, nor listen to wise counsel, are precisely the people it is necessary to reach. So common sense suggests some liberalization of controls in relation to testing. For example, it should be possible to test blood, which has been taken for other purposes, for the virus. It should also be possible for medical personnel, including dentists, to ask for a test report before embarking on treatment that may carry additional hazards for them. It should be a matter of routine to investigate for AIDS when treating any kind of sexually transmitted complaint, unless a patient specifically requests that this should not be done. (This power of veto would perhaps be necessary to ensure that people

would not forego essential treatment through reluctance to be tested.) Such extensions of testing could remove the principle objection to testing, in that being tested would no longer be in itself a suspect matter, and therefore not an appropriate subject of enquiry by insurance companies or employers.

"Drug use, prostitution, and, to a lesser extent, homosexuality, characterize the less affluent subcultures."

Finally, whether compliance is total or not, the burden should be put, as it is in Sweden, on the individual who has encountered a risk of infection, either sexually or through the sharing of needles, to take the initiative in seeking a test. Anonymity could be guaranteed in the case of a negative result and confidentiality ensured between doctor and patient in the case of a positive result, providing the doctor's advice for subsequent behavior is accepted. (The doctor would report a positive result by number rather than name.) As for the special categories singled out for compulsory approach in some countries, the case of immigrants will be discussed later; the case for applicants for marriage licenses is open to argument; while the case of prisoners must be accepted for the sake of the prisoners themselves. To confine a person where he may be at risk of, and unable to avoid, sexual assault with serious consequences for health and life is itself criminally irresponsible. Those who run prisons have an obligation to take what action they can to avoid these unintended consequences of incarceration, and therefore to acquire the knowledge that will make this possible.

Ethical considerations, then, do not rule out some kinds of mandatory testing, subject to safeguards for the individual. In addition, through the principle of care for others, they suggest a more positive approach to voluntary testing, which should clearly be made available as cheaply and as conveniently as possible, and in conditions of maximum confidentiality.

Blood that has been donated for medical purposes such as transfusions raises other considerations. Most countries now accept the need to test blood that is being donated to blood banks and will be used for transfusions to third parties. But should this screening be done in a way that makes it possible to trace the donor of infected blood? Where it is possible to do so, would-be donors may be informed in advance, as they are in the United Kingdom, that their blood will be tested and that they will be told of a positive result. This gives them the opportunity to withdraw, and so avoid placing themselves in the situation of taking a test without due consideration. It is an arrangement that removes any possible ethical dilemma from the shoulders of those collecting the blood as to whether to inform or not; in this case, they *will* inform. The overwhelming moral priority here, however, must be the protection of those who may receive donated blood, and international guidelines might well be agreed to on this, with financial assistance available where cost alone may be preventing the monitoring of blood supplies. Blood that is collected for other purposes, however, and indeed blood collected for research and survey purposes, must be freed from restrictions argued for on so-called ethical grounds—i.e. because it may be impossible to give test results to those found positive. The priority is to control the spread of the virus, and for this, statistical estimates need to be replaced as far as possible with properly researched factual data.

> ## "Many of the arguments . . . about the ethical and legal aspects of AIDS have been arguments for *in*action."

It is only in the light of such information that demands for mass compulsory testing of whole populations can properly be assessed. Clearly,

such a strategy, because it is both expensive and coercive, should be contemplated only as a last resort. It should not be undertaken for a problem on a modest scale confined to fringe groups. But it is vital to know whether that *does* accurately describe the nature of the problem, for the time lag between infection and disease, which may be a matter of years, will make genuinely last-resort measures ineffective. This is a wider application of the principle generally applying in the case of this disease; that the obligation to save life overrides many other ethical considerations, and that the right to life is the first and foremost of human rights.

Containing AIDS

It is because they have failed to take account of this point adequately, that many of the arguments advanced by people concerned about the ethical and legal aspects of AIDS have been arguments for *in*action. Some who have argued against legislative change, however, have done so for a different reason. They have argued that in most countries the law as it stands is already adequate to cover the risks to second and third parties that are implicit in this disease. Against this consideration, however, it is necessary to weigh the fact that it is unlikely that cause and effect could be effectively demonstrated in such circumstances; again, we are in the presence of the lethal time lag that makes AIDS the problem for the world that it in fact is. The argument for inactivity may suggest the possibility of interesting legal cases or potential compensation suits, but it cannot be accepted as an argument against introducing more specific laws placing stronger duties on individuals, both to seek testing and to avoid risks to others.

The law is sometimes criticized in this, as in other areas, for protecting the wealthy and strong against the poor and weak. Those who claim this are likely to claim that internationally as well, coercive policies may be directed at protecting rich and powerful nations against poorer and less influential nations in the Third World. In considering these charges, it must be conceded that drug use, prostitution, and, to a lesser extent, homosexuality, characterize the less affluent subcultures of societies. Nor is it surprising that it is amongst those subcultures that AIDS first manifested itself. The standard pattern of such sociological presumptions is, however, skewed, not only by the fact that homosexuals and bisexuals may be wealthy, respected members of the mainstream establishment culture, but also by recent findings about racial or ethnic differences in susceptibility. According to findings in Trinidad, for example, Asians may be less susceptible than people of African descent, not to infection, but to the disease. Parallel findings in the U.S. and Britain suggest a genetic component in certain populations in these countries as well, irrespective of social factors. Nevertheless, the poor do remain susceptible, as is demonstrated by the case of people of Hispanic descent in the U.S. and Brazil. However, the moral to be drawn from this is that these vulnerable groups need the *protection* of soundly constructed legal and social policies; it is not a question of policing vulnerable groups as criminals, but of protecting them as potential victims.

"The health testing of immigrants remains the prerogative of sovereign nations."

As for the protection or policing of whole nations, the question remains as to whether it makes sense for some countries to try to keep people who are infected with the virus out, using immigration controls. Certainly, whenever this is proposed, it is bound to be a politically popular move, for those affected have no constituency, and those who *have* a constituency—a vote—see themselves as being offered protection. But this is a virus that knows no boundaries, and once it is rife *within* a population, external protection becomes a somewhat pointless curb on freedom of movement. It is an irony, then, that such mea-

sures are often most vociferously proposed in countries that are themselves amongst those most affected by the presence of AIDS, such as the U.S. One significant fact to consider here is that the more permissive, or sexually liberated, a society, the greater the toll that this disease will exact. And it is undoubtedly the case that the U.S., Australia, and the countries of Western Europe have moved much further in this direction than the countries of Eastern Europe. Russia's recent decision to test visitors and students, then, is rational in view of the fact that three-quarters of its small number of AIDS cases have been visitors. It is a somber thought that the Iron Curtain, which has controlled the freedom of movement between East and West for decades, may prove a *cordon sanitaire* against the AIDS virus. In the end, the health testing of immigrants remains the prerogative of sovereign nations, and each will form its own judgment as to whether the AIDS threat is greater from without than within.

AIDS Legislation

The three parameters that ethical and compassionate considerations jointly suggest for any proposed AIDS legislation are: 1) that it should guarantee strong action against discrimination where this is appropriate, 2) that it should promote essential measures to protect public health, and 3) that it should free from legislative control aspects of life that it has in the past seemed immoral for society to recognize, in order to bring them within the orbit of health promotion measures.

This three-pronged approach is to be contrasted with the one-sided and divisive proposals of those who set civil rights in opposition to public health, and vice versa. Individuals can only be expected to cooperate in necessary public health measures if they can be assured that the law will protect them in their personal lives from intimidation and discrimination. This enables those, for example, who are affected by a long-term episodic illness to continue, as long as they are able, to earn a living and maintain residence in their own community.

Law is a blunt instrument for bringing about the enormous changes in behavior necessary to remove the threat posed by this new disease. Sex, as the philosopher Santayana said, is nature's categorical imperative, and so people will continue to take enormous risks, both with their own health and with that of others, under the overwhelming pressure of this drive. Changes in behavior that regulate people's sex lives—fewer partners or, more strongly, premarital chastity and faithful monogamy—while they may be recommended, will continue to be honored as much in the breach as in the observance. Education is, of course, essential, and indeed it is the only tool available in the absence of a cure or vaccine. But what should be the burden of that education?

Shocked by the implied acceptance of immorality, the religious right in some countries is opposed to sex education in schools, explicit public education campaigns, and most particularly to education and advertising about condoms. They see in AIDS a tool to turn back the wheel of the sexual revolution, and certainly AIDS is a deadly chain letter for sexually liberated societies. To those who think like this, it must be said that historically good advice has never been lacking, but that it is often the fate of good advice to be ignored, particularly by the young and headstrong. The young are willing to take risks, even with their lives. . . .

Invisible Menace

Any educational strategy that is to be successful must embrace, as lovingly as do the young themselves, the reality of sexuality. This means not only the forms of sexuality that furnish ideals for literature, poetry, and religion, but also sexuality for money, sexuality for release, sexuality for one, sexuality for same-sex partners. Some will find this repugnant, but they will have to ask themselves whether they can take responsibility for the safety of their own young in a world overlaid by the invisible menace of the AIDS virus.

The key and salient need here is to understand the nature of the threat that is posed. This is a virus that attacks us—human beings, that is—in our reproductive function. If there is to be a future for the human race, there must be young people who have never encountered the virus. (And where premarital sexual relationships have been the norm, prenuptial testing makes noncensorious sound sense.) There must also be people who can know and trust each other enough to keep the threat away from their own relationship, at least for the childbearing years. For in this context, "safe sex" is not an option.

"If there is to be a future for the human race, there must be young people who have never encountered the virus."

Outside the crucial area of life where sex is intended for generation, the condom, at present, is in a literal sense the only physical barrier and protection from this disease. Moral protection is indeed to be sought as well. But this will come, not from setting unrealistic goals for other people, but from renewed attention to older and more central moral values—values such as honesty, openness, and concern for each other. In practice, being directed by these values dictates, first, that the facts uncovered by AIDS research, no matter how unpalatable, be confronted by both governments and individuals without prevarication or dissimulation; and second, that policies based on those facts must not ignore the need to protect those so far unaffected from the threat to their life and health posed by this microscopic enemy. Finally, it means taking account, too, of the claims of future unborn human beings, whose very existence may be in question if nature or science do not quickly restore the old order of things. AIDS *is* a moral issue—one urgently requiring human beings to reach a consensus on the promotion of an appropriate range of moral values, values which have the capacity, like the virus itself, to transcend the boundaries of culture, class, color, and religion.

Is AIDS Testing Necessary?

No: AIDS Testing Violates Civil Liberties

AIDS Testing Is Ineffective and Discriminatory
Physicians Should Not Be Tested for AIDS
Testing Immigrants for AIDS Is Harmful

AIDS Testing Is Ineffective and Discriminatory

Sandor Katz

About the Author: *Sandor Katz is a writer and AIDS activist. His work appeared in* OutWeek, *a gay magazine published in New York City.*

As the AIDS crisis in the United States accelerates into its tenth year, panicked health authorities are adopting counterproductive and coercive policies instead of confronting the difficult realities of treating people with AIDS and halting the spread of HIV [human immunodeficiency virus], the virus believed to cause AIDS. Policy-makers in search of a magic bullet have focused on testing people for the presence of HIV antibodies, reporting to health authorities the names of people who test positive and finding and notifying their sexual and needle-sharing partners. Despite evidence that these measures discourage those at greatest risk of getting AIDS from seeking information and care, almost half the nation's states now report, in most or all cases, names of people who are HIV positive. In December 1989 the American Medical Association officially endorsed mandatory name reporting and called for aggressive contact tracing as well (contact tracing is when authorities notify sexual or needle-sharing partners of the HIV infected that they are at risk). But aside from advocating widespread HIV testing, "most of the nation's physicians are still failing to take part in the fight to treat and control the deadly disease," according to a recent investigation by Bruce Lambert of *The New York Times*. The medical establishment's response to AIDS mirrors that of the federal government and many states and localities, where the focus of AIDS policy is identification of the infected rather than care and prevention.

Social control in the name of public health has a long and illustrious history in this country. The legacy of wholesale quarantines of immigrants and prostitutes gives other disenfranchised groups good reason to fear name reporting of people who are HIV positive. Given the stigma of AIDS and the vulnerability of the groups hardest hit by it so far—gay men, drug addicts and their partners and children—there is an ever-present danger that public health officials will trample on civil liberties in their zeal to do something (or at least to appear to be doing something to fight AIDS.) New York's recently departed Health Commissioner, Stephen Joseph, was condemned by virtually every AIDS service-providing agency in the city for his proposal to compile lists of the names of people testing HIV positive. In a *New York Times* Op-Ed piece in February 1990, Joseph wrote, "Concern for the individual liberties of those currently infected must take second place to the protection of the uninfected and the larger community."

> **"Almost half the nation's states now report, in most or all cases, names of people who are HIV positive."**

But do the civil liberties of the HIV infected really conflict with the protection of the uninfected? Dr. Mervyn Silverman, president of the American Foundation for AIDS Research and the former San Francisco Health Commissioner who made the controversial decision to close the gay bathhouses in that city in 1984, thinks not. "Whenever there is a conflict between public health and civil liberties, public health always wins," he says. But in the case of AIDS, he continues, "they are consonant. If I can make it safe for you to come in [for testing and health care], you'll do it. If you think you'll lose your civil liberties, you won't come in." Ronald Johnson, executive director of New York's Minority Task Force on AIDS, concurs in saying that any public health policy that arouses fears of repression "would be counterproductive to public health goals because it would drive people away" from testing and care.

"Contact tracing raises frightening civil liberties questions when it moves beyond the purely voluntary."

HIV testing has raised the specter of discrimination in employment, housing, health insurance and other areas. When the HIV test was still in development in 1984, for instance, Florida health authorities received a request from a school district to use the test to screen out gay teachers, which they properly denied. A national survey conducted by the Robert Wood Johnson Foundation and the University of California at Los Angeles found that, despite promises of confidentiality, two-thirds of the nation's hospitals indicate HIV status openly on patients' medical charts, and many hospitals routinely test patients without their knowledge or consent. Stories abound of test results leaking out, and insurance companies routinely test applicants and share the names of HIV-infected individuals. Due to the lack of effective legal protection from discrimination on the basis of HIV status, most AIDS activists have opposed anything but anonymous and voluntary testing. Blood samples tested anonymously are identified by a number to insure that the name of the tested individual is never known.

The appeal of name reporting for health authorities is that it gives them greater control over any follow-up procedures. But there is convincing evidence that such policies backfire. A now-classic University of South Carolina study, presented at the Fourth International Conference on AIDS in Stockholm in 1988, charted changes in HIV testing patterns after South Carolina repealed anonymous testing in 1986 and established mandatory name reporting. The number of gay men tested dropped by 51 percent. While the total number of people tested increased slightly, the overall rate of seropositivity among those being tested decreased by 43 percent. The study demonstrates that ending anonymous testing and requiring the reporting of names serve to scare away from diagnostic information and health care those people at greatest risk. Despite the evidence that mandatory reporting is a counterproductive health policy, it is winning widespread support. With the passage of a New Jersey law, twenty-five states now require name reporting in most cases; nine of those states do not allow anonymous testing at all.

Contact Tracing

Mandatory name reporting is usually accompanied by contact tracing. It is desirable for people to inform past and present partners who may be at risk and not know it. Discussion of notification procedures is an important component of the post-test counseling process, and every state has voluntary partner notification programs in which people can ask counselors to notify partners for them. But contact tracing raises frightening civil liberties questions when it moves beyond the purely voluntary. Patients can feel coerced into revealing the names of partners, fearing that services will be withheld if they don't, and doctors and health authorities frequently breach confidentiality to inform partners without the patient's consent. Because of the stigma attached to AIDS and the sexual and drug-using behaviors with which it is generally associated, people often are afraid to inform partners. Many doctors and public health authorities feel that, justified though the fear of telling partners may be, it is unconscionable not to tell them, and that it is their medical duty to inform the partners if the HIV-infected patient refuses to do so. The gay community has taken a firm position opposing such breaches of confidentiality, arguing that, as with name reporting, the threat of such action is *precisely* what will keep people away from testing and health care. "If your primary goal is to notify unsuspecting partners," says Nan Hunter, director of the A.C.L.U.'s AIDS and Civil Liberties Project, "you can be damn sure you'll never get to them if their partners don't come in in the first place."

There is no unanimity among AIDS activists on contact tracing; class, race, gender and sexual orientation all come into play. "I think the gay community has valid and serious concerns about contact tracing," says Debra Fraser-Howze, executive director of New York's Black Leadership Commission on AIDS. But Fraser-Howze believes that for women the issues are different: "We are beginning to ask, Why are we not letting these women know they are at risk?" For Marie St. Cyr, executive director of New York's Women and AIDS Resource Network (WARN), the question of breaching confidentiality is more complex. "Contact tracing tends to be coercive and punitive toward women," she says, noting that partner notification for HIV-positive women often results in physical violence against them from the men informed.

"Locating and testing identified contacts solves nothing when everyone is potentially at risk."

Opponents of contact tracing also note that it can drain resources from treatment and education programs. Multiple contacts, and lack of information about how to reach them, create vast logistical challenges. "A lot of people can be going on a lot of wild-goose chases," cautions St. Cyr. A study of the contact-tracing provisions of Representative William Dannemeyer's Proposition 102, defeated by California voters in 1988, estimated initial costs of $765 million and ongoing costs of $25 million a year for a state in which total AIDS spending in the 1988-89 fiscal year was below $75 million. This study's authors,

University of California, Berkeley, economists Robert Anderson and John Quigley, concluded that "adoption of Proposition 102 would have required a massive diversion of funds from other programs, including, in all likelihood, proven programs for prevention of HIV transmission."

Personal Survival

The spread of AIDS can be halted only by appealing to the rationality of human beings bent on personal survival. If human behavior can be changed—and the experience of the gay male community in the first decade of the epidemic suggests that it can—it will take aggressive education efforts. This entails explicit risk-reduction information from an early age, targeted education efforts, mass-media reinforcement and support from existing institutions, from health and social service agencies to churches and schools. "If we are looking seriously at prevention, it needs to be a global approach," St. Cyr says, in support of the idea that locating and testing identified contacts solves nothing when everyone is potentially at risk. Mervyn Silverman concurs: "Our goal is to get the emphasis and mindset on educating everybody."

The alternative places the full burden of responsibility on the HIV-infected individual. This is the view that supports breaches of confidentiality and the logic of incarcerating people who have sex without announcing they are HIV positive. Indiana's health department, under Dr. Woodrow Myers, put two HIV-infected people in "isolation" and issued pre-quarantine warnings to ten others, threatening that "engaging in an intimate sexual act *even with the use of barrier technique* (condoms or rubbers), without informing your partner that you carry HIV," could lead to detention. [Emphasis added.] Myers has since been named New York City Health Commissioner by Mayor David Dinkins, over the vocal objections of the AIDS Coalition to Unleash Power (ACT UP) and many AIDS service providers and gay groups.

Many public health advocates and civil libertarians interviewed in the course of researching this article believe there are behaviors that expose others to HIV risk and should be subject to state control, such as quarantine. They recount worst-case scenarios which vary in detail but generically consist of a vindictive "AIDS monster" deliberately infecting scores of innocents, à la Gaetan Dugas as he was sensationalized as "Patient Zero" in Randy Shilts's book *And the Band Played On*. But even in the worst-case scenarios, punishing such individuals as a matter of public policy would do little to protect anyone from AIDS, for it does nothing to alter anyone else's risky behavior.

"There is an attitude that the people involved in this [AIDS] are disgusting scumbags to begin with."

The HIV virus is not easily transmitted. It can be forced on a well-informed person only through rape or physical assault. Aside from those exceptions, people can protect themselves from it. But they can protect themselves only by behaving as if every sexual partner is HIV infected. Screening partners is ineffective. The facts of HIV are that it takes from several months to several years after transmission of the virus to develop antibodies, and people can live with HIV for many years without symptoms. If people know what sexual acts are unsafe and how they can be made safer with condoms and dental dams (for cunnilingus), then it doesn't matter what a partner's status is, whether the partner knows his or her status or whether the partner chooses to share that information. A urine test to detect HIV antibodies has been developed by New York University researcher Alvin Friedman-Kien, who envisions its use as a home test to "check out your lover" before having sex. Such screening promotes a false sense of security, due to the lag between the time of HIV infection and the appearance of antibodies. People who engage in unsafe behavior do so at their own risk.

Until there is a cure, we are all living with AIDS.

Regarding the possibility of quarantine, the A.C.L.U.'s Nan Hunter says that "it's certainly conceivable that it could be justified," so long as the state "first exhausts every possible less restrictive alternative, proves that there is an imminent risk to others and affords full due process." But these lines are already being crossed. In Indiana an HIV-infected person (and the state knows who that is, thanks to name reporting) is considered an imminent risk to others if he or she does not announce his or her HIV status to sexual partners, even if they are practicing safer sex. Some states' HIV laws refer not only to people infected with HIV but those "suspected" of it. "Remember, there is an attitude that the people involved in this [AIDS] are disgusting scumbags to begin with," notes Rodger Pettyjohn, a nurse formerly at New York's Community Health Project who has AIDS himself. The prospect of quarantine laws being abused is a chilling one. What could be more appealing to opportunistic politicians functioning in a climate of panic?

Testing and Quarantines

No less horrific a figure than Adolf Hitler devoted his attention to the control of syphilis. In "the medical struggle against the plague," the Führer wrote in *Mein Kampf*, "there must be no half-measures; the gravest and most ruthless decisions will have to be made. It is a half-measure to let incurably sick people steadily contaminate the remaining healthy ones." Hitler's ideological descendants recognize AIDS as a potent issue to mobilize fear. North Carolina Senator Jesse Helms advocates universal testing and says, "I think somewhere along the line we are going to have to quarantine, if we are really going to contain this disease." Lyndon LaRouche's unsuccessful 1986 ballot proposition calling for the quarantine of all HIV-positive individuals was supported by 2 million California voters. In this atmosphere, would you want the government to know you were HIV infected?

It is against this backdrop that the overall role of HIV testing in the fight against AIDS must be understood. One important political appeal of testing is that it is cheap and easy. Public health officials generally view testing as part of prevention. But where is the rest of the strategy? Providing drug treatment to intravenous drug users is difficult and expensive, and provision of explicit safer-sex education and clean needles is controversial and therefore easier not to do. The isolationist approach to AIDS prevention, which costs relatively little compared with universal education and gives the appearance of action, is HIV testing, contact tracing and the threat of quarantine.

Increasingly, the HIV test is being viewed as a diagnostic tool for purposes of treatment. Aerosolized pentamidine can prevent pneumocystis carinii pneumonia, the single biggest killer of people with AIDS, and low doses of AZT, or azidothymidine, may slow the virus's effects. With the advent of such early intervention treatments for asymptomatic HIV-infected people, many AIDS activists have begun to warm to testing, although generally with the caveat that the decision of whether to get tested is complex and must remain up to the individual.

For most AIDS activists, the primary consideration in thinking about testing is access to quality health care (as well as supportive social services), without which it is not possible to take advantage of early intervention therapies. And, as Stephen Beck, former executive director of the National Association of People with AIDS, points out, "That's not a reality for most people." In New York, waits of several days in hospital emergency rooms are common, while waiting lists for primary health care clinics are measured in weeks and months. St. Cyr of WARN laments, "Without the support network, I really have to think, What is it that I am offering someone [by getting them tested]? What is the level of psychological punishment that I am asking people to take?" Rodger Pettyjohn asks, "Since the needs of people already diagnosed aren't being met, how are we supposed to believe that the government will do anything more for more people?" The expected passage of $600 million in emergency federal AIDS assistance will be an important step in the right direction, but providing adequate health care will require a far greater commitment of spending.

"The government is not mobilizing to help people with AIDS survive or to stop the spread of HIV."

Federal AIDS research has so far yielded little, being driven more by scientific egos and the pursuit of pharmaceutical profits than by health needs. While the National Institutes of Health reorganizes its data, new drug trials are being held up. Progress has instead come out of places like New York's Community Research Initiative, where the tests for aerosolized pentamidine were conducted, and which the feds have refused to fund. In case after case, the Food and Drug Administration has failed to release promising drugs until AIDS activists forced them to.

A Cry for Leadership

The government is not mobilizing to help people with AIDS survive or to stop the spread of HIV. "All across the country there is a cry for leadership from the Federal Government," stated the National Commission on AIDS in its April report to President George Bush, who refused to address the Sixth International Conference on AIDS held in San Francisco. This dismal record leaves AIDS activists suspicious of the focus on testing and frightened of what the future appears to hold.

Physicians Should Not Be Tested for AIDS

Larry Gostin

About the Author: *Larry Gostin is executive director of the American Society of Law and Medicine in Boston. He is also an associate professor in health law at the Harvard University School of Public Health in Cambridge, Massachusetts.*

In 1988, I was invited by the Hastings Center to prepare a position paper asserting that patients had the right to be protected against exposure to HIV in health care settings. Believing, rather naively I fear, that I was being asked to defend the rights of patients, I happily accepted. My paper examined such areas as the patient's right to be informed if her surgeon was HIV-infected, along with the prevailing professional duty of health care providers to protect patients from avoidable harms.

When I arrived at the debate forum, I looked up to see my friends—humane public health officials, civil libertarians, and AIDS activists—on the other side of the table. It dawned on me that the debate was not about *patients'* rights at all, but about restricting the *employment* rights of HIV-infected health care professionals. Still, I argued at that time, and have continued to assert in the Centers for Disease Control [CDC] review process, that HIV-infected health care professionals ought to refrain from the practice of seriously invasive procedures.

At the core of my argument is a common sense, patient-oriented approach. The CDC has long advocated, quite correctly, that restrictions on the rights of persons infected with HIV in employment, education and housing are not justified because the mode of transmission of HIV is sexual or blood-borne and not casual. The CDC, then, could hardly sustain a public position favoring the continuance of seriously invasive procedures by infected professionals—health care professionals whose hands are immersed in a bodily cavity, using a sharp implement with demonstrable epidemiologic evidence of a high rate of torn gloves and cut hands.

On the "letters" page of *JAMA* [Journal of the American Medical Association] in July 1989, the CDC was urged not to wait for the first case of professional-to-patient transmission before developing a clear policy. Days after the publication, that first case was reported by the CDC: it appeared that a Florida dentist had transmitted HIV infection to a patient. Two further cases of transmission to patients by that same dentist were reported in January 1991; CDC epidemiologists were investigating a possible fourth case. The strain of the AIDS virus that infected the three patients was identified as the same as in the infected dentist. The CDC was able to identify breaks in infection control procedures such as failure to change gloves between patients. The most likely explanation for the transmission was direct blood-to-blood transfer of the virus, perhaps by bleeding into the oral cavity. Another possible explanation was that HIV was transmitted through instruments contaminated by blood from the dentist or another patient.

> **"The debate was not about *patients'* rights at all, but about restricting the *employment* rights of [the] HIV-infected."**

Shortly after the first Florida case, Johns Hopkins Hospital sharply criticized the CDC for the absence of clear guidance. The hospital decided to write to all patients of a surgeon who died of AIDS and inform them of the possible risk. The

Larry Gostin, "The HIV-infected Health Care Professional: Public Policy, Discrimination, and Patient Safety, *Law, Medicine & Health Care*, Winter 1990. Reprinted with permission.

Johns Hopkins case added to the debate not just the professional question as to whether infected surgeons ought to refrain from practicing, but also the legal/ethical question as to whether their patients have a "right to know." The ethical conundrum becomes all the more apparent when one factors in the finding that a significant number of health care providers claim the "right to know" if their patients are infected and, in fact, test them without consent. With both sides claiming a right to know, and with the careers of dedicated physicians at stake, some rational line must be drawn which separates real risks from speculative risks, and that protects patients without wholly disproportionate economic and human rights burdens. I suggest separate questions that need to be asked for a rational resolution of this health policy puzzle.

"Warning patients would represent a deep invasion of privacy for [HIV-infected] workers."

Should health care professionals be required to disclose their serologic status to patients?

American society has become obsessed with the "right to know" even remote risks to health or safety. Numerous examples can be cited. They range from the disclosure of environmental risks to workers to the disclosure of risks of sabotage to air travelers. The American Medical Association asserts that HIV-infected practitioners have an ethical obligation to warn their patients or give up invasive procedures. But warning patients would represent a deep invasion of privacy for workers, while achieving very little public health benefit. At its most basic level, the duty to warn breaches confidentiality by requiring disclosure of sensitive health care information. The professional herself is a patient who is being treated for HIV disease by her physician. Forced disclosure of that privileged information to a third party (i.e., the infected physician's pa-

tient) is a classic case of breach of confidence. The invasion of privacy goes much deeper, for inevitably the information will spread to many patients and professionals, and ultimately may become public knowledge in the community.

Health Care Workers

The infected health care professional does not merely lose her privacy, but also her career and livelihood. It is unrealistic to expect that if professionals informed their patients of their health care status they could continue to practice. Disclosure of information that the professional has a transmissible, potentially lethal infection would be ruinous to the professional's career. Such a serious invasion of human rights might be warranted to achieve a compelling public health benefit, but no such unequivocal benefit arises.

Informing patients that their caring professional is infected with HIV would produce a great deal of anxiety in most patients. Studies suggest that the majority of patients would not want to be treated by an infected physician. More importantly, merely possessing information about a caring professional's serologic status does not produce any direct benefit. If the information is given *retrospectively* (i.e., after the professional/patient relationship has ended), the patient's anxiety is provoked needlessly. The chance that the patient contracted the infection in a health care setting is minute. Moreover, patients cannot take any action to avoid harm, because their interaction with the infected professional is now in the past. Certainly, they could be tested and, if positive, receive early treatment. But this goal could be achieved as well by routine testing of hospital patients, already recommended by the CDC.

Patients' Concerns

If the information is given to patients before any treatment occurs, the only way for the patient to eliminate the perceived risk is to seek another professional. If the risk is so low that patients have no justified concern, then it would be inequitable to discriminate against a professional because of her health care status. Requiring the professional to warn her patient implicitly condones the discrimination that will occur as a result of the disclosure.

Those who argue that patients have the right to be informed use the doctrine of informed consent as a justification. The law of informed consent, however, does not require the disclosure of highly remote or unforeseen risks. Nor would the ethical principle of autonomy support disclosure. A patient's decision-making is aided only by relevant information that helps her balance benefits against realistic risks and adverse effects. The patient may face many low risks of nosocomial infection or other unforeseen events in a hospital which are not routinely disclosed. Indeed, significantly higher rates of success for more experienced centers in areas such as coronary bypass surgery have been reported. Yet, patients are not routinely informed about infections acquired in hospitals or the varying degrees of success or failure of different providers. A clear justification would have to be provided before discussing a professional's HIV status, but not her other infectious conditions or her record of success.

> ## "Screening is so costly and cumbersome . . . that the [work] restrictions themselves must be abandoned."

If the risks of contracting HIV were indeed significant in relation to particularly invasive procedures, then informing patients would not suffice. The doctrine of informed consent was developed to assist patients in making decisions about the benefits and risks of medical treatments, and not to protect them against incompetent or dangerous physicians. If a physician is impaired or there is a real risk of transmission of infection to her patient, then this is a problem that should be remedied by professional standards and licensing requirements. Patients must be protected against unreasonable risks posed by practitioners; obtaining the patient's consent does not obviate the need for professional and licensing standards necessary to protect the patient.

Thus, a professional's intimate health care status which may, or may not, affect her ability to perform the job competently and safely is not a matter for patients, but for employers and licensing authorities, whose job it is to ensure the highest professional standards. Disclosure to patients rather than employers means that the professional's private life will be a matter of public record, and will foster discrimination based upon irrational fears or prejudice. . . .

Health Care Screening

[Should] health care professionals . . . be subject to screening?

Perhaps the strongest, and most persistently made, argument against *any* restrictions on the practice of infected physicians is that restrictions can only be enforced through screening. Screening is so costly and cumbersome, it is argued, that the restrictions themselves must be abandoned. There is a simplicity and consistency to this argument that makes it appealing. However, if perfect enforcement of an ethical or professional rule were always a necessary condition for the rule itself, the health care professions would have very few rules to ensure high performance, quality care, and patient safety. The fact is that the professions quite properly impose upon themselves a number of rules with which they expect compliance, and so do not rigorously monitor. Health care professionals are not permitted to conduct medical procedures on patients under the influence of drugs or alcohol, or subject to other impairments, and they are required to report weeping sores or airborne infections which may endanger patients. Yet, few health care facilities or licensing authorities require blood alcohol or drug tests, or systematically monitor the professional for physical or mental impairments or dangerous infectious conditions. The rules are enforced by professional sanctions, even legal action, when an infringement is reported.

"Facilities might also have to decide whether to disclose the information to patients or third parties."

Screening without consent or as a condition of licensure represents an invasion of human rights by undermining the person's autonomy and physical integrity. It, therefore, requires a justification in its own right, apart from any justification for the professional rule itself. Required screening of health care professionals would indeed be ironic when programs for prisoners, immigrants, sex workers, and others at higher risk have been rejected. The disadvantages of screening health care professionals are similar to those in other low risk populations, and have been explicated elsewhere.

Screening health care professionals for HIV has disproportionate human and economic costs when compared with the benefit to be achieved. The human cost is that the professional is asked to forego the right to consent to medical testing. Testing for HIV, moreover, is qualitatively different from other testing since it may suggest that the person has engaged in behaviors disfavored in society, and it makes the individual confront a dire prognosis without voluntary agreement and advance counseling.

Public policy experts spend considerable time trying to impress upon professionals the importance of obtaining informed consent for medical procedures. Virtually all state legislatures have specifically required written informed consent before testing for HIV. Why should professionals adhere to the rule of informed consent for their patients if it is so easily dispensed with for themselves?

A negative test result does not guarantee that a professional is free from infection. A period of six weeks or more must transpire before many infected persons produce antibodies which are detected by current assays. The professional could also contract the infection at some future time. To be certain that professionals are free from infection, facilities would have to periodically re-test at considerable expense.

Systematic collection of highly sensitive health care data would place considerable burdens on facilities. They would be required to keep the information confidential and could be liable for intentional or negligent disclosure. Facilities might also have to decide whether to disclose the information to patients or third parties under a duty to inform theory. The CDC has also said that pre- and post-test counseling is professionally desirable, adding substantial cost to a screening program.

Benefits of Screening

The benefit of screening from a public health perspective is that it might catch a few infected physicians who do not honestly disclose. The decision not to screen would rely upon the professional integrity of health care providers to comply with the requirements of their professional bodies and licensing authorities. A professional rule which is subject to the usual ethical expectation and possible sanctions of the licensing authority is far preferable when compared with the inordinate human, social and economic costs of screening. Ultimately, one has to consider what the health care system will be like if patients and practitioners each have a distrust of the other. Both sides will call for a "right to know" and the right to test. The expense will be inordinate and the morale of both patients and professionals will be depleted.

Testing Immigrants for AIDS Is Harmful

Marc Ramirez

About the Author: *Marc Ramirez is an associate of the Center for Investigative Reporting in San Francisco. He has been a reporter for* The Wall Street Journal *and the* Phoenix Gazette.

Luis is nervous and his hands are sweating. Ben, his lover, sits quietly at his side. Neither has given his real name. As Luis talks, he pulls at his fingers, one at a time, big brown eyes scanning the surroundings, a downtown Los Angeles office.

"My family, they know," he says. "My mother told me, 'You knew what you were doing, you knew the risks, you live with it.'" Luis has tested positive for HIV [human immunodeficiency virus], the virus that can cause AIDS.

A native of Mexico in his mid-twenties, he is a hairdresser, fashionably dressed, charming in a way that belies the anxiety he feels, uncomfortable discussing his situation. The United States has been Luis's home for ten years now, long enough to qualify him for legal residency under the Immigration Reform and Control Act of 1986. He missed the law's original deadline, but he is still eligible through a special category set up for people who failed to apply because they were misinformed the first time around.

But Luis's eligibility is in jeopardy. HIV testing is required by law for amnesty applicants and other immigrants. Unless Luis can meet conditions necessary for waiver of his test result, he will be refused legal status in the country where he has lived since he was a teen-ager.

Marc Ramirez, "AIDS and the INS," *The Progressive,* May 1990. Reprinted by permission from *The Progressive,* 409 E. Main St., Madison, WI 53703.

"There are people who have been here ten, fifteen years who are HIV positive," he says. "Obviously, they got it here. There's no right to throw them out."

Luis is one of a growing number of immigrants who feel threatened by the HIV testing program. From San Francisco to Miami, their advocates complain that a combination of misleading information and inadequate education is leaving people desperate and frightened. Federal policy has misfired, creating an underground society of people who, afraid to surface, are being denied the treatment and counseling they need to avoid spreading the virus.

And that means the program is harming not only immigrant communities but also the very thing it was supposed to protect—the public health of the United States.

Many aliens do not know the Immigration and Naturalization Service [INS] can grant waivers for HIV-positive applicants, say immigration attorneys. Others know, but they don't trust the INS. And some, fearing they will soon be dead, wonder why they should bother about legalization.

Attorneys are concerned that, among the conditions for receiving a waiver, the applicant's coverage by private health insurance may be a key element in INS decision-making. And that's a qualification many immigrants won't be able to meet. The costs of treating an AIDS patient—as high as $30,000 a year—are well known, and it's an expense taxpayers will end up footing for those without insurance.

> ### "The program is harming not only immigrant communities but . . . the public health of the United States."

"It's not an immigration problem," says Phoenix attorney Roxanna Bacon. "It's a health problem. The policy that the INS ought to be looking for is one that best serves the public good, that doesn't penalize people for having this disease, that encourages them to come forward, and I have not seen any of that."

To apply for amnesty, a person must have lived in the United States since at least 1981. The thought of being returned, after so many years, to a country no longer familiar, where economic conditions may be desperate, where cultural attitudes toward AIDS may be harsh, or where health care falls far below U.S. levels, is not welcome.

"I was hearing that people who tested positive won't get amnesty."

Obviously, many HIV-infected people will opt instead for a life of false names, constantly changing addresses, and the abysmally low-paying jobs available to the undocumented. No one can know how many infected aliens there are, but knowledgeable people estimate the number runs well into the thousands.

It was February 1986 when Luis found out he carries the HIV virus, nine months before President Ronald Reagan signed into law the most sweeping immigration reform in American history.

The Immigration Reform and Control Act of 1986 was supposed to grant permanent residence to foreigners who already lived in the United States and close the border to newcomers. The Act brandishes employer sanctions as its primary weapon—those caught hiring illegals are subject to severe fines. The idea is that immigrants without work authorization, unable to get jobs, would return home, and others would be discouraged from crossing at all. Border-apprehension statistics have been cut nearly in half since the law's passage, but even the INS admits an estimated 300,000 to 500,000 people still cross annually without being caught.

About three million people applied for temporary residency during the new law's first phase. The second phase, for permanent residency, began in December 1988. But while immigrants were busy collecting documents—old utility bills, school records, and the like—to prove they had lived here since 1981, something else that had infiltrated American borders was drawing Federal attention—the disease known as Acquired Immune Deficiency Syndrome, AIDS.

By 1986, the epidemic had prompted increasing calls for funds and action. Some pushed for education to combat the rapidly spreading virus; others believed mandatory testing was the right approach.

In June 1987, a measure calling for mandatory AIDS testing for certain immigrants shot through the U.S. Senate by a vote of 96-to-0. The affected aliens included those applying for legalization under the new immigration law. Two months later, the Justice Department added HIV infection to its list of "dangerous contagious diseases" that serves as basis for denial of U.S. residency, a list that includes gonorrhea, infectious syphilis, and active tuberculosis.

Immigration Questions

Immigration lawyers began to take a barrage of new kinds of phone calls: What if I test positive? Can I still apply for amnesty? Will I be deported? Why should I care about amnesty?

There was hope for those seeking information. The INS said it would consider, on a case-by-case basis, waivers for anyone denied residency for medical reasons. Such waivers might be based on humanitarian reasons, to preserve family unity, or when it is otherwise in the public interest to do so. That avenue remains open to HIV-infected applicants, provided they can establish three things:

• They pose a minimal threat to public health.

• The possibility of the disease's spread is minimal.

• No cost will be incurred by any Government agency without its consent.

Early in the program, there was widespread confusion. Many HIV-infected applicants believed they were ineligible for amnesty. One of those people was Luis, who knew he was otherwise eligible but was afraid his medical condition automatically disqualified him.

"I was hearing that people who tested positive won't get amnesty," he says. "That was everywhere—TV, papers, everything."

Whether Luis misunderstood or was misinformed—both scenarios were common—the result was the same. He missed the application deadline. Another HIV-positive man living in California, sure he would be deported, quit his job and moved to Illinois. He also missed the deadline, says his Chicago attorney.

Waiver Problems

Many other immigrants affected by the HIV testing program are in similar situations. And there are other problems as well:

• Many physicians are unaware of the possibility of a waiver. San Francisco attorney Ignatius Bau attended a conference on minorities and AIDS. Several physicians, he says, admitted they were telling their HIV-positive patients their hopes for amnesty were unfounded. J. Craig Fong, a Los Angeles attorney, reports similar cases.

"Someone with no immigration expertise would be telling a person, in a foreign language, that he has AIDS."

• Many INS interviewers are unaware of the waiver. San Francisco attorney Patricia Dunn tells of an incident in late 1988: "I went to an INS interview with my client," she says, "and I didn't want the examiner to freak out. So I said, 'Here's the medical exam. He's tested positive. We'd like to apply for the waiver.' She said, 'Oh, okay,' and then went to her supervisor and I heard her saying, 'This attorney thinks there's a waiver.' A few weeks later, one of our volunteer attorneys went to the same adjudicator and she said the same thing."

• Some clinics that conduct the tests aren't approved by the INS. Barbara Effros of the National Center for Immigrants' Rights in Los Angeles says she had a client whose test result was rejected by the INS because the testing facility wasn't INS-approved. "This particular clinic just didn't know," she says. "The applicant just has to retest. But it could have hurt someone who was near the deadline."

• Some physicians don't inform patients of their test results, and such applicants don't find out they're positive until they reach the INS interview. "It's difficult to do when you have to translate from English to Spanish," says an adjudicator in Phoenix. "And then you have to explain what AIDS is."

• Physicians and INS staffers are often confused about the responsibility for counseling, and the infected person ends up with none at all. "There are people who think they're just going in to get their green card, and they have this bombshell dropped on them," says Judy Rabinovitz of the American Civil Liberties Union in New York. She tells of one man whose doctor provided the positive test result and nothing more. "Luckily this person had enough together," she says, "that he saw a sign on the bus and called an AIDS organization. But he felt like he wanted to kill himself when he got out of [the doctor's office]."

Roxanna Bacon, the Phoenix attorney, says the list of INS-approved doctors ballooned once HIV testing was mandated. The newer ones, she charges, "had no training and no understanding of what they were doing or why. They would do the exam, the alien would leave, then come back and pick up the sealed envelope." In some cases, she says, clients received their test results from temporarily hired INS front-desk staffers. "Someone with no immigration expertise would be telling a person, in a foreign language, that he has AIDS. It's the equivalent of finding out you have brain cancer from the person who's supposed to give you your driver's license."

Counseling for those who test HIV-positive is

essential. They need to hear that the result doesn't necessarily mean they will develop AIDS, but that they can transmit the virus to others. And they need to know that a waiver is possible.

Lawyers cite cases of immigrants calling them for advice but then never calling back. They remember occasions on which clients referred to them by doctors never showed up. A public-health worker in Tucson says he has been unable to track down at least half a dozen amnesty applicants. "For the people we come in contact with, fine," says Nancy Warren of the Brooklyn AIDS Coalition in New York. "But I have a feeling we're just hitting the tip of the iceberg."

And from immigration attorney Fong in Los Angeles: "By the time they get to me, I'm educating them. I try to talk; I say, 'Do you have any friends who are hiding out?' But even though they are coming to trust me, that is not something they're going to talk about."

Immigrants and the INS

Luis isn't sure what he will do if he is denied residency. He says that although his family, like most in Mexico, disapproves of his lifestyle, they are understanding of his situation. If he has to, he says, he can return home. "But most people," he says, "have nothing to go back to. I am here by choice. I come from a middle-class family. But the others. . . ."

Most of these immigrants came here from Latin America to escape extreme poverty. They knew the wages they would earn, though meager by U.S. standards, would be more than they could dream of back home. They expected to give up the freedoms of legal existence, to be on constant guard against detection by immigration agents—*la migra*. But they never counted on AIDS.

Those who work with Latino immigrants say homosexuality is more common than widely believed in this culture that has a hard time admitting it. Fong, who directs Downtown Immigrant Advocates run by Asian Pacific Legal Center in Los Angeles, says AIDS information in the Hispanic community is several years behind the

norm; meanwhile, the Hispanic rate of HIV infection is four times that of Anglos.

"I'm not a social worker," Fong says. "But I've had to hold hands, tell people it's not that bad. These people are running scared. Not only do they have immigration to worry about—now it's a matter of life and death."

Dave Still, an INS official in San Francisco, says not many people have turned up positive under the amnesty testing program. "I don't know of any cases where someone tested positive and hence failed to apply at all," he says. "How would we know?"

The latest tally shows seven waivers approved and two denied throughout the country. About a hundred applications are pending, and many more remain to be filed. But until further decisions are made, no one can assess how difficult it is to obtain one. Waiver requests aren't submitted at all, as a rule, unless attorneys think their clients have strong cases.

The national network of immigration lawyers shares frequent conference calls about the latest regulatory changes, procedural problems, special cases, and waiver-application strategies. The Coalition for Immigrant and Refugee Rights and Services in San Francisco has even compiled its own list of INS-approved physicians to whom applicants should be referred, a list based on a survey assessing the doctors' sensitivity, thoroughness, and reliability.

"Not only do they have immigration to worry about—now it's a matter of life and death."

"A lot of people are testing positive," says San Francisco attorney Patricia Dunn of the Coalition. She knows of 180 HIV-positive immigration cases in the Bay Area alone. Nationwide, there are hundreds more, with the hardest-hit areas being Los Angeles, New York, and Miami.

The Senate approved the program "pretty fast, without debate," Still concedes. "I don't think they thought about all the ramifications when they passed it."

But Joseph Cuddihy, an INS examinations officer, says he's starting to take the complaints leveled by advocacy groups less seriously. "I would tend to think that the amount of rhetoric these groups put forth would be more detrimental to the process than the problems they're talking about," he says. "If you cry, 'Fire,' long enough, eventually a fire will start."

Cuddihy adds that, because physicians are responsible for informing infected applicants about available services, even those who decide not to pursue amnesty should know where to go for education and counseling. Those who leave the country because of positive test results, he points out, are departing "of their own free will" since the information is used only to deny legal status and not for deportation purposes.

"I don't think the answer is to close our eyes to the law," says Cuddihy of calls for slackening the waiver requirements. The solution? "I don't know that a problem exists," he responds.

Cultural Attitudes

Guille Sastre was once one of those people desperate enough to seek hope in the illegal life in the United States. Now in her mid-twenties, Sastre works with the National Women and AIDS Risk Network Project in Phoenix. Like many of those she counsels in the hidden communities of the city, she is an amnesty applicant and a native of Mexico. She says cultural attitudes in Mexico and Central America make it impossible for many of those diagnosed HIV-positive to return. At the same time, attitudes and conventions in the immigrant community sometimes clash with safe-sex practices.

In many cases, religious beliefs label condoms as birth-control devices and therefore immoral. In some families, male authority is so unquestioned that the man dictates whether a condom is used. Many people don't understand that the HIV virus can be transmitted heterosexually. And, she says, "There is a lot of denial." She cites a case in which the woman refused to have sex with her husband if he wore a condom, even though she knew he had tested positive for the HIV virus.

Sastre works in the Project office of Phoenix director Jan Kenney, who also knows of people who tested positive and then chose not to complete their amnesty applications. She complains of divisiveness among local AIDS agencies and decries public attitudes toward the disease.

"There's not a lot of talk about this problem in Phoenix," she says, adding sarcastically, "because we don't have prostitution here, we don't have drugs here. We don't have AIDS here."

But, of course, they do. "There is a whole underground of people who chose not to apply," Kenney says, "who would probably have qualified if they did." The street talk was that if you tested positive, you might as well stay underground. "People felt very vulnerable," she says. "There are people dying of AIDS in this community who don't even know they have AIDS. They're not going to seek health care unless it's an emergency."

If you've got two gallons of water and you throw out a couple of drops, can you tell the difference?

That's the way D.A. Henderson, dean of the Johns Hopkins School of Hygiene and Public Health and former coordinator of the worldwide effort to eliminate smallpox, sees the issue of testing immigrants for the HIV virus. "We have 1.5 million people infected, and to add maybe a thousand more over a very large base is not very much," he says. "We are not effectively containing the disease."

"The street talk was that if you tested positive, you might as well stay underground."

Health officials and others argue that testing this immigrant population is a waste of money, and that the underground society it has created contradicts the program's original intent.

Those who choose to stay in the United States despite HIV infection will always face the possibility of developing AIDS. Because of the types of jobs they typically hold, they aren't likely to have health insurance and will end up relying on the American taxpayer. And there is always the danger that those who don't get counseling and education will unwittingly pass the virus to others. But by the time an illegal's fear of dealing with public institutions succumbs to his fear of dying, many advocates fear it will be too late.

Those who do return to their native countries face inadequate, outdated health care and education, as well as harsh cultural attitudes toward AIDS. In Mexico, infected people often are ostracized; others' access to health care is severely limited because clinical attendants are afraid of them, sometimes refusing to bring them food or wash them.

"The bitter irony is, where did they get the disease?" says attorney Crystal Williams of the American Immigration Lawyers Association in Washington, D.C. "They didn't get it in Peru. They got it in the United States. We're trying to send people back to their countries so they can spread the disease there."

One of the Lucky

Opponents of the testing program believe it would be better to incur the costs of granting the waivers and letting these people stay than to send them to uncertain fates back home. "I think anyone who looks at the balance sheet," says one Washington lawyer, "would come up with the conclusion that it would be in our best interests to grant these waivers."

For now, that is all that infected amnesty applicants have to hope for—that is, if they even know a waiver is possible.

Carlos, a Guatemalan immigrant in his late twenties, came to America more than ten years ago. He is one of the lucky ones. As a child, he says, he used to paint pictures of the Golden Gate Bridge and has wanted to come to the Bay Area, where he now lives, ever since reading about it as a teen-ager.

When he arrived he knew no English but learned quickly after landing his first job as a dishwasher in Los Angeles. Now self-employed, he hopes to run his own house-cleaning business some day. His mother doesn't know he has tested HIV-positive, doesn't even know he is gay, and he wants to keep it that way.

> ### "He was surprised to hear that . . . he was one of only four people to have been granted a waiver."

Carlos says he wasn't surprised when he got his waiver. "I've been lucky," he says. "I believe that if you don't do bad, you don't expect bad things to happen to you." He was surprised to hear that, at the time of our interview, he was one of only four people to have been granted a waiver.

"You know, it makes me wonder why," he says. "I don't understand—why me? Why not these other people? I was very confident I would get it, because I feel like I deserve it. I never felt like a stranger in this country."

He is perfectly healthy, he says, and he knows all about his condition and its ramifications. He hates going to AIDS counselors. "It's depressing," he says. "They make you feel like you're already dying." Carlos says he has better things to worry about, like paying the bills. He says he eats well, sleeps well, takes good care of himself. Why should he think he's sick?

"I get depressed sometimes—but then everybody does. There's too much I want to do before I die." His eyes moisten and he looks away momentarily.

Now that he has been granted the waiver, he says, "I feel good. It's my dream come true. San Francisco is my home. I belong here. Nobody will take me away from here until I die."

Chapter 4

How Can AIDS
Be Treated?

AIDS Treatment: An Overview

Geoffrey Cowley, Mary Hager, and Ruth Marshall

About the Authors: *Geoffrey Cowley is a senior editor at* Newsweek, *a weekly newsmagazine. Mary Hager works at* Newsweek's *Washington, D.C. bureau. Ruth Marshall works in the Paris bureau.*

Editor's Note: Perhaps no other disease in history has been the target of such intense study and research as has AIDS. Since the discovery of the virus in 1981, the world's scientific community has studied AIDS in an effort to make it a treatable rather than life-threatening sickness. While scientists have made much progress in prolonging the lives of AIDS patients with promising drugs such as AZT, they have yet to succeed in finding a cure.

While researchers struggle to find a medical cure, many AIDS patients are seeking other, nonmedical treatments for the disease. Among these treatments are dietary changes, meditation, and a reliance on ancient therapies such as acupuncture.

The following overview, written by Geoffrey Cowley of Newsweek *magazine, details how the AIDS virus debilitates the immune system. Cowley profiles several experimental AIDS drugs and provides an update on the treatment of AIDS as the disease enters its second decade.*

A sense of crisis is hard to sustain. It thrives on earthquakes and tornadoes, plane crashes and terrorist bombings. But forces that kill people one at a time have a way of fading into the psychic landscape. So, if you've stopped thinking of AIDS as an emergency, consider a few numbers. In 1984, when scientists identified the virus that causes the illness, fewer than 4,500 Americans

had been stricken. Today more than 3,000 cases of AIDS are reported every month in this country; the total tops 130,000. An estimated 1 million Americans are infected with the virus—and by the end of the decade, most of those people will be sick.

The AIDS epidemic is far from over. It's not even under control. "The worldwide situation is deteriorating," says Dr. Jonathan Mann, former director of the World Health Organization's Global Program on AIDS. "We are facing a decade in the 1990s that will be far more difficult than anything we saw in the 1980s." The WHO estimates that as of 1990, 700,000 people have developed AIDS worldwide and 6 million to 8 million have contracted the virus that causes it. By the end of the decade, an estimated 5 million to 6 million will be sick, and the total number infected may approach 20 million. Worse still, the situation isn't expected to stabilize for several more decades.

Already, the AIDS virus infects a third of the population in some parts of Africa. This nation's most desperate neighborhoods appear headed in the same direction. Regional surveys have turned up infection rates of 5 to 12 percent among pregnant women in the Bronx, 25 percent among young men surveyed in Newark, N.J. But the poor aren't the only ones suffering. Dr. June Osborn, chairman of the National Commission on AIDS, foresees a time when most Americans may know someone with AIDS. "By the end of the 1990s," she says, "people will be shaking their fists and saying, 'Why didn't you tell us?' That's going to hurt, because we did.". . .

> ## "The AIDS epidemic is far from over. It's not even under control."

No longer just a medical problem, AIDS has become a pock on the social order, a festering emblem of countless other ills. Federal spending for AIDS research and treatment has climbed to $1.6 billion in just nine years. Scientific progress has been brisk. Yet for many of the afflicted, here and throughout the world, minimal health care is still a distant hope.

"There are still unanswered questions about the human immunodeficiency virus."

Though AIDS is spread solely through the exchange of blood or other body fluids, local conditions have a lot to do with who gets sick and how. In Africa, the virus is transmitted almost exclusively through heterosexual contact. In Thailand—where the number of infected people has shot from 1,000 to roughly 50,000 in just three years—the epidemic apparently started among intravenous drug users and spread into the heterosexual community. In Eastern Europe, AIDS has been spreading mainly through unsafe medical practices.

The U.S. epidemic has always been concentrated in major cities, among gay men and IV [intravenous] drug users. But that pattern is changing as the epidemic matures. In 1989 AIDS incidence rose nearly four times as fast in the nation's smallest cities as in its largest ones. And while the number of new cases rose by 11 percent among gay males, it increased by 36 percent or more among heterosexuals and newborns. By the year 2000, says Dr. James Chin, an epidemiologist in charge of AIDS surveillance at the WHO, "heterosexual transmission will predominate in most industrial countries." The growth of the epidemic may be slower among heterosexuals than it has been among gays or IV drug users, but it will be implacable nonetheless. "AIDS is a sexually transmitted disease," says Dr. Robert Redfield of the Walter Reed Army Medical Center, "and the fact is that most of us in society are heterosexual."

Monogamous couples are not at risk, but there's no evidence that Americans are about to become wholly monogamous. Syphilis and gonorrhea—diseases that not only indicate unsafe sexual practices but facilitate the spread of the AIDS virus—have skyrocketed in recent years. At the same time, the crack epidemic has created a whole new class of high-risk heterosexuals: women who trade sex directly for the drug. "We've seen the rate of syphilis in various parts of the country quadruple because of sex associated with crack," says Don Des Jarlais of the Chemical Dependency Institute at New York's Beth Israel Hospital. "The same thing could happen with AIDS."

With or without crack, American teenagers are ripe targets for AIDS: they're already experiencing 2.5 million cases of sexually transmitted disease every year, and nearly a million unintended pregnancies. "We know their sexual behavior results in significant risk for infection," says Dr. Gary Noble of the federal Centers for Disease Control. Indeed, at least 20 percent of today's AIDS patients were probably infected as teens.

Americans at Risk

As long as we fail at sex education and drug-abuse treatment, millions of Americans will remain at risk. And clearly we are failing. Medically, though, the past decade has brought remarkable successes. No one had heard of AIDS when doctors started describing the syndrome in 1981. Since then, scientists have not only identified the human immunodeficiency virus (HIV) but learned a great deal about how it infects cells and ruins the immune system. The 1980s brought a diagnostic test, a safe blood supply and several useful treatments. Thanks to drugs like AZT and pentamidine, patients who would once have died within months of developing AIDS are now surviving a year or more.

In the short run, treating the myriad infections and cancers that actually kill AIDS patients is the surest way to extend their lives. Activists have long accused scientists, drug companies and federal agencies of neglecting these secondary complications, of preferring the higher drama of fighting the virus itself. The criticism has had an effect. Dr. Anthony Fauci, director of the National Institute of Allergy and Infectious Diseases (NIAID), says the proportion of federally funded AIDS studies relating to opportunistic infections has risen from 10 to 20 percent, and may eventually grow to 30 or 40 percent. Yet treating symptoms won't solve the problem. AIDS patients who survive early bouts with *pneumocystis carinii* pneumonia and other once lethal infections are now falling prey to an array of other maladies. Among San Francisco AIDS patients, the number of lymphomas rose by 48 percent in 1987 alone. Until the AIDS virus can be locked out of the body, or paralyzed from within, the plague will spread and the afflicted will die.

The epidemic has prompted a resurgence in the study of infectious disease. Antiviral drug research, long stagnant before AIDS struck, is now among the hottest fields in medicine. And the quest for a vaccine, though far from fruition, is proceeding briskly. Can this virus be stopped? What are the strategies? What are the obstacles? These turn out not to be simple questions, for the battle against AIDS is being fought inside the cell, amid genes and proteins and enzymes and antibodies. But the questions are worth grappling with. All of humanity has a stake in the answers.

What HIV Does to Cells

Just nine years ago, epidemic diseases were a thing of the past. Modern medicine, having subdued The Germ with vaccines and antibiotics, was busy saving us all from cancer and heart disease. Then came AIDS, and the realization that a devious bug could still cause a worldwide plague. At first no one knew what was causing the mysterious illness, but scientists in Paris and Washington soon linked it to an infectious agent known as a retrovirus. Today there are still unanswered questions about the human immunodeficiency virus, such as why it causes illness so much faster in some people than in others. But its basic mechanisms are now well understood.

HIV has no life of its own. Unlike a bacterium, it doesn't absorb nutrients, generate waste or reproduce by dividing. It's just a protein capsule containing two short strands of genetic material (RNA) and a few enzymes. It happens to use human cells to perpetuate itself. After infecting someone, HIV may spend 10 years or more quietly ensconced within various tissues and organs. But when activated, it turns certain immune cells into virus factories, which produce a flurry of new virus capsules and die. Other cells become infected in the process, and the immune system falls like a house of cards.

"Just [a decade] ago, epidemic diseases were a thing of the past."

The immune system is an elaborate, internal defense network that includes different types of blood cells. Among these immune cells, the ones that identify an intruder and authorize an attack on it are called T4 lymphocytes, or (imprecisely) "helper T cells."

Every T4 cell has appendages called CD4 receptors, through which it exchanges information with other immune cells. And it is through these CD4 receptors that HIV attacks. The outer shell of the HIV capsule (known as the envelope) is equipped with an appendage called gp120. This distinctive protein molecule happens to fit the CD4 receptor as a plug fits a socket. When the two molecules dock, the contents of the viral capsule—the RNA and the enzymes—flow freely into the cell's interior.

Once inside, HIV becomes a permanent feature of the cell. First, an enzyme called reverse transcriptase uses information encoded in the RNA to manufacture a double strand of DNA—a piece of software that can direct the cell to manufacture more virus. This DNA, known as the provirus, then integrates itself into the host cell's chromosomes. It represents just a tiny segment of the cell's genetic code. Once activated, however, it's the only segment that counts.

The trouble begins when the provirus starts directing enzymes in the host cell to produce new strands of viral RNA. These rogue pieces of RNA serve as a blueprint, from which other enzymes start churning out the raw material for new virus capsules. These raw materials (long protein molecules) get chopped into shorter pieces by an enzyme called protease. Those pieces then clip together to form new HIV particles, which burst from the surface of the host cell and float off to infect others. The host cell is killed in the process.

One reason HIV poses such a challenge is that the infection itself is not even theoretically curable: modern biologists, for all their ingenuity, are far from knowing how to purge unwanted DNA sequences from human chromosomes. Still, scientists are hopeful that by keeping the virus from replicating so wildly, they will gradually make it less deadly. Scores of researchers are working on drugs to interfere with HIV's production cycle at one stage or another. Twenty-one such drugs are now under development in this country alone. The hope is that they'll work, in some felicitous blend, to make AIDS a chronic, manageable condition, much like diabetes or high blood pressure.

"If we could vaccinate everyone, the epidemic might really be stopped."

So far, only one of these drugs has been approved as a treatment for AIDS. Zidovudine, or AZT, attacks the virus after it has wormed its way into the cell but before it has integrated itself into the host cell's chromosomes. Specifically, it impedes the "reverse transcription" of viral RNA into DNA. The only way HIV's reverse transcriptase enzyme can manufacture DNA is by gathering up chemical units called nucleosides and matching them to the pattern on the viral RNA. AZT looks just like one of these nucleosides. In

fact, reverse transcriptase prefers it to the real thing. But AZT turns out to have a slightly different structure. When it's clipped on to a growing chain of DNA, the next link doesn't fit and the whole production is foiled.

Conceived as a cancer treatment back in the 1960s, AZT found no use until 1986. It now earns the Burroughs Wellcome Co. well over $100 million a year. The big comeback started when scientists noted a decline in infection and death among AIDS patients taking a daily dose of 1,200 milligrams. Despite a number of side effects—ranging from headaches, vomiting and malaise to bone-marrow suppression and anemia—AZT sped through the drug-approval process in record time. In March 1987, the Food and Drug Administration approved it as a treatment for patients with symptoms of AIDS or with T4 counts below 200 (the normal range is 600 to 1,200). Since then, AZT has been found to work just as well at half the original dose, and federal guidelines have been changed to recommend the drug for any infected person whose T4 count dips below 500— even if no sickness has set in.

A Minor Adjustment

That may sound like a minor adjustment, but it pushes the number of potential AZT users in this country from 40,000 to more than 600,000. A panel convened by the National Institutes of Health made the early-treatment recommendation, after two studies showed that AZT could delay the initial appearance of AIDS. But many experts consider the move premature and potentially dangerous. They note that several ongoing studies have so far failed to show the same beneficial effect. Moreover, they say, the NIH studies didn't compare the advantages of early and late treatment. They compared early treatment with no treatment. "We don't know that it ultimately does you any good to delay crossing the 200 mark by a few months," says Dr. John Hamilton, chief of infectious diseases at the Durham, N.C., VA [Veterans' Administration] Medical Center and cochair of an AZT trial designed to answer that question. "If you're building up resistance to AZT by taking it early, when you're still feeling fine, you may be losing a crutch you could use later."

Even the proponents of early treatment agree that AZT leaves much to be desired. First, it's quite toxic: even with lower doses, nearly a third of those taking the drug develop grave bone-marrow problems within a year. Second, it's not cheap. Burroughs Wellcome has twice reduced the price but still charges $1.20 for every 100-mg capsule—more than $200 for a month's supply. Third, while it does help ward off opportunistic infections in AIDS patients, it doesn't prevent the outbreak of lymphomas or tumors such as Kaposi's sarcoma. Most important, it seems to become less effective as the virus mutates out of its range of action.

Researchers are hopeful that AZT's close relatives DDI and DDC, both now in clinical trials, will help address some of these problems. DDI and, especially, DDC are toxic in their own right: both cause a painful nerve irritation called peripheral neuropathy, and DDI can damage the pancreas. But they could provide alternatives for people who can't tolerate AZT or who develop resistance to it. Both drugs are also being tested in low-dose combinations with AZT. The hope is that patients will get cumulative benefits but, because of the lower doses, experience less toxicity and resistance. "The way to go," says Dr. Samuel Broder, head of the National Cancer Institute, "is not to discard drugs that show promise, even with side effects, but to find ways to use them more creatively."

Breaking the Cycle

AZT and its kin all attack HIV at the second stage of its life cycle—after it has entered the host cell but before it has integrated itself into the cell's DNA. But there are several other possibilities. One is to keep the virus from entering the cell in the first place. To do that, one would have to keep HIV from plugging its distinctive appendage—the gp120 envelope protein—into the CD4 receptors on target cells. Several laboratories have designed synthetic, free-floating CD4 receptors with just that thought in mind. In principle, flooding the blood with this "soluble CD4" should inactivate the virus by covering all its plugs before they find real sockets. That's exactly what happens in a test tube. There is no evidence yet on whether soluble CD4 will help infected people, but toxicity tests have shown no serious side effects. In an interesting variation on this same approach, the Upjohn Co. and others are now working on molecules that combine CD4 and a potent synthetic toxin. When the CD4 binds to the viral envelope proteins protruding from infected T4 cells, it's supposed to release the poison and kill them. Unfortunately, there is at least one large drawback to the whole CD4 approach. The molecule is very expensive to make, and it breaks down so fast that it has to be taken—by injection—every few hours.

"To be of real use, a preventive AIDS vaccine would need to have a lasting effect."

Suppose the virus eludes both CD4 and AZT, penetrating the cell and infiltrating the local DNA. There are still possibilities for checking its growth. Opportunity No. 3 arises shortly after the provirus (the integrated viral DNA) starts running off RNA copies of itself. The enzymes that manufacture the raw materials for new virus particles from this RNA use its chemical sequence as a blueprint. If the enzymes can't read the blueprint, they can't do their work. And it's possible—using genetically engineered "antisense" molecules—to make the blueprint illegible. By zipping itself onto a crucial segment of the viral RNA, an antisense molecule blots out the vital information, and protein production grinds to a halt.

Antisense represents a whole new approach to drug design, and HIV is not its only potential target. Traditionally, notes biochemist Jack Cohen of Georgetown University Laboratories, researchers have treated people with various organic compounds in the hope that one would prove therapeutic. With antisense, he says, "you figure out exactly what genetic process you need to alter and design a molecule accordingly." In test-tube experiments, antisense molecules have slowed production of the AIDS virus by 90 percent. The catch is that they're still difficult—and exceedingly expensive—to make. "We've been working on [an antisense drug] for a year," says Dr. Jeffrey Laurence of the Laboratory for AIDS Virus Research at Cornell University Medical College. "I'm promised that by the end of the summer we'll have enough to treat one mouse."

While awaiting affordable antisense, researchers are targeting still later stages in the viral life cycle. A fourth possible strategy is to keep HIV's protease enzyme from milling the construction materials into pieces that can form new virus particles. A number of companies have developed drugs that work at this stage, and human trials are expected to start. These "protease inhibitors" have performed well in test-tube experiments, and animal tests have turned up no serious side effects. That's not surprising. For unlike AZT and its kin, which disrupt a number of cellular processes, the protease inhibitors affect only a single enzyme. As a result, researchers expect them to be far less toxic.

"HIV is not a single, well-identified target."

In other labs, scientists are working with a fifth group of antiviral agents, known as interferons. These are antiviral chemicals produced naturally by cells. Drugs that step up production of interferons can help control the growth of tumors—and at high doses, the same drugs seem to impede the budding of new virus particles from infected cells. NIH researchers conclude that alpha interferon can have a "significant antiviral effect" in patients whose immune systems are still largely intact. In a small trial involving asymptomatic patients, the investigators found that 41 percent of those getting the drug became "culture negative," meaning the virus dropped temporarily out of sight in their blood samples. Only 13 percent of the untreated subjects became culture negative (a common but temporary occurrence). Moreover, T4 counts held steady in the treated patients but declined slightly in the others. There is a catch, of course: the treatment was so toxic that a third of those receiving it dropped out of the trial.

A Vaccine in the '90s?

Antiviral drugs aren't the only hope for eliminating AIDS. If we could vaccinate everyone, the epidemic might really be stopped. Vaccines have triumphed famously over other viral diseases, from measles to smallpox to polio. The approach consists of exposing people to a virus in some harmless form to provoke a natural immune response without causing serious illness. Unfortunately, the AIDS virus is well designed to foil that approach. One problem is that no one knows what natural immunity would consist of. Infected people produce a flurry of antibodies directed at different parts of the virus, but those people don't end up safe from future infection. They end up dead, as the virus destroys the system producing the antibodies. It's possible that one or more of those antibodies *would* prevent infection in healthy people, but there's no guarantee. A second problem is that HIV is not a single, well-identified target. Like a cold virus, it varies widely and changes fast. There are dozens of strains of HIV, and a vaccine that worked against one might prove worthless against another.

Despite these and other obstacles, the quest for a vaccine is gaining momentum. "A year ago I wouldn't have been able to say whether we would ever have a vaccine," says Fauci, of the NIAID. "I think most scientists are now reasonably optimistic that some time, hopefully in the 1990s, we will." The change of heart stems from a handful of recent experiments. Two research teams have succeeded at protecting monkeys from SIV (the simian AIDS virus), and two other groups have protected chimpanzees from HIV itself. Still other scientists have shown that infected women who produce large amounts of a particular antibody are less likely to bear infected children—a finding that could lead directly to a prenatal vaccine. In the monkey trials, conducted at primate-research centers in Massachusetts and Louisiana, scientists injected animals with whole, inactivated SIV to produce an immune response and then challenged them with unadulterated virus to see what would happen. The New England researchers managed to protect two out of six monkeys from infection, the Louisiana group eight out of nine.

The chimpanzee experiments involved a different approach. Researchers at two biotechnology companies—Pasteur-Vaccines in Paris and Genentech in South San Francisco—inoculated their animals with "subunits" of the human AIDS virus before injecting them with the whole agent. (HIV infects chimps but doesn't cause illness.) In the Pasteur experiments, two chimps resisted infection after receiving cocktails of several HIV fragments. The Genentech vaccine, based on a fragment of HIV's gp120 envelope protein, also protected both of the chimps that received it.

"Two chimps resisted infection after receiving cocktails of several HIV fragments."

However impressive, none of these feats means that school kids will soon be lining up for inoculations against AIDS. To be of real use, a preventive AIDS vaccine would need to have a lasting effect against a wide range of virus strains. The animals in these experiments were tested at the peak of their immune responses, and they received the same strains of virus they had encountered in their vaccines. "If we had a simple vaccine that worked in chimps," says Marc Girard, the virologist who directed the

French experiments, "it would be five years before it could be used in man, with toxicity tests and all that. And we're very far from that takeoff point." Even a vaccine that proved effective in chimps might perform miserably in people. And finding out would be a challenge in itself, since human subjects can't be purposely exposed.

One virtue of trying to block mother-to-child transmission is that success is easier to gauge. Since 30 to 40 percent of the children born to infected women are themselves HIV positive, a vaccine that changed that ratio would clearly be making a difference. No one has yet tested such an agent, but Dr. Arye Rubinstein, director of the Center for AIDS Research at New York's Albert Einstein College of Medicine, is rapidly laying the groundwork.

Infected Mothers

Intrigued by the fact that many infected mothers *don't* bear infected children, Rubinstein and his colleagues set out to identify specific antibodies that might set those women apart. In a study of 15 AIDS pregnancies, the researchers described such an antibody. Of the 11 women in the study who bore infected babies, not one was producing an antibody directed at the HIV envelope protein's so-called principal neutralizing domain (PND), a short molecular segment that is common to many different strains of the virus. By contrast, the PND antibody was present in three of the four mothers who bore healthy babies. "We suspect the fourth mother had the antibody," Rubinstein says, "because it showed up in the baby."

The PND antibody doesn't seem to help people once they're infected; the mothers who produce it suffer the same fate as those who don't. But if that antibody is the reason some babies are born uninfected, then protecting others might be fairly simple: you would simply inoculate mothers with the tiny piece of the virus that engenders it. Dr. Yair Devash of Ortho Diagnostics has already fabricated the viral fragment, and Rubinstein has incorporated it into a vaccine that could be given to pregnant patients.

He's now testing it for toxicity in animals and expects to start a human trial later this year. If the vaccine were to succeed at protecting babies, he notes, it might protect other uninfected people as well.

Preventing infection is not the only goal of vaccine research. Scientists are also testing vaccinelike agents designed to boost the defenses of people who are already infected. These researchers study the body's production of antibodies to different parts of HIV, then try to amplify the most useful responses. Several preliminary studies show promise. Dr. Robert Redfield of the Walter Reed Army Medical Center has observed that when some patients are exposed to a synthetic fragment of gp160 (a large envelope protein that includes gp120), they produce antibodies directed specifically at that fragment and their T4 cells die less quickly. Allan Goldstein of George Washington University has sparked potentially useful immune activity by exposing people to a piece of the virus core. And Jonas Salk, inventor of the polio vaccine, has reported beneficial effects in about half of the patients he has treated with whole virus stripped of its envelope.

Again, because HIV can hide in places that are beyond the reach of the immune system, none of these therapeutic vaccines could root out the infection completely. But as Salk observed recently, winning and losing are not the only alternatives in the battle against AIDS. A negotiated settlement may still be possible.

Raging Epidemic

AIDS, unfortunately, is not just a medical challenge. Science will eventually produce better treatments, maybe even a vaccine. The question is whether these costly advances will reach the populations most in need. It's clear that the burden of sick people will rise steeply during the 1990s, but not at all clear that the world's health systems are prepared to respond. "My fear," says Dr. Ruth Osborn, of the National Commission on AIDS, "is that [scientific progress] will be overwhelmed by a health-care disaster."

All over the world, the epidemic is raging most fiercely within groups that are most removed from education and health care. One major exception is the U.S. gay population. Since the epidemic began, homosexual men have fought discrimination, demanded treatment and research, and reaped the rewards of safe sex and blood testing. In large groups that have been followed over the past decade, the proportion becoming infected each year (not developing AIDS but contracting the virus) has fallen from 7.5 percent in the early 1980s to 1 or 2 percent today. Studies also suggest that infected gay men are living longer thanks to AZT and new treatments for secondary infections.

> ## "Infected gay men are living longer thanks to AZT and new treatments."

The experience of inner-city minorities could hardly be more different. Infection rates have not declined substantially among intravenous drug users. And as the epidemic spreads to their sex partners and children, new treatments are making little difference. "These people are intensely poor, alienated, powerless," says Dr. Harold Freeman of Columbia University and Harlem Hospital. Last fall Freeman coauthored a study showing that black men in Harlem were less likely to reach 65 than men in Bangladesh. The data were collected before AIDS even struck. "This is a disaster on top of a disaster," he says. "The people who are suffering need to cry out. But the people involved in this problem have no voice."

Minority women who are infected by their partners may *avoid* seeking treatment for fear they will lose their children to foster homes if their illness is discovered. Maria, a 31-year-old Hispanic woman in Chicago, is the widow of the man who infected her after contracting the virus through his own drug use. Now, with three children to care for (one of them HIV positive), she is suffering full-blown AIDS. Yet she and her family keep her illness a secret. They fear that if others knew, the children would be excluded from school and they from their jobs and their church congregation. Maria's family *curandera*, a traditional healer who treats patients with herbs, incantations and prayer, believes persistent illness is a sign that the sufferer has strayed too far from Latino culture and is being punished by God.

Lagging Health Care

Inner cities aren't the only places health care is lagging. Consider rural Georgia, where AIDS rates have soared in recent years. None of the 14 hospitals in the Southeast Health Unit, a 16-county area roughly the size of Massachusetts, can afford to buy the $80,000 machine needed to test patients' T4 counts. "The problem is real critical now," says Dr. Ted Holloway, director of the Southeast Health Unit. "There is a limited amount of AZT that we can give to indigent patients, but we have to have a T-cell count." The problem is compounded by a lack of physicians willing to treat the disease. "No one wants to be the AIDS doctor," says Holloway. "If you set up a service, people are going to come from miles away."

"No single government initiative is going to solve the AIDS crisis."

Because people who are infected with HIV can't buy private insurance, Medicaid has become a major source of care. Roughly 40 percent of AIDS patients end up on Medicaid, and the federal portion of AIDS-related Medicaid spending has soared from $10 million in 1983 to an anticipated $670 million. Yet many infected people who need the assistance don't qualify: besides being poor, one has to be over 65 or a member of a family with dependent children or

totally disabled. For many people, that means no medical care until total disability sets in. When AIDS patients finally do qualify for Medicaid, they're often hospitalized for illnesses that might have been prevented through earlier intervention.

To eliminate the Catch-22, Congress is now considering legislation that would let states approve outpatient services for infected people as soon as treatment is needed to prevent a decline in health. And the House and Senate have recently passed bills that, if signed into law, would provide an additional $600 million to $700 million for AIDS care each year. To Ruth Osborn, head of the National Commission on AIDS, such efforts are mere "fingers in the dike." The federally appointed commission issued a report to the president, decrying a lack of leadership from the federal government and repeating its demand for a national AIDS plan with clear roles for federal agencies, state governments and the private sector. To date the report has elicited a *pro forma* letter of appreciation.

A Global Crisis

No single government initiative is going to solve the AIDS crisis. The crisis is global, and it is magnifying social problems that were already enormous. But complacency would be a mistake. Jonathan Mann, the former WHO official, argues that the world has actually been lucky with the AIDS epidemic so far. Had the virus had a longer latency, the disease might just now be coming to light, in a much greater number of people. The next such virus—and there will most assuredly be others—may be more devious than this one. What HIV teaches us about retroviruses, and about the necessity of education and basic health care for all, could turn out to be valuable. "It takes a lot of hubris to imagine that this couldn't happen again," says Mann. "It could be happening right now."

How Can AIDS Be Treated?

Medical Methods Can Effectively Treat AIDS

AZT and Other Drugs Prolong the Lives of AIDS Patients
Vaccines May Effectively Treat AIDS
Early Intervention Can Extend the Lives of AIDS Patients
The CD4 Synthetic Protein Can Fight the AIDS Virus

AZT and Other Drugs Prolong the Lives of AIDS Patients

Douglas Sery

About the Author: *Douglas Sery, who now lives in Germany, is the former editorial coordinator for* Editorial Research Reports, *a weekly publication analyzing national issues.*

Since 1987 there has been a single approved drug to fight the AIDS virus—azidothymidine, or AZT. Invented in 1964 as a cancer therapy, the drug proved ineffective for its initial task, but in 1974 AZT was rediscovered as an effective agent against retroviruses, the family of viruses of which AIDS is a member. Nevertheless, it languished again until the mid-1980s, when the National Cancer Institute began a screening program for potential AIDS drugs. In 1985 the first human trials were begun with 33 patients. Although the study was small, the results were encouraging, and more testing was undertaken. By early 1986 the drug's effectiveness was so apparent that the trials were stopped; patients who had been given a placebo were switched to AZT. Later in the year, the drug received federal approval as a treatment for AIDS.

Although AZT was not a cure, it did represent some hope for the thousands of Americans who had AIDS. Unfortunately, there are hundreds of thousands more who are infected with HIV but have not come down with AIDS. AIDS has a long dormancy period, and people who were infected with HIV had little choice but to wait for what seemed like the inevitable. In 1989, they got a

Douglas Sery, "Good News and Bad News About AIDS," *Editorial Research Report*, vol. 2, no. 13 (1989), pp. 554-566. Reprinted by permission of Congressional Quarterly Inc.

double dose of good news: AZT apparently can *stave off* AIDS, and, for people who are infected with HIV but show no symptoms of the disease, it seems to work quite well in relatively low, and therefore less expensive, doses. It all amounted to what Health and Human Services Secretary Louis S. Sullivan called a "significant milestone in the battle to change AIDS from a fatal disease to a treatable one."

The news came from two nationwide clinical trials coordinated by the National Institute of Allergies and Infectious Diseases (NIAID). The first study, known as Protocol 016, began in August 1987. It involved 713 people infected with HIV. All of them had early AIDS-Related Complex, or ARC, a fuzzy midpoint between asymptomatic HIV infection and full-blown AIDS, with symptoms such as diarrhea, chronic rash, and thrush, a mouth infection. Also, all of the patients showed reduced counts of T4 cells, white blood cells that are an important part of the immune system. A normal T4 cell count ranges between 800 and 1,200. The patients in the study all had counts between 200 and 800. A patient with full-blown AIDS typically has a count of less than 200.

The patients, who were from 29 locations around the country, were split into two different groups. One group received 1200 to 1500 milligrams of AZT a day—a normal dosage for patients with full-blown AIDS—and the other group received a placebo.

> ## "Although AZT was not a cure, it did represent some hope for the thousands of Americans who had AIDS."

Thirty-six patients who received the placebo developed AIDS, but only 14 of the patients taking AZT came down with the full-blown disease. By showing that early treatment with AZT could slow the onset of AIDS in people showing only symptoms of ARC, the NIAID estimated that between 100,000 to 200,000 people infected with HIV could benefit from the drug—up to five times as many Americans as have AIDS.

There was scarcely time to react to that good news before there was more. Just two weeks after NIAID released the results of Protocol 016, it released the results of another promising study, this one involving 3,200 people who were infected with HIV but showed *no* symptoms.

The second study, called Protocol 019, began in July 1987 with two groups of subjects. Neither group showed symptoms, but one had T4 cell counts of less than 500, and the other had T4 cell counts of more than 500. In each group, some patients were given 500mg of AZT per day, some were given 1500mg, and the rest were given a placebo.

"Like AZT, ddI appears to prevent the AIDS virus from replicating."

Of the 1,300 people with low T4 cell counts, those taking AZT were almost half as likely as those taking a placebo to develop AIDS or complications associated with AIDS. As a result, NIAID estimated, about 400,000 more Americans could benefit from AZT treatment—in addition to the 100,000 to 200,000 extra beneficiaries recognized by Protocol 016 and the approximately 42,000 with full-blown AIDS.

Perhaps just as important, Protocol 019 showed that patients taking the lower 500mg dose did just as well as those taking the higher level. And that was good news on the medical as well as the financial front.

Since AZT's approval in 1987, there have been two major drawbacks to its use. The first was AZT's toxicity. Between 40 percent and 80 percent of all AIDS patients who have taken AZT have had to discontinue treatment because of side effects such as anemia or bone-marrow suppression brought on by the drug. Although both studies showed that infected individuals

without full-blown AIDS had fewer serious side effects anyway—less than 5 percent of the patients in the first study, for example—virtually none of the patients receiving the lower 500mg dose of AZT in the second study had any serious side effects (3 percent reported some nausea, but not serious problems).

The Cost of AZT

The effectiveness of AZT at lower levels was also important in regard to the second drawback of AZT—its cost. At first, a full 1200mg daily dose of AZT cost about $10,000 per year. The manufacturer soon cut the cost to about $8,000, and in 1989 cut it again to about $6,400. But it is still one of the most expensive drugs on the market. And even though the cost for infected individuals without full-blown AIDS will be $3,000 or less per year, that is still a hefty amount for treatment year after year.

In cutting the price by 20 percent—from $1.50 per capsule to $1.20 per capsule—Burroughs Wellcome, the drug's manufacturer, said it was reacting to a sudden increase in demand for the drug. But the high price has long been a matter of protests, and a spokeswoman for the company, Karen Collins, told the *New York Times* that the protests were a factor in the price-cut decision. "We are certainly mindful of the needs of the patients and the desire for a price change in the medical community," she said.

Critics of Burroughs Wellcome said they were pleased with the price cut, but they said the company could and should do much more. Sidney Wolf of the interest group Public Citizen, for example, accused Burroughs Wellcome of continuing to make an "immoral, unethical, obscene amount of profit." The company has never released details about its costs of researching and producing the drug, but independent estimates place the cost of manufacturing each capsule anywhere between 7 and 53 cents—far below what the company charges for it.

Whatever the cost, the news about the apparent effectiveness of AZT was extremely encouraging. But there are caveats. First, AZT does not represent a "cure" for AIDS. And second, there unfortunately are some indications that the body can develop a resistance to the effects of AZT. A study published in *Science* magazine in 1989 showed increased levels of resistance to AZT in AIDS patients who had been taking the drug for at least six months. In some cases, the patients were 100 times more resistant to the effects of AZT on the AIDS virus than they had been when they began taking the drug. This is a particular concern in light of the new studies, which indicate that many people may be taking AZT for much longer periods of time, although no one knows whether infected individuals without full-blown AIDS will experience the same resistance

Thus far, AZT has shown the most promise in fighting the AIDS virus. In fact, it is the only drug the FDA [Food and Drug Administration] has approved for that purpose. Many other drugs, however, are now undergoing testing. Among the most promising are these:

• Dideoxyinosine (ddI). On Sept. 28, 1989, the government announced that ongoing tests of this chemical relative of AZT were so encouraging that it would make the drug widely available while the safety and efficacy trials continued. According to Kathryn Bloom of Bristol-Myers Co., which holds the license to manufacture ddI, the expanded distribution is "conceptually very much the same" as the government's so-called "parallel-track plan." Under parallel tracking, which was announced by the government in 1989, testing of promising drugs would continue in rigorous trials while the drugs were simultaneously distributed to patients who were not taking part in the trials. . . .

Encouraging Results

Like AZT, ddI appears to prevent the AIDS virus from replicating. A study published in *Science* by researchers from the National Cancer Institute showed encouraging results. Of the 26 patients enrolled in the study, 13 exhibited an increase in immune system cells and a decrease in the AIDS virus. Also, a number of the patients

reported they were less fatigued and were gaining weight. Another favorable sign was that the drug showed fewer side effects than AZT. However, the Department of Health and Human Services, in making the ddI announcement, noted that the drug does have some serious side effects—painful nerve damage and damage to the pancreas—at high doses, but the side effects appear to be reversible if they are detected early and the drug is stopped.

"If there could ever be a magic bullet for HIV disease, it's CD4."

Under the plan, the drug will be tested against AZT on about 2,600 people with AIDS or ARC in 50 sites around the country, according to Bristol-Myers. It also will be given to people not in the test who cannot take AZT or whose disease is progressing despite taking AZT. All the patients taking the drug, in and out of the formal trials, will receive it free of charge. After it is approved, Bristol-Myers will be allowed to charge for the drug, but a second approved AIDS drug could provide competition for AZT and, therefore, keep down the price of both drugs.

AIDS activists have been pressing for parallel tracking for a long time. They argue that with a fatal disease like AIDS, patients and their doctors should be allowed to assume the risk of experimental treatment. FDA Commissioner Frank Young, in announcing the ddI distribution plan, seemed to agree with the activists when he said, "The AIDS epidemic is extraordinary, and it must be met with extraordinary means." Mark Harrington of the New York-based AIDS Coalition To Unleash Power (ACT-UP) called the decision "a good precedent [to] build on."

Some scientists expressed concern, however, about the possible problems that widespread distribution of unproven drugs could cause. "My guess is we will see some late-arriving side effects, and some price will be paid," said Dr. Jere Goyan, a former FDA commissioner and now dean of the school of pharmacology at the University of California at San Francisco. "The question is how high a price will society have to pay? Suppose someone who experiences side effects sues and wins? Maybe this is the right experiment to do, but I hope in doing it we don't destroy the clinical trials, and lose the information that will tell us whether this drug works."

• Dideoxycytidine (ddC). This drug, a relative of ddI, is further along in clinical trials than ddI. Hoffman LaRoche, the manufacturer of ddC, began tests in July 1989 at 25 sites around the country. About 600 patients are participating in the study. Although ddI is used by itself, ddC is used in combination with AZT, in order to lower the necessary dose of AZT to temper AZT's potential toxicity.

• CD4. CD4 has potential both for preventing HIV from infecting immune cells and for killing infected cells. CD4 is a protein on the surface of certain immune system cells that HIV infects and destroys. The virus uses the protein as an entry point into the immune cells. Initially, scientists manufactured the synthetic version of the molecule in the hope that it would act as a biological sponge, soaking up the AIDS virus and keeping it away from the natural CD4. However, early results showed that the synthetic protein had a short lifespan, which meant that the drug would either have to be given in extremely large doses or almost continuously. In February 1989, scientists reported a novel approach to treating HIV. Attaching a human antibody to the synthetic protein, they created an artificial antibody with a strong response to HIV. Although natural antibodies have proved ineffective against the AIDS virus, the artificial antibodies, called immunoadhesins, stimulate responses in the immune system that seem to be effective against the virus. There is some fear, though, that an infusion of antibodies would increase the risk of HIV infection in some cells. As of yet, that fear hasn't been realized.

While immunoadhesins are still in prelimi-

nary trials—so far they have been tested only in the test tube and in animals—there are a couple of reasons why the new drug is so promising. Immunoadhesins last more than 200 times longer than CD4 used by itself. And, unlike many experimental drugs, if initial trials with the immunoadhesins fail, the drug can be redesigned to compensate for mistakes. For example, a Swiss study showed that a different class of antibodies could be "1,000-fold more effective" in its inhibitory effect on HIV. CD4's promise as an effective AIDS treatment was endorsed by noted AIDS researcher Dr. Robert Gallo, who said at the Fifth International AIDS Conference in Montreal, "If there could ever be a magic bullet for HIV disease, it's CD4."

Other AIDS Drugs

• GLQ223, or Compound Q. The purified form of a Chinese cucumber root, GLQ223 may be the first drug to kill only the cells harboring the AIDS virus. The drug, which has been used for centuries in China to induce abortions, attracted some adverse publicity because three patients died in connection with an unofficial test of the drug. There was also some concern that AIDS patients had been acquiring unpurified samples of the drug, which can be fatal. Despite the furor, Project Inform, the organization that funded the unofficial study, is now working together with Genelabs, the manufacturer of GLQ223, and the FDA.

"AIDS is an indirect killer."

AIDS is an indirect killer. It attacks the immune system, making the body easily susceptible to other diseases. It is those other diseases that eventually cause death.

For that reason, while researchers scramble for ways to defeat the virus, they also are moving toward new ways to battle the infections and diseases that tend to accompany AIDS. One of the most common of these opportunistic infections is *pneumocystis carinii* pneumonia (PCP). And on June 15, 1989, the FDA approved the use of the drug pentamidine in aerosol form as a prophylactic against PCP.

Drug Trials

Although pentamidine has been approved for use intravenously since 1984, doctors and patients have been experimenting with it in an aerosolized form for just as long. Treatment with intravenous pentamidine was effective, but patients often experienced adverse reactions to the drug that required them to be taken off of the treatment. Side effects from aerosolized pentamidine have been minimal.

In February 1989, the FDA gave aerosolized pentamidine a license as an investigational drug, thus approving its use in certain conditions. Then the drug skipped the traditional trials necessary for conditional approval. Four months later, after additional FDA trials, it was given full approval for use as a treatment for PCP.

The drug is approved for use in patients who have experienced at least one bout of PCP or who have a diminished immune system. The drug is relatively expensive, around $300 a month, not including the cost of administering the drug, according to Dr. Peter Hawley, medical director of the Whitman-Walker Clinic, in Washington, D.C. Because pentamidine now has been approved by the FDA, private insurance generally will pay for those who are covered.

Vaccines May Effectively Treat AIDS

Peter Radetsky

About the Author: *Peter Radetsky teaches science writing at the University of California at Santa Cruz. He has written numerous articles for* Discover, *a monthly science magazine.*

Murray Gardner is excited. He paces his office, gesticulating vigorously. Gardner directs the Center for AIDS Research at the University of California at Davis, one of the front-runners in the race toward the ultimate weapon against AIDS—a vaccine. "Scientists who want to get in on the vaccine effort are suddenly coming out of the woodwork," he exclaims. "They're coming at me from all directions."

The telephone rings: a Swedish pharmaceutical company is on the line, eager to work with the Davis research team. Three other calls await Gardner's attention. For the past several years the 60-year-old researcher has played a somewhat evangelical role, as he puts it, boosting morale and bringing a message of hope to a despondent flock of AIDS vaccine researchers. Now, with the announcements of the first real successes in the field, Gardner's message is falling on very receptive ears. "They just point me somewhere, and I go and talk," he says. "I feel like a nonstop mouth."

Indeed, the world desperately wants to hear what Gardner has to say. For the first time, after millions of dollars and half a decade of intense effort, a vaccine against HIV, the lethal human immunodeficiency virus, is beginning to look like a real possibility. The optimism in scientific

Peter Radetsky, "Closing In on an AIDS Vaccine," *Discover,* September 1990. Copyright © 1990 Discover Publications. Reprinted with permission.

circles is guarded but genuine.

"Over the past several years, the feeling was we might never get a vaccine against HIV," says Dani Bolognesi, a virologist at Duke University Medical Center and one of the first to do AIDS vaccine research. Earlier prototypes had by and large met with disappointment. Although they stimulated the immune system to make antibodies, they elicited neither enough antibodies nor the right kind, apparently, to immobilize the elusive virus. "We felt we probably couldn't dominate the virus, given all its evasive strategies," says Bolognesi. "But now that pessimism has faded. It's no longer a question of whether there will ever be a vaccine. I think it's within reach."

The codiscoverer of the AIDS virus, Robert Gallo of the National Cancer Institute, agrees. "There is a real glimmer of hope now," he says. "A couple of years ago, nobody held out much of a glimmer at all."

Some of the most involved participants in the effort, however, aren't talking—except, perhaps, among themselves. They are members of a hardy, abundant, easily bred monkey species called rhesus macaques, and at Davis 3,000 of them scoot about on 300 acres of fertile farmland set in the Sacramento Valley. These animals and their kin at primate centers around the country are the reason for much of the new optimism concerning AIDS vaccines.

> ## "Scientists who want to get in on the vaccine effort are suddenly coming out of the woodwork."

Why monkeys? Because monkeys, researchers discovered in 1985, are also prey to a type of AIDS. The culprit is the simian immunodeficiency virus, or SIV, which under the electron microscope is virtually indistinguishable from the virus that causes the human disease. "You can hardly tell the two apart," says Gardner. "They're the same size, same shape. The simian virus enters the cell using the same receptor as does HIV, causes disease in the same way, and as far as we know, provokes the same immune response in the host."

But whereas humans may not exhibit the first signs of AIDS for as much as ten years, monkeys show symptoms in a matter of months, typically succumbing to their disease in little more than a year. That sad fact has made them ideal subjects for experimental vaccines. "The macaques are the bridge between test tubes and humans that we simply have to have," says Gardner. "We feel that if vaccines work in them, they're going to work in people."

"There exists not simply one strain of the AIDS virus but many."

And vaccines have begun to work. First out with promising results was Ronald Desrosiers at the New England Regional Primate Research Center near Boston. In August 1989 Desrosiers published a study showing that of six monkeys he and his colleagues had vaccinated, two later resisted infection when injected with SIV. Then, in December 1989, Michael Murphey-Corb of the Delta Regional Primate Research Center outside New Orleans reported that of nine monkeys vaccinated at her facility, eight had resisted infection. Finally, in April 1990, Gardner and his colleagues at the California Primate Center in Davis revealed that all three monkeys injected with a prototype vaccine had successfully fought off the virus. They, like the other monkeys that responded well to vaccination, continue to remain virus-free.

The strategy that worked for each of these groups was surprisingly straightforward. Unlike most of the previous, failed vaccine efforts, it involved no slick genetic-engineering methods to make vaccines from mere pieces of the virus. Instead, all three primate centers reverted to the tried-and-true approach of using a whole virus that had been killed. The virus could no longer

cause disease but could fool the immune system into making an arsenal of antibodies able to recognize the live virus, latch onto it, and put it out of commission. It was, as Gardner likes to say, the classical approach to making vaccines, the one that gave us the Salk polio vaccine. Only the unfamiliarity of the virus itself held up the work for so long. HIV was an enemy no one had grappled with before, and it took several years of painstaking effort to culture the virus en masse, to test different killing strategies, and to work out vaccine recipes (which contain not only killed virus but immune-system enhancers known as adjuvants).

After vaccination the monkeys in these tests were injected with ten times the amount of virus needed to infect them, an amount that simulated an infectious dose in a human. When word spread that many of these animals had responded by making antibodies that would ward off infection, you could almost hear the collective sigh of relief. "People had been throwing up their hands, saying, 'My God, there's no hope, we can't do it,'" recalls Gardner. "Now, finally, we had something to build on. Starting with a positive result is a lot better than wallowing around looking for one. We've had enough of that."

Despite the euphoria, these successes are clearly just a beginning. The vaccines have shown that human protection might be possible, but by their very nature they illustrate a number of problems that remain to be solved.

Problems of Experiments

The first is a risk inherent to all killed-virus vaccines. Suppose by accident some virus escapes being killed? The 1950s witnessed just such a catastrophe when a manufacturing error loosed into the population a number of doses of Salk vaccine that contained live virus; they caused a rash of vaccine-induced polio cases that almost derailed the fight against the disease.

With AIDS the consequences of such a mistake could be even more devastating. All viruses subvert cells by ordering them to make new viral offspring instead of new cells. But the AIDS virus takes subversion one step further: it not only invades the cell, it splices its genes into those of the cell and then hides there indefinitely, invisible to the immune system. All it might take to cause disease, then, is a single escapee, just one live virus. Says Desrosiers, "Once HIV gets a foot in the door and infects a single cell in your body, it's there for life. It might take one year, it might take five years, but when the virus reproduces it will probably get you."

That's why most researchers, including Gardner, contend that the eventual goal must be to devise a vaccine lacking any viral genes whatsoever. And that means continuing the effort to develop a vaccine that uses only pieces of the virus to trick the immune system into thinking it's under attack by the whole thing.

The second problem is that the monkey experiments were a tame reflection of what goes on in the real world. "It's important to remember," says Desrosiers, "that these experiments were done under highly idealized lab conditions. We tried to stack the deck in our favor, so as to get vaccine protection." For example, the macaques were challenged with live virus soon after they were vaccinated and at the peak of their protection. And they were challenged with only one virus strain, the same one used to make the vaccine.

Yet in reality the AIDS virus is highly variable. At least 20 different strains are known to exist. While all the strains resemble one another, they differ in specific ways by as much as 20 percent. And they are continuing to change, mutating more quickly than any other virus known. A practical vaccine will have to deal with this knotty problem of variability, perhaps by incorporating a "cocktail" of different strains or some stable feature that is common to them all.

Finally, the monkeys were exposed to live virus only by injection, a mode of transmission that most closely mimics the experience of intravenous-drug users or other recipients of contaminated blood. In these circumstances the virus enters the bloodstream as a free-floating parti-

cle. An effective vaccine, therefore, must produce the kind of antibodies that circulate in the blood, ready to neutralize the invader before it can infect cells. But in reality the most common means of human infection is sex. And during sex the virus doesn't slip into the bloodstream; rather, it directly infects cells in the mucous membranes of the sexual organs. Nor during sex, does the virus necessarily enter free-floating; it can also arrive hidden inside cells in semen.

"Long absent from the vaccine wars, [Jonas] Salk has returned to launch an ambitious campaign against AIDS."

Stopping this route of infection calls for cellular immunity, a quite distinct arm of the immune system that employs antibodies in the fluid surrounding mucous membranes as well as marauding white blood cells called killer T cells. Whether the SIV vaccines can also call up this army is still not known, but all three primate centers are planning to find out.

A Slice of Virus

Macaques are not the only animals vaccine researchers are using. For while rhesus macaques succumb to a simian variant of the AIDS virus, our closest genetic cousin, the chimpanzee, can be infected by HIV itself. But chimps, which are on the endangered species list, can be used only in very small numbers and with the utmost of care. Moreover, although they're susceptible to infection by HIV, as far as researchers can tell, chimps simply don't come down with disease— they don't get AIDS. In fact, until Scott Putney came on the scene, few people had gotten very far with chimps at all.

Putney, a 36-year-old molecular biologist, heads the AIDS vaccine program at Repligen, a pharmaceutical company in Cambridge, Massachusetts. His work paved the way for the development of the first vaccine to protect an uninfected chimp from HIV, in the fall of 1989.

"It's not a perfect experiment," Putney says. "But it's very promising." Moreover, the goal of his effort is to develop a vaccine for humans that employs not the whole virus, but merely a tiny, synthesized portion of its outer surface. Such a vaccine could be effective, economical, and because it contains no viral genes at all, absolutely safe.

Under the electron microscope HIV resembles a tiny sphere studded with protruding proteins. These protrusions are made up of an outer knoblike part, dubbed gp120, and a smaller protein, gp40, that anchors the knob to the cell membrane. The entire unit bears the designation gp160 and serves as a docking mechanism: it attaches to receptors on the cells the AIDS virus attacks.

Putney and his colleagues' first step was to mass-produce these "envelope" proteins in the laboratory, which they did by inserting the appropriate viral genes into bacteria: the bugs then dutifully manufactured millions of copies of the proteins. Next the researchers needed to verify that it was indeed these proteins and not some other part of the virus that elicited antibodies. To do that, they injected the proteins into a variety of animals. "We used goats, rabbits, guinea pigs, mice," says Putney. "All made antibodies to the proteins."

> ## "What can provoke an immune response in an infected person might do even better in an uninfected person."

The next step was to check whether the antibodies could actually stop HIV from infecting cells. "We sent samples to Gallo's lab and to Bolognesi's lab at Duke," recalls Putney. "They mixed the antibodies in a test tube with the virus, then took that mixture and tried to infect human immune cells." Within a week the labs had returned their verdict: no infection. What

that meant, says Putney, was that the proteins had elicited virus-neutralizing antibodies, and thus the proteins alone, rather than the entire virus, might serve as the heart of a vaccine.

But that was just the beginning. Although Putney had identified a tiny fragment of a microscopic virus, he wanted to fine-tune things even further. He wanted to pinpoint the exact spot on the protein knob—the antigen—that the antibodies targeted.

"We wanted to narrow it down," says Putney, "so we would know how much variability might actually affect a vaccine. Also, we knew a smaller fragment could be synthesized more easily."

Molecular Biology

Working the magic of molecular biology, Putney's team sliced the protein into three parts, hoping that one of them would contain the site he was after. He got lucky. When the original test was repeated at Duke, it showed that the two outside parts were superfluous. "What worked," says Putney, "was the middle third. We then dissected that portion into smaller and smaller sizes. And we found that there was this structure on the surface of the protein, a loop, which was just thirty-six amino acids long. Although it was only about four percent of the whole protein, this loop proved to be the only place that elicited neutralizing antibodies."

As it turned out, not even the whole loop was necessary. Chopping the protein even further, Putney discovered that the antibody target site consisted of "ten to fifteen amino acids from the very top." That simplified the process of reproducing the antigen considerably. When a structure is that small, researchers can make it from scratch, by stringing together the requisite amino acids in a machine called a peptide synthesizer.

So far, so good. But as the researchers knew only too well, there exists not simply one strain of the AIDS virus but many, and even within those strains there are variations. How could Putney be sure that his antigen remained common to them all—that it was, in the language of the trade, "conserved"? There was only one way: examine as many varieties of HIV as he could find.

So, with help from Duke, the Veterans Administration, and the Air Force, which routinely tests recruits for HIV, Putney and his colleagues collected a vast inventory of viruses. After sequencing the loops from more than 250—representing each of the 20 known strains several times over—they found out that the tip of the loop did indeed have some conserved parts to it. "That was very good to see," says Putney. "It meant that this highly critical site on the virus didn't just vary infinitely—there were conserved parts that we could use in a vaccine." It was another important step toward solving what Gallo calls "the singular problem staring us right in the eyeballs: the variation problem."

"The next logical step was to challenge the chimps with live HIV."

Now all was in place. Putney had found his vaccine antigen, could produce it readily in the laboratory, and had evidence that it showed up in numerous strains of virus. It was time for the moment of truth: would this prototype vaccine prevent infection in an animal as well as in a test tube?

Before Putney could find out for himself, Marc Girard of the Pasteur Institute in Paris gave him the answer. Girard, head of the French AIDS vaccine effort, had been trying to immunize chimpanzees for more than two years. He and his French and American colleagues had already injected several HIV concoctions into two chimps at the LEMSIP primate center, in Sterling Forest, New York, though with little success. While the animals displayed some buildup of neutralizing antibody, it was considerably lower than Girard had hoped for.

By the spring of 1989, frustrated with the way his research was going, Girard decided to gener-ate his own version of Putney's loop and inject it into both of the chimps. Girard's collaborator, Patricia Fultz of the Yerkes Primate Research Center in Atlanta, states the results succinctly: "We got a significant increase in neutralizing antibodies."

The next logical step was to challenge the chimps with live HIV to see if their new antibodies would ward off infection. With some apprehension—there had not been any instance of a chimp truly immunized against HIV—Girard and Fultz injected live virus into the veins of their animals. That was in August 1989. As yet, they have not been able to find any virus in the chimps. "We can't say they're free of infection," Fultz says. "It may be that the virus is not in such a concentration or form that we're able to detect it." Yet for Putney, the news is nothing less than exhilarating. "We're very, very excited," he says.

Still, because the chimps had previously been given other test vaccines, it's not entirely clear what caused their high antibody levels. Was it the combined effect of the loop and the other injections, or was it the loop alone? In collaboration with pharmaceutical giant Merck Sharp & Dohme, Putney intends to find out: he is now repeating Girard's experiment with his own vaccine prototype in fresh chimps at the Southwest Foundation for Biomedical Research in San Antonio. With Murphey-Corb in New Orleans, Putney is also testing the fledgling vaccine in AIDS-susceptible macaques to see if the antibodies it produces can also prevent disease. "If results are positive," Putney says, "we'll start human trials as soon as possible."

Key to Protection

Another strong indication that the loop may be the key to protection was provided by the biotechnology firm Genentech, which announced that it too had immunized two chimps against HIV infection. While the Genentech vaccine consisted of the entire outer knob of the protein, tests showed that the chimps' antibodies targeted the tip of the loop, in an area that almost exactly corresponded to the 15-amino-acid sequence identified by Putney. 'We see this as confirming the loop's importance," says Putney. "That's very nice."

Salk Returns

Of course, it would also be nice to be able to do something for the vast throngs of people—more than one million in this country and six million worldwide—who are already infected with the AIDS virus. While the macaque and chimp experiments have provided the first ray of hope for someday preventing the disease, that promise provides scant consolation for those in whom, as Jonas Salk says, "the clock is already ticking." Long absent from the vaccine wars, Salk has returned to launch an ambitious campaign against AIDS, focusing on people already infected with the virus.

It is not an entirely new strategy. In collaboration with Gallo, Daniel Zagury of Pierre and Marie Curie University in Paris was already experimenting with HIV-infected people when Salk began his campaign. In fact, the Zagury-Gallo team was the first ever to try immunizing humans against HIV. Their experiments, begun in 1986, involved injecting infected people who already had symptoms with a genetically engineered vaccine containing an HIV envelope protein—the same one Putney started out with. The vaccine incorporated the HIV protein into the harmless vaccinia virus, originally used in small-pox inoculations, which has become an all-purpose carrier for engineered vaccines.

Soon afterward Zagury expanded the study to include uninfected volunteers. One year later, albeit with the help of an impractical regimen of booster shots, it was clear that the vaccine could indeed beef up immune defenses against HIV. Zagury himself served as one of the volunteers in the experiment; needless to say, he stopped short of actually challenging himself with the virus.

Salk is taking a rather similar tack, and there is no mistaking his sense of urgency about the problem. "The idea is to prevent disease now," he says, "even in the presence of infection—to see if we can intervene early, before symptoms arise." He argues that since AIDS symptoms typically don't develop until years after the initial infection, there may be a way to augment the body's immune defenses before it's too late. "I call this approach immunotherapy," he says, "to distinguish it from what people conventionally think of as a vaccine."

Salk begins with the premise that, once in the body, HIV's main mode of spread is not through the bloodstream but from cell to cell. Infected cells often fuse with healthy ones to form unwieldy clumps filled with virus. By destroying diseased cells you may thus destroy much of the resident virus. And that's exactly what Salk wants to do. He hopes to prevent disease in people already infected by shoring up their immune system's ability to destroy infected cells—so-called cellular immunity.

"Salk is relying on the proven techniques that served him so well with his polio vaccine."

Salk is relying on the proven techniques that served him so well with his polio vaccine. In contrast to Zagury and others who are using genetically engineered vaccines containing pieces of HIV, Salk's preparation contains the actual killed virus.

"I'm only interested in solving the problem, and I don't care how." he says. "My style is old-fashioned. I don't know how else to do it. I have nothing to contribute from a molecular biology point of view—it's not my field. All I need is the antigen in a harmless form. My job is to inactivate the virus and present it in a form that will trick the immune system into reacting."

In a further departure from the approach favored by most others, Salk's killed virus contains no envelope proteins, the very part considered by Putney to be the focus of neutralizing antibodies. The envelope falls away during the process of readying the virus for use in Salk's preparation. But for what Salk is after—the destruction of infected cells rather than free-floating virus—the loss of the outer proteins may not be crucial.

"With infected people, I don't believe that neutralizing antibody—the kind that circulates in the blood—is of primary importance," Salk says. The real key in his view is cellular immunity. And that kind of immunity, he believes, is induced by the other remaining proteins in the virus, such as the ones surrounding its genes.

Virus-Free Chimps

To test his theory, Salk first tried his preparation in animals, with results that suggest the remaining proteins do indeed elicit cellular immunity. In the spring of 1987 his collaborator Clarence Gibbs, a microbiologist at the National Institute of Neurological Disorders and Stroke, in Washington, D.C., injected the killed-virus preparation into two chimps infected with HIV. To the delight of everyone, Gibbs subsequently could no longer detect virus in the infected animals. A year later Gibbs challenged them with doses of live HIV. They've continued to remain virus-free. "If they've got it," Gibbs says, "we can't find it."

"We're trying to remove their death sentence."

Still, as far as Salk is concerned, humans are ultimately the only valid model. "Only in humans can you test those already infected in significant numbers," he says. Accordingly, in November 1987, with the chimp study only just begun, Salk launched experiments aimed at testing his preparation's safety in HIV-infected humans. His co-experimenter, Alexandra Levine of the University of Southern California Medical School, has so far injected the killed-virus preparation into 82 patients carrying the virus or in the early stages of disease (the condition known as AIDS-related complex). "The first thing everybody asked was, will this make things worse?" Salk says. "It didn't." The treatment hasn't accelerated the course of the disease. In fact, only one of the 82 patients has developed an opportunistic infection.

Yet it's one thing to inject the killed virus into people who are already infected, people for whom the outlook is clearly grave, and quite another to expose uninfected people to the same relatively untested preparation. When Los Angeles archbishop Roger Mahoney raised the possibility of the Catholic clergy receiving Salk's preparation, it quickly made headlines. PRIESTS, NUNS MAY TEST AIDS VACCINE screamed the *New York Post*.

Salk considers the reaction typical of the way the press misrepresents his efforts. While it is true that he plans to inject killed virus into uninfected volunteers, the goal is not to test the preparation's effectiveness nor to immunize these people against infection—they will not be challenged with live virus. Rather, he says, the project is another attempt at immunotherapy. Essentially he's asking ten volunteers to be living factories for the manufacture of killer T cells and antibodies to the virus, which will then be culled and given to people in the later stages of HIV infection. He hopes the injections will provide patients whose own immune systems are failing with "passive immunity," thereby stalling the disease's progress. "We're trying to remove their death sentence," says Salk. He now awaits official approval to go ahead with the trial, which attracted more than 200 volunteers.

Still, some fellow researchers have expressed concern. "Why do we need to jump so fast into people with a whole virus particle?" asks Bolognesi. "How much better might it be if we engineered antigens to do the job and removed any possible risks? What worries me is the pressure to do too much too soon in man. It's untested and untried."

Gallo echoes the point. "I think Salk's program is important. But unless somebody can prove otherwise, unless it were an absolute, total emergency, I wouldn't move with a killed virus in uninfected people. That's my judgment. I just think there are better alternatives."

Larger Studies

Salk agrees that there may be. He considers his approach one way of finding out. "Does it mean this shouldn't be done?" he asks. "The real question is what's going to work? You may come up with something that's safe but doesn't do anything. I feel a sense of responsibility to contribute how I can." He also plans to conduct much larger studies with infected people. One, involving 200 patients, will focus on the body's immune response to the preparation; a second will assess its disease-fighting ability in another 800 volunteers. Owing to the slow nature of HIV infection, these studies will take one to two years to complete. Meanwhile Salk hopes to test a true vaccine, one designed to prevent disease, in rhesus macaques. If these experiments are successful, he envisions pursuing a vaccine for humans in earnest.

Thus, in the end, although their styles couldn't be more different, the aims of Salk and researchers such as Zagury and Bolognesi are not so far apart. "Immunotherapy and vaccine are parallel work," says Gallo. "What can provoke an immune response in an infected person might do even better in an uninfected person. Out of the work on therapy, we're learning about prevention. It's a lead toward which direction to go for a vaccine."

Exactly where those leads will take them, and when they'll arrive at the end of their journey, remains to be seen. "It's pointless to project a timetable," says Salk "AIDS is a problem such as we've not seen before."

"These viruses know how to hang in there," says Gardner, reflecting on the tough agenda ahead. "They can outsmart nature, so it's up to us to come up with something that does the job." Pacing up and down his office, he looks like a man impatient to get on with the task. "We're going to have to do a lot of grunt work. But I think it's possible."

Early Intervention Can Extend the Lives of AIDS Patients

Larry Josephs

About the Author: *Larry Josephs is director of public affairs for the New York State Urban Development Corporation.*

As a heart monitor beeped at my side and an automatic blood-pressure machine quietly inflated and deflated, the nurse started the infusion. Doctors and more nurses hovered nearby. The drug dripping into my vein was dideoxyinosine, or DDI. Thus, on July 22, 1989, I became one of about 100 people in the United States to receive what was being described in the press as a "promising" new AIDS drug. But at that moment I knew the doctors and nurses at the National Institutes of Health were thinking not about how promising the drug was, but about seizures. Several people who had received intravenous infusions of the drug had experienced them, and, while the doctors felt it was unlikely the seizures had been caused by the drug, they were still nervous—and prepared.

A young nurse was instructed not to leave my side while the infusion progressed. It was her first day on the job, and I wondered if I were to begin convulsing whether she would actually know what to do. As I lay there we chatted, and I asked her why she was at the N.I.H., as opposed to a private hospital. Had she wanted to work with AIDS patients? I was surprised by her answer. "A member of my family is HIV positive," she said. "My uncle." I could not help thinking

that this is part of the story of AIDS in this country—the evolutionary process by which more and more Americans become acquainted, first-hand, with the most insidious epidemic of our time.

It's an epidemic whose shape has begun to change. Though AIDS must still be considered a fatal disease, advances in the development of antiviral drugs—and learning how and when to administer them—and of prophylactic therapies to prevent deadly infections like *Pneumocystis carinii* pneumonia have begun to offer hope that AIDS may be on its way to becoming a serious chronic disease, like diabetes, that only occasionally leads to fatal complications. I am an example, indeed a beneficiary, of the change in strategy being developed by AIDS researchers. Summed up, it can be described in a simple two-word phrase: early intervention.

I learned in 1987 that I was HIV positive, not because I had sought out the antibody test, but because it was offered and I rather passively agreed to take it. I was participating in a psychological study by the Columbia University School of Public Health on the reaction of healthy gay men to the AIDS epidemic. The study involved being visited by a friendly interviewer who asked dozens and dozens of questions about everything from my sexual history to how I was coping: Was I afraid? Had I changed my life-style in response to the crisis?

> **"AIDS may be on its way to becoming a serious chronic disease . . . that only occasionally leads to fatal complications."**

When the doctors in charge of the study decided to correlate their psychological profiles with HIV positivity, we were asked if we wanted to take the test, and, more crucially, if we wanted to know the results.

I knew a few other people in the study, and

discussed the pros and cons with them, enacting on a small scale a debate that was taking place in gay communities across the country. The risks of knowing one's HIV status were clear. In some places, people who tested positive had lost jobs, health insurance, even apartments and houses. But to me, and to most gay men, the possibility of overt prejudice—which we live with constantly—was less troubling than the uncertainty of how our already battered psyches would process this information. The crisis had made all gay men feel vulnerable. To be told yes, you harbor the virus, might unleash a storm of depression. Ultimately I decided that more information was better than less.

"It didn't take me long to decide that I should be on AZT."

It's strange to think back to those weeks of waiting after taking the blood test, turning an impossible proposition over in my mind again and again. A negative result would mean I could continue to think about the future, think about moving to another city if I wanted, about changing jobs, finding a lover and settling down. If it were positive, all bets were off. The idea of making plans of almost any sort would become a grotesque joke.

When the dreaded letter from Columbia arrived, I wondered if I would have the courage to open it. Normally, such test results are not sent through the mail, but I had prevailed upon the director of the study to make an exception for me. I could still choose not to know—throw it in the garbage, torn into a dozen little pieces.

My then-roommate, a man with whom I shared an apartment but was not particularly close, was, coincidentally, also in the study.

"Are those your Columbia test results?" he asked.

"I guess so," I said. I took the envelope to my room.

The debate did not last long. I ripped it open.

The words cut like a blade. "Your results are confirmed positive."

Strangely, my first inclination was simple disbelief. For days I read everything I could on the accuracy of AIDS testing. I even devised a journalistic pretext for visiting a New York City AIDS testing laboratory (the putative purpose of which was to obtain photos of Western blot tests for possible publication) and grilling one of the technicians about how the test worked.

After several weeks, the ghastly truth settled over me like a shroud. And it was not long before I had to swallow the additional bad news that not only did I harbor the virus, but it had begun to damage my immune system.

I had recently switched to a new doctor, Jack Weissman, who had a large AIDS practice. He began monitoring my immune system using relatively new tests to measure the count of T-4 cells. In the great pageant of the body's immune defenses, the T-4 "helper" cell is something between stagehand and director, allowing other cells to correctly identify and attack infections. T-4 cells also happen to be the favorite target of the AIDS virus. As their numbers decrease in test results from the normal range of between 700 and 1,200, it is a sure sign that the virus has begun to replicate and destroy cells. His first tests of me indicated that while my T-4 cell count was low, in the mid-200 range, it was still sufficient to fight infection.

Numb Terror

When Jack called me one morning to say that my T-cell count had fallen to 160, I felt a kind of numb terror.

"I think you'd better come in so we can talk," he said. "But you might as well start thinking about whether you want to go on AZT. Any count under 200 qualifies you for it."

I was stunned. AZT had been approved in March of 1987, and it was clear that it was a mixed blessing. My first thought was that it was crazy to consider taking a highly toxic drug when I didn't even feel sick. I found myself in Jack's office, listening as he described in detail just how serious a falling T-cell count was—though he made no reference to the ultimate prognosis. The thing that bothered me most was that I felt completely healthy and well. I hadn't even had a bad cold in years.

"Not to be difficult, Jack," I said, "but I feel fine."

"It's not necessary that you feel sick in order to be sick," he replied. "There are many diseases, like hypertension, where the person feels nothing—until, that is, he has a stroke. In your case, think of your body as an office building whose sprinkler system is out of order. Everything is fine, as long as there is no fire."

He explained that the drug did indeed have toxic side effects, but said there was evidence that the toxicity was better tolerated by healthier people. It didn't take me long to decide that I should be on AZT. Jack recommended a pharmacy that had a pretty good price. The cost of AZT at that time was running about $1,000 a month. (Burroughs Wellcome, the manufacturer, has since instituted two separate 20 percent price cuts under pressure from AIDS activists and legislators.) In one of the oddest transactions I have ever been part of, I picked up my prescription for a month's supply of AZT and handed over $900 in cash. Fortunately, my insurance reimbursed me for 80 percent of the cost of the drug. I also went out and bought a timer so that I wouldn't forget to take my pills every four hours. After a while the drill became second nature, and for 18 months I took the pills on schedule almost instinctively.

If there are ironies in dealing with serious illness—and doubtless there are many—one of them surely is the contrast between how easily human beings can adjust to the physical demands and how difficult they find handling the psychological impact. This became clear to me as I pondered how and whom to tell about my condition.

Painful Decisions

Initially, at least, I had decided not to share the news of my positivity with anyone but immediate family and one especially close friend, Diana. But with the decision to go on a drug whose effects on me were potentially hazardous, it became clear that I would have to share the information with my friends. What ensued were among the most difficult, painful encounters I was to have with the people closest to me. I discovered that no matter how optimistically I tried to portray my situation, the message everyone was hearing was the same: death.

"I have been fighting the virus all the way, trying to keep it in check and prevent it from gaining the upper hand."

In fact, though I didn't talk much about it, I, too, became obsessed with the idea. I thought about my funeral, where it should be held (my family wouldn't be wild about coming into Manhattan, but all my friends were here), whether music would be appropriate (I weighed the possibility of writing a letter to Kathleen Battle asking her to sing at my funeral). Who would take Sandy, my dog?

In most cases, it was difficult for my friends to disguise their shock and sadness. My parents were stoic, but often they would hang up the phone after an update from me and cry together. (My father died of a heart attack just before I began taking AZT.) When I called a friend in San Francisco, Melinda, she said she had dreaded getting such a call from me, and wept openly.

In a variation on a theme, I had a similar conversation with a young man I had met and wanted to date. Naturally, I had to tell Craig the awful truth. This time it was I who almost cried as he told me that he didn't care, that he wanted to pursue a relationship with me. With some reassuring advice from Jack Weissman about just how difficult the virus is to transmit, we embarked on a relationship that included "safe" sex. Though it's impossible to deny that the virus—invisible but omnipresent—occasionally intrudes into our intimacy, for the most part we've learned how to live with it, if not entirely make peace with it. Craig and I have now been together almost two years; he continues to test negative for HIV.

As a newly "sick" person, with a T-cell count below 200, I began seeing Jack every four weeks, for blood tests and monitoring, and we became friends. At one point, he suggested I take an unproven concoction called aerosolized pentamidine, to prevent *Pneumocystis carinii* pneumonia [PCP]. I resisted at first, on the grounds that AZT was supposed to be protecting me. Jack informed me that, even among people on AZT, PCP was an all-too-common first infection unless they were taking pentamidine.

As it turned out, Jack and other doctors who prescribed AZT to their "healthy" HIV-infected patients were right: in August 1988, the results of a study by Dr. Margaret Fischl at the University of Miami confirmed that AZT given to mildly symptomatic HIV-infected individuals slowed the progress of the disease significantly. A few weeks later, the N.I.H terminated a study of asymptomatic HIV-infected people on AZT because the results had become so dramatically clear: even among those who showed no clinical signs of illness, AZT slowed the progress of the virus. Jack was also right about aerosolized pentamidine, which, along with other systemic drugs like Bactrim is today considered standard prophylactic treatment for the prevention of PCP in HIV-infected individuals.

Change in AIDS Treatment

In many ways, I represent the rapidly changing face of AIDS treatment in the 1990's. At a time when many people argued against testing, I was tested. Instead of waiting for a serious opportunistic infection, I made a pre-emptive strike with AZT. I began prophylactic treatment against PCP before the treatment was even approved by the Food and Drug Administration. And when my time on AZT expired, I sought out another antiviral drug, DDI. The result is

that I have not yet had an infection serious enough to put me in the hospital.

Some people would argue that in that case I don't have AIDS. According to the Centers for Disease Control, that's true. I have what is commonly called AIDS-Related Complex, or ARC. But the dramatic change in the way doctors approach the treatment of AIDS is diminishing the usefulness of these definitions. While I may not have had PCP or another serious infection, that is not because the AIDS virus hasn't attacked my immune system with all its might—it's because I have been fighting the virus all the way, trying to keep it in check and prevent it from gaining the upper hand.

"So far, the evidence indicates that DDI is relatively effective."

By early 1989, I began to suffer from AZT-related side effects—night sweats and weight loss. My red-blood-cell count, or hematocrit, began to drop, resulting in anemia, and I found myself out of breath at the top of the subway station stairs each morning. I felt like I was 82, not 32. In June, Jack took me off AZT, saying that we'd wait awhile and see whether my bone marrow could recover. That was the last conversation I had with Jack. Three weeks later, I received word that he had died.

Though I knew he had been quietly fighting AIDS himself for more than two years, and had been taking AZT, Jack's death hit me hard. I suppose it was because I felt that, as a doctor, he was invincible. And the fact that he continued to work and flourish with AIDS made me feel optimistic about my own future. Now, I felt vulnerable again. If Jack couldn't keep himself alive, how could I expect to remain healthy? My search for a new doctor was somber but urgent; I knew that as long as I was off AZT, there was a greater—and growing—risk of infection. But it wasn't clear to me what the options were. As far as I could tell, there were no options. It was AZT or nothing.

It didn't take long for me to locate a new doctor, Jeffrey Greene, and find out that in the six or eight weeks since I had last been tested my T-cell count had dropped to 60. I was advised to enter a drug trial, something Jack had mentioned as the next step if I couldn't tolerate AZT. With the help of a friend who is well-connected in Washington, I gained entry to a DDI study being conducted at the N.I.H. The problem was that this involved not only an extended hospital stay, but weekly follow-up visits to Bethesda, Md.

I consulted with my boss at the New York State Urban Development Corp., Harold Holzer, who already knew about my condition and had been very supportive. His inclination was not to tell the rest of our department, mainly, I think, because he wanted to protect me from negative reactions. Yet, with my having to stay in Washington for up to two weeks, and then having to travel back one day a week for six weeks, it seemed impossible not to tell them. A colleague, Carl Weisbrod, head of the 42d Street Development Project, joined us for a drink to discuss the situation. Carl had dealt with the issue of "AIDS in the workplace," as it had come to be known, at his previous job as executive director of the New York City Planning Commission. His advice: tell everyone, and tell them the truth.

We agreed that I would inform my office, and hope for the best. As it turned out, everyone, including Vincent Tese, the chairman of the U.D.C., was understanding and warm. I packed my bags and headed for Washington.

The DDI Program

After a day-long screening process, during which what seemed like gallons of blood were drawn and analyzed, I was accepted into the program. From the time I received the initial intravenous infusion, I had no major problems taking DDI, and, happily, did not develop any seizures. While I was an in-patient at N.I.H., I was visited by Dr. Samuel Broder, the head of the National Cancer Institute. The DDI drug trial is being run by N.C.I., and Broder was upbeat

about the prospects for the drug. He was also upbeat about the prospects for getting me out of the hospital sooner than expected. As Dr. Robert Yarchoan, the head of the drug trial, later explained, it was likely that DDI was going to be in the hands of thousands of AIDS patients within a few short months, such was the promise of the drug—and the pressure from AIDS activists to release it. The knowledge to be gained from keeping me—a late entry into this Phase I trial—in the hospital another two weeks, receiving the drug intravenously, was minimal.

"Early intervention is the best hope for the million or so Americans who carry the virus."

I headed back to New York after five days, carrying an enormous shopping bag filled with drug vials, bottles of liquid antacids, syringes and other paraphernalia needed to administer the rather primitive oral formulation of DDI. The flight attendant on the Pan Am shuttle regarded my shopping bag and cheerily asked, "Do you sell pharmaceuticals?"

So far, the evidence indicates that DDI is relatively effective, with antiviral properties similar to those of AZT, the only drug approved for treatment of the underlying viral infection in AIDS. But the reason it has become the hot drug of the moment has less to do with what it does than what it doesn't do: so far, DDI does not appear to attack the bone marrow, something that seems almost inevitable with prolonged use of AZT at high doses, or cause deterioration of large muscles, as AZT sometimes does. Some patients, most of them on higher doses, have experienced peripheral neuropathy, a painful nerve disorder of the feet, or inflammation of the pancreas. But at lower doses most experience only minor side effects, like headaches and irritability.

It appears DDI will be very much in the news in the near future. The drug attracted front-page news coverage a few days before I traveled to Bethesda when Bristol-Myers agreed to supply large quantities free-of-charge to AIDS patients. In the last week of September 1989, the F.D.A. [Food and Drug Administration] approved distribution of the drug to thousands of patients, a move notable because it is the first time the Federal Government has encouraged the widespread distribution of a drug at such an early stage of the F. D. A. approval process. Initially, at least, the drug will be made available to patients who can no longer tolerate AZT. It remains to be seen, when the drug is widely distributed, whether serious side effects will be a problem.

"Early intervention has meant I have suffered only minor infections."

There are an estimated one million HIV-positive Americans. At this point, medical experts expect most of them to develop signs of immune damage from the virus they carry. The attention of the media has tended to focus on the dangers of transmission, with scant attention paid to this time bomb ticking away in our society. The evidence that AZT, even at low doses, can forestall the progress of AIDS should change the shape of the epidemic, and the toll it takes. Those who suspect they may be at risk now have reason to be tested; those who test positive can monitor their immune systems and begin antiviral therapy when signs of damage appear.

And yes, even with further reductions in the price of AZT, the costs will be enormous. But not so enormous that they will eclipse other serious illnesses that cost our nation billions of dollars a year, like heart disease and cancer. The key to gaining the upper hand in the fight against AIDS is early intervention, and it appears that, short of a cure, early intervention is the best hope for the million or so Americans who carry the virus.

Intervention Success

For me, early intervention has meant I have suffered only minor infections that have been dealt with on an outpatient basis, like oral thrush. And while my T-4 cell count has never recovered, and was 29 when last measured, DDI appears to be effectively suppressing viral activity in my body. The measure of viral activity, known as the p24 antigen test, like the T-cell count, yields a number: the lower the number, the less viral presence. At the beginning of the DDI trial my p24 was 329; when last tested it had dropped to 179.

Though this development is encouraging, it doesn't and can't answer the question that haunts me. How effective will my body be at fighting off deadly infections as I am exposed to them? How long can someone in my immuno-compromised state actually expect to live? I, and thousands like me, have no choice but to wait, and hope that as much progress is made against AIDS in the next few years as has been made in the last few.

The CD4 Synthetic Protein Can Fight the AIDS Virus

Marilyn Chase

About the Author: *Marilyn Chase is a staff reporter for the* Wall Street Journal, *a daily business newspaper.*

In the photograph, a strand of chromosomes glows red, like links of neon sausages. But the strand is also touched by spots of glowing gold where scientists have spliced in genes to design a drug for acquired immune deficiency syndrome [AIDS].

Taken under fluorescence and high magnification by scientists at Genentech Inc., the photo shows but the latest twist in a process known as "rational" design, which aims at a specific target. It requires finding a weak link in the life cycle of a microbe, and tailoring a drug to attack it. Here, the product is a hybrid that links the human protein CD4 with an antibody in the hope of boosting their power against the AIDS virus. . . .

While scores of compounds have entered clinical tests, many have been existing drugs, pulled off the shelf and tested randomly for traits that could defeat the virus. AZT, a failed anticancer drug that languished for 20 years on the shelf, was reprised after such a random screening. Now it helps about half of AIDS patients live longer. Scientists continue to screen stuff as diverse as Chinese tubers and Caribbean sea sponges.

Increasingly, however, laboratories are relying on rational drug design to make molecules that, like CD4, can specifically attack the AIDS-virus life cycle. The subject was a hot topic at a conference of AIDS researchers at Tamarron, Colo., in February 1989.

"In two years, we'll know the molecular biology of this virus," said Nobel medical laureate David Baltimore. This knowledge will enable medicinal chemists to design smart drugs like CD4, though it doesn't guarantee their practical success. Only one in 10 drugs of rational design, for a wide variety of diseases, has worked.

The odds are no less daunting with AIDS. Mutable, omnivorous and evasive, its virus has proved a formidable foe for any therapy. The virus now is believed to seek out and infect not only the white blood cells of the immune system known as T-helper cells but also other cells of the blood, brain, skin and bowel.

It is a parasite with a refined palate. Different strains show tastes for different cell types. David Ho, a scientist at the University of California at Los Angeles, believes the enterprising bug may use a different "receptor," or doorway, to enter and infect these different cells. Also, the virus may mutate into a more virulent, or drug-resistant, strain as the disease worsens.

The virus may have another chilling trait, says Jay Levy, of the University of California at San Francisco: Paradoxically, it may be "enhanced" by the very antibodies that the immune system musters to fight it.

> **"Of all the possibilities, CD4 so far has sparked the biggest scientific stampede."**

All this makes the development of an AIDS drug a tough and complicated job. It's just such difficulty that draws scientists to the art of rational design.

If one approach works, scientists someday will design agents to block an AIDS-virus enzyme, the protease, that the virus needs in order to mature and infect human cells. But of all the possibilities, CD4 so far has sparked the biggest scientific stampede. Since researchers in London and Paris first identified the protein in 1985, more than half a dozen research groups have embraced it.

"Flooding the body with the synthetic copies might decoy the AIDS virus, sparing healthy T-cells from infection."

Besides Genentech, of South San Francisco, competitors include SmithKline Beckman Corp. of Philadelphia in collaboration with Columbia University and the University of Pennsylvania; Biogen Inc. of Cambridge, Mass., with Massachusetts General Hospital; Dana-Farber Cancer Institute of Boston with Harvard University; the Basel Institute for Immunology in Basel, Switzerland; Ortho Pharmaceuticals Corp. of Raritan, N.J., with California Institute of Technology and the University of Alabama; and GeneLabs Inc. of Redwood City, Calif.

As ever in AIDS research, there are disputes over who came first with the idea that CD4 could block the virus. Genentech published the first peer-reviewed scientific journal article, the usual evidence of priority, in *Science* in December 1987. Most scientists accept the claim by Genentech, which needs CD4 to restore its prestige after disappointing heart-drug sales. But Biogen argues it was earlier, with a paper it presented at a gathering in Cold Spring Harbor, N.Y.

The competitors' common target, CD4, is a protein on the surface of certain white blood cells. Normally, it helps these cells, called T-helper lymphocytes, to recognize foreign invaders and summon an immune response. "But CD4," says SmithKline scientist Raymond Sweet, "has been subverted in man to serve as the receptor for HIV"—the AIDS virus—as it commandeers T-cells to serve as viral factories. As new

viruses burst out, the T-cells rupture and die.

CD4 is now "one of the most intensively studied receptors of any enveloped virus," says Robin Weiss of Chester Beatty Laboratories, London.

The efforts to develop synthetic CD4 are the first to employ recombinant DNA technology— or gene-splicing with deoxyribonucleic acid—to focus on a part of the AIDS viral life cycle for a potential therapy.

Scientists have taken CD4 protein's gene-encoding program and inserted it into cells that act as a factory to synthesize more of the protein. They think that flooding the body with the synthetic copies might decoy the AIDS virus, sparing healthy T-cells from infection and destruction. It works in the test tube. Now at least three of the half-dozen or so research rivals have begun human tests of CD4. . . .

Before CD4 went into a single patient, it generated more than its share of controversy. At the Fourth International Conference on AIDS in Stockholm, William Haseltine of Dana-Farber publicly predicted CD4 would fail. Between 10% and 20% of AIDS patients develop an antibody against their own CD4, in what is known as an autoimmune reaction. Mr. Haseltine said the synthetic CD4 would similarly elicit antibodies, much as insulin does in some diabetics, "raising serious problems for the use of CD4 as a therapy."

So far, at least, CD4 doesn't seem to be producing auto-antibodies. Nor has it been found toxic. Still, several groups of scientists already consider that it will take more than CD4 alone to defeat AIDS.

Improving the Original

For one thing, CD4 in the body is short-lived; small as it is, it is quickly filtered out of the blood by the kidneys. And though CD4 alone blocks free-floating viruses, it alone won't kill infected cells. "It is limited," Genentech scientist Daniel Capon acknowledges. "At most, it could only be capable of a passive defense."

So a whole round of efforts aims to improve upon CD4. In September 1988, a National Institutes of Health group began arming CD4 with a poisonous bacterial byproduct, pseudomonas exotoxin, to home in on the virus with a cell-killing warhead. The question remains whether scientists can give enough of the poison to kill infected cells effectively without harming the patient.

Genentech next linked CD4 with the common workhorse antibody, Immunoglobulin-G (IgG). Company scientists took genes for the CD4 and for IgG and spliced them into the Chinese hamster cells that acted as a factory to churn out the fused antibody. The combination lasts 200 times longer than CD4 in animals' blood. The combination also ferries CD4 across the placenta, enabling doctors in theory to treat infected children before birth. Finally, CD4-IgG could potentially rally an active immune response.

Scientists liken it to a bloodhound-policeman team. "CD4 sniffs out the virus, and the immunoglobulin radios for the troops," Drs. Robert Yarchoan, Hiroaki Mitsuya and Samuel Broder, of the National Cancer Institute, wrote in a report.

Moreover, the CD4-IgG combination is specifically designed not to elicit the antibodies that have worried Mr. Hazeltine and others. Says Dr. Jerome Groopman, of Harvard University and the New England Deaconess Hospital: "This shows how rational drug design can enable you to jump some of the hurdles" posed by the virus. . . .

The CD4-IgG presentation at Tamarron impressed more than one battle-scarred veteran of the AIDS drug development wars. "I'm very optimistic now about therapies," said Angus Dalgleish, of MRC Clinical Research Centre, in Harrow, England. And Anthony Fauci, director of the National Institute of Allergy and Infectious Diseases, says he is "cautiously optimistic" about CD4 and a number of other therapeutic approaches, including DDA and DDI.

DDA and DDI are among several sister compounds of AZT. Like AZT, they inhibit an enzyme (reverse transcriptase) that the virus needs to reproduce itself. In the first reported results of a continuing human study, the DDA and DDI compounds caused a rise in T-cells and a decline in the virus, along with increased energy and appetite, and weight gain. Dr. Yarchoan said side effects were mainly limited to headaches and insomnia. . . .

In another plan of attack, Dr. Mitsuya and colleagues at the Cancer Institute are targeting the very gene that activates the virus, named "rev." They're using a new technology called "antisense," in which a synthetic strand of deoxyribonucleic acid (DNA) is made to block out the rev gene's message, much as white correcting tape covers up a typographical error.

"CD4 sniffs out the virus, and the immunoglobulin radios for the troops."

Still another feature of the AIDS virus, the sugars stuck to its outer coat, is becoming a target for rational drug design. The G.D. Searle unit of Monsanto Co. is developing a drug to alter the sugars to disrupt the binding of virus to the cell.

Merck & Co., SmithKline and others are targeting the protease enzyme that helps make AIDS so deadly. Christine Debouck, a scientist at SmithKline, says the company is doing both random screening and rational development. She calls it "playing with peptides"—protein building-blocks that might keep the protease from doing its job.

Tinkering with CD4

A group led by George Kenyon at the University of California at San Francisco is using the computer to examine protease's crystal structure and then rationally design molecules, like a three-dimensional puzzle piece, to block it.

Nor are scientists finished tinkering with CD4. In the next stages of refinement, scientists may soon attempt to paint CD4 with radioactive isotopes, or other virus-killing agents. Other groups are trying to strip the molecule to its smallest active part to avoid provoking an autoimmune reaction. British researcher Robin Weiss hotly dismisses concern over the molecule's size as "a bubble." But other scientists at Caltech and at GeneLabs consider it a real issue.

A critical question is whether CD4 can protect brain cells, where AIDS infection hides and causes devastating dementia. Dr. Groopman found that certain brain cells called glial cells were indeed protected by CD4 in the test tube. Mr. Weiss disputes this, saying that in his lab, CD4 "didn't block infection very well [in these cells], though Jerry Groopman will tell you that it does." Further research is needed to settle the question.

It has become plain that a perfect AIDS drug must do many tasks: outmaneuver the virus on many fronts, kill infected cells while protecting healthy cells, and do so with little or no toxic side effects to the patient. Amid such complexity, scientists are reaching a quiet consensus that no single drug may ever suffice to quell AIDS in all its forms. Multiple drug regimens—combining antiviral drugs with drugs that boost the immune system, for example—are likely to predominate in AIDS therapy, just as they have in cancer treatment, many believe.

"Certain brain cells called glial cells were indeed protected by CD4 in the test tube."

"It's a mistake to think that every drug must be all things to all people," concludes Dr. Broder. "What we are building," he says, "is an armamentarium."

How Can AIDS Be Treated?

Nonmedical Methods Can Effectively Treat AIDS

Positive Thinking Helps AIDS Patients
A Macrobiotic Diet Can Help People with AIDS
Acupuncture Can Help Treat AIDS
Marijuana Can Help AIDS Patients

Positive Thinking Helps AIDS Patients

Mary Morton

About the Author: *Mary Morton is a free-lance writer in Evergreen, Colorado. She is the principal author of a series of articles on holistic healing for* East West, *a monthly natural health magazine.*

Dr. Donald Pachuta has declared war. The enemy is ignorance—ignorance about AIDS. "Since the beginning of the AIDS epidemic," he says, "we have been bombarded by a great deal of negativity. We have been led to believe that this will be the first epidemic in history with a 100 percent mortality rate: everyone with Human Immunodeficiency Virus type 1 infection [HIV-1, the virus believed to cause AIDS] will eventually develop AIDS, and, therefore, the presence of HIV-1 in a person is a death sentence. This simply isn't true."

Many scientists, medical doctors, and health care providers have recently joined ranks and agree with Pachuta. Dr. John Bartlett, chief of the Division of Infectious Disease at Johns Hopkins University School of Medicine in Baltimore and one of the foremost experts on AIDS, says, "The intensive scientific study of this disease during the past years has resulted in an extraordinary assembly of scientific information; this once mysterious disease is now well understood in terms of its biology and clinical features. Perhaps most important are the very recent developments permitting medical intervention at relatively early stages of the infection when the patient lacks symptoms." Doctors John Zurlo and H. Clifford Lane of the National Institute of Allergy and Infectious Diseases in Bethesda, Maryland, state, "A disease [AIDS] once viewed as an automatic death warrant is now in the process of becoming a chronic, potentially long-term treatable illness." The final and indisputable proof is the hundreds, maybe thousands, of long-term survivors of AIDS.

The facts—the new facts—about AIDS inspire optimism, not fear.

Fact: Not everyone who is exposed to HIV-1 becomes infected.

As guest editor of the February 1990 issue of the *Maryland Medical Journal*, Pachuta and the Medical and Chirurgical Faculty Committee on AIDS devoted the entire issue to supplying data that supports the premise "Living Long and Living Well with HIV and AIDS—An Idea Whose Time Has Come." According to Pachuta, "In Los Angeles, [D.T.] Irnagawa and his colleagues studied 133 homosexual men (selected because they continued to engage in sexual activities that put them at very high risk for HIV-1 infection) who tested antibody negative. Only 31 (23 percent) of these men grew HIV-1 on culture, and 27 of them remained seronegative [antibody negative] up to 36 months. . . . Despite very high risk sexual behavior 77 percent of these men remained antibody and HIV-1 culture negative." Pachuta says that the authors concluded that a prolonged period of latency may be much more common than previously realized, suggesting that some people may harbor this virus and never seroconvert or never get ill.

> ## "We have been led to believe that . . . the presence of HIV-1 in a person is a death sentence. This simply isn't true."

Pachuta goes on to note that the data on infestations of health professionals are well known. "The statistical risk of contracting HIV-1 infection from needle stick and other exposures is between 0.1 and 0.5 percent per exposure," he

Mary Morton, "Surviving AIDS." Reprinted from the January 1991 issue of *East West: The Journal of Natural Health and Living,* Box 1200, 17 Station St., Brookline Village, MA 02147. Subscriptions $24/year.

says. "There has been no HIV-1 transmission to a surgeon or other physician doing invasive procedures (or from a doctor to a patient) despite numerous needle sticks, splashes of blood, and secretions."

Fact: Not everyone who is infected with HIV gets AIDS.

The *Maryland Medical Journal [MMJ]* demonstrates that all the projections are based on an extremely biased statistical subgroup of men from San Francisco, who, not knowing they were infected, did not alter their sexual behavior or lifestyle for several years. They continued to engage in high-risk sexual behavior, and followed a fast-paced lifestyle including frequent alcohol consumption, smoking, and recreational drugs, which did not help their immune systems. "Despite all this," Pachuta says, "at the end of the ten years only a minority of these individuals have developed AIDS. If only 48 percent developed AIDS after a decade of being HIV-1 seropositive, without early changes in behavior, the possibilities are legion of altering the outcome considerably by changing attitude, lifestyle, and behavior."

Fact: Not everyone with AIDS dies from it.

Dr. Luc Montagnier, a Nobel prize candidate and co-discoverer of the AIDS virus, says, "AIDS does not inevitably lead to death, especially if you suppress the co-factors that support the disease. It's very important to tell this to people who are infected. Psychological factors are critical in supporting immune function. If you suppress this psychological support by telling someone he's condemned to die, your words alone will have condemned him. It simply isn't true that the virus is 100 percent fatal. If you lead a normal life—sleep regularly at night, avoid alcohol, coffee, and tobacco—your immune system could perhaps resist the disease for ten to fifteen years. By then, we might have found an effective therapy. The Centers for Disease Control statistics are biased. They're based on a single homosexual population (San Francisco) with a lot of co-factors aiding the disease."

The real evidence is the survivors. As Dr.

Bernie Siegel wrote in the *MMJ*'s February issue, "We should study success by looking at people who survive life-threatening illness. . . . The common denominator of long-term survivors of AIDS, cancer, and other life-threatening illnesses is that they take charge of their lives."

Creating the Space for Healing

In the summer of 1985 Ron Webick waited tables to pay for an upcoming trip to Europe. Suddenly he began to lose his sight. After extensive testing, his doctor informed Webick that he had an AIDS-related brain disease and gave him four months to live. Six weeks later, paralyzed on his left side, he was flown to his mother's home in St. Petersburg, Florida to spend his last days. Webick became determined to regain the use of his legs, however, and began a slow but sure road to recovery without the use of any medical drugs. Pachuta described Webick's case in the MMJ. *He said, "I met a man who was sent home to die in a few months with AIDS and progressive multifocal leukoencephalopathy (PML). He had dementia, was nearly blind, and could barely walk and talk. . . .When he went home to die, all his mother did was love him; apparently that stimulated his immune system. No one has survived PML with AIDS for more than a few months. He is completely well five years later." The following is Webick's story.*

"The common denominator of long-term survivors of AIDS . . . is that they take charge of their lives."

"The first time I heard anyone talk about being a long-term survivor of AIDS I thought, 'This guy was one of the lucky ones. It could never happen to me.'

"At the time I was bedridden and was suffering from the effects of the AIDS virus in my spinal fluid as well as a brain disease. Briefly put, it is a disease that progresses relentlessly to paralysis, blindness, coma, and then death. I was already paralyzed on the left side, and I was losing my vision. So I could never even think that I would be a long-term survivor. I don't recall what that man said because I was searching as to how to even begin!

"Weeks passed before I realized that I had to make some choices. My first choice was to try—not only for myself but for those who loved me. As those of us who get a diagnosis of AIDS know, we are not the only ones who have AIDS—the people who are around us and our family will be suffering with us.

"We have a commitment—to life, to others who will have AIDS—to make a prognosis of living long and living well."

"So in my travel of getting better, I was doing what most of us talk about—eating well, getting rest. I continued to get better. It seemed like almost a year had passed before my health lifted to the point where I trained myself to walk again by using walkers and canes.

"It was about that time that I was fortunately pushed to a Louise Hay meeting in Key West. I had heard this theory of positive thinking and that it could help AIDS patients. I thought, 'This is really ridiculous.' It just didn't seem that anyone could recover just from a change in attitude.

"So I went. A protégé of Louise Hay's talked about the benefits of positive thinking that helped him recover from cancer. It all started to make sense to me. I decided to try because I started to see love enter my life. For more than six months before there was a lot of hatred and anger.

"When I started to lift all that anger there was some space for healing to begin. I started to do Uncle Bernie's [Dr. Bernie Siegel] work. One thing struck me about cancer patients [in Bernie Siegel's book *Love, Medicine and Miracles*] is that they are recovering. If cancer patients and other people with so-called terminal illnesses can recover, why can't we?

"As I was going into my second year of wellness or recovery, a lady friend of mine gave me a wonderful book called *Man's Search for Meaning*, written by Viktor Frankl, a survivor of the Holocaust. It talks about how people in the concentration camps survived. It explains that everyone who suffered had a common element between them. They had hope—hope that their lives would be liberated and they would be free. It inspired me so much that I felt that maybe I was experiencing my own holocaust. Maybe AIDS was a holocaust of its own. After diagnosis we [persons with AIDS] feel, 'What is there left to look forward to in life? We have AIDS. There is nothing more.'

"But there is a greater question. What is life expecting from us? Maybe we have a commitment—to life, to others who will have AIDS—to make a prognosis of living long and living well.

"In my public speaking many times they ask me, 'How did you get well?' As Frankl explains, it is not only the question of how you get well but why you get well. I chose to get well because I wanted to help other people and make a difference. It is really the basic reason that has sustained my life for almost five years."

The Gift of Life

In 1985 Robert Mehl, while working as executive director of the American Foundation for AIDS Research, noticed a swollen lymph gland in his leg. Soon after, his physician performed a biopsy and found the gland to be malignant with AIDS-related KS cancer. Because of the tremendous stress that his job placed on his health, Mehl retired to Baltimore, Maryland, to "grow tomatoes and bake bread." Two months into retirement, he knew he needed to be active again. Soon he was back in action as coordinator of Positive Directions, Preventative Medicine and Epidemiology for the Baltimore City Health Department. He also founded Movable Feast, an organization that delivers balanced meals to homebound adults and children diagnosed with AIDS. Today Mehl is certain that it is his work that has saved his life.

"I'm going into my fifth year since I was diagnosed with full-blown AIDS. How do I survive? I think that the most important thing I do is work with other people with AIDS and with health care providers like nurses, doctors, and dentists. I change their opinions. I turn them around. They, in turn, go back to their clients and have a much more sensitive, caring approach.

"Without self love, without the feeling that the healing is inside you, the drugs are all for naught."

"Many of the people I speak to have never met anyone with AIDS. It is a nonentity they don't know how to deal with. Now they have to confront me as a real live person. First, I tell the audience that I think my diagnosis was a gift. Those four years have been the best, the most rewarding. Every year at the anniversary of my diagnosis, I have a party and open a bottle of champagne because it is like a new birthday. It is special for me. I have a shelf of them already lined up.

"When I say this to groups, there is usually an audible shock that goes through the room. 'How can you say that something so horrible is a gift?!' But I really didn't live until this disease. Now I really know how to live and I can confront whatever my eventual death is. Who knows what it is?

"I tell them about AIDS transmission. It is not transmitted by casual contact with door knobs or toilet seats, or through mosquito bites. These are misconceptions. There are really only two ways to transmit the disease: sexual intercourse and sharing of infected needles. You really have to work hard to get this disease. It is not going to happen to you on a bus. Quite often [after I speak] people come up to me and they feel the need to hug me or hold my hand. It is a way for them to say that they aren't scared anymore.

"The question I get the most from people I speak to is, 'How come you're not dead yet?' They really put it quite that way—as if they are offended. I admit that I don't know why I'm still alive. Someone once said about me, 'Bob will use anything to make himself well. He'd munch on goat droppings!' I'm just very pragmatic because I'm going to beat this thing.

"I was on AZT for two and a half years, which is an awfully long time to tolerate AZT. I had very little trouble for most of the time I was taking it, but in the end I was having to take transfusions because it was destroying my white blood cell count. So I went off that and the only other alternative was DDI, an antiviral drug. That was a disaster. I got pancreatitis and almost died from the effects of the drug. Sometimes I think that all the push for the FDA [Food and Drug Administration] [to release drugs] has gone too far in allowing pharmaceutical companies to put drugs on the market without adequate testing. Whatever you die from, DDI or AIDS, you're still dead.

Healing

"Really the healing is within you. The drugs can be great and I'll still try whatever I think is going to help me. But without self love, without the feeling that the healing is inside you, the drugs are all for naught.

"Nutrition is a very underrated component of this disease. I realized there was no nutritional support system here in Baltimore, so I started a meal program for people with AIDS called Movable Feast. We now have sixty clients. Most are indigent. Some are minority women with children. We serve only fresh food, no frozen or canned. We even make our own juices. Nothing is prepackaged. It is all made from scratch. Part of what we do is to educate our clients about what is good nutrition because they don't know.

"We have devoted people who spend a lot of time and effort. We also encourage the participation of our board and of our staff by people who have AIDS and who are HIV-positive. It is a means for them to get constructively involved, which has proven to prolong the life of people with AIDS. It gives us a purpose. I know that if I had stayed in New York and not started these programs, I would not be alive today."

Lon Nungesser, an AIDS survivor of eight years, is considered one of the healthiest of long-term survivors. Using his regimen of nutrition, exercise, and meditation he has brought himself from near death, without medication of any kind. As a noted staff psychologist at Stanford University and author whose works include Axioms for Survivors *(IBS Press, 1990), which details his work on self-healing methods, Nungesser has shared his techniques, his experience, and his compassion with others having terminal diseases. In recognition of the success of Nungesser's research, counseling, and teaching, the University of Michigan at Ann Arbor has acquired his life's work, unpublished autobiography, and photo albums in a special collection called, "The Nungesser Papers: Hope For Humanity."*

"I was just finishing a Ph.D. program in social psychology and had taken a full-time job as a foreign student advisor for Stanford University when I noticed I had some strange bumps on my skin. I had already started working with a group of psychologists and medical doctors and saw the emergence of this new disease that was called 'grid' at the time.

"The first lump appeared in May of 1983, and by September of that year I had fourteen lumps which looked like very large tumors. I was diagnosed with Kaposi's sarcoma, an AIDS-related terminal cancer, determined as permanently disabled, and was told I had three to six months to live.

Taking Charge

"I was angry that at thirty years of age I was facing death and no one could do a damned thing about it. I held on to that anger and used it to mobilize myself to gather information. I went to medical libraries and read everything I could about the disease. The information gathering process was powerful and informative. It is probably 80 percent of the reason I recovered. The very act of taking charge and feeling you are in charge of your medical care—and the medical knowledge surrounding your health care—has a direct immunological and physical effect.

"It was clear to me [from my research] that taking immunosuppressant treatments for benign symptoms would be dangerous. I would confront my doctors and say, 'I know that what you are doing is primarily experimental.' I refused chemotherapy and told them, 'You can't mess around with my immune system.'

"I began to see that maybe 'no treatment' was the best idea. I went home and decided to take a cancer approach to my illness. It's a psychoneuroimmunological approach that includes diet and spirituality. I went on a low-fat, high-fiber diet. The cornerstones of my supplement program were the vitamins A, C, and E, thymus, and bone marrow glandular because they seemed to make sense to me. I also took high doses of selenium. I do aerobic exercise with light weights three times a day.

"Talking to people—telling them what is going on—is a part of my recovery."

"I have a positive attitude about survival. Although I realize I am mortal, I don't see death as failure. If you have loved, you haven't failed. I have a strong sense of purposefulness both in my thoughts and in my activities. I feel committed to life, connected to my profession. I think I was born to serve a purpose. It is still here and my work isn't done.

"AIDS is a compromised immune system I have to live with. In 1985 I got a splinter in my leg while gardening. The emergency room that I went to refused to treat me because I was HIV-positive. They said, 'Come back when you develop an infection, then we can see where it is.' I said, 'That doesn't make sense.' The doctor didn't know as much as I did about AIDS. I said, 'If we don't mount an initial response for infection, and we wait three days, then it will be too late to deal with it. I'll have a systemic infection.' That is exactly what happened.

"In spite of my immune weakness, my program has worked. I haven't had one opportunistic [AIDS-related] infection during the entire eight years. I have put myself into complete remission from KS cancer without any medical treatment. I have no lesions left, only what is called a 'tattoo' on my left calf. Some friends jokingly say that I am holding onto it as my purple heart.

"A diagnosis is an event to be adapted to, not a death sentence to be compliant with. I've offended a lot of doctors by being alive. Now they're starting to call me for advice."

Ninety-Two Or Bust

Diana Nova learned that she had AIDS when her doctor examined the bluish lumps on her ankle. She was overwhelmed. As an upper middle class divorced woman living in Santa Fe, New Mexico, Nova does not fit the profile of a person with AIDS. How did she contract the disease? Was it from an unscreened blood transfusion thirteen years ago? Or did she contract AIDS during an affair she had with a man who enjoyed recreational drugs? Whatever the cause of her disease, Nova has chosen to live. Although for months she feared sharing her diagnosis with anyone outside of her immediate family, Nova now finds that sharing publicly her experience with AIDS supports her recovery. Today, speaking about AIDS is a substantial part of her life.

"Because of my history, I feel I can survive this disease. I am planning to live to be ninety-two, at least. There is just no room for anything else. I am convinced that I am not going to die from this disease.

"In 1968, at the age of eighteen, I got Hodgkin's disease [a chronic condition characterized by progressive enlargement of the lymph nodes]. At the time, it was considered fatal. I met my husband then, and he said he was going to cure me.

"We both went on strict vegetarian diets. I gave up ice cream. I chewed my food a hundred times. It took me two and a half hours to eat a meal. My husband refused to eat with me. I was completely miserable.

"Still, the disease came back! I started thinking that something else was going on. I read Carl Simonton's first book and that changed my life. I realized that I had some control over this disease and I wasn't just a victim. It is more than twenty years later and I am still alive!

"In 1974, because of chemotherapy, I ended up getting a serious case of pneumonia, which I was told has a death rate of 90 percent. I learned I can't always listen to doctors because they don't necessarily know. All those experiences—all those awful experiences have taught me that I can survive this too.

"In 1985, I started getting those little red spots on my legs. They were biopsied and tested benign. Then in July of 1987 they biopsied a growth that had been removed and grew back. It was Kaposi's sarcoma—cancer and AIDS.

"I thought, 'I have had enough of this. I don't want to try to get better again.' I was completely devastated. I cried for the first two weeks.

"I told only my parents, my ex-husband, and my sister that I had AIDS—that was it. I was so ashamed. I couldn't tell my friends. Then I realized that I was losing my friends because I was lying to them. When they would ask me, 'What are you doing?', I'd say, 'Nothing.' Everything was 'Nothing.' I couldn't say, 'Well, I went to four doctors just trying to find one who wouldn't look at me like I was going to die in two years.' I felt like I was in prison.

"I feel that AIDS fits perfectly in my personality."

"I finally decided that if I was going to get well I had to stop lying to people. I had to go out and do what I had to do. So I called my best friend who was going to move to New Mexico to start a business with me. I was really terrified. She had a six-month-old and a two-year-old. I said, 'Kathy, I just have to tell you that I have AIDS. If you don't want me to come over to your house anymore I'll understand. If you don't want me to hug your kids anymore I'll understand'—which wasn't true. I would not have understood! She said, 'No, Diana, I just don't want you to have sex with my kids.' We both laughed and I was really grateful to have friends who understand.

"It has been three years since I was diagnosed. I have not been rejected by anybody. Nobody has fire-bombed my house. People always say they can't tell. I look like a normal person.

"Talking to people—telling them what is going on—is a part of my recovery. I tell them that I don't think AIDS is worse than any other disease, and some people get angry when I say that.

The worst thing about this disease is the stigma, which is really awful. I encourage everyone who has AIDS to speak out. Maybe when everyone finds out that the person who looks normal sitting next to them has AIDS, we'll get rid of all this stuff.

"I basically feel that I am a healthy person. When I look back on it, I feel that AIDS fits perfectly in my personality. I am a fighter and I really like being different. I survived Hodgkin's. I survived pneumonia. That was different. Now I'm a woman, not a drug abuser, and I have AIDS—that is different. I'm going to survive this. That is a good way to be different."

A Macrobiotic Diet Can Help People with AIDS

Tom Monte

About the Author: *Tom Monte is the co-author of* Recalled by Life: The Story of My Recovery from Cancer *and the author of* The Way of Hope, *from which this viewpoint is excerpted.*

This is the story of desperate men who dared to hope—AIDS patients who volunteered to participate in a therapeutic program based on an ancient philosophy and a simple diet. The program sounded unbelievably simple when compared with the complex solutions being explored by the medical establishment. Yet it was not without some scientific support. An abundance of research has demonstrated that a healthy diet and a positive attitude enhance immune function. But to the scientists who followed the progress of these men, such a program seemed to be the softest and least effective of the therapies being proposed to combat the devastating disease of AIDS. The results, therefore, were all the more remarkable. Virtually all the men who participated in the study saw an improvement in AIDS-related symptoms; several of the men are still alive years after diagnosis. But for Michio Kushi, the man who guided the participants along *The Way of Hope*, such progress was not at all surprising.

In the spring of 1983, ten men with AIDS (acquired immune deficiency syndrome) volunteered to participate in a study examining the effects of a diet and life-style on the course of their disease. The program they followed was macrobiotics, which included a diet composed chiefly of whole grains, land and sea vegetables, beans, fish, and fruit.

All the men were homosexuals living in Manhattan. They were professionals, generally affluent, ranging in age from their mid-twenties to mid-forties. Before beginning macrobiotics, their life-styles could be characterized as materially oriented and hedonistic. They were concerned primarily with advancing their careers and enjoying a fast-paced social life. Each man consumed, on a regular basis, quantities of drugs, especially cocaine, marijuana, and a variety of amphetamines; each also engaged in promiscuous sex. In short, these men fit the profile of the homosexuals at risk of contracting AIDS. Like many who get AIDS, they also developed a type of skin cancer called Kaposi's sarcoma.

Several of the men had begun macrobiotics well before the study was initiated. There was little medical science could offer as treatment for their disease, especially in 1982 and 1983, and consequently they had little to lose by adopting an alternative health approach. That macrobiotics could be used in conjunction with other conventional medical modalities, such as chemotherapy or radiation for cancer, made the program all the more appealing.

> ## "The central idea of macrobiotics is that through proper eating and living, one can establish balance and harmony."

The men had other reasons for adopting macrobiotics. For one thing, a growing body of scientific evidence demonstrated that nutrition played an important role in the maintenance and enhancement of the functioning of the immune system. Second, the macrobiotic diet and philosophy was an alternative to surrender. By practicing a healthful diet and a life-supporting philosophy, the men gained a degree of control over their lives, their fears, and their health.

Macrobiotics gave them a tool with which to fight their disease, and it gave them hope. An abundance of scientific evidence shows the positive effects of hope and will on immune response.

"The macrobiotic diet these men followed has applications for a wide diversity of illnesses."

The Boston University (BU) study began in May 1983. It was conducted by BU researchers Dr. Elinor Levy and Dr. John Beldekis, both of the department of microbiology and immunology at BU. Dr. Martha Cottrell, a medical doctor and director of health at the Fashion Institute of Technology of New York City, monitored the health of the men and periodically drew blood samples from each participant. The blood was sent by overnight courier to BU, where it was analyzed by Levy and Beldekis. These blood values were compared with the original tests, or baseline results, obtained at the outset of the study.

The official number of men who participated in the study went from ten to twenty. The men were followed for three years, during which time their blood values were analyzed at regular intervals.

The men were guided in their approach to macrobiotics by Michio Kushi, the leading teacher of macrobiotics, and a number of senior macrobiotics teachers from New York and the surrounding states. While the program is grounded in a sound diet, it also includes the broader principle of maintaining balance in one's life. One of the practical aspects of such a philosophy is that it teaches one to avoid extremes in behavior that tend to have extreme consequences on health. Moderate actions have milder effects on health. The central idea of macrobiotics is that through proper eating and living, one can establish balance and harmony in all aspects of life. The macrobiotic philosophy also embraces the concept that life is everlasting

and that at the time of physical death, one's life merely changes form, but one continues living through infinity.

Levy presented her findings at the Third International Conference on Acquired Immunodeficiency Syndrome (AIDS), which took place in Washington, D.C., during the first week of June 1987. There she reported that of the twenty men studied, eight had died. The rest experienced an increase in the number of lymphocytes, or white blood cells, and a diminution of AIDS-related symptoms, including night sweats, fatigue, and weight loss. Remarkably, Levy had found that the number of T4 cells had increased over time during the first two years of the study. T4 cells, which direct the immune system's attack against disease, are destroyed by the AIDS virus. In the majority of AIDS patients, the number of T4 cells steadily declines, thus rendering the immune system incapable of responding to an illness. In addition, the men had survived well beyond the twenty-two-month average life expectancy for men with AIDS. Several were alive five years after diagnosis. . . .

Effective Diet

Elinor Levy's findings may point the way to the first real chance of prolonging life, or improving the quality of life, for anyone infected with the AIDS virus or now suffering from AIDS.

Moreover, Levy's work is directly relevant to every man and woman who is concerned about his or her health. AIDS continues to spread through all segments of the U.S. population. . . .

In the October 1988 issue of *Scientific American*, William L. Heyward and James W. Curran, both of the Centers for Disease Control, wrote: ". . . given the fact that the virus is transmitted through sexual contact, through the traces of blood in needles and other drug paraphernalia and from mother to newborn infant, one can envision many possible chains of infection, which leave no segment of the U.S. population completely unaffected by the threat of AIDS."

The macrobiotic diet these men followed has applications for a wide diversity of illnesses and, indeed, can be effective in preventing many diseases long before they manifest. Levy's findings suggest that there is much every one of us can do to strengthen his or her own immune system and to prevent the onset of disease. Even after one has contracted a serious illness such as AIDS, there are measures that can be taken to enhance immune function and improve and prolong the quality of life.

The current methods of treatment, including AZT (azidothymidine), do not constitute a cure for AIDS. In addition, most of the drugs currently available have severe side effects. There is no vaccine and likely will be none in this century, according to former U.S. Surgeon General C. Everett Koop.

Diet therapy is neglected by most researchers today despite the abundant scientific evidence demonstrating that the immune system is dependent upon nutrition for health. Certain nutrients, such as zinc, selenium, beta-carotene, and others, strengthen immune response, making white cells more effective against disease. Conversely, the absence of certain nutrients, and an abundance of fat, weaken immune response. The studies are unequivocal on these points. However, just as scientists were reluctant to appreciate the role of diet in the onset and prevention of cancer and heart disease—even after the studies were available—many remain unconvinced of the importance of nutrition in the treatment of immune-related illnesses.

"A healthy diet and positive attitude can do much to enhance immune function, even for those . . . [with] AIDS."

Michio Kushi offers a bold challenge to the thinking of every American. Kushi maintains that AIDS is not a disease confined to the homosexual community. The sudden advent of "new" immunodeficiency diseases—including Epstein-Barr, chronic fatigue syndrome, and others—represents yet another slide downward in human health. The human capacity to deal effectively with antagonists in the environment is weakening. The cause, says Kushi, is the daily torrent of poisons being ingested by the body. These poisons are often hidden, for example, in processed food that are laden with fat, sugar, chemical additives, and pesticides. The diet is often deficient in many vitamins and minerals that are essential to healthy immune function.

Diet and Behavior

Kushi maintains that unless rapid changes are made in eating patterns and life-style, human health will continue to degenerate and other more frightening diseases will manifest themselves among people from all walks of life.

But there is hope. The men [in the study] abused their health, became deathly ill, and still managed—through appropriate nutrition and life-style—to continue living.

The macrobiotic approach is exactly opposite to that being employed by scientists. Rather than relying on any single weapon, such as a drug or genetic clone, macrobiotics addresses the human being as an entity composed of body, mind, and spirit, all of which need to be nourished properly in order to restore health.

There is no single factor—no nutrient, no mantra, no magic—that can be gleaned from the program and placed in a pill or potion. The strength of the program lies in its totality. It is only through the transforming effects of the diet and philosophy that macrobiotics can help stimulate the patient's own healing capabilities.

The program does not constitute a cure for AIDS. It is a multifaceted approach that can, in some people, have a positive influence on health. It may prolong life in some and improve the quality of life for others. The sciences of nutrition and psychoneuroimmunology suggest that a healthy diet and positive attitude can do much to enhance immune function, even for those who face a life-threatening illness such as AIDS.

Acupuncture Can Help Treat AIDS

Leon Chaitow and Simon Martin

About the Authors: *Leon Chaitow practices osteopathy, a therapy based on the manipulation of bones and muscles. Simon Martin is a free-lance investigative journalist specializing in health issues.*

Modern scientific research confirms that acupuncture can directly influence the physiology of the body in general and the immune system in particular. T. Cracium and colleagues have shown that acupuncture on humans increases phagocytic activity (phagocytes are part of the immune system's defence against invading micro-organisms) by 55.6 per cent and fibrinolytic activity by 79 per cent. The reasoning is that acupuncture stimulates regions of the brain controlling these activities via nerve and hormone links.

Eastern European studies have shown that the insertion of a needle into a single point (Stomach point 36 Tsusanli) below the knee, for 30 minutes, has a double effect. For the first 30 minutes or so after treatment there is a fall in the blood level of leukocytes (their job is to take care of disease-causing micro-organisms), then they increase to a level well above that before acupuncture. This lasts for some three hours before returning to normal.

Chinese research more or less confirms this with slight variations in the findings. These showed that needling of Stomach 36 produced an increase in leukocyte count rising to 70 per cent above average three hours after acupuncture. After 24 hours the levels were still 30 per

Excerpted, with permission, from *A World Without AIDS* by Leon Chaitow and Simon Martin, published in 1988 by Thorsons of HarperCollins Publishers Limited, England.

cent above pre-acupuncture levels. Just to check, the researchers also needled non-acupuncture points and this failed to produce any rise in leukocyte levels. Doctors at George Washington University have shown the beneficial effects of acupuncture on the immune system in animal studies.

These experimental studies show that there are definite effects on the immune function by acupuncture. If a drug was found to have these beneficial results with no side-effects, doctors would surely be clamouring to use it.

Acupuncture has been used to treat addiction and a wide variety of health problems in Europe and the USA for some 25 years, and disease in general in China and Japan for thousands of years. Orthodox medicine may ignore its potential but the public will not. Indeed, its usefulness in the treatment of AIDS is proving its enormous potential.

Dr Michael Smith, director of the acupuncture clinic at Lincoln Hospital New York City is probably the foremost MD involved in this aspect of AIDS treatment in the USA. He points out that acupuncture has a balancing effect. In a sense the body uses the stimulus of the needle, providing it is correctly sited, according to its own needs.

> **"[Acupuncture's] usefulness in the treatment of AIDS is proving its enormous potential."**

Dr Smith says: 'We often use the same acupuncture point for treating low blood pressure as we do for high blood pressure and the same point for low as for high thyroid. Another way is to say acupuncture improves body vitality.'

How can this work?

Operating in the body is a mechanism called homoeostasis. This represents the combined activity of many systems and organs and is the factor which restores balance in response to all the multiple and constant demands made on the body.

If we walk out of a hot room into cold air, a vast number of changes are taking place involving the nervous system, circulatory system and the hormonal system which alter the various heat control mechanisms in the body in order to adapt to this new need. This sort of thing is happening countless times daily in all areas of our lives and it represents homoeostasis, the balancing of physiological demands and requirements.

"Almost all our patients have T-cell increases on acupuncture and this seems to upset the physicians."

Homoeostasis is the reason for the response described by Dr Smith. The body wishes to restore normality (blood pressure, say) and given a stimulus to which it can respond (the needling of a specific area) it will do so, whether the blood pressure is high or low.

Now, depending on the causes of this altered blood pressure, such a response may be very temporary indeed and the problem might be expected to return, unless underlying causes are also dealt with.

As Kimball Chatfield, a certified acupuncturist, states in *The Textbook of Natural Medicine* (and provides full references for the statement):

> Modern scientific methods have unlocked many of the mysteries of acupuncture. An impressive number of endogenous chemicals [substances produced by the body itself] have been shown to be stimulated by acupuncture. They include, but are not limited to, beta-lipotropin, beta-endorphin, growth stimulating hormone, serotonin, ACTH, norepinephrine, prolactin, oxytocin, thyroid hormones and insulin. Plasma cholesterol and triglyceride levels have been lowered and citrate metabolism and white blood cell production increased, all by acupuncture.

Immune function can clearly be influenced beneficially by acupuncture. We've already seen from the experimental examples that there can be a temporary improvement in immune function, in response to acupuncture, but that is merely one part of an overall approach to the current needs of the body.

The enhanced (albeit temporary) immune function assists in dealing with the infecting agents in the body while other things are being done, such as nutritional restructuring, the use of herbal therapies, and mental assistance to the healing process.

Acupuncture is used for people with AIDS in other ways as well. It can be shown to deal very effectively with the major symptoms such as night (and day) sweats, diarrhoea, muscle and joint aches and so on. (The decision as to which points to use is made on an individual basis which precludes the giving of a 'prescription' of points to use in AIDS.)

Dr Misha Cohen, of the Quan Yin Centre in San Francisco, says that acupuncture offers help on the three most important fronts at the same time. It can help build the immune system back to strength; it can mobilize the body's anti-viral defences; and it can also stimulate relaxation and meditation, helping people begin the vital 'inner work'.

'Acupuncture does a lot of these things in one package, so it reduces people's need to do lots and lots of things,' says Dr Cohen.

Chinese Medicine

The concepts in Traditional Chinese Medicine (TCM) that explain how and why acupuncture works relate to energy imbalances and channels of energy known as meridians. The fact that a phenomenon is understood in different ways in different cultures does not negate the value of the use of that phenomenon. Both concepts may contain elements of the truth or they may both be right but simply use different terminology to describe the same factors.

The major energy channels or systems (meridians) which are employed in the TCM approach to AIDS, relate to digestive, kidney, spleen, respiratory and skin functions.

Where acupuncture is used in treating AIDS/ARC [AIDS-Related Complex] it is always part of a wider approach, using also TCM and Western herbal remedies, nutrition, massage or other forms of body-work, and various aspects of meditation/visualization often at the same time as orthodox drug therapy.

Dr Smith states: 'Our clinic makes no effort to be a diagnostic centre for AIDS and we have no interest in trying to be the sole treatment for these patients.'

"The communal acupuncture-based programme . . . vindicates alternative/complementary medicine's methods."

In fact many of the people he and colleague Dr Naomi Rabinowitz see continue with various forms of chemotherapy. However, the results with acupuncture show through. 'Acupuncture definitely improves T-cell ratios,' Dr Smith reports. 'Our first patient went from 0.3 to 2.3 in three months and he has done well, functions professionally and gets by without having to take three or four naps a day. Eighty per cent of the time, patients who complain of weight loss, night sweats and lymphomatous type of symptoms start to improve by three treatments, and acupuncture protects them against recurrent infections.'

This, remember, is acupuncture applied by a medically qualified doctor, operating out of a medical hospital in New York City. What is the reaction from fellow-doctors to his extraordinary results and claims, relating to the greatest health challenge of the century? Are they clamouring for a chance to use the same methods? Are the representatives of the media clamouring for interviews to publicize this message of hope?

Sadly, very little positive response is evident from his medical colleagues or from the media.

'Almost all our patients have T-cell increases on acupuncture and this seems to upset the physicians who follow them up elsewhere,' states Dr Smith. 'Some hospitals keep asking us four and five times to give them our data but nothing ever comes of it. The idea that someone outside the medical mainstream might be helping these patients is upsetting to the physicians at the conventional centres.'

In a decidedly non-hospital setting, Chicago acupuncturists have created a traditionally Chinese atmosphere. The room is busy, but not crowded, and four or five people are receiving 'treatment' at once. The first thing you notice is the warmth and gentleness of the practitioners and their clients. There is no panic here, no fear, just relaxed banter. It's hard to remember that some of these people are actually dealing with what the outside world believes is an invariably fatal disease.

Here, licensed acupuncturists (not MDs) have established a community clinic by the simple method of turning their own consulting room into a free clinic two days weekly. On these days people with ARC/AIDS visit, some on their own initiative, some as a result of referral from broadminded MDs. They receive Chinese medical help in the form of counselling regarding diet, herbal medication (Traditional Chinese and Western) and acupuncture. They are not charged fees.

Health Not Profit

Mary Kay Ryan, one of the dedicated acupuncturists involved in this project, explains: 'Our motivation is healthcare not profit. This is a community clinic and we remain steadfast in our goal to integrate our clinic's concepts with the rest of the AIDS healing community.

'Often we refer patients to many of the area's physicians, as well as new patients being referred here. This open communication is truly unique to the Chicago area.'

The communal atmosphere, where four to five patients at a time receive acupuncture in one large room, is deliberate. It breaks down barriers of isolation and actually engenders an atmosphere, if not exactly of fun, at least of companionship and shared experience. It also allows the small premises available to be used to their optimum advantage.

People receive treatment twice weekly at least, and more if needed. This is considered essential in the early stages of dealing with the myriad problems involved in AIDS/ARC, but places great strain on the extremely limited resources of this type of self-funded clinic. Body-workers (masseurs, Rolfers etc.) also come voluntarily to this clinic to treat, with tenderness and love, the people in need.

Results? It is early days but many of the patients seen are improving symptomatically. All are also receiving other therapy, conventional and/or unorthodox. All are encouraged to attend classes on visualization and meditation.

The communal acupuncture-based programme has grown out of the need of desperate individuals, and the success of such a holistic approach vindicates alternative/complementary medicine's methods and ideals, just as surely as it shows the weaknesses and flaws in the conventional, orthodox approach to AIDS.

Marijuana Can Help AIDS Patients

Robert Randall

About the Author: *Robert Randall is president of the Alliance for Cannabis Therapeutics (ACT), a patients-rights group in Washington, D.C. Randall, a glaucoma patient, became the first American to receive legal, medical access to marijuana in 1976.*

In the last decade of the millennium we are haunted by a pandemic plague which threatens to destabilize nations and impoverish entire continents. AIDS has brought many ancient and evil superstitions alive, mocked the modernity of our sciences and strained the capacity of our societal compassion.

In the midst of these titanic consequences we have discovered a commonplace, easily grown weed has beneficial properties which, while not curative, can greatly ease the torment which afflicts HIV [human immunodeficiency virus]-positive people. As fate would have it, the plant, Cannabis sativa, is universally prohibited and subjected to an unrelenting global assault by law enforcement bureaucracies who have, without much protest from eco-freaks, publicly proclaimed their intent to eradicate this most helpful plant species from the face of the earth.

Is this crazy? Sure. And welcome to the club. AIDS joins a long list of medical conditions including cancer, glaucoma, multiple sclerosis, paralysis, phantom and chronic pain, which respond favorably to marijuana therapy.

While the bulk of this viewpoint will focus on marijuana's use in AIDS therapy, it's important to quickly review the basics. . . .

In 1970, Congress created the Controlled Substances Act. Under the CSA marijuana was listed as a Schedule I drug. Schedule I drugs are defined as drugs with "no accepted medical use in treatment in the United States." They are also deemed to be "unsafe for use under medical supervision."

In an effort to scientifically confirm this absolute legal assumption Congress authorized federal agencies to conduct research. The first two directors of U.S. marijuana research were fired because they felt scientific inquiry should be neutral and directed at an honest evaluation of the plant's properties. They were hastily replaced by more malleable men dedicated to making a buck off the bureaucrats by trying to scientifically demonstrate the law enforcement assumption that marijuana is purest evil straight from Hell.

The feds have now spent over $200 million in this effort to demonstrate marijuana's evil character. As a result of this obsessive evaluation we know more about marijuana than we know about any of the commonly prescribed drugs marketed to us daily. For the last twenty years a scientific paper a day has explored marijuana's myriad possibilities.

This frantic investigation has unintentionally unearthed marijuana's long forgotten medicinal properties. So obvious are these therapeutic benefits that they surfaced despite the best efforts of bureaucrats and their research hacks to avoid such discomforting realities.

> ## "For the last twenty years a scientific paper a day has explored marijuana's myriad possibilities."

In 1970, researchers at UCLA accidentally discovered marijuana lowered eye pressure. This information, of tremendous import in the treatment of glaucoma, the nation's leading cause of blindness, was not trumpeted. It was suppressed.

In 1972, cancer specialists in Houston and Boston realized that young cancer patients were not vomiting after receiving their highly toxic chemical therapies. Why not? The young patients were smoking marijuana.

Even earlier, physicians walking the paralyzed wards at VA [Veterans Administration] hospitals, packed with returning casualties fresh from Southeast Asia, noted many of the newly disabled vets were smoking pot in their hospital beds and seemed to have fewer problems with muscle spasms.

"AIDS patients were quick to realize marijuana's therapeutic benefits."

Marijuana's medical use, historically documented and clearly outlined in the streams of data flowing into federal drug agencies, was not compatible with the legal imperative of an absolute prohibition. So the bureaucrats ignored the human benefits which might be received by patients from a rational, scientific exploitation of marijuana's therapeutic properties.

This policy of benign ignorance only lasted until 1976, when a glaucoma patient, arrested for growing four marijuana plants, argued his use of marijuana was not criminal, but an act of "medical necessity." The case, supported by two controlled medical studies which showed marijuana was not merely beneficial, but critical to the maintenance of this patient's vision, persuaded the court.

It was the first time any government body in the post-prohibition era had proclaimed marijuana a useful substance It was also the first time a court accepted a plea of medical necessity.

It was a decision which saved my sight. Marijuana has afforded me with fifteen years of sight I might not otherwise have enjoyed. So I know firsthand how important medical marijuana can be.

Since I first gained legal, medical access to marijuana in 1976, many patients have medically benefitted from marijuana. Most, unfortunately, have had to break the law to obtain the marijuana they medically needed.

Marijuana Prohibition

Working together, patients with life- and sense-threatening diseases have tried to break the bureaucratically imposed medical prohibition against marijuana.

In 1978, New Mexico became the first state in the nation to recognize marijuana's medical value in the treatment of cancer and glaucoma. Thirty-four states have enacted similar legislation.

Federal drug agencies, however, have blocked the implementation of these state laws. Most states never made marijuana available to any patients. Six states, however, provided marijuana to nearly 1,000 cancer patients in the early 1980s. The resulting studies clearly show marijuana is one of the most effective anti-vomiting drugs known to man.

For two years, from 1986 to 1988, the Drug Enforcement Administration (DEA) held public hearings on marijuana's medical use. At the end of these extensive hearings DEA's Chief Administrative Law Judge ruled marijuana has important medicinal properties and should be available by prescription. DEA refused to abide by the verdict and has blocked marijuana's medical use. In April 1991, the U.S. Court of Appeals in Washington ordered DEA to reconsider its opposition to marijuana's prescriptive medical use.

AIDS patients were quick to realize marijuana's therapeutic benefits. The Alliance for Cannabis Therapeutics (ACT), a Washington-based patient-rights group which monitors marijuana's medical use, began hearing from HIV-positive people in the mid-1980s.

HIV-positive people consistently reported three distinct, but critically important, therapeutic benefits;

1. Marijuana helped reduce the intense nausea and vomiting caused by HIV infection and the highly toxic drugs used to treat AIDS.

2. Marijuana makes patients hungry and able

to eat. As a result they were able to counteract the "Wasting Syndrome" and maintain or even increase their weight.

3. Finally, marijuana allows HIV-positive people to function normally, and to cope with the consequences of having a poorly understood and invariably lethal disease.

For the remainder of the 1980s the Alliance continued to collect such reports. But, despite offers of assistance, no HIV-positive patient wanted to "go public" and ask for legal access to marijuana.

Legal access to marijuana? Yes. In 1978, around the same time New Mexico was legislatively abandoning the medical prohibition, the FDA [Food and Drug Administration] began its so-called Compassionate IND [Investigational New Drug] program. Under the program seriously ill patients were told they could legally obtain marijuana for legitimate medical purposes.

This was not exactly true. The paperwork involved in a Compassionate IND request overwhelmed even the most well intentioned physician. The Compassionate IND program was compassionate in name only. But, a few patients with glaucoma, cancer and chronic pain managed to use the Compassionate IND system to legally obtain medical access to marijuana.

AIDS patients, ill in the midst of a War on Drugs, were already subjected to tremendous societal pressures, to fear.

In October 1989, Steve L., a 34-year-old Texas AIDS patient arrested for possessing marijuana, phoned the Alliance and asked for our help. He got it.

"When I smoke marijuana I'm living with AIDS. When I don't smoke marijuana I'm dying of AIDS."

"When I smoke marijuana I'm living with AIDS. When I don't smoke marijuana I'm dying of AIDS," Steve said. As any patient can tell you,

that's a hell of a difference.

The San Antonio AIDS Foundation helped the Alliance locate a physician and, within two weeks, Steve L. became the first AIDS patient to ask FDA for Compassionate IND access to marijuana. Under constant pressure from the Alliance, FDA approved Steve's request for medical marijuana in early December 1989.

The Politics of Compassion

The Drug Enforcement Administration tried to block Steve's FDA-approved shipment of medical marijuana. DEA did not want AIDS patients to secure marijuana because DEA was in court arguing marijuana had no medical value. For six weeks, while Steve's condition eroded, DEA delayed his first shipment. Finally, Steve "went public." The next day DEA permitted Steve's marijuana to be shipped.

I met Steve in person at the San Antonio VA Hospital the day before he received his first legal joint. Later, we smoked together. Two weeks later Steve died. Just before AIDS overwhelmed him I sent Steve a copy of a news story about him from an English-language paper in Tokyo. Steve died knowing he'd sent other AIDS patients a message. Two messages really. First, marijuana works! Second, you can make the bureaucrats give you marijuana if you demand it.

I was still missing Steve when I received a phone call from Kenny Jenks and his wife, Barbra. Kenny and his wife had been arrested for growing two marijuana plants. They got out of jail, bought a magazine and discovered an article about Steve.

"It was just like reading about us," Kenny Jenks said.

Kenny Jenks has hemophilia and got AIDS from a tainted blood transfusion he received in the early 1980s. Before he learned he was infected, Kenny transmitted the deadly HIV virus to his wife, Barbra. They were young. Kenny was 28. Barbra was 23. Could the Alliance help?

The Alliance helped Kenny and Barbra find a good doctor who applied for Compassionate IND access to marijuana. We also found Kenny and Barbra a good criminal lawyer. In June 1990 the doctor asked FDA for legal access to marijuana. In July, the young couple went on trial facing three felony charges which carried a five-year sentence.

The local court refused to hear Kenny and Barbra's "medical necessity" defense, despite testimony from two physicians who concluded marijuana was critical to their medical welfare. Medical records showed Barbra Jenks nearly died in early 1988 when her weight collapsed from 155 lbs. to 113 lbs. After she started smoking marijuana she regained nearly 25 lbs.

"Without marijuana my wife would be dead by now," Kenny Jenks told the court.

FDA "lost the paperwork" three times! After six months of delay, however, FDA granted their Compassionate IND request in December 1990. DEA blocked the shipment for another two months. But, in late February 1991, Kenny and Barbra Jenks gained legal, medically supervised access to federal supplies of medicinal marijuana.

During 1990, the Alliance helped one other HIV-positive person, a Virginia health care professional, gain legal access to marijuana. "Danny" received his first legal joint on Thanksgiving Eve.

Seeking Approved Marijuana

The Alliance realized in mid-1990 that it was going to be overwhelmed by HIV-positive people seeking legal, medical access to marijuana. In an effort to empower HIV-positive people and their physicians, the Alliance, working with Chicago financier Richard J. Dennis, launched the Marijuana/AIDS Research Service.

The MARS Project was publicly announced in Chicago on February 28, 1991. Kenny and Barbra Jenks were joined by Jim Barnes, a Michigan AIDS patient, Richard Dennis and myself.

MARS provides HIV-positive people and their physicians with all the paperwork required to file for Compassionate IND access to FDA-approved medical marijuana.

The MARS Project was an immediate success.

Within hours of the official announcement the first MARS packets were mailed from Washington, D.C.

In May 1991, Kenny and Barbra Jenks took the MARS Project to the 4th Annual AIDS Update Conference in San Francisco where they were overwhelmed by requests for MARS information.

The impact of MARS on federal drug agencies was striking. FDA approved more Compassionate IND requests in the first six months of 1991 than in the previous thirteen years.

"Depriving the desperately ill of needed medical care for symbolic reasons is barbaric."

By early June 1991, the Alliance had sent out several hundred MARS-based INDs. Additionally, the Alliance authorized AIDS support groups around the country to copy MARS materials. Cure AIDS Now, a Miami-based AIDS support group, distributed more than 1,000 MARS INDs to patients in South Florida.

Then, in late June 1991, major news organizations including the *Washington Post,* United Press International and the Associated Press revealed a secret FDA plan to terminate the Compassionate IND program. FDA officials, startled by the secret plan's sudden public disclosure, admitted they were shutting the program down because hundreds of AIDS patients were demanding medical access to marijuana.

The primary reason the drug bureaucrats gave for closing down the program was the "message" giving AIDS patients medical marijuana might send to America's young.

This is an absurd and brutal basis for public policy. Depriving the desperately ill of needed medical care for symbolic reasons is barbaric.

In place of marijuana, federal drug agencies are telling AIDS patients to take an officially sanctioned synthetic substitute marketed under the brand name Marinol.

Marinol is not marijuana. Marinol is a synthetic drug chemically constructed to mimic THC, the most powerfully psychoactive chemical in marijuana.

Marijuana, like all living things, is chemically complex. There are over 400 chemicals in marijuana, 60 of which appear nowhere else in nature except the human brain.

Some argue synthetic drugs are better than natural drugs. These people are called chemists who would be out of work if people didn't use synthetics. They have a bias. They pretend this bias is "science." In fact, this bias is more honestly called "profit."

The economic difference between marijuana and Marinol is striking. Marijuana can be grown, processed and delivered to patients for about a penny per dose. Real cheap. And marijuana grows in nearly any type of soil from the equator to the poles. So what we have here is a plant anyone can grow for nearly nothing in their backyard. Companies can't make money from something like this.

"Marijuana's most common side effect: it makes patients feel good."

Marinol is made in a factory with expensive chemicals. The result is an extremely expensive product which retails for $8 per dose. FDA is so anxious to impose Marinol on HIV-positive patients it has granted Marinol orphan drug status to prevent other manufacturers from entering the market with THC that can be far more inexpensively extracted from organic marijuana.

According to Kenny Jenks, "FDA is selling AIDS patients to the pharmaceutical companies like slabs of meat."

The therapeutic difference between marijuana and Marinol is nearly as profound as the profit differences.

Bioavailability is a measure of how fast a drug gets into the body and does some good.

Marijuana, when smoked, has an almost immediately positive effect. HIV-positive patients notice a sudden and prompt decline in vomiting and nausea within 5 to 10 minutes. Hunger asserts itself within 30 to 45 minutes after smoking,

Marinol is swallowed. Many patients simply vomit it up. Assuming a patient manages to keep the pill down it takes from *one to four hours* for Marinol to begin to work. If it works at all. An internal National Cancer Institute memo from 1987 describes synthetic THC (aka Marinol) as "erratic" and "unpredictable." That's an understatement.

Therapeutic utility is a measure of how well a drug works. Marijuana works. Studies on cancer patients in New Mexico, New York, California and Michigan consistently found marijuana reduces nausea and vomiting in 90% of patients *who failed to respond to conventional anti-nausea drugs.* And this high level of utility is repeatable from dose to dose, day to day, week to week. Marijuana retains its medicinal properties.

Marinol proved much less reliable with a positive effect in only 50-70% of patients only 50% of the time. And Marinol rapidly loses whatever therapeutic benefits it has over time. Marinol gets less and less effective with repeated use. Put simply, patients given Marinol start to throw up.

A 1979 National Cancer Institute (NCI) study clearly demonstrated these differences. The NCI study also confirmed that patients who failed to respond to Marinol still responded well to marijuana.

Adverse effects measure the unintended consequences associated with a drug's medical use. Marijuana's most common side effect: it makes patients feel good. Its second most common side effect: it makes you hungry. Third most common side effect: it makes you sleepy.

Adverse Reactions Minimal

Not a single cancer patient in the New Mexico program suffered an adverse side effect from smoking marijuana. Three patients given synthetic THC experienced panic reactions.

Marijuana makes patients feel "euphoric."

This translates into a "sense of well-being." Marinol causes intense anxiety, loss of control, mental confusion, depression, and it makes you very sleepy or manic, depending.

Marijuana, in short, works faster, more predictably and with greater safety than does Marinol, the FDA-sanctioned synthetic substitute.

"There is no clinical or research evidence which demonstrates marijuana injures the human immune system."

There is one final, very important difference between marijuana and Marinol. With marijuana the patient has complete control over the dose. This is called self-titration. It empowers the patient.

How does self-titration work? Simple. You smoke marijuana until the nausea and vomiting subside. Then you stop smoking. Put simply, your body tells you when you've had enough. When you stop smoking, you've stopped delivering any more drug.

With Marinol you lose control the second you swallow the pill. Anxiety attacks and full-blown panic reactions are commonplace as a result of the absence of patient control overdose.

The safest, most effective way to medically use marijuana is smoking. Smoking delivers the drug to the body quickly, relief is prompt and you have good control over the dose.

But some HIV-positive people can't smoke. Marijuana can be made into teas or baked into cookies. Eating products with marijuana to achieve a medical effect is tricky. Dosing control isn't very good. It's easy to eat too much or too little. And it takes a lot longer to get relief. This lag time means patients who ingest marijuana are less likely to get the therapeutic benefits they are seeking.

Federal drug agencies have tried to frighten AIDS patients away from marijuana. The most commonly used excuse is that marijuana "might" damage the immune system.

First, many drugs do, in fact, damage the immune system. Often these drugs are employed in AIDS therapy because their beneficial effects are thought to warrant their damaging consequences.

Second, there is no clinical or research evidence which demonstrates marijuana injures the human immune system. More than thirty-five studies of marijuana's effects on the immune system have been conducted over the past two decades. None of these studies has found persuasive evidence that marijuana use suppresses or significantly alters immune system response. Several studies actually suggest marijuana may enhance immune response.

Based on available data, marijuana does not pose a significant threat to the human immune system. The most recent study (and the only one using humans as opposed to test tubes or white rats) was published in 1989 in the *Journal of Steroid Biochemistry*. The findings? "No endocrine or immunological alterations were observed." The conclusion? "[A]t least some of the previously described immunosuppressive effects of THC may be nonspecific effects secondary to very high doses of THC used for study." Translation? Early studies purporting harm to the immune system were seriously flawed in their methodology.

Unregulated Marijuana

The fact that most HIV-positive people are forced to illegally acquire marijuana to meet their legitimate medical needs does create potential problems. First, there is no assurance the substance you get is actually marijuana. Second, there is no guarantee of potency. Third, the product you buy on the street may contain contaminants or be adulterated with other drugs. . . .

Marijuana works. Federal drug agencies are trying to force AIDS patients to take an expensive, medically inferior substitute. Don't accept second-class care from a second-class government. Break the law. Get the medical care you need and demand that they change the law.

Chapter 5:
How Can the Spread of AIDS Be Prevented?

Preface

Soon after scientists discovered how the AIDS virus was transmitted, both the government and the medical community implemented efforts to inform the public about ways to prevent it. These efforts included sending brochures about the disease to households throughout the U.S., public service announcements on radio and television, and billboard advertisements. Such informational messages often recommended the use of condoms during sex to avoid AIDS infection.

While some people have welcomed these messages as a step toward containing the deadly disease, others have objected to the public discussion of sensitive and personal issues such as the use of condoms. Perhaps the most controversy has been generated by the inclusion of condom information in school AIDS education programs, which are sometimes part of sex education classes.

Many AIDS experts advocate programs that explain the use of condoms to children and adolescents. By educating students about AIDS at an early age, experts contend, future generations may be able to use the information to avoid contracting the disease. One of the most outspoken advocates of such education is former U.S. surgeon general C. Everett Koop. In a 1986 report, Koop urged that AIDS education be taught in schools from grades three through twelve. While he stressed the greater importance of mutually faithful relationships and abstinence from sex, Koop recommended informing students about the use of condoms as a means of preventing AIDS.

Many Americans agree with Koop. In a June 1991 Roper poll, 47 percent said condom information and distribution should be part of AIDS education curricula as early as junior high school. Despite such widespread support, many school districts in the U.S. have debated adopting such programs. The New York City Board of Education has perhaps gone the furthest toward making condoms part of its AIDS education program. In February 1991, it narrowly approved a plan to make free condoms available to 221,000 high school students. In addition, each city high school is mandated to offer a minimum of ten class periods per week where staff and volunteers provide condom information.

Safe-Sex Education

Not all Americans welcome these safe-sex campaigns. The idea of teaching children about condoms or distributing them to students disturbs many parents, teachers, and community and religious leaders, who argue that such plans take the wrong approach to preventing AIDS. They believe these strategies encourage teenagers to have sex, thereby increasing the risk of HIV infection rather than decreasing it.

According to writer William F. Jasper, these programs "show nothing less than a deliberate, widespread campaign to sexually corrupt our nation's youth." Critics of condom programs, such as E.W. Habert, say that abstinence, or avoiding sex, is the only certain way to prevent AIDS. Says Habert, a college professor, "To present this concept of chastity to our students may be one of the most urgent roles of education in the last part of the twentieth century."

Since AIDS has no cure at present, prevention is the key to controlling the disease. Whether explicit AIDS education for youth will help stop the spread of the disease is one of the topics debated in the following chapter.

Using Condoms Can Help Prevent the Spread of AIDS

Robert A. Hatcher and Melissa Sammons Hughes

About the Authors: *Robert A. Hatcher is a professor of gynecology and obstetrics. Melissa Sammons Hughes is a graduate of Emory University School of Medicine in Atlanta, Georgia.*

In most societies condom use is minimal. Throughout the world condoms are used by only 5% of reproductive-age couples. Clearly, if condom use is going to play a significant role in the prevention of the spread of human immunodeficiency virus (HIV) infection, condom use must increase in the near future. Of the most populous nations in the world, condom use is most extensive in Japan where condoms are used by 43% of married reproductive-age women. This falls to 18% in the United Kingdom and to 10% in the United States. Condoms are used by 2% or less of married couples in Indonesia, Brazil, Bangladesh, Pakistan, Egypt and Nigeria.

The data come from the most recent national survey for each of the countries—the 1982 National Survey of Family Growth (NSFG Cycle III) in the case of the United States. More recent data for the United States are available from a series of Ortho birth control studies which have been carried out annually for almost two decades. The Ortho surveys have included unmarried women for the past decade and 15-17-year-olds since 1985. In the United States, condom use increased by 33% from 12% to 16% from 1982 to 1987. Use of condoms by married women increased insignificantly from 14% in 1982 to 15% in 1987, but increased from 9% to 16% among unmarried women in the same time span. Even more dramatic was the increase in favorable attitudes toward condoms. From 1977 to 1982 favorable opinions of the condom remained stable at about 40%. Favorable opinions of the condom fell to 38-39% from 1982 to 1984. Then, favorable opinions of the condom rose sharply to 60% in 1987. Increased use of condoms and more favorable attitudes toward condoms appear to be related to growing interest in avoiding sexually transmitted infections.

"Condom use is going to play a significant role in the prevention of . . . HIV infection."

In his study of condom use in developing nations, H.I. Goldberg found that 1% or less of married women aged 15-44 used condoms in 36 of 66 nations, including eight of the 15 nations where 100 or more cases of AIDS have been reported to the World Health Organization as of February, 1988.

Condoms are used for two major purposes: to prevent pregnancy and to prevent infection. In neither case is protection 100%. J. Trussell and K. Kost's extensive review suggests three failure rates for condoms as contraceptives in the first year of use. The authors' best estimate of the failure rate among couples using condoms consistently and correctly is 2%. Among typical users the first year failure rate is 12%, while the lowest reported failure rate in first year users is 4%. For typical users of condoms, the failure rate is lower than for typical users of the diaphragm, sponge, cervical cap, spermicides or fertility awareness methods.

Condoms do break and it is important to remember that postcoital contraception may at times be indicated. As long as condoms break; inclination and opportunity unexpectedly converge; men rape women; diaphragms and cervical caps are dislodged; people are so ambivalent about sex that they need to feel "swept away"; IUDs [intrauterine devices] are expelled; and pills are lost or forgotten, we will need morning-after birth control.

In an attempt to determine the likelihood of condom breakage, 282 attendees of family planning and reproductive health conferences; 86 university students; and 89 women attending a municipal hospital family planning clinic were asked several questions about condom use, condom breakage, and pregnancies specifically attributable to a condom that broke. The overall rate of condom breakage was one break per 105 acts of intercourse. However, women seen at the public family planning clinic had a breakage rate 10 times higher than the reproductive health employees (1:16 *vs.* 1:161). The university students averaged one break per 92 condom uses, which was intermediate between the other two groups in the study. Compared to family planning clinic patients, the employees working in the reproductive health field were older (mean age 37) and had used condoms more often (an average of 139 times per person). The average clinic patient was 23-years-old and had used a condom only 27 times per person.

"Consistent condom use . . . helped decrease HIV transmission from 82% to 17%."

In two states, Minnesota and Pennsylvania, more detailed information was collected from 195 individuals working in the field of reproductive health. Condom breakage was more than four times as likely to occur among women who had used condoms less than 100 times than among women who had used condoms more than 250 times. This suggests that frequent condom use teaches women how to use condoms more effectively. Moreover, when condoms did break they were less likely to lead to pregnancy among women who had used condoms more than 250 times (one pregnancy per 31 condom breaks) than in women who had used condoms 100-250 times (one pregnancy per nine condom breaks) or in those women who had used condoms less than 100 times (one pregnancy per 13 condom breaks). This suggests that once a pregnancy results from a broken condom, a woman will not return to the use of condoms, while if pregnancy does not occur, a woman may persist in using condoms. For example, one woman in the study had experienced 15 condom breakages using condoms 1,250 times, but had not experienced a pregnancy attributable to a broken condom.

Condom Effectiveness

How effective are condoms at preventing transmission of the virus which causes AIDS? In one study of heterosexual transmission of the human immunodeficiency virus (HIV), 79% of the couples using condoms experienced condom breakage at least once in the 18-month study period. Another 8% experienced leakage at least once. The heterosexual partners of HIV-positive individuals were least likely to seroconvert if abstinence was employed (0% or zero of 12). Of the 18 couples using condoms consistently, three (17%) seroconverted to become HIV-positive over 18 months. If condoms were not used or were used erratically, as was the case in 17 couples where one person was infected with HIV, then 82% (14 of 17) became HIV-positive during the study period. Consistent condom use thus helped decrease HIV transmission from 82% to 17% but did not eliminate the risk of HIV transmission. An investigation of prostitutes in Zaire demonstrated an association between condom use and protection against HIV infection. W. Cates concludes that clinical studies suggest "that the protective effect of condoms against many STDs [sexually transmitted diseases] is real and clinically important."

Natural membrane condoms, often called "skin" condoms or "natural skin" condoms, are actually made from the caecum of lamb intestine. Most are produced in Australia. The hepatitis B virus (HBV), which is approximately $42\,nm$ (nanometers) in diameter, has been demonstrated to pass through natural membrane condoms. The same investigator found that larger viruses such as the retrovirus causing AIDS (HIV, $100\text{-}150\,nm$), cytomegalovirus (CMV, $150\text{-}200\,nm$), and herpes simplex virus (HSV, $150\text{-}200\,nm$) did not pass through natural membrane condoms. Other investigators have found that the human immunodeficiency virus has passed through pores in natural membrane condoms. At a conference convened in early 1987 to discuss the use of condoms in the prevention of sexually transmitted disease, a number of participants expressed the opinion that they could "see no reason why anyone would recommend natural skin condoms for the prevention of disease." Even stronger was a statement by Malcolm Potts, a longtime student and advocate of condoms, who said, "I would ban the use of natural skin condoms until they have been proven safe." Potts recommends the use of spermicidal latex condoms if the prevention of sexually transmitted infections is a major reason for using condoms. Another position is that natural membrane condoms, which act as barriers to all but the smallest viral particles, should not be too strongly discouraged, particularly in view of the finding that natural membrane condoms are the only condoms acceptable to some sexually active men.

"Where there is a clear and present danger of . . . HIV infection or any other STD, condoms make extremely good sense."

A strong word of caution has now been sounded suggesting that clinicians counsel men and women that natural membrane condoms or "skin" condoms are not quite as effective a barrier as latex condoms. Latex condoms, and in particular latex condoms with an effective spermicide added, appear to be the best choice, particularly if the prevention of infection is a high priority for an individual or a couple using condoms.

Condom detractors suggest that condom breakage leading to potential spread of the human immunodeficiency virus is too catastrophic an outcome to even consider their recommendation. Do condoms lead to safe sex? No, but most counsellors would suggest that condoms certainly do make sex safer. If condoms are used *when sexual intercourse definitely would have occurred, condoms or no condoms*, then condoms clearly do make sex safer than it otherwise would have been. Organizations providing condoms might consider developing a rejoinder to condom detractors.

HIV Status Is Critical

If a person who is not HIV-infected is about to have intercourse, far more critical than condom use or the lack of it is the HIV status of the second person with whom the noninfected person is about to be intimate. However, only a small fraction of the U.S. population has been tested for HIV. And the possible window of time it can take before a person becomes HIV antibody-positive keeps getting longer. So knowledge of another person's HIV status is imperfect. Moreover, even when one or both people who are about to enter into an intimate sexual relationship have been tested recently and know their HIV antibody status, there is no guarantee that they will be able to summon the courage to discuss it; or that, if they do discuss it, the information shared between the two people will be honest. In sum, a noninfected individual may not accurately know the HIV antibody status of a person with whom he or she is about to have intercourse.

Sexually transmitted infections may complicate pregnancy for a pregnant woman, her partner(s) and/or her child. In the following situations, the provision of condoms to a pregnant woman should be carefully considered:

1. A pregnant woman whose partner is diagnosed as having herpes simplex virus (HSV) infection, chlamydia infection or nongonococcal urethritis (NGU), human immunodeficiency virus (HIV) infection or acquired immunodeficiency disease (AIDS), venereal warts, trichomoniasis, gonorrhea, syphilis, or hepatitis B. (Or if one of the above infections has been strongly suggested.)
2. A woman whose partner is likely to have multiple partners during the course of her pregnancy or whose partner is an intravenous drug abuser.
3. A pregnant woman who is diagnosed, herself, for any of the following infections: HSV infection, HIV infection, chlamydia, pelvic inflammatory disease, mucopurulent cervicitis, venereal warts, trichomoniasis, gonorrhea, syphilis or hepatitis B.
4. A pregnant woman who indicates that she is quite likely to have multiple partners during her pregnancy.

Condoms are not perfect at preventing either pregnancy or HIV infection. For sexually active couples, there are more effective ways of preventing pregnancy. For couples committed to having sexual intercourse where the prevention of HIV transmission is a goal, the best intervention to employ, once the decision to have intercourse has been made, is a condom. In most instances, the condom will not break.

Abstinence

There are many, many couples—throughout the world in different cultures—of different ages and at various degrees of risk of exposure to HIV infection, who would be much wiser not to have intercourse at all. We, in family planning and sex education programs, have been praising the option of abstinence for the past two decades. Often our "love carefully," "save it for later," "how to say no" or "how to say not now" messages have been appreciated and abstinence has been fostered. But our messages also fall on completely deaf ears, in some instances. Where there is a clear and present danger of possible transmission of HIV infection or any other STD, condoms make extremely good sense. The debate should end. It has gone on too long.

Education Can Help Young Adults Avoid AIDS

Linda Marsa

About the Author: *Linda Marsa is a frequent contributor to* Omni, *a monthly science magazine.*

A slightly built young man in jeans and a work shirt pads across the stage of the National 4-H Center auditorium in Chevy Chase, Maryland, and introduces himself to the audience—a cross section of 100 teachers and students from Washington, DC's public high-school system. The two-day conference, called "Live-In-Learning: AIDS Prevention Education Experience," is sponsored by Washington's DC Public Schools AIDS Education Program. Its goal: to teach ninth, tenth, and eleventh graders—kids too young to vote or buy a drink—peer counseling techniques they can use to help their fellow students avoid AIDS. Later in the day, the group will see *Don't Forget Sherrie,* a Red Cross docudrama about a girl their age who got AIDS after a single instance of unprotected sex with her boyfriend.

"Does anyone here know someone who has AIDS?" asks the man onstage, a representative of a local AIDS support network called LifeLink. No one moves.

"Now you do," he says. "I have AIDS."

The audience gasps. "I was shocked," says Carolyn Hunter, an eleventh grader at Wilson Senior High School in northwest Washington. "I suddenly realized that AIDS was a reality that could happen to me." Meeting the man from LifeLink and watching *Don't Forget Sherrie* had

Linda Marsa, "Teaching AIDS," *Omni,* April 1990. Reprinted by permission of *Omni,* © 1990, Omni Publications International, Ltd.

the most profound impact on the students of all the events that weekend, recalls Hunter. "These people weren't actors; they were *real* people," she says. "After talking to someone with AIDS and seeing kids my own age who are infected with the virus, it really hit home."

The kind of unflinching frankness that characterized the Live-In-Learning conference has made the DC AIDS education program one of the nation's most innovative and therefore effective efforts. Thirty-three state legislatures now require AIDS education in their districts' schools, but both content and approach vary widely. Most school systems try to balance state mandates to provide precise information against parents' desire to prolong their children's innocence. Washington educators, however, deliver the goods with a special urgency. An overwhelming proportion of their students live in neighborhoods rent by poverty, violence, teenage pregnancy, and drugs. They are routinely exposed to (and tempted by) drug use and needle sharing, sex with multiple partners without protection, and prostitution—the so-called high-risk behaviors that lead to contracting HIV, the virus that causes AIDS. What these kids learn in school could save their lives.

"I suddenly realized that AIDS was a reality that could happen to me."

Kids growing up in cities like Washington, New York, Los Angeles, and San Francisco, beset by disproportionately high rates of HIV infection, might seem to have a more critical need for information about AIDS than their peers in other areas. Alarming new data, however, indicate that an entire generation of young people may be in jeopardy of contracting the deadly virus. By October 1989 the federal Centers for Disease Control (CDC) had recorded 1,908 cases of full-blown AIDS among children under thirteen in addition to 439 cases among teen-agers—a jump of 40 percent in the last two years. Even more chilling, a fifth of the men and a quarter of all the women who have AIDS are under thirty: The incubation period can last ten years, meaning most in this age group were infected as adolescents.

"The youngsters who are most susceptible to HIV infection . . . often fall between the system's cracks."

The CDC refuses to make future projections or comment on the specter of an epidemic among adolescents. And in reality, the number of full-fledged AIDS cases among teenagers remains relatively low—in line, the CDC says, with figures for the general population. The causes for concern are manifold, however, given young people's sexual habits. Each year, two and a half million American teenagers—or one out of every six—contract a sexually transmitted disease. Another million get pregnant—an incidence of teenage pregnancy unequaled in the Western world.

These behaviors have spawned a nationwide scramble to implement AIDS education programs. That's no easy task, given that sex remains a stumbling block in mainstream America. While adding AIDS instruction to sex education classes for the postpubescent may seem reasonable preparation for life in the nineties, some of the new programs target children as young as five.

Warning Children and Teens

The question of age appropriateness sometimes collides with the mandate for AIDS education. Jackie Walton Sadler, director of the DC public schools program, says that even the youngest children should be warned about needles. Preschoolers and second graders run the risk of picking up contaminated works on the school ground and playing with them or trying to use them as they've seen on TV, she says.

Some teachers warn second graders against the ancient childhood rite of pricking their fingers in "blood brothers" ceremonies. In Washington anal intercourse is raised at the junior high school level but is not associated specifically with homosexuality. "We don't talk about high-risk groups; we talk about high-risk behaviors," says Sadler.

Most schools, however, have bowed to parental and political pressure and watered down safe sex instruction to the point where it does not address sexual behavior explicitly. If teachers discuss sex at all, they preach the joys of abstinence and mutually exclusive heterosexual relationships. Even mentioning the word *condom* is taboo in many districts as well as most parochial schools.

"Most of these programs give out plenty of information about AIDS but do virtually nothing to show teenagers how to practice safe sex or to abstain," says Debra Haffner, executive director of the New York-based Sex Information and Education Council. "They need to tell teenagers *how* to say no when someone is pressuring them into having sex and how to avoid potentially dangerous situations. They need to show teenagers how to use condoms and where to buy them—or even give them out for free. The underlying problem is that as a nation we are unwilling to acknowledge our teenagers as sexual beings. But until we start being more honest, lots of young people will die."

Nationwide just a handful of programs deal sensitively and realistically with the subject of sex in the hope of persuading teenagers to AIDS-proof their sex lives. San Francisco's Wedge Program and Kansas City's Good Samaritan Project use interaction with AIDS patients to raise teens' consciousness about the disease. In New York the Red Cross is developing a classroom game designed by a high-school administrator from the Bronx, where, she says, the students don't say "No" to anything. The game uses dice and a "sexual wheel of misfortune" to teach students the consequences of unsafe sex and demonstrate the idea that each time they go to bed with someone, they are in effect having sex with all of that person's previous partners. . . .

Students and Dropouts Targeted

The DC public schools program has become a beacon because its message seems to be reaching its audience. "It's working," says Sadler. "The kids appreciate the opportunity to go out and network. They feel comfortable with the material and their knowledge level has increased. Their parents accept it and their teachers appreciate the fact that the peer educators augment what they teach in class."

At the Chevy Chase conference, participants devised slogans, skits, and rap songs they could use to educate their classmates about AIDS transmission and safe sex. They learned how to use condoms effectively and role-played situations in which young women persuaded unwilling partners to wear them. Back at school the students festooned their campuses with signs reading LATEX IS THE MORAL FIBER OF AMERICA and VIRGINS ARE FIRST CLASS PEOPLE and distributed booklets with suggestions for buying condoms.

The youngsters who are most susceptible to HIV infection, however, often fall between the system's cracks and never receive any information. Among adolescents living on the streets, the virus has already spread rapidly. A survey of 1,800 teenagers conducted by Covenant House, a network of privately funded shelters for homeless teenagers and runaways, revealed that 7 percent were infected with AIDS. "We're getting discouraged about trying to reach kids exclusively through the schools," says Devon Davidson, project director of the AIDS Education Project for the National Coalition of Advocates for Students, a nonprofit student-advocacy group headquartered in Boston. "That's because the adolescents who are at highest risk are not in school; they either attend sporadically or they've dropped out. We're trying to figure out where these kids gather and how to reach them."

The Los Angeles Free Clinic (LAFC) is making some headway: It sponsors a theater troupe production of a play about eight homeless teens and their effort to grapple with a friend's death from AIDS. In the past year the semiprofessional troupe has performed before more than 5,000 teenagers at runaway shelters, juvenile halls, church groups, and universities. After each performance the actors hold an informal rap session to answer questions about AIDS and provide information about using condoms correctly and cleaning shared needles.

"We don't preach because if we do, they won't listen to us," says Jack Carrel, the LAFC's adolescent education coordinator. "These kids don't believe they're vulnerable: AIDS has such a long incubation period, and they rarely know anyone who has been diagnosed with the disease. We not only have to make AIDS real to them," he says, "but we must show them *how* to protect themselves. Doing anything less is irresponsible, and expecting them to 'just say no' is wildly unrealistic."

"We not only have to make AIDS real to them, . . . but we must show them *how* to protect themselves."

Peter S. is a case in point. At thirteen he began running away from his home in a working-class suburb of Los Angeles. Each time he left, he lived on the streets and had sex with men in exchange for food and a place to stay. Peter didn't think he was at risk for AIDS because he doesn't think of himself as gay: Now sixteen, he has a girlfriend at the high school he attends sporadically, and they started having sex two years ago. Neither saw a need to use condoms. In 1989 Peter went for an AIDS test; the results came back positive. Although he remains symptom-free, the teenager is consumed with guilt about the possibility that he could have given his girlfriend AIDS. He is reluctant to make plans for the future because no one can tell him how much time he has.

Partner Notification Can Control AIDS

Larry Katzenstein

About the Author: *Larry Katzenstein is a senior editor for* American Health, *a monthly health magazine.*

"Some people break down and start sobbing. Others sit back in shock—numb. And some get furious with me for tracking them down," says Wisconsin health worker Juana Sabatino, whose job it is to find the partners of people infected with the AIDS virus and inform them that they, too, may have been infected. "But I sit there and hold their hands and say, 'Look, I'm here to help you. I'm here because I care about your health. And I can help you get the care you need if you're infected, or help you learn how to protect yourself if you're not.' It might take 45 minutes, but then they calm down. Most people are grateful that I've come. One even called me an angel from heaven." They have good reason to be grateful. If you're a partner of someone infected with HIV [human immunodeficiency virus], the virus that causes AIDS, a visit from someone like Sabatino can be a lifesaver. If you're not infected, you can take steps to minimize the risk that you will be. And even if testing shows you're infected, the AIDS drug AZT can delay illness in infected people who don't yet have symptoms. But will people at risk be warned? The question is especially crucial for women.

Women are all too often the unsuspecting

partners of HIV-infected people, especially bisexual men. According to an estimate by Dr. Bruce Voeller, president of the Mariposa Education and Research Foundation in Topanga, CA, there are 10 million bisexual men in the U.S.—twice the number who are exclusively gay. Bisexual men often have many male partners, which puts them at high risk for AIDS. The overwhelming majority, say psychiatrists and sex therapists, conceal their bisexuality from wives or girlfriends for fear of losing them or their jobs if word gets out.

"Women are all too often the unsuspecting partners of HIV-infected people, especially bisexual men."

In addition, the HIV virus is transmitted much more readily from men to women than from women to men, making it especially crucial to warn the female partner of an infected man. A study followed two groups of heterosexual couples—one where the female partners were infected, the other where the male partners were infected. 20% of the women became infected—nearly 10 times the percentage (2.4%) of men who became infected.

Partner notification has become ensnared in controversy. As states bolster partner notification programs, their efforts are colliding with the right to anonymous testing for the AIDS virus.

And so, behind the lines of the war against AIDS, a second battle is raging between the patient's right to privacy and the partner's right to know, between individual rights and public health. The key question: Should states abandon anonymous AIDS testing and require all who test positive for the virus to be identified so their partners can be warned?

In a free society, people can't be forced to divulge intimate information about themselves— even if it bears on the health of others. But states are implementing programs that, short of coercion, will increase the odds that the partners of HIV-infected people will be warned that they may already be infected or face the risk of becoming infected. In programs throughout the U.S., thousands of people have already been notified—and many have responded by getting tested and taking precautions against infection.

Anonymous testing, available at some clinics in most states, remains the main method. People are given confidential code numbers to use when they call back for the test results. Only that person knows if he's infected. People tested by their own doctors enjoy similar protection, since most states don't require that doctors report the names of those who test positive to the health department.

But while anonymous testing assures maximum confidentiality—a legitimate concern, since people known to be infected often face discrimination—it hinders efforts to warn their partners of the risks they face. Now, largely because of the proven benefits of early medical intervention, the trend is away from anonymous testing. The American Medical Association, the CDC [Centers for Disease Control] and many state health departments now favor reporting the names of people who test positive.

Preventing HIV Infection

By obtaining the names of HIV-infected people, health departments can help them get medical attention before they get sick. Symptoms of AIDS generally don't appear until five to 10 years after infection, and early treatment with the drug AZT can help infected people stave off illness. Equally important, name reporting provides health departments with a crucial link to the partners of infected people.

Health department workers can contact people who've tested positive and ask their cooperation in alerting their partners that they may be at risk for AIDS. As a result, some could be saved from infection; those unknowingly infected could receive early treatment; and the spread of AIDS could be slowed. Anonymous testing, on the other hand, leaves notification largely up to

those who are infected—and they often don't notify their partners.

"We have found in Colorado that if you leave notification up to the patient, only one in 10 give it any thought at all," says Fred Wolf, chief of the AIDS section of the sexually transmitted disease program at the Colorado Department of Health in Denver. Studies tend to support his pessimistic view.

"Those unknowingly infected could receive early treatment; and the spread of AIDS could be slowed."

Researchers interviewed 66 sexually active gay and bisexual men who went for anonymous testing in California's Alameda County. One in eight said they would not tell their steady partners if they tested positive; one in four would not tell their casual partners.

Another study, involving 93 gay or bisexual men living in San Francisco, found that 77% of men who tested positive had informed their steady partners; 60% had told their former or casual partners; and only 51% had informed their new partners—men they began having sex with *after* they learned they were infected.

HIV-infected women are also reluctant to break the news to current and former partners. A study of 25 HIV-infected women in New Jersey found that almost none of them intended to tell their partners.

Name Reporting

States increasingly are cutting back on anonymous testing; eight have eliminated it entirely. Instead, to bolster partner notification efforts, they require that names of infected people be reported to the health department. But name reporting is a trend that some people—particularly gay- and civil-rights activists—find worrisome.

Keeping lists of infected people, they say, invites breaches of confidentiality that may ruin lives. They also warn that apprehension about being on a list will drive people away from testing and counseling. "Whether it's realistic or not, most people have a gut reaction to the government's knowing they're HIV-infected. It's called fear," says Chai Feldblum, legislative counsel for the American Civil Liberties Union AIDS project. The concern that mandatory name reporting will jeopardize privacy may no longer be justified, however. Courts are granting AIDS-related matters stronger privacy protection, and sanctions for confidentiality breaches have become more severe, according to David Schulman of the Los Angeles City Attorney's office. Also, at least 30 states have passed laws that protect the confidentiality of HIV-related information; others have strengthened confidentiality provisions of sexually transmitted disease laws already on the books. "These laws protect the identity of people who get tested, their test results and medical records," says Larry Gostin of the American Society of Law and Medicine.

"Partner notification could mark a major advance in the battle against AIDS."

So far, 25 states have adopted some form of "mandatory name reporting," with more states expected to follow suit. Those tested are of course informed of the results. But in addition, as the term implies, doctors and test centers must report the names of people testing positive for HIV to state health departments. Then a department employee contacts them—and, later, searches for their partners.

"I call the client and always verify that I am talking to the right person," Sabatino says of her initial contact. "Then I say I'd like to get together. I don't go into detail on the phone because of confidentiality.

"If the person agrees, we set up a time to meet—generally at their home, at their conve-nience, any time, night or day. I'll go anywhere.

"I tell them just what HIV infection means— that it does not mean they have AIDS, but it does mean they can transmit the virus. I tell them about safer sex practices, show them how to use a condom. I explain that I can hook them up with all the services in their community— support groups, programs for families, medical and mental health facilities."

Voluntary Notification

Sabatino then brings up the subject of partner notification. "I say, 'We'd like your help in notifying anyone you might have had contact with, including needle-sharing partners and sexual partners.' I will ask not only for each partner's name, address and phone number, but also for a complete description—height, weight, hair color, any identifying marks, where they work, where they hang out—to make sure I contact the right person. There might be more than one person in the neighborhood with the same name."

Even at this point, people can decide to notify partners themselves. If so, the public health worker prepares them for the anger and blame they're likely to encounter. But if they prefer not to do it themselves, Sabatino and her fellow workers will do the notifying for them.

Partner notification is nothing new. As recently as 10 years ago, when having a sexually transmitted disease usually meant having either syphilis or gonorrhea, partner notification was called "contact tracing." What is new is the misunderstanding that now surrounds it.

"There has been a lot of criticism of partner notification, but it has come from not understanding what it is," says Wolf. The first misconception, he says, is that people who test positive for the AIDS virus will somehow be forced to reveal their partners' names. They won't. Their cooperation is entirely voluntary.

The second misconception is that partner notification can jeopardize the confidentiality of HIV-infected people. That's extremely unlikely. Stringent safeguards prevent partners from discovering the identity of the person who may have infected them. Even critics are unable to point to instances where someone's HIV status was wrongfully disclosed.

Ensuring confidentiality ranks as a top priority for Sabatino when she contacts a partner at risk. "I meet with the partner and say that someone cared enough about their health to warn them that they may have been exposed to HIV infection. I can't tell them who gave me their name, not even if it was a man or a woman. I just say it could be anyone they had sex or shared needles with in the last 10 years.

"People always ask, 'Who gave you my name?' But we will never reveal that. You can do anything to me and I will not tell you the name."

Support for Notification

Partners are urged to get tested for the AIDS virus. And they're given information about HIV infection, how the virus is transmitted, safe sex practices, and medical and mental health facilities available in their areas. Partners are also asked for names of people they may have exposed. And so the process goes.

How do notified partners react to the programs? Critics contend that partner notification will alienate them by prompting fears of infection, discrimination or privacy violation. But a South Carolina study found otherwise. Only 12 of 132 notified partners had suspected that they might have been exposed to HIV. When asked if the health department had done the right thing in telling them about their exposure, 87% responded "yes." And 92% said the health department should continue notifying partners at risk.

Other studies clearly show the value in finding unsuspecting but infected people who can benefit from early treatment:

• Over a 10-month period in Florida, some 1,500 HIV-infected people gave the health department the names of more than 2,000 partners. Nearly three-fourths were located and counseled. Of 1,286 partners who agreed to be tested, 390, or 30%, tested positive.

• In a Belgian study, infected women and men were enrolled in a partner-notification study. They provided the names of 92 heterosexual partners, who in turn were notified and tested. 36 of them, or 39%, tested positive.

If adopted with vigor nationwide, partner notification could mark a major advance in the battle against AIDS. The evidence so far shows that partner notification programs can safeguard the confidentiality of HIV-infected persons. And for people who are at risk of infection but don't know it, partner notification can save lives.

Needle-Exchange Programs Can Prevent Drug Users from Spreading AIDS

Rod Sorge

About the Author: *Rod Sorge is a needle-exchange-program coordinator for the AIDS organization ACT UP (AIDS Coalition to Unleash Power) in New York City. Sorge is also assistant editor of* Health/PAC Bulletin, *a quarterly publication of the Health Policy Advisory Center in New York.*

We have understood HIV [human immuno-deficiency virus] transmission for years. The routes are obvious, limited, and modifiable, yet HIV seroprevalence has steadily increased around the world. There have been only limited medical advances in the treatment of HIV-related illness. Because of a lack of federal leadership on all fronts, from funding to discrimination, misguided research priorities at the National Institutes of Health (NIH) and the Food and Drug Administration (FDA), and because the virus continues to confound researchers the more it is studied, the dream of making AIDS a chronic but manageable condition remains mostly a dream as we start to live through its second decade.

Instead of producing safer sex education for men who have sex with men, the government still demands an end to such sexuality; and instead of producing safer drug use education, the government demands an end to drug use by force rather than treatment. Many of our laws

Rod Sorge, "Drug Policy in the Age of AIDS," *Health/PAC Bulletin,* Fall 1990. Reprinted with permission.

and cultural mores regarding sexuality (like prostitution and sodomy laws) and drug use (such as hypodermic possession and drug paraphernalia statutes) only create a climate that promotes silence, secrecy, hate, and shame at a time when we need to be talking openly about sex and drug use. It is not surprising, then, that most of the AIDS prevention education that has been effective has been developed outside of government agencies and in the communities at which it is aimed.

> ## "Community-based needle exchange programs . . . prevent further HIV infection among [drug addicts]."

As the "second wave" of the epidemic crests, and seroprevalence reaches staggering levels among intravenous drug users (IVDU's), there is a growing movement among providers, AIDS activists, researchers, and policymakers toward a drug policy paradigm aimed not at incarcerating and punishing users, or at positing absentionism as the only alternative to drug taking, but at educating users about how to reduce drug-related harm. AIDS activists across the country are establishing, often illegally, programs in which drug users can exchange used needles for new ones and learn how to clean their works with bleach to help limit the transmission of HIV from the sharing of contaminated needles. Once again community activists have refused to wait out the prevention debates—quagmires of personal anti-drug morality and local politics—and have taken public health into their own hands. This viewpoint attempts to articulate some of the arguments and developments in the U.S. movement for harm reduction.

Nowhere has the debate about needle exchange and safer injection education been as intense as in New York City. The complex racial realities and politics that dominate many aspects of New York life have likewise influenced this discussion. Where three socio-epidemics—homelessness, drug addiction, and AIDS—intertwine to devastate communities of color, some argue that needle exchange or bleach distribution programs are merely a way of ignoring the scope and gravity of these epidemics, paltry interventions that mock the realities of many people's lives. Most opponents of needle exchange programs believe that drug treatment should be given top priority, and that anything less is a non-solution. Some contend, despite much evidence to the contrary, that needle distribution would add to the problem by encouraging drug use or, at the very least, by sending "mixed messages" about drug use.

In their search for a single and immediate solution, opponents of harm-reduction measures simplify the complex phenomenon of drug taking and the complex lives and motivations of drug users. Their arguments reflect a lack of knowledge about addiction as it currently exists in New York City, the realities of the services that are needed, how much they will cost, and how long it will take for them to be actualized. What may seem like an inadequate response to AIDS and drug-related harm from the vantage point of a policymaker or church leader can nevertheless be a life-saving strategy from a drug user's viewpoint. Proponents of needle exchange and distribution programs do not support such programs as solutions to the AIDS epidemic or drug-related harm. But that these programs *can* help prevent HIV infection, and help prevent those already immunosuppressed or HIV infected from contracting life-threatening infections, is undeniable.

"While clean needles should be a public health issue, they remain a drug policy issue."

The issue of risk-reduction education has been largely portrayed as a controversy between black church and political leaders on the one hand and white health officials on the other. However, such a generalization eclipses the fact that many Latino and African-American AIDS advocates and service providers have spoken out in support of the immediate implementation of needle exchange programs and do so with input from drug users themselves and from those who live in neighborhoods affected by AIDS and drug-related harm. Debra Fraser-Howze, director of the Black Leadership Commission on AIDS, an organization that is one of the most outspoken opponents of needle exchange, admitted that needle exchange, bleach distribution, and safer injection education "are not about AIDS, but about power and control." But in the struggle over who will determine drug and AIDS policy, those who most require empowerment and control are continually left out: active and former drug users themselves.

Just Say No to 'Just Say No'

Drug use as it exists in the United States is largely the result of diverse forms of socio-economic coercion, but the sources of that coercion are made diffuse and indirect, shifting the focus away from the physical considerations and the origins of addiction to the presumed recalcitrance of the individual user. The "just say no" approach to drug "education" typifies this attitude: the recalcitrant individual is the one who won't or can't say no. The "choices" are clearly set forth. What type of person are you/will you be? The life conditions that often lead to drug-related problems are seldom raised in the mainstream discourse about drug addiction. Rather, the addict is solely accountable for her or his addiction, while racism, classism, poverty, and heterosexism almost never enter the picture. Each addict is viewed as a separate case, a separate individual having made a personal choice to use drugs. In the age of AIDS, the logic goes, choosing to become addicted and choosing not to end one's addiction makes HIV a self-inflicted condition. The just-say-no approach also denies the fact that drugs can be used more safely than they often are, and establishes the equation drug *use* = drug *abuse*. Our culture hypocritically calls those who use heroin and cocaine "drug abusers," while "social drinkers" and cigarette smokers escape even the label of "drug user."

"Just say no" introduces the appearance of a choice when in actuality often no choice exists, thereby establishing a structure through which blame and accountability can be meted out. Drug-related harm prevention programs aimed at intravenous drug users and their sexual partners and families are essentially non-existent in New York, except for the work of ADAPT (the Association for Drug Abuse Prevention and Treatment) and a few other community-based organizations that distribute bleach kits and show addicts how to clean their needles. Drug addicts must be given realistic choices if they are to avoid health problems and change their drug-taking behavior: there must be immediate implementation of community-based needle exchange programs and the decriminalization of hypodermic needles and drug paraphernalia to prevent further HIV infection among this population. Such measures must be seen as components of a larger effort that includes drug treatment and health care for users. U.S. drug policy must be reworked to acknowledge and confront the AIDS crisis and the realities of addiction. HIV will continue to spread unchecked until effective needle exchange programs and safer drug use education are standards of preventive care for drug users.

"Along with getting needles and bleach kits, drug users get counseling sessions where they can ask questions . . . about HIV."

Drug users will not be given choices—of treatment, needles, or safer injection education—if, as is currently the case, they are considered to have relinquished some of their rights merely by using drugs. In the United States, an addicted person is expendable. That intravenous drug users are prohibited from obtaining life-saving clean needles and unable to obtain drug treatment constitutes a government-sanctioned violation of their human and constitutional rights. The user's right to the pursuit of life has been abandoned.

AIDS and Drug Users

Intravenous drug users constitute the second-largest but fastest-growing AIDS caseload in New York State. Compared to the rest of the United States, people with AIDS in New York are three times as likely to be IVDU's. For 1988 and 1989, heterosexual drug users made up a larger proportion of AIDS cases in New York City than gay men (43 percent versus 41 percent in 1988, and 43 percent versus 40 percent in 1989). Findings from studies of clients in methadone programs and detoxification units estimate 50 to 60 percent HIV seropositivity among these clients. The New York City Department of Health estimates that by 1993, 50 percent of New York City's AIDS cases will be among IVDU's.

Just as drug addiction has devastated communities of color, so HIV infection among IVDU's disproportionately affects Latinas, Latinos, and African-Americans. However, a large proportion of deaths among New York City's HIV-infected IV drug users is not classified by the Centers for Disease Control (CDC) as AIDS; similarly, HIV manifestations in women—especially gynecological symptoms—do not fit the CDC's definition of AIDS. Thus, there is a relative undercounting reflected in the statistics that purport to show the impact of AIDS on drug users. . . .

Intravenous drug users commonly contract bloodborne infections and diseases like hepatitis, encephalitis, endocarditis, and sexually transmitted diseases; develop abscesses that promote infections; and suffer from other conditions that are a direct result of using unclean injection equipment. Though HIV-related illness may be the most well-known, it is only one of many health problems an injecting drug user faces. This fact was recognized early in the Netherlands, where needle exchange programs were originally developed to help prevent the spread of hepatitis B.

Clean injection equipment for drug users is a form of preventive health care. In the United States and other "first world" countries, it would be unthinkable for a person to visit a hospital or doctor's office and be injected with a needle that was previously used on another patient. But receiving an injection in a hospital and injecting "illicit" drugs, while they entail the same physical act and thus the same physical risks, are perceived as moral worlds apart and therefore are judged differently. Although sterile needles and syringes could prevent drug users from contracting HIV and a host of other infections, users are denied access to such instruments and can even be arrested for having them. While clean needles should be a public health issue, they remain a drug policy issue. But U.S. drug policy, of course, is synonymous with law enforcement. Not only is access to medical treatment for drug users non-existent, but simple, cost-effective preventive health care measures like needle exchange are actively disallowed and criminalized. With AIDS, this prohibition means legally sanctioning a public health disaster.

"Advances will come . . . only when drug users gain their rights, and are treated as people rather than criminals."

Members of the AIDS activist community of New York City, most visibly embodied in the organization ACT UP (the AIDS Coalition to Unleash Power), have taken control of their lives in many ways despite AIDS. They often know more about treatments for HIV-related conditions than doctors do. They have created clinical drug trials separate from those of the government, tested drugs the government would not test, found ways to get drugs to those who couldn't afford them, and found ways to care for their

sick when no one else would. They have struggled against the ghastly media depictions of people with AIDS and provided alternative representations. And they have cast off the smothering label of "AIDS victim": they are people living with AIDS. This change was much more than a linguistic one.

New York City's IV drug users who have AIDS or are HIV positive are not living with AIDS. For them, HIV is a death sentence. Their day-to-day struggles for basic necessities preclude any possibility of mobilization or political action or community building to demand access to drug and medical treatment. Needle exchanges can be a departure point for a user's process of empowerment and can even serve therapeutic purposes for active and former users involved in needle distribution.

In countries with a national health plan, adequate housing, and other services—in short, where the quality of life for drug users is much better—addicts have successfully organized themselves to fight for their human rights and against stereotypic and degrading images of drug users. Groups like the *Junkiebonden* (junky unions) of Amsterdam, the Western Australia Intravenous Equity (WAIVE), and Queensland Intravenous A.I.D.S. Association (QuIVAA) of Queensland, Australia, have done for addicts many of the things ACT UP and other AIDS organizations have done for and as people with AIDS. In Amsterdam, the first syringe exchange established to prevent HIV transmission was initiated by a user-based organization called MDHG in 1984. And the Rotterdam Junky Union was distributing clean syringes in high-drug-use areas of Rotterdam as early as 1981. The IV drug user's condition in New York City and the United States is situational, not necessary.

Needle Exchange: One Model

The terms "needle exchange" and "needle distribution" do not do justice to the concepts that they try to name. The words refer to only a small part of the event that needle exchange is. "Harm reduction" is the term most often used to describe the drug policy paradigm upon which needle exchange is predicated. The First International Conference on the Reduction of Drug Related Harm was held in April 1990 in Liverpool—a new force on the drug policy scene. The term "risk reduction" rather than "harm reduction" might sound better to ears in the United States, where it has become a staple in the discourse of AIDS education, particularly when talking about safer sex. The analogue to "safer sex" is "safer drug use." The fact that the latter phrase is never uttered is telling.

"The analogue to 'safer sex' is 'safer drug use.'"

ACT UP/New York's Needle Exchange Committee is currently operating the only needle exchange programs in New York City, with four "permanent" sites in three of the city's boroughs—as permanent as they can be considering that the possession and distribution of needles are criminal activities in this state. Along with needles, ACT UP outreach volunteers hand out kits that contain bleach, clean water, cotton, cookers, condoms, referral information, and illustrated instructions on how to wear condoms and how to clean works. Alcohol pads, medicine for abscesses, and lubricant (to use with condoms as well as to lubricate needles that may become stiff from bleach) are distributed when the committee can obtain them. And they try to have several types of condoms on hand, especially for sex workers who use the service.

ACT UP runs a very user-friendly project. Addicts are not required to give a needle in order to get one. Because the group's resources are currently limited and because the program is completely run by volunteers, it operates only two days a week. A 24-hour, seven-day-a-week program might have stricter return criteria. In addition, many of those who use the exchange are homeless, so it is unrealistic to demand that addicts save their works from one exchange to the next, when exchanges happen only twice a week. In fact, a majority of New York's addicts—whether homeless or not—do not carry works with them unless they intend to use them immediately, for fear of getting arrested. Despite this situation, at the six-month mark of ACT UP's project in August 1990, many needles were being collected. At the oldest site, an almost one-for-one exchange occurs each week. It is clear that many users are willing to risk arrest to use this program.

What is often overlooked or ignored by critics of needle distribution is the interaction that takes place during the encounter. It is this interaction between the giver and receiver of the needle that is the significant component of needle exchange, especially when encounters are repeated, and trust—maybe even friendship—is established.

Along with getting needles and bleach kits, drug users get counseling sessions where they can ask questions—sometimes for the first time—about HIV transmission, receive advice on how to care for their abscesses, or simply have an opportunity to talk to someone who will listen to what they have to say. The exchange comes to encompass more than the needle.

Obtaining Needles

ACT UP's Needle Exchange Committee has ironed out most of the practical problems it faces in order to operate viable programs: obtaining needles, which is, of course, illegal in New York State; having enough supplies; maintaining a consistent exchange schedule; and setting up *pro bono* legal support and a bail fund for addicts or outreach volunteers who are arrested during an exchange. The group is now trying to set up opportunities for users to receive more far-reaching care by connecting them with medical services, drug treatment, and other services from community-based organizations (the "bridge" concept). These services should all be a part of needle exchange. In Australia, where needle exchanges are located in the same building as drug treatment facilities, the connection between AIDS prevention and other services is difficult to ignore.

But while the concept of needle exchange as a "bridge" to drug treatment is important, needle exchanges must be viewed as helpful and life-saving *independent of further linkages*. In a place like New York City or Newark, New Jersey, where very little drug treatment exists and primary care for drug users is extremely limited, needle exchange can be a bridge to other services only insofar as those services exist. The drug treatment that is available in New York and New Jersey is mostly methadone based, so that many methadone patients who are addicted to more then one drug are shooting cocaine or other non-opiates while "in treatment." In addition, recovery from drug addiction is usually a long process with much recidivism. And, finally, there are many people who will use a needle exchange program who do not wish to stop using drugs at that point in their lives. While needle exchange can and should be viewed as one step in a continuum of care, an addict must be able to use it to the extent she or he wishes. If that means going no further than obtaining needles to shoot up more safely, this must be respected.

"Needle exchange must be viewed as a medical intervention against infection that results from the fact that people use drugs."

Because the personal interaction that occurs during a needle exchange is so important, decriminalization of needle possession in itself would not be a sufficient AIDS prevention measure for IVDU's. Even if the needle possession statute were removed, deeper-rooted cultural stereotypes about drug users and drug use would persist as barriers to easy access to needles and syringes. Members of ACT UP's Needle Exchange travel to states without paraphernalia laws to purchase needles, but are often perceived as drug users and thus refused service. In England, where syringes have long been legally available from pharmacies and where the philosophy of harm reduction is much more widely accepted, many drug users have traditionally been turned away, and thus do not consider this a viable route for obtaining injection equipment. Finally, although needles are less expensive in pharmacies than on the street, all economic restrictions are lifted in free needle exchanges. The street price for a needle in New York City is currently two to three dollars.

Prevention Methods

Reflecting back on the years of the AIDS epidemic we have lived through so far, it is clear that the most effective prevention methods and systems of care have been community-initiated and based. Needle exchange programs will not be helpful if they are inconveniently located, staffed by judgmental people, or coercive in any way. They must be located in neighborhoods where people buy and use drugs, be staffed by people who know the language spoken there (both the ethnic and street language), and offer points of identification and support to a user of the exchange. This means having active and former addicts and HIV-positive people involved, as well as residents of the neighborhood in which the exchange site is located. Needle exchange on a significant scale cannot take place without the removal of hypodermic and paraphernalia statutes, but the repeal of such laws would not make needle exchange unnecessary.

There must be a shift in drug policy from the punitive, law enforcement philosophy that now serves as its base to an understanding that drug use is a socio-medical phenomenon that cannot be "treated" by jailing people. It is this mindset that is responsible for keeping needle exchange interventions so limited in the United States. Needle exchange must be viewed as a medical intervention against infection that results from the fact that people use drugs, and must be recognized as providing real, life-saving options to users. These advances will come, however, only when drug users gain their rights, and are treated as people rather than criminals.

Strict Regulation of Blood Supplies Can Prevent the Spread of AIDS

Theresa Crenshaw

About the Author: *Theresa Crenshaw is a former member of the Presidential Commission on the HIV Epidemic, a committee formed by the Reagan administration to study the AIDS crisis. Crenshaw is a noted author and lecturer on AIDS issues.*

In the age of AIDS, the HIV epidemic dominates our thinking on sex because, after all, sexual transmission is still the main method of spreading the virus. However, getting lost in the overall picture is the relentless spread of HIV through blood transfusions. It is true that the number of people infected by transfusions is a small fraction of those infected through sex, but transfusion-related AIDS is not insignificant. Ask anyone who got infected that way. Even if the risk is small, which it is not, the consequences are enormous.

The best illustration of current problems with the blood supply is the case of Dorothy Polikoff and her husband, Bill. Their circumstances came to my attention in a most personal way, since Dorothy and Bill were friends of my mother. They were unable to get the cooperation of their physicians when they requested HIV testing several years after Bill had received a blood transfusion. Close to despair, they called me for help, knowing that I was active in the issue of AIDS. Dorothy speaks most eloquently for herself in the text of her testimony before the Presidential Commission on the HIV Epidemic.

"Transfusions—It's a Bloody Shame" by Theresa Crenshaw first appeared in the May/June 1989 issue of *The Humanist* and is reprinted by permission.

Dorothy participated in a panel that I chaired to explore the value of intraoperative autologous transfusion (IAT) as an alternative to traditional blood transfusion. IAT is a method of recycling blood lost during surgery and returning it to the patient's bloodstream, often eliminating the need to use banked blood and thus eliminating the risk of transfusion-related AIDS. On the panel with her were three physicians, all of whom were visibly moved by her experience. Members of the audience were crying, and I don't think there was a dry eye among commission members.

Individual experiences like these brought home to our hearts the crucial issues that must be grappled with in order to prevent unnecessary suffering. In fact, in order to prevent similar tragedies from happening to others in the future, we must reform our national blood strategy.

> ## "Many hospitals and blood banks are not notifying those who have received infected blood."

No one knows when an emergency requiring surgery and perhaps a transfusion will strike. Others, if they have had surgery in the past ten years, may have received transfusions without even knowing it. Doctors often don't think to mention that a few units of blood were transfused during surgery any more than they would say what style of stitch closed the wound or whether metal or silk sutures were used. However, because of the catastrophic consequences of HIV infection resulting from transfusions, this issue deserves closer attention.

According to the *Final Report of the Presidential Commission on the HIV Epidemic:*

> The initial response of the nation's blood banking industry to the possibility of contamination of the nation's blood by a new infectious agent was unnecessarily slow. . . . Some regional blood centers have been hesitant to promote

strategies that minimize the use of transfusion therapies since their operating income is derived from the sale of blood and blood products. . . . Many physicians and hospitals do not have an adequate understanding and, therefore, have not adequately informed their patient population about the availability of alternatives to traditional transfusion therapy.

Unfortunately, our recommendations are gathering dust on a shelf somewhere because they have not yet been transformed into policy.

"If units of blood from the same donor were kept together, the risk of exposure to HIV would be significantly reduced."

Due to the reluctance of the blood bank industry to respond to the HIV crisis and, in particular, to the economic conflict of interest surrounding blood banks, new legislation is necessary in order to modernize our national blood strategy. Not only must we protect the individual from transfusion-related HIV infection but we should do everything reasonably possible to insure that the best systems are in place in order to protect society against the next blood-borne disease to challenge humankind. Such legislation will provide procedures for implementing the most advanced technology as it becomes available so that transfusion therapy does not lag ten years behind technology.

National Blood Strategy

Some of the provisions of a new national blood strategy should include the following:

Informed consent for all transfusions. The President's Commission on HIV recommends that:

Informed consent for transfusion of blood or its components should include an explanation of the risks involved with the transfusion of blood and its components, including the possibility of HIV infection and information about the appropriate alternatives to homologous blood transfusion therapy, such as pre-dona-

tion, plasmapheresis, and intraoperative autologous transfusion.

Preoperative consent forms for patients should include a paragraph to the effect that:

I have been advised of the possibility that I might require a transfusion as a result of this procedure. Alternatives to homologous transfusions (those performed with someone else's blood) have been discussed with me prior to surgery. I have also been advised that my options include pre-donation of my own blood and intraoperative autologous transfusions (having my blood suctioned from the wound during surgery and returned to me during surgery after a filtering process) et cetera.

This statement should be made a standard part of preoperative consent forms and be required for accreditation of hospitals. Intraoperative blood recycling is widely available but not widely utilized, and it will take many years for the general public and physicians to become aware of the value and availability of these procedures. Introducing this wording into preoperative surgical consent forms will expedite not only the discussion of these alternatives but the education of both physician and patient.

Insurance coverage for autologous transfusions. Health care financing plans should treat autologous transfusion therapy no differently than homologous transfusion therapy. Coverage should apply to both.

Autologous blood, or the patient's own, including but not limited to pre-donation and intraoperative autologous transfusion, should be covered by insurance. Homologous, or banked blood, is covered by insurance. Autologous blood is covered in many states and by many policies but not consistently or comparably to homologous blood. Since autologous blood is safer, consistent insurance coverage of autologous blood would actually be cost-effective because many diseases in addition to AIDS will be prevented by this process.

Notify all recipients of transfusions since 1977. Agencies which license and certify health care facilities should make as a condition for licensure a program to notify all recipients of blood or blood products since 1977, and their sexual partners, of their possible exposure to HIV.

The Presidential Commission on the HIV Epidemic recommended that

> as soon as is practically possible, but no later than July 1, 1989, agencies which license and certify health care facilities should make a condition for licensure a program to notify all recipients of blood or blood products since 1977 of their possible exposure to HIV. . . . If licensing agencies do not take such immediate steps, Congress should then enact a law that requires it.

Look-back programs that notify recipients of infected blood are taking an average of several years before the transfusion recipient is notified. Many hospitals and blood banks are not notifying those who have received infected blood or their sexual partners. Those institutions that are doing so are often delaying the process. One blood banker who prefers not to be identified explained that if he waits long enough, the transfusion recipients of infected blood will already have died and not be able to sue.

Knowingly donating infected blood should be a felony. People who know they are infected with HIV should not donate blood. Unfortunately, some continue to do so. The president's commission report recommends criminal sanctions for those who continue to donate blood in spite of knowing that they are infected.

Safeguard Blood Supplies

Establish an independent commission for the advancement of blood safety. A commission for the advancement of blood safety should be established to advise the blood banking industry, the private sector, and research programs. The purpose of this committee would not be to find fault or cast blame but to help the industry best respond to future challenges and to make recommendations for improvement as appropriate.

Keep blood from the same donor together. Units of blood and blood products taken from a single donor should be kept together and distributed for transfusion to the same patient whenever possible to minimize exposure to multiple donors.

The standard practice of transfusion medicine involves no effort to keep blood from the same donor together. As a result, someone who requires two or three units of blood typically gets two or three units from two or three separate individuals. If units of blood from the same donor were kept together, the risk of exposure to HIV would be significantly reduced. This is a record-keeping matter that requires redesign of certain procedures. It is being implemented in certain regional blood centers successfully already but should be a national standard of practice. There are various other provisions in this proposed legislation, but these are the key points.

"The systems put into place today will protect society against the diseases that are transmissible through blood."

The blood bank industry insists that the blood supply is safe and that the risk of HIV infection is negligible. The Centers for Disease Control still states that the risk of getting AIDS through transfusion is only one in one hundred thousand. However, the figures more commonly accepted by the medical community are one in forty thousand, and an article published by the *New England Journal of Medicine* indicates the risk may actually be one in five thousand and, in high-incidence areas such as New York, San Francisco, and Los Angeles, as high as one in five hundred.

In addition, approximately two million unnecessary transfusions are given each year. Several years ago, a seventeen-year-old girl was given a transfusion of two units of blood. She could have been anyone's daughter. Due to heavy menstrual bleeding, she underwent a dilation and curettage. Because she was somewhat anemic, she received a transfusion. She would have lived without this extra blood, but she won't survive too many more years because of it. It took two years before the blood bank notified her that she had received HIV-infected blood. By that time, she was not only infected but engaged to be married.

The High Cost of Blood

Dorothy Polikoff, her husband Bill, this young teenager, and many others would all have been protected from this deadly disease if the policies within the blood banking industry had caught up with currently available transfusion technology and guidelines.

Should economic interests determine protocols for the health of our nation? Short-term thinking would conclude that maximizing the utilization of using your own blood, whether through pre-donation, IAT, or other methods, is dangerous to the survival of the blood bank industry. However, long-term economic thinking makes clear that not to use autologous blood to the fullest potential is an economic disaster. Aside from the cost in human lives, which can't be measured in dollars, the use of autologous blood is, in fact, not only economical but cost-effective. Let's look at some of the specific costs involved.

"As a general rule, it is always best to use your own blood whenever possible."

Two million units of banked blood used in transfusions can be eliminated altogether at a savings of approximately $350 million to the health industry and patients. This savings is arrived at by calculating a cost of $175 per unit for banked blood. Any surgical procedure requiring two or more units of blood saves the patient and his or her insurance company money by using IAT. For example, the cost to the patient for twenty units of banked blood (at $175 per unit)

is $3,500, while the cost for IAT involving twenty units of recycled blood is $350 to $650. Moreover, these figures do not take into account indirect costs such as medical care for those who become infected or ill as a result of transfusion with banked blood.

One of the primary reasons why I have taken such an interest in transfusion medicine is that there are ready solutions to transfusion-generated HIV infection. Most areas of AIDS—whether prevention, research, or treatment—are economic black holes with cautious predictions for success. Nonetheless, they must be pursued. The blood transfusion picture, however, is brighter. If we adopt a national blood strategy that conserves banked blood by maximizing the use of autologous blood, we will simultaneously relieve the blood shortages you hear so much about while minimizing transfusion-related disease. In the future, the systems put into place today will protect society against the diseases that are transmissible through blood and, ideally, equip every hospital with the capacity to recycle blood during surgery.

All of these procedures are established and workable. They could have been put in place years ago. Now is an improvement on never, and sound legislation will accelerate the pace.

The blood supply is not as safe as it could be. While it can and must be improved, it will never be completely safe. As a general rule, it is always best to use your own blood whenever possible. There are a variety of methods that can be used.

Pre-donation is the best known, but it possesses some limitations. During the month prior to scheduled surgery, a person can usually donate about four units of his or her own blood. However, pregnant women are often unable to pre-donate because of anemia and other problems. Most babies and children are too small to pre-donate adequate amounts of blood prior to surgery. Pre-donation applies only to elective procedures, not emergency surgery. When more than four units of blood are required, pre-donation is not adequate. Nonetheless, pre-donation should be encouraged as a general rule whenever possible and supplemented by other methods when necessary. *Frozen blood* can be preserved for ten years, and there are new services that will ship frozen blood to any place in the United States within hours. Freezing and storing blood for future use is becoming more popular, but there are fees for storage and delivery that make it economically unavailable for many people.

Intraoperative autologous transfusion is the best method for using your own blood during surgery for both elective procedures and emergency situations. A machine suctions the blood you lose during surgery, cleans it, and returns it to you within minutes. Approximately half the hospitals in the United States have IAT equipment. The informed patient can request admission to a hospital that can provide IAT.

For hospitals that do not have IAT equipment, national companies like PSICOR provide twenty-four-hour service to hospitals in various cities by supplying both the equipment and trained personnel. Some Red Cross centers also provide IAT equipment and personnel to hospitals. Haemonetics Corporation is the largest manufacturer of this equipment and has even developed a portable unit that may someday be available in ambulances.

Alternatives to Banked Blood

Plasmapheresis is an additional procedure important for surgeries when high-volume blood loss is expected, such as open heart surgery. A certain amount of plasma is drawn from a patient while he or she is being anesthetized which is returned at the end of surgery. This fluid is rich in platelets and clotting factors that can be washed away when too many units of blood are recycled with IAT. Instead of getting someone else's platelets at the end of an operation, you get your own back, thus avoiding exposure to anyone else's blood. IAT and plasmapheresis when used together can insure that many patients *receive no* banked blood, even when thirty or forty units of blood are required.

"Pharmaceutical manufacturers are also contributing drugs that can help reduce the need to rely upon banked blood."

Pharmaceutical manufacturers are also contributing drugs that can help reduce the need to rely upon banked blood. Ortho Pharmaceuticals has developed a product called erythropoietin. It helps a patient who has lost blood manufacture it approximately twice as fast by stimulating the bone marrow, thus further reducing the need for transfusions. Likewise, Alcide Corporation is performing research on methods of sterilizing platelets and red blood cells in the hope that those who must receive banked blood or blood products will receive a safer product.

These are some important examples of available, or soon to be available, resources for someone needing surgery.

Getting a Blood Safety Act passed into law takes time. Therefore, until such a bill is introduced and passed, anyone requiring surgery must protect him- or herself by making informed decisions. Make sure that you don't receive an unnecessary transfusion. Use your own blood whenever possible and discuss various alternatives with your doctor. Keep informed of new advances in transfusion therapy and support legislation that promotes a safe national blood strategy by sending a letter of support to the AIDS Prevention Council, 1380 Garnet Street, Suite E 200, San Diego, CA 92109.

A National Sex Survey Could Target Groups for AIDS Education

Michael Specter

About the Author: *Michael Specter is a science and medical writer for the* Washington Post, *a daily newspaper in Washington, D.C. Specter is based in New York City.*

Nothing scares Americans more than sex. We are obsessed by it, but it also seems to repel us. Doctors keep saying that "normal" sex is an essential part of a healthy life. They have also suggested the opposite: Sex that isn't "normal" isn't healthy.

But who knows what normal sex is? Most of us think we have an idea, and yet we know astonishingly little about the true nature of American sexual behavior. For most of the past decade we have been battling a lethal new epidemic with data from a limited study conducted by Alfred Kinsey more than 50 years ago. Federal scientists have designed a comprehensive and sophisticated new survey that would finally move beyond Kinsey, but our government's absolute fear of sex—masked as fiscal prudence—has stopped it at every turn.

Sex is an important and increasingly dangerous fact of life in the United States, and experience from 1940 will no longer answer our questions. In 1989, for example, there were nearly 3 million unwanted pregnancies. Raging epidemics of syphilis, chancroid and other venereal diseases have become massive public health threats. And AIDS, the most feared of all sexually transmitted diseases, has already killed nearly 80,000 people in this country alone.

You can't find a scientist who fails to recognize the overwhelming need to gain a better understanding of our sexual behavior. That's why the National Institute for Child Health and Human Development devised such a significant study. The proposed $15 million "National Survey of Health and Sexual Behavior" is long overdue. The proposition is simple; its execution has turned out to be anything but.

"The initiative was designed to provide the medical and scientific community with information on how and to what extent the general population is engaging in behaviors that might put them at risk of HIV infection, or of AIDS," according to the original prospectus.

"We have been battling a lethal new epidemic with data from a limited study conducted . . . 50 years ago."

Without it, public health officials cannot possibly assemble the information they need to gauge the scope of the AIDS epidemic. The endless pop surveys spewed out by women's magazines and pseudoscientists such as Shere Hite are of passing interest at best, but they are worthless as reliable guides to patterns of national behavior.

The Kinsey report was a landmark. But because he decided whom to interview—rather than selecting the subjects randomly—the study was skewed heavily to well-educated, white middle-class Americans. Useful as it has been, it lacks the scientific rigor we now need to make accurate policy judgments about the AIDS epidemic. But even if the study were a perfect snapshot of 1940, it couldn't help us much today. It is likely that sexual behavior has changed dramatically in the past half-century.

For years, many of our best scientists have made an urgent case for a comprehensive national survey. Researchers at the National Institutes of Health [NIH] have labored over the extremely detailed and—admittedly—unusually frank questionnaire, which they devised over five years. ("When you had sex with your partner how often did you have an orgasm?" "Have you injected drugs in the last five years?" "Did you give your partner money or drugs in exchange for sex?") But so far the study has gone nowhere.

Obstacles to the Survey

It would be wonderful if we lived in a world where these questions were of interest only to the prurient. Unfortunately, we don't. Without knowing much about what America does in bed, our best guesses about how many people are infected with HIV (which range responsibly from 500,000 to 3 million) remain just that—guesses.

The best knowledge we have about the natural history of HIV comes from gay men who were infected in San Francisco more than a decade ago. But the "fast track" gay men with hundreds of annual sexual partners who were infected in the first stages of the epidemic don't accurately represent the sexual patterns of the majority of homosexuals. They certainly have little to tell us about the rate of infection among heterosexuals, or so most researchers think.

"Without [a national survey], our best guesses about how many people are infected with HIV . . . remain just that—guesses."

Yet politicians, federal health officials and bureaucrats at the Office of Management and Budget [OMB]—all petrified by the notion of asking the nation highly personal questions about sex—have frozen the study in committees, conferences and councils.

"Let's face it, sex makes people crazy," says Ward Cates, Director of the Sexually Transmitted Disease program at the Centers for Disease Control (CDC). Like virtually every researcher in the field, Cates says that more knowledge about our sexual behavior would help disease prevention and planning efforts immensely. "Most of our knowledge on HIV comes from groups at highest risk," he says. "We run a very big danger of drawing conclusions about the entire nation based on the small groups we do know something about."

Dozens of other people, professional organizations and agencies such as the General Accounting Office and the Presidential AIDS Commission have made similar points. But they have watched in dismay as Congress, OMB, NIH and HHS [Health and Human Services] have taken turns passing the hot potato. When you ask any of these people, all of whom are paid to govern, whether the country needs a sex survey, they immediately say yes.

A spokesman for Dr. James O. Mason, assistant secretary for health, says Mason has been urging the NIH to "get the sex survey back to him as soon as possible." But one day after receiving a letter from OMB director Richard G. Darman which challenged the "general" nature of the survey, Mason directed the Public Health Service to "conduct a vigorous reexamination of the proposed survey" to ensure that it was scientifically sound and to make certain that "issues of personal privacy are properly balanced against important public health needs." OMB has used the Paperwork Reduction Act, a law designed to prevent excessive record-keeping, as a weapon against surveys and studies that administration officials don't like.

In his letter to Mason, Darman made it clear that he did not question the government's need to get a better picture of the potential threat posed by AIDS and other sexually transmitted diseases.

"This surely would seem to justify federal initiatives to learn more about and to understand better how these diseases are transmitted. . . ," he wrote to HHS Secretary Louis W. Sullivan. "The important thing is that any government survey which potentially intrudes into sensitive and private aspects of individual behavior should be reasonably focused and directed toward the advancement of an essential federal interest."

Darman needn't have feared. In July 1989, the House Appropriations Committee decided the survey was too controversial, that it "did not appear to be an appropriate use of public funds," and deleted from the budget the $11 million Congress had originally intended to spend on it.

The sex study clearly could be considered intrusive, but it would draw on a representative group of up to 20,000 volunteers who would answer detailed questions about their sex lives, and about other practices—such as drug use—that could put them at high risk for AIDS and other illnesses. They would not be forced to answer the questions, and strict confidentiality would be guaranteed to all who participated. Most experts agree that the results of the study—a clearer picture to help predict the future patterns of HIV infection—would save the Treasury far more than the $15 million taxpayers would have to spend on it.

"[A survey] would almost certainly provide the first accurate estimates of the number currently . . . at risk of HIV infection."

Armed with a reliable survey, public health officials could then zero in on the people who most need education. If they find out, for example, that teenagers are frequently engaging in sex without condoms, money could then be directed to making certain they know the risks. If it turns out that most urban heterosexuals in the Southwest are monogamous, then we won't need to waste millions of dollars telling them that fewer partners means lower risk.

We shouldn't underestimate the importance of such a study. It would almost certainly provide the first accurate estimates of the number currently engaging in behaviors that put them at risk of HIV in-

fection. Without the study, CDC will have to continue trying to stop a lethal epidemic by changing behavior. They just won't know much about the behavior they are trying to change.

"Right now we are making billion-dollar decisions with no real facts to back them up," says William Bailey, AIDS policy director at the American Psychological Association. "People want the study to go away because they are just too reluctant to accept the fact that sexuality is a regular part of human life."

Importance of Education

House conservatives, led vociferously by Rep. William Dannemeyer (R-Calif.), have opposed the survey on many grounds, saying that it is not needed, that its comparative nature will "undermine human intimacy," that the investigators carry a "bias in favor of laissez-faire sexual attitudes," and that it will "sway public opinion to liberalize laws regarding homosexuality, pedophilia, anal and oral sex, sex education and teenage pregnancies."

A more stubborn obstacle lies in our cultural attitudes about health care. Americans have come to identify medicines with technology and disease with cures. When they go to the doctor, they want to be told that a cure is available, and that drugs are waiting at the pharmacy to make them better. Behavioral science does not work that way. It seems "soft," and we think we ought to be able to figure it out without paying federal dollars. It's the type of study for which William Proxmire might have erroneously awarded a Golden Fleece.

But it's time Americans—particularly those worried how much we spend on health care—started appreciating the value of studies that focus on disease prevention. For every ten dollars the National Institutes of Health spends searching for an AIDS cure it could just as effectively spend one dollar on education and prevention. That is almost always true with medicine. It is a lot easier to teach a young girl not to smoke than it is to treat her for emphysema or lung cancer 30 years later, when she will die in a hospital at great cost to society.

The same is almost certainly true of AIDS. We have seen dramatic reductions in infection rates over the past decade among gay men in major cities mostly because they have responded to education. But what works well with sophisticated, prosperous gay men doesn't work with minority drug users or suburban teenagers. That should be of no surprise. Cigarette warning labels scare off a lot of well-educated pregnant women and older men. But youngsters need a different message—one that portrays smoking as a repulsive turnoff—before they see the light. By now we should have learned what tobacco companies know so well. Different groups of people need to be targeted in different ways.

But in order to target information properly, public health officials need to know who to spend their money on. It would seem stupid, for example, to blanket a midwestern college with safe-sex videos if we knew that students there were already fully aware of what the films contained.

Other Countries

Other countries are already way ahead of the United States here, as they are ahead in developing new methods of birth control and many other preventive public health measures. We have lived too long under the general belief that what we don't know won't hurt us. The truth, as a visit to any hospital will show you, is just the opposite.

Promoting Abstinence Will Stop AIDS

Herbert Ratner

About the Author: *Herbert Ratner is a doctor and editor of* Child and Family, *a quarterly magazine. Ratner is also a member of the medical advisory board of the American Life League, a Stafford, Virginia, organization that promotes family values.*

Acquired Immunodeficiency Syndrome (AIDS) is expected to be with us for a long time. Treatment has not controlled infections or stopped deaths, and vaccines are not in sight. The highly publicized prophylactic, the condom, which has been with us throughout the 20th century, has marked limitations. The continuous parade of new contraceptives attests to the condom's notably poor record in preventing pregnancy. If the much larger sperm can get through, so can the AIDS virus. It has a worse record in preventing sexually transmitted diseases, the incidence of which today has never been higher.

Epidemiologically the AIDS virus's primary spread is through multiple sex partners. Each new partner sharply increases the risk of becoming infected with the AIDS virus, particularly if the partner has ever used intravenous (IV) drugs, engaged in homosexual practices, or has had relations with someone who has. With the continuing spread of the virus into the public at large, the risk of a new partner having the virus becomes greater.

There is now general agreement, even among homosexuals, that abstinence or exclusive contact with an uninfected partner are the only sure

Herbert Ratner, "Condoms and AIDS," *The Wanderer,* June 8, 1989. This article first appeared in *ALL About Issues* and is reprinted by permission of the American Life League.

protections against the AIDS virus. Today abstinence and monogamy are no longer disdainfully dismissed as religious impositions. Rather they are seen as the pragmatic answer to a pressing problem, since the condom is admittedly inadequate. It may delay but does not prevent eventual infection.

At another level, there is even a growing appreciation that nature is trying to tell us something: that abstinence before marriage and monogamy thereafter are sexual norms which serve the survival needs of the human animal. Accordingly, the effective public health approach is not a nationwide push for a condomized society, starting with the very young, but a nationwide effort to curb the generation of multiple sex partners, whose primary source comes from the sexually active young.

The fact is that year after year, generation after generation, millions of preteens and teenagers enter into the stormy sea of precocious and premature genital sex. And the consequences as Kinsey researchers point out, are clear: "Once persons begin premarital coitus, they seldom recant and remain abstinent until marriage. It is a crossing of the Rubicon in life history." When the young give up abstinence, monogamy is rarely the outcome. Sex education which explicitly or implicitly condones genital sex by featuring condoms as the answer for our young people, simply accelerates the process.

> **"Abstinence or exclusive contact with an uninfected partner are the only sure protections against the AIDS virus."**

Actually the major accomplishment of the condom campaign to prevent AIDS is to impress the promoters, politicians, and the public at large that something is being done; and although well-intentioned, it offers more of a placebo than a panacea.

Publicizing the condom to the four winds is, for the most part, the bravura of a Puritan who is trying to prove to the world that he is not a Puritan. To concentrate on the mechanical aspects of the sex act to the exclusion of the emotional and psychological aspects (which the condom campaign ignores) is the essence of Puritanism. The only difference between the new and the old is that while the traditional Puritans were alleged to believe that sex was something to be isolated and repressed, neo-Puritans accept sex as something to be isolated and exercised. Rollo May states that the new Puritanism is "the same old Puritan form: alienation from the body and feeling, and exploitation of the body as though it were a machine."

"Condom information is a simplistic answer to the guidance of youth."

Furthermore, what the Greeks knew, and what today's sex educators seem to have forgotten, is that the young "have strong passions, and tend to gratify them indiscriminately. Of the bodily desires, it is the sexual by which they are most swayed and in which they show absence of self-control" (Aristotle, *Rhetoric*, 1389a 2-1389b 11). Since this is so, it should be obvious that the message on condoms included in the federal government's *Understanding AIDS* brochure, which was mailed to each household in the United States, is waste of effort and money.

Condom information is a simplistic answer to the guidance of youth. It will not convert immaturity into maturity. Formation, not information, is needed. Rather than the facts of the condom, it would have been more to the point to equip parents with the appropriate knowledge needed to educate their sons and daughters on the value of abstinence, and to supply through the parents the understanding that boys and girls need to place their energies in other directions, and that girls need to fend off opportunistic boys. Per-

haps the next great advance will be made when chastity, as with abstinence and monogamy, will no longer be viewed as a religious imposition.

Primary Prevention

The basic, though long-range, answer, then, to the control of AIDS, is primary prevention. It is to get at the young before they get started on precocious and premature sex—the inexorable path to multiple sex partners, and AIDS. Public health strategists in the United States Public Health Service have no difficulty with primary prevention in the case of smoking and drug misuse by getting to the youth before they get started. What prevents them from doing the same in the case of AIDS? To assume that all preteens and teenagers are automatically going to become prematurely sexually active is a defeatist attitude.

Seen from another angle, our problem is that in today's culture, fidelity is not characteristic of young love. And love without commitment is counterfeit love. Without real love, abandonment is common, and sex partners come and go with the attendant heartbreaks. This becomes part of the breakdown of young people's self-esteem and the loss of self-identity.

Having multiple sex partners not only places them on the road to AIDS, but sooner or later brings in its wake a whole series of destructive social ills: not only disruption of personal growth and development, but unwanted pregnancies, abortion with its physical and psychological sequelae, sexually transmitted diseases, drugs, alcohol, suicide, and the weakening and breakdown of present and future family life.

The Gift of Fertility

Perhaps worst of all is the loss of the gift of fertility. To discover in later life, when the urge to have a child is so great, that one's earlier promiscuous life-style has rendered one sterile is a great tragedy. Those who flock to birth-control clinics early in life often find themselves at sterility clinics later in life. The younger generation needs to have impressed on it that nature gives them only one body; that it is not a rehearsal body to be turned in when the fun is over; it has to last a lifetime.

Condoms Encourage Sex

The problem, then, is to rescue the young from the clutches of a freedom run rampant. The condom fosters neither abstinence nor monogamy; rather it does the opposite. Those who stress condom usage only put the seal of approval on active genital sex. The message it communicates is that the condom is a good which converts irresponsible sex into responsible sex, giving it the appearance of acceptability and respectability. It is the old refrain of birth controllers which has only resulted in more and more adolescent pregnancies.

The advocates of the condom seduce our young people into deep waters from which they seldom emerge. Its intensive promotion does more to arouse and stimulate the imagination and encourage genital sex among the young than to curb unprotected sex among the promiscuous. Such promoters are in effect sorcerer's apprentices, unable to stop the flow which they have fostered. One cannot bail out the ship when the water keeps rushing in.

Concerned adults need to re-examine certain contemporary shibboleths that underlie the promotion of the condom: that genital sex is a good at any age and in any manner; that the promotion of abstinence in sex, unlike abstinence from tobacco, alcohol, and drugs, is a religious imposition that has no place in a secular society; that the poor and the underprivileged are uncontrollable in their passions, uneducable, and beyond improvement. This is an elitist position that has no place in a country that purports to be a democracy.

> "The condom fosters neither abstinence nor monogamy; rather it does the opposite."

There is a saying that the longest way around is often the shortest way home. Perhaps if we put our energies to educating and persuading young people, boys and girls, men and women, to think "no", to say "no", and to act "no", we would get much further in curbing AIDS than by urging them to carry condoms in their purses and wallets.

Bibliography

Books

Jad Adams — *AIDS: The HIV Myth.* New York: St. Martin's Press, 1990.

Dennis P. Andrulis — *Crisis at the Front Line: The Effects of AIDS on Public Hospitals.* New York: Priority Press, 1989.

Gene Antonio — *The AIDS Cover-Up?* San Francisco: Ignatius Press, 1987.

Mary Catherine Bateson and Richard Goldsby — *Thinking AIDS.* Reading, MA: Addison-Wesley, 1988.

Ronald Bayer — *Private Acts, Social Consequences: AIDS and the Politics of Public Health.* New York: The Free Press, 1989.

Michael Callen — *Surviving AIDS.* New York: Harper Collins, 1990.

Inge B. Corless and Mary Pittman-Lindeman — *AIDS: Principles, Practices, and Politics.* New York: Hemisphere Publishing, 1989.

Elizabeth Fee and Daniel M. Fox, eds. — *AIDS: The Burdens of History.* Berkeley: University of California Press, 1988.

Joseph Feldschuh and Doron Weber — *Safe Blood: Purifying the Nation's Blood Supply in the Age of AIDS.* New York: The Free Press, 1990.

T.C. Fry — *The Great AIDS Hoax.* Washington, DC: Life Sciences Institute, 1989.

Michael Fumento — *The Myth of Heterosexual AIDS.* New York: Basic Books, 1990.

Robert Gallo — *Virus Hunting: AIDS, Cancer, and the Human Retrovirus.* New York: Basic Books, 1991.

David G. Hallman, ed. — *AIDS Issues: Confronting the Challenge.* New York: The Pilgrim Press, 1989.

William B. Johnston and Kevin R. Hopkins — *The Catastrophe Ahead: AIDS and the Case for a New Public Policy.* New York: Praeger, 1990.

Helen Singer Kaplan — *The Real Truth About Women and AIDS: How to Eliminate the Risks Without Giving Up Love and Sex.* New York: Simon & Schuster, 1987.

Nancy F. McKenzie, ed. — *The AIDS Reader: Social, Political, Ethical Issues.* New York: Penguin Books, 1991.

Eleanor D. Macklin, ed. — *AIDS and Families.* New York: Harrington Park Press, 1989.

William H. Masters, Virginia E. Johnson, and Robert C. Kolodny — *Crisis: Heterosexual Behavior in the Age of AIDS.* New York: Grove Press, 1988.

Heather G. Miller, Charles F. Turner, and Lincoln E. Moses — *AIDS: The Second Decade.* Washington, DC: National Academy Press, 1990.

Barbara A. Misztal and David Moss, eds. — *Action on AIDS: National Policies in Comparative Perspective.* New York: Greenwood Press, 1990.

Tom Monte — *The Way of Hope: Michio Kushi's Anti-AIDS Program.* New York: Warner Books, 1989.

Eve K. Nichols — *Mobilizing Against AIDS.* Cambridge, MA: Harvard University Press, 1989.

Alan E. Nourse — *AIDS.* New York: Franklin Watts, 1989.

Bruce Nussbaum — *Good Intentions: How Big Business and the Medical Establishment Are Corrupting the Fight Against AIDS.* New York: Atlantic Monthly Press, 1991.

Padraig O'Malley, ed. — *The AIDS Epidemic: Private Rights and the Public Interest.* Boston: Beacon Press, 1989.

Panos Institute — *AIDS and the Third World.* Philadelphia: New Society Publishers, 1989.

Cindy Patton — *Inventing AIDS.* New York: Routledge, Chapman and Hall, 1990.

Christine Pierce and Donald VanDeVeer	*AIDS: Ethics and Public Policy.* Belmont, CA: Wadsworth Publishing, 1988.
Ines Rieder and Patricia Ruppelt, eds.	*AIDS: The Women.* Pittsburgh: Cleis Press, 1988.
Enrique T. Rueda and Michael Schwartz	*Gays, AIDS and You.* Old Greenwich, CT: Devin Adair Co., 1987.
Susan Sontag	*AIDS and Its Metaphors.* New York: Farrar, Straus & Giroux, 1989.
Rose Weitz	*Life with AIDS.* New Brunswick, NJ: Rutgers University Press, 1991.

Periodicals

Lawrence K. Altman	"AIDS Testing of Doctors Is Crux of Thorny Debate," *The New York Times,* December 27, 1990.
Robert Bazell	"Vaccination Market," *The New Republic,* July 1, 1991.
Gene Bylinsky	"A Promising New Assault on AIDS," *Fortune,* February 26, 1990.
Peg Byron	"HIV: The National Scandal," *Ms.,* January/February 1991.
Mona Charen	"Are Heterosexuals Responsible for AIDS?" *Conservative Chronicle,* July 11, 1990. Available from PO Box 11297, Des Moines, IA 50340-1297.
Commonweal	"Unholy Protest," January 12, 1990.
Geoffrey Cowley	"How Safe Is the Blood Supply?" *Newsweek,* June 3, 1991.
Susan Dentzer	"Why AIDS Won't Bankrupt Us," *U.S. News & World Report,* January 18, 1988.
Lisa DePaulo	"Alison Gertz: Champagne, Roses . . . and AIDS," *Mademoiselle,* December 1990.
Peter H. Duesberg and Bryan J. Ellison	"Is the AIDS Virus a Science Fiction?" *Policy Review,* Summer 1990.
Peter Dworkin	"The AIDS Threat to Teenagers," *U.S. News & World Report,* October 23, 1989.
Steven Findlay	"The Worsening Spread of the AIDS Crisis," *U.S. News & World Report,* January 29, 1990.
Bill Gentile	"Doctors and AIDS," *Newsweek,* July 1, 1991.
Christine Gorman	"Returning Fire Against AIDS," *Time,* June 24, 1991.
Robert K. Gray	"AIDS: We Will Win the War," *Vital Speeches of the Day,* March 1, 1990.
David Holzman	"AIDS Fear Alters Surgeons' World," *Insight,* October 15, 1990.
Mark S. Kaplan	"AIDS: Individualizing a Social Problem," *Society,* January/February 1990.
John Leo	"When Activism Becomes Gangsterism," *U.S. News & World Report,* February 5, 1990.
Paul Likoudis	"The Threat of AIDS Terrorism," *The Wanderer,* April 19, 1990. Available from Wanderer Press, 201 Ohio St., St. Paul, MN 55107.
Terence Monmaney	"The Return of AZT," *Discover,* January 1990.
National Review	"AIDS: Here, There—And Everywhere?" January 22, 1990.
John Cardinal O'Connor	"Who Will Care for the AIDS Victims?" *Origins,* January 18, 1990. Available from Catholic News Service, 3211 Fourth St. NE, Washington, DC 20017-1100.
William T. O'Connor	"AIDS, Discrimination, and Self-Protection," *New Dimensions,* January 1990. Available from *New Dimensions,* Subscriptions Department, PO Box 811, Grants Pass, OR 97526.
Brian O'Reilly	"The Inside Story of the AIDS Drug," *Fortune,* November 5, 1990.
Edmund Pellegrino	"Ethics in AIDS Treatment Decisions," *Origins,* January 18, 1990.
Andrew Purvis	"Forging a Shield Against AIDS," *Time,* April 1, 1991.
Joe Queenan	"Straight Talk About AIDS," *Fortune,* June 26, 1989.
Eloise Salholz	"The Future of Gay America," *Newsweek,* March 12, 1990.
Phyllis Schlafly	"Liberal 'Solutions' Make Problems Worse," *The Phyllis Schlafly Report,* February 1991. Available from The Eagle Trust Fund, PO Box 618, Alton, IL 62002.
Jean Seligmann	"A Very Risky Business," *Newsweek,* November 20, 1989.
Dick Thompson	"Longer Life for AIDS Patients," *Time,* June 19, 1989.
Anastasia Toufexis	"When the Doctor Gets Infected," *Time,* January 14, 1991.
Isabel Wilkerson	"AMA Approves AIDS Testing for Doctors and Health Workers," *The New York Times,* June 22, 1991.

Organizations
to Contact

The editors have compiled the following list of organizations that are concerned with the issues debated in this book. All of them have publications or information available for interested readers. The descriptions are derived from materials provided by the organizations. This list was compiled at the date of publication. Names and phone numbers of organizations are subject to change.

AIDS Coalition to Unleash Power (ACT UP)
135 W. 29th St., 10th Fl.
New York, NY 10001
(212) 564-2437

ACT UP is a group of activists committed to informing the public about the AIDS crisis. The group seeks to increase public awareness and government involvement in the fight against AIDS, and lobbies for government approval of experimental AIDS drugs. Publications include the quarterly *ACT UP Reports* and the weekly *Treatments and Data Digest.*

**American Enterprise Institute for
Public Policy Research (AEI)**
1150 17th St. NW
Washington, DC 20036
(202) 862-5800

The institute is a research and educational organization that aims to assist policymakers, scholars, businesspeople, and the public by providing analysis of reports on AIDS and other national and international issues. Publications include the monthly *AEI Economist* newsletter and various pamphlets, which contain occasional reports on AIDS.

American Foundation for AIDS Research (AMFAR)
1515 Broadway, Suite 3601
New York, NY 10036
(212) 719-0033

AMFAR promotes the urgent need for biomedical research on AIDS. The group advocates the development of AIDS treatments, vaccines, and an improved understanding of AIDS. Publications include *The Facts About AIDS* and the monthly *AIDS Targeted Information Newsletter.*

Eagle Forum
PO Box 618

Alton, IL 62002
(618) 462-5415

Eagle Forum is dedicated to preserving traditional family values. It believes homosexuality is morally wrong, and it opposes behaviors, such as IV drug use and homosexuality, that are often associated with AIDS. Publications include the monthly *Phyllis Schlafly Report,* which frequently reports on AIDS topics.

Family Research Council (FRC)
700 13th St. NW, Suite 500
Washington, DC 20005
(202) 393-2100

The FRC focuses on issues such as parental responsibility, disadvantaged families, and adolescent pregnancy. The council objects to admitting immigrants with HIV or AIDS into the U.S. and has worked to maintain a ban on such immigrants. The FRC publishes *Washington Watch,* a monthly newsletter concerning legislative action on AIDS and other issues.

Foundation for the Advancement of Compassion and Truth (FACT)
PO Box 90140
Arlington, TX 76004

FACT supports traditional public health measures, such as quarantining, to control the spread of infectious diseases, particularly AIDS. The group advocates tracing and contacting sexual partners of HIV-infected people and mandatory HIV testing as preventive measures against AIDS. FACT publishes the monthly *International Healthwatch Report* newsletter.

Free Congress Research and Education Foundation (FCREF)
721 Second St. NE
Washington, DC 20002
(202) 546-3004

This foundation conducts research on policies that affect the stability and well-being of American family life. It opposes life-styles often associated with AIDS, such as homosexuality and illicit drug use. Publications include the book *Gays, AIDS and You.*

Gay Men's Health Crisis (GMHC)
132 W. 24th St.
New York, NY 10011
(212) 807-6655

GMHC is an educational and support agency for people with AIDS. Programs include crisis intervention counseling, group therapy, and legal, financial, and health-care advocacy. Its library contains information about AIDS and safe sex. Publications include the bimonthly *Health Letter* and the pamphlets *Legal Answers About AIDS; Women Need to Know About AIDS;* and *The Safer Sex Condom Guide.*

The Heritage Foundation
214 Massachusetts Ave. NE
Washington, DC 20002
(202) 546-4400

The Heritage Foundation is a conservative public policy research institute that studies many national issues. It conducts policy research on AIDS and other sexually transmitted diseases and on gay rights. Publications relating to AIDS include the quarterly journal *Policy Review* and *Red Tape for the Dying: The Food and Drug Administration and AIDS.*

The HIV Eradication Foundation (HIVE)
PO Box 808
Vacaville, CA 95696

HIVE offers information on the dangers of HIV, including updates of the most recent epidemiological findings. The organization believes the U.S. has failed to adequately warn people of the dangers of AIDS. HIVE opposes AIDS antidiscrimination laws and it advocates mandatory testing of high-risk AIDS groups. Publications include the booklet *AIDS: The Alarming Reality* and the pamphlet *Saliva and HIV.*

Human Life International (HLI)
7845-E Airpark Rd.
Gaithersburg, MD 20879
(301) 670-7884

HLI is an educational and service program that conducts research on sexuality, family planning, and other human life issues. It opposes programs that distribute condoms and needles to drug addicts and others. The group advocates abstinence in sex and intravenous drug use as preventive measures against AIDS. HLI publishes the monthly newsletter *HLI Reports.*

National AIDS Information Clearinghouse (NAIC)
PO Box 6003
Rockville, MD 20850
(800) 458-5231

The clearinghouse, operated by the U.S. Centers for Disease Control, is a federal organization that provides information on AIDS and AIDS-related services. It distributes free AIDS and HIV publications such as the pamphlets *What Everyone Should Know About AIDS; The Surgeon General's Report on AIDS; Facts About AIDS and Drug Abuse;* and *AIDS and Your Job: Are There Risks?*

National Association of People with AIDS (NAPWA)
PO Box 34056
Washington, DC 20043
(202) 898-0414

NAPWA is comprised of people who have been diagnosed as having AIDS, AIDS-related complex, or HIV. NAPWA advocates access to AIDS treatment for early intervention against the disease. It also advocates increased funding for direct AIDS services, such as health care for people with HIV or AIDS. The association publishes the monthly *NAPWA News.*

People with AIDS Coalition (PWAC)
31 W. 26th St., Fifth Fl.
New York, NY 10010
(800) 828-3280

PWAC was founded as an educational and support group for people with AIDS and AIDS-related complex. The group's primary goal is to provide all available information to people with AIDS to facilitate personal decisions on such matters as how to treat their disease. Publications include the monthly newsletter *PWA Coalition Newsline,* the quarterly *SIDA Hora* in Spanish, and the book *Surviving and Thriving with AIDS.*

Project Inform (PI)
347 Dolores St., Suite 301
San Francisco, CA 94110
(800) 822-7422

Project Inform is an information clearinghouse and hotline providing updated information on experimental drug treatments for persons with AIDS or HIV. It also provides information on organizations through which treatment drugs for AIDS can be obtained. Publications include the quarterly *PI Perspective* and an information packet.

San Francisco AIDS Foundation (SFAF)
PO Box 6182
San Francisco, CA 94101
(415) 864-4376

The foundation is a regional organization whose goals are to educate the public on the prevention of AIDS and to make social service programs, such as emergency housing and food services, accessible to people with AIDS. Publications include the quarterlies *Impetus* and *Bulletin on Early Intervention Treatments for AIDS* and the monthly newsletter *Advance.sponse to the HIV/AIDS Crisis.*

Women's AIDS Project (WAP)
8235 Santa Monica Blvd., Suite 201
West Hollywood, CA 90046
(213) 650-1508

Believing that women with AIDS are often overlooked, WAP provides education and support to such women. WAP also provides HIV testing and other health-related services. Publications include the pamphlet *Women Address AIDS.*

Index

human papillomavirus (HPV)
women and, 96-97
Hunter, Nan, 33, 134, 135

influenza epidemic of 1918, 25
International AIDS Conference
fifth, 161
first, 106
fourth, 28, 53, 58, 133, 199
CD4 drug and, 178
sixth
George Bush and, 70, 136
third, 190
George Bush and, 70
intravenous drug abusers (IVDA)
as AIDS risks, 18, 19, 21, 60, 62
defined, 49
education of, 88
lack of health care for, 18, 21
men as, 18
needle exchange and, 215
New York City and, 18, 19, 57, 215
statistics regarding, 45-46
teenagers and, 37
treatment for, 88
women as, 18

Jacobson, Amy, 40
Jaffe, Harold, 56, 59
Jarlais, Don Des, 149
Johnson, Ronald, 29, 133
Johnson, Virginia
AIDS survey conducted by, 28
disagreement with, 52, 54
Johnston, William, 52, 53
Joseph, Stephen, 132
Josephs, Larry, 171
*Journal of the American Medical
Association*, 32, 54, 108, 137
Judson, Franklin, 106
Jue, Sally, 100

Kaposi's sarcoma lesions, 186, 187,
189
AZT and, 152
defined, 95
Katz, Sandor, 132
Katzenstein, Larry, 211
Kennedy, Edward, 84
Kenney, Jan, 145
Kenyon, George, 179
Keyworth, George A., 28
Kimberly Bergalis Patient and
Health Providers' Protection Act,
102
Kinsey, Alfred, 226, 230
Koch, Robert, 44
Kolodny, Robert, 52, 54
Koop, C. Everett, 25, 38, 63, 76
mandatory AIDS testing and, 109
"Report on AIDS" and, 39
vaccines and, 191

Kost, K., 204
Kramer, Larry, 70, 71, 72
Krauthammer, Charles, 72, 74
Krim, Mathilde, 30, 97, 100
Kushi, Michio
macrobiotics and, 189, 190, 191

Lambda Legal Defense and
Education Fund, 81, 98
Lambert, Bruce, 132
Lane, H. Clifford, 182
Langmuir, Alexander D., 44, 58
LaRouche, Lyndon, 135
Laurence, Jeffrey, 153
Law, Bernard F., 41
Lekatsas, Anna, 51
lesbians, 99
Levine, Alexandra, 169
Levy, Elinor, 190
Levy, Jay
research of, 177
Liebling, Linette, 40
lymphomas, 150

McArthur, Lynne, 34
McConnell, Stephen, 66
McGovern, Theresa, 98
McGuire, Jean, 65, 67
McKenzie, Nancy F., 16
macrobiotics, 189-191
Maggenti, Maria, 30, 32
Maier, Catherine, 30, 34, 35
Maki, Dennis G., 112
Mann, Jonathan, 148, 156
Marijuana/AIDS Research Service
(MARS), 199
marijuana therapy, 196-201
Marinol, 199, 200, 201
Marsa, Linda, 208
Marshall, Ruth, 148
Martin, Simon, 192
Mason, James, 108
Masters, William
AIDS survey conducted by, 28
disagreements with, 52, 54
Mehl, Robert, 184-185
Melchiono, Maurice, 39
Meyers, Abbey, 66
Minority Task Force on AIDS, 29
Mitsuya, Hiroaki, 179
Montagnier, Luc
co-discoverer of AIDS virus, 183
Monte, Tom, 189
Morella, Constance, 100
Morton, Mary, 182
Movable Feast, 184, 185
Murphey-Corb, Michael, 164, 167
Myers, Woodrow, 134

National Commission on AIDS, 85
duties of, 86
National Institute of Allergy and

Infectious Diseases (NIAID), 78
funding for research, 97
testing of drugs
AZT, 158
on men instead of women, 33,
94-95
on pregnant women, 96
National Institutes of Health (NIH),
33, 65, 74, 75, 78
AZT approval and, 151
CD4 research and, 178
Office of Research on Women's
Health, 100
proposed programs of, 92
National Organization Responding
to AIDS (NORA), 81
National Women and AIDS Risk
Network Project, 145
newborns and AIDS, 22, 23, 96
natural antibodies of, 154
testing of, 120
Noble, Gary, 149
Norwood, Chris, 50, 53, 54, 56
Nova, Diana, 187-188
Nungesser, Lon, 186-187

Osborn, June, 148
Osborn, Ruth, 155, 156

Pachuta, Donald, 182
Padian, Nancy, 56, 76
Pasteur, Louis, 44
pentamidine. *See* aerosolized
pentamidine
People with AIDS Coalition, 31
Peterman, Thomas, 56
Pettyjohn, Rodger, 135, 136
pneumocystis carinii pneumonia
(PCP), 136, 150, 162, 171
AIDS definition and, 30
treatment of, 136, 162, 174
Polk, B. Frank, 59
Portner, Jessica, 81
Potts, Malcolm, 206
Presidential Commission on the
Human Immunodeficiency Virus
Epidemic, 31, 33
AIDS testing and, 112
children and, 34
prevention of AIDS
abstinence and, 230-232
condom use and, 204-207
safe sex and, 126
short-term, 21
Project Inform, 21
approval of new AIDS drugs and,
72, 161
prostitutes
as source of AIDS transmission,
32-33, 62
Putney, Scott
research of, 165-167